CRAIG
WLCH
Y
ÔCH

Prentêg

A498

h y Môch Garage
rol . . . . Parking
é . . . . Campsite

GW00360426

Tremadog

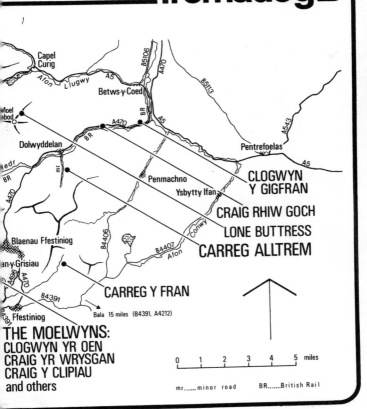

Capel
Curig

Afon   Llugwy   A5

B5106   A470

B5113

Betws-y-Coed

Moel
abod

A470   BR

BR

A5

A543

Dolwyddelan

Pentrefoelas

A5

edr

BR

A470

Penmachno

Ysbytty Ifan

CLOGWYN
Y GIGFRAN

CRAIG RHIW GOCH
LONE BUTTRESS
CARREG ALLTREM

B4406

Conwy

Blaenau Ffestiniog

an-y-Grisiau

B4407   Afon

A496   A470

B4391

CARREG Y FRAN

Ffestiniog

Bala 15 miles (B4391, A4212)

THE MOELWYNS:
CLOGWYN YR OEN
CRAIG YR WRYSGAN
CRAIG Y CLIPIAU
and others

0   1   2   3   4   5 miles

mr......minor road   BR......British Rail

Entering the crux crack of the Wasp, Craig y Castell.
Photo: Paul Williams

Andy Pollitt on Psyche 'n Burn, Craig Pant Ifan.
Photo: Glenn Robbins

CLIMBERS' CLUB GUIDES TO WALES
Edited by Geoff Milburn

8

Tremadog and

Cwm Silyn

by **Mark Pretty, Dave Farrant and Geoff Milburn**

Diagrams by **Greg Griffith**

Cover photographs by
Glenn Robbins and Paul Williams

 Published by the CLIMBERS' CLUB

1960 Snowdon South — First Edition
by C T Jones and J Neill.

1966 Snowdon South — Second Edition
by C T Jones and J Neill.

1970 Snowdon South — Third Edition
by C T Jones and L R Holliwell.

1970 Snowdon East — First Edition
by A J J Moulam.

1971 Cwm Silyn and Cwellyn — First Edition
by Mike Yates and Jim Perrin

1978 Tremadog and the Moelwyns — Fourth Edition
by Mike Mortimer.

1983 Tremadog — Fifth Edition
by Leigh McGinley

1989 Tremadog and Cwm Silyn — Sixth Edition
by Mark Pretty, Dave Farrant and Geoff Milburn

© The Climbers' Club 1989

British Library Cataloguing in Publication Data
Pretty, Mark
   Tremadog. – 6th. ed. – (Climbers' Club guides to Wales)
   1. Gwynedd. South-eastern Snowdonia. Rock climbing
   I. Title   II. Farrant, Dave   III. Milburn, Geoff   IV. Series
   796.5'223'0942925

   ISBN 0-901601-45-4

front cover:	Martin Atkinson on Dream Topping,
	Craig Bwlch y Moch
	Photo: Glenn Robbins
back cover:	Andy Grondowski on the exposed
	Crimson Cruiser
	Photo: Paul Williams

Prepared for printing by: Synergy, Royal Oak Barn, Cartmel,
Cumbria, LA11 6QB.
Produced by: The Ernest Press, Glasgow.
Distributed by Cordee, 3a De Montfort Street, Leicester, LE1 7HD.

4

CONTENTS

Editorial Introduction

The 1983 Tremadog guidebook has been out of print for some time now and being one of the best-selling North Wales guidebooks it has meant that a replacement is urgently needed to satisfy the considerable demand.

The original plan was to amalgamate the Cloggy and Cwm Silyn guidebooks to produce one volume but as the Cwm Silyn section was not ready the Cloggy volume had to go ahead on its own.

The decision to amalgamate the Tremadog and Cwm Silyn guidebooks was then made on several grounds. Geographically it made sense to put all the South Snowdon crags into one volume and certainly there was an overlap within the Cwm Pennant valley. In addition Moel Hebog is just up the hillside from the Aberglaslyn cliffs, and the climbing at Castell Cidwm is very similar to that found at Tremadog. There is also the point that many climbers have explored the whole of this new area at various different times as can be seen by the First Ascents list.

A certain amount of controversy has also gone on during this guidebook's embryonic stages and there was a strong body of opinion which suggested that the previous guidebook to Tremadog should be reprinted with the new routes included. This was partly due to the fact that some climbers felt that it would be wrong to have a pro-bolting author actively placing bolts (albeit in another area) while writing a C.C. Welsh guidebook. This is an over simplification of a complicated issue and it is sufficient to record that it was decided to go ahead with the manuscript as it existed. Recognition however, given to the solid basic groundwork laid down by Mike Mortimer, Mel Grifiths, Geoff Milburn and Leigh McGinley in the previous two Tremadog guidebooks.

At a late stage the Editor was prevailed upon to take the whole project in hand and to finish off all the incomplete sections, with the utmost speed. (Also helping were Greg Griffith on the diagrams, Paul Williams and Ian Smith who read the script and cast the net for suitable photographs.) This has now been done and rather than delay any further the guidebook is going to the printer.

G.M.

TREMADOG AREA

by Mark Pretty

ACKNOWLEDGEMENTS

I would like to thank the following:

The many people who offered advice, information, death-threats! etc. on all aspects of the guide. Particularly Andy Pollitt, for information on all the routes I can't do, John de Montjoye for commenting on the script, and Geoff Milburn for his enthusiastic devotion to the guide and its writer's blood pressure. Thanks to George White and Mick Smith and all the team at the Lichfield MC without whom many of the easier routes would have gone unchecked.

All the previous authors; I now know what you went through!

To Mandy, Alix, Karen and Jacky for helping me through my mid-guidebook life crisis. This is for you.

M.P. 1988

Introduction

This guide follows the same format as Leigh McGinley's 1982 Tremadog guide.

Most of the crags in this guide are low-lying, valley cliffs out of the main mountainous (and wet) Snowdon area. The variety of rock types is unusual to the area with the steep clean crags of the Glaslyn Estuary changing to the easier-angled mountain crags of The Moelwyns. Even slate gets a mention at Moel y Gest Quarry. The general atmosphere is rather more akin to the gentle scenery of Derbyshire with just a hint of the seaside for added flavour. The low-lying, coastal location makes the crags a particularly fine, wet-weather alternative to the main Snowdonia areas.

Unlike the last guide all routes that have been claimed over the years have been written up and incorporated into the text. Although there are several routes of a poor quality it is probably better to include them for the sake of posterity (and future guidebook writers!).

Climbs are described from left to right as the climber faces the crag. Stars are used to indicate quality; perhaps less sparingly than before. The number of aid points (if any still exist) are indicated after the grade.

Please: when 'on the crag' treat it, and the surrounding area, with due consideration, DON'T leave litter, take care not to damage any fences, don't block access when parking, avoid disturbing wildlife and try not to 'clean' too vigorously.

The inclusion of a crag or the routes upon it in this guidebook does not mean that any member of the public has the right of access to the crag or the right to climb upon it.

Historical

The exploration of the southernmost areas of the Snowdonia area occurred very late in the climbing history of Wales, except in the mountainous Gwynant Valley area where such evil boulder problems as the *Gwynant Crack*, and the equally thrutchy *Lockwood's Chimney*, were climbed in the early years of this century.

No records of further explorations in the next twenty-five years exist, until Colin Kirkus, on a rare trip to the Moelwyn's found, and climbed, the classic *Kirkus's Climb* on Clogwyn yr Oen. In the 1930s R. Elfyn Hughes climbed many routes, albeit of a slight nature, on the different Moelwyn crags, paving the way for future development.

Several climbers, including P.L. Roberts (the hero of Main Wall) and the enigmatic Menlove Edwards, had tried lines on the Tremadog cliffs but all attempts had failed. The main occurrence there, at this time, being an enormous rock-fall (not the last!) from the Avalanche Buttress area of Pant Ifan which even managed to sweep across the road into the fields on the other side.

Dave Thomas 'rediscovered' the cliffs whilst flying at a low-level in a bomber – unable to stop at that moment he returned later, only to be rebuffed.

The area maintained a low profile for the next few years though by the early 1950s Paul Work had explored the Aberglaslyn Pass and those early 'slateheads' Showell Styles, Nea Morin and Bill Tilman, of the MAM, had made a few climbs on Moel y Gest in preference to the nearby Tremadog cliffs. Clearly they were climbers ahead of their time!

Finally, Tremadog gained its first worthwhile route with *Hound's Head Buttress* which was destroyed by council vandals in 1963. The route was the work of Tony Moulam who also added such modern day classics as *Shadrach*, *Scratch*, *Christmas Curry* and *Merlin*. At the same time John Cunningham, Bill Smith and Pat Vaughan led a northern raiding party to Craig y Castell. The result, *Creagh Dhu Wall* became, and still is, one of the great Welsh classics. At the same time interest picked up in the Gwynant Valley. Menlove Edwards climbed what were probably his last two routes with *Tenth Rib* and *Side Entry* on Clogwyn y Bustach while down the road at the Wenallt Johnny Lees succeeded on the excellent *Oxo*. His partner in crime on that route, G.D. Roberts, returned later in the year for *Carol Crack*.

1953 saw the first ascent of *Clutch* by Moulam, significant, at the time, for its use of pegs for aid, the first but by no means the last route of this type. These days the whole issue of aid-climbing has been forgotten but in the 1950s, with the advent of all-out aid extravaganzas on the limestone of Derbyshire and Yorkshire, there were those who were worried that it would spread to Wales with Tremadog being an obvious outcrop target. At that time there was some justification for using aid, on many routes, as they were covered in vegetation. At Tremadog the 'anything goes' attitude of the 1970s and 80s found early expression with pre-placed protection, abseil inspection and even prior top-roping. That aid was used, was freely admitted at the time, and as it turned out nobody was really bothered!

One of the keenest climbers of that time was Harry Smith who was living in the Pant Ifan farmhouse in 1954. His finest contributions were *Grim Wall* and the stunning *Stromboli*. The following year Don Whillans payed a visit to the crag and produced the evil, and totally terminal, *Strapiombo*.

In 1953 Moulam discovered the secluded Carreg Alltrem. *Penamnen Groove*, by Bob Downes, was the first hard route there, climbed just before his untimely death in the Himalayas. It was around this time that Trevor Jones, one of the keenest and most enthusiastic of Tremadog climbers, appeared on the scene to produce, between 1956 and 1969, several fine routes, including *Great Western*, *The Brothers*, *One Step in the Clouds* and *Kestrel Cracks*.

Over in the Gwynant Valley Claude Davies added, in 1957, one of the best routes in the area, with the fine *Bovine* on the Wenallt, a route with the most surprising of pitches.

Fresh from success in other parts of Wales, Joe Brown, the 'big daddy' of Welsh climbing appeared on the scene. First stop was, again, the Wenallt where he climbed *Ferdinand* and *Torero* in 1959. The year after Brown 'hit' Tremadog, the resulting routes, *Leg Slip*, *First Slip* and *The Wasp* are all fine classics, but it was *Vector* that really set the cat amongst the pigeons. At the time its reputation attained ridiculous heights and a steady stream of exciting failures did nothing to lessen it. Meanwhile, Brown had blown wide open that belayers' nightmare, Carreg Hyll-Drem, with *Primus*, *The Hyll-Drem Girdle* and the very technical *Hardd*.

The production of the 1960 Snowdon South guide provided added impetus to the new route rush. Brown again was the main culprit with a string of classics including *Striptease*, *The Grasper*, *The Fang*, *The Neb* and *Nimbus*. Although they all used the odd point of aid they were essentially free routes in the traditional ethic.

A retrograde style set in with the occurrence of several totally artificial routes, even more surprising when one considers the free routes being produced at the time. Then, as now, the easiest answer was to free the aid routes, a good example being John Clements' free version of *Falcon*, within two years of its first ascent.

Besides Brown's hard routes there were several lower-grade classics:- Ron James's *Lavaredo Wall* at Carreg Alltrem – one of the best VS's in Wales and his excellent *Meshach* on Bwlch y Moch. *Scratch Arête* and *The Struggler* by Baz Ingle and Hugh Banner's excellent *Mangoletsi* were all fine routes. Inevitably, however, the plums went to Brown with the superb *Tensor* and *Pellagra*. In 1964 Rowland Edwards added some hard new routes, the best being *Geireagle* and *Erebus*. When the 1966 guide came out Tremadog was at the forefront of Welsh climbing in terms of popularity and difficulty with all but a very few of the big names operating there. The most significant omission being Pete Crew whose sole new route was the virtual aid ascent of *Zukator* followed by a youthful and, as ever, clownish, Al Harris (dressed in a cow-gown and winklepickers!).

Although Crew wrote a guide to the Tremadog cliffs later on, he was never interested in the area, his attitude well summed up in the comment "Dismantle Vector Buttress stone by stone and rebuild it in The Pass and you could blow up the rest of Tremadog for all the good it is."

1966 saw the ascent of *Itch* by the Holliwell brothers plus their development of the terminally loose Moel y Gest Quarry – most sane people stayed well clear!

Soloing was in vogue at that time and Eric Jones found time to solo *Grasper* whilst Richard McHardy was typically cool on *Vector*. 1969 was also the year of TWO guides to Tremadog, one by Trevor Jones, for the CC, and the previously mentioned Crew guide.

The first few years of the 1970s saw climbers' interests stray elsewhere, however, one of Tremadog's finest routes, *Silly Arête*, was climbed in this period by Hank Pasquill. It was head and shoulders above any other offering of this time.

By 1975 climbing had gone through a metamorphosis – a new 'professional' attitude, combined with serious training (plus chalk!) created a breed of superfit rock cougars who started demolishing all the accepted standards. First off was Alec Sharp who climbed the fierce *Vulture*, followed by Rowland Edwards's *Void* and Peter Livesey's exhausting *Fingerlicker*. Livesey was criticised at the time, by Sharp, for 'yo-yoing' the route but praised by many others for this new addition to the climber's armoury.

At the same time as this activity at Tremadog, Jim Perrin was developing the Pennant cliffs with the fine *Exterminating Angel* in 1974 followed by other routes such as *The Widening Gyre* and *The Second Coming* in 1975.

In 1976 Livesey was back at Tremadog to free Zukator and this soon became one of the most tried (and failed!) pitches in Wales. With fellow Yorkshireman, Ron Fawcett, he produced *Cream* – a stunning route left of Void. Meanwhile, yet another Yorkshireman, Ian Edwards, produced the infuriating *Venom*. Next year saw *Steelfingers*, *Scarecrow* and *Tall Dwarfs* by Jim Moran and *Mongoose* by Pete Gomersall. Mongoose caused much controversy by Gomersall top-roping the route first, then leading it with side-runners (a man ahead of his time!).

However, the plum of the year was the first free ascent of Vulcan by Fawcett giving one of the best pitches in Wales. Fawcett also climbed the excellent, though rather scary, *Marathon Man*, to the right of Zukator.

1977 was the year of yet another rock-fall on Pant Ifan and the banning of climbing there for a time whilst 1978 saw the evergreen Rowland Edwards, along with Paul Williams and Dave Roberts, cleaning and developing the area of rock right of Belshazzar; the best product being *Daddy Cool*. Edwards and Roberts sieged the fierce *Groove of Horror* on Pant Ifan only to have it freed later in the year by 'Boris' Hannon. Livesey visited Craig y Llyn and climbed a typically bold route with *Wailing Wall*.

The 1978 guide by Mike Mortimer sparked off yet another wave of exploration just as people were beginning to think that the area was worked out.

1979 saw the addition of the pleasant *One Step in the Crowds* by Al Evans but it was 1980 that saw major developments. Paul Williams added *The Weaver*, an excellent pitch on Vector Buttress, whilst John Redhead climbed the 'thuggish' *Atomic Finger Flake* underneath the Ochre Slab. Redhead then climbed the buttress right of Stromboli with the superbly technical *Sexual Salami*. The main exponent at this time was Fawcett and his valiant efforts on the crack left of Cream; after two days of effort he had to concede defeat only 10 feet from the top. He returned the following weekend, pre-placed his gear and ropes and did the route in one push. Although something of a non-ascent by today's style *Strawberries* is still considered Fawcett's route and the stunning quality of the route ensures its popularity.

Redhead immediately retaliated with *Bananas* which started life at 7a, and was soon down to 6b! *Sultans of Swing* an exposed girdle of Vector Buttress was another fine route from Redhead.

Fawcett, meanwhile, had strayed up to the Moelwyns where he bagged the biggest prize in the area with *The Crimson Cruiser* plus the excellent *Non Dairy Creamer*. Not content with this he then freed Poacher on the Wenallt to produce a difficult testpiece. Later in 1981, the up-and-coming Jerry Moffatt repeated Strawberries; later interrogation revealed that he had used several rest points! The first 'proper' ascent of Strawberries came a year later from Johnny Woodward.

Meanwhile, back in 1981, Redhead had added the difficult *Hitler's Buttock* on Stromboli Buttress and over in the Moelwyns Mel 'the Mole' Griffiths had climbed several excellent new routes including *Nosferatu*, *Return of the Horseman* and *The Non Dairy Creaming Start* whilst in 1982 he added the scary *Widowmaker*. Steve Haston solved two problems at Hyll-drem with his start to Hardd, – *The Wildebeest* and the obvious extended 'bolder' problem – *The Weirpig*. The best addition of 1981 was the ascent by Jerry Moffatt of the bald left wall of Vulcan to give the serious and technical *Psyche 'n Burn*.

Andy Pollitt added a couple of excellent pitches to Tremadog with *Blade Runner*, a classic arête, and *The Unreal Finish* which gives a technical finish to the Lee brothers' *Surreal*. 1982 saw the publication of Leigh McGinley's Tremadog guide. Since then development has slowed somewhat with new routes of quality becoming very difficult to find at Tremadog and a consequent reawakening of interest in the smaller crags.

Little happened in the golden summer of 1983 though *Emotional Rescue* by Andy Andrews was a worthwhile addition.

1984 saw several major additions; first off was Pat Littlejohn with the obvious roof crack left of Raging Bull on Hyll-Drem; *Raving Lunatic* is a typical Littlejohn addition and is probably destined for few repeats.

Limited Editions and *The Sandbagger* were two hard eliminates, by Pete Gomersall, on Pant Ifan but it was Martin Atkinson who stole the limelight with his ascent, over several days, of the direct finish to *Dream Topping*. The style of the ascent – pre-practised and with pre-placed wires – left little to be desired but the achievement was still a very fine effort.

On the Wenallt Redhead climbed part of one of the best new routes left to do there, to give *Fishbox* – the continuation has yet to be freed. 1985 saw a smattering of short pitches on Pant

Ifan and throughout the Moelwyns but there was little of any significance.

1986 was another quiet year; the best new routes being *Quite Easy for Bigheads* by Craig Smith on Bwlch y Moch and the excellent move of *Honorary Grit*, by Johnny Dawes, on Craig y Llyn.

1987 has seen a further scouring of Tremadog and Dawes succeeded on what is perhaps the last, last great problem of Vector Buttress with the frighteningly exposed *Llanberries*.

It was left to a Lakeland raiding party, comprising Al Phizacklea and Dave Lampard, to make one of the best finds, or rather re-discoveries of the year. Straying over to Cwm Pennant on a busy bank holiday they at once spotted the potential of Craig Cwm Trwsgl – four excellent new routes were added making this long-neglected crag well worth a visit especially when the other crags are filled to overflowing.

Back at Hyll-Drem R. Griffiths solved the long-eyed problem, left of Wildebeest, to give *Gwyddbwyll* while George Smith undertook some spacewalking up the wild scoop right of Raging Bull to give *Total Bull*.

At Tremadog, Strawberries received its final subjugation with an on-sight 'flash' from visiting German superstar Stefan Glowacz, a fitting climax perhaps to Tremadog's history.

The future development in the area would appear to lie on the small, previously overlooked crags – routes such as *Bleed for the Dancer* on the Gwynant Crack buttress, perhaps point the way, whilst down at Tremadog there is little prospect of anything particularly outstanding being climbed. However, Tremadog will always maintain its position as one of the most enjoyable outcrops to climb on in Wales – and what better epitaph for a crag is there than that?

CWM PENNANT

This beautiful and lonely valley has several small but pleasant outcrops and one rather more significant cliff. The rock is like that found on the Tremadog cliffs, and the weather is similarly mild although Craig Cwm Trwsgl being higher and vegetated is subject to wetter weather and is much slower to dry.

The first cliff can be found above Dolbenmaen Church:

Craig y Llan (Crag of the Church)   O.S. ref. 507 434
These small buttresses are very obvious from the Caernarfon – Porthmadog road. To get to the cliffs drive down the Cwm Pennant road for about 300 yards past the church. A gate is then visible on the left; pass through this and go up to the cliffs. Several routes can be done but only two are worthy of specific mention.

About 300 yards along the track through the gate, and a little higher on the hillside is a prominent steep grey pillar of rock with a fine crack line running up it; this is **Buzzard Crack**, 90 feet, Very Severe.

Grave Matters   90 feet   Hard Very Severe   5b
Climb the buttress immediately left of Buzzard Crack.

Craig Isallt (Crag of the lower slopes)   O.S. ref. 533 450

The end of a spur running down from Moel Hebog into Pennant provides the cliff. The crag is reached through a gate just beyond the bridge after Llanfihangel y Pennant. There are several facets of rock of varying quality. The main (south-west) face is heavily vegetated and although climbed upon is of little value (except to the desperate!). Farther right are some slabby walls of 70 – 80 feet, which give excellent pitches from Severe to Very Severe. Also some excellent bouldering can be found by the road on bulging outcrops of pillow-lava and also on a steep quarry wall. Farther on towards the main crag more excellent bouldering can be found. The bouldering is well worth a visit unless on holiday in the Lleyn Peninsula when a trip to Criccieth Castle will prove more rewarding!

SOUTH-WEST FACE
This is the vegetated face below the highest point of the outcrop and directly above the bands of shale left by the quarry workings. In the centre of the cliff immediately above a dark band of shale are two large trees on the right of which is a clean

rib running up to the left end of a large field half-way up the face; this rib provides the first pitch of Owl which is the only worthy route on the face. Immediately above the field is a stretch of overhanging rock.

Owl   270 feet   Severe   (1954)
The large field is reached by the prominent rib below its left-hand end, after which the overhanging upper wall is taken on the right. Start at the base of the rib which is split by a crack.
1   110 feet. Climb the rib to belays on the edge of the field.
2   60 feet. Go up and slightly right to a tree under a line of overhangs. Climb up rightwards and awkwardly go round on to the face of the buttress. Traverse right to the belays below the grooves on the right.
3   100 feet. Climb the groove, keeping to the right at first, until an exit can be made to a shelf on the left. Traverse left and go up easily to a belay. Scrambling remains.

The buttress to the right of the Owl is heavily vegetated. Farther right is:

SOUTH-EAST WING
The first feature of the wing is a steep buttress above a fence which forms the right-hand edge of the South-West Face.

Ivy Buttress   180 feet   Severe   (1956)
A pleasant route which takes the buttress direct. Start below an obvious break about 20 feet right of the fence.
1   60 feet. Go up a small crack to a ledge on the left-hand edge of the buttress, then go straight up the corner to a good ledge.
2   60 feet. Climb the slab above the ledge to a large tree; then follow the arête to a large oak tree and good belays.
3   60 feet. Ascend the easy-angled rib to the overhang. Surmount this on the right and continue up the slab above to finish.

Easter Wall   160 feet   Very Severe   (1956)
A fine pitch, steep and delicate with some dubious holds. Start about 40 feet right of Ivy Buttress, below a clean orange-coloured wall.
1   100 feet. Climb up rightwards to a small tree then go straight up a faint weakness in the wall above to a large grassy ledge and belay over on the left beside an oak tree.
2   60 feet. Go up the rib behind the belay to the overhang, surmount this and the slab above to finish (pitch 3 of Ivy Buttress).

Beyond Easter Wall is a recess (**The Cracks**, 100 feet, Very Difficult), followed by a narrow ivy-covered buttress terminating in a pinnacle beside a large tree, this buttress is bounded on the right by a deep cleft capped by a large jammed block (The Chasm, 100 feet, Severe).

Swept Wall   100 feet   Severe   (1956)
A fine steep pitch, rather easier and better protected than Easter Wall. Start at a shallow groove in the centre of the right-hand wall of The Chasm.
1   80 feet. Ascend the groove and the wall above to two large spikes. Traverse up rightwards then go leftwards to the top of the wall.
2   20 feet. The short wall at the back of the bay leads to the top.

Oak Tree Wall   100 feet   Very Severe   (1956)
A good delicate pitch, although rather more broken and artificial than the other two walls. It ascends the next slab to the right of Swept Wall. Start on a pointed block below an ivy-choked chimney just to the right of the lower section of the slabs.
1   100 feet. Step left from the block on to the slab and move across into a shallow groove. Ascend this to a large oak tree on the left. Follow the diagonal crack up rightwards to the top (or better, from a few feet up the crack, traverse right and ascend the delicate slab bearing right.

The cliff now rapidly deteriorates, becoming much shorter and is covered with ivy.

Craig Cwm Trwsgl (Crag of the Rough Hollow)

O.S. ref. 550 494

At the head of Cwm Pennant is a large cliff of superb, rough dolerite lying on a northerly shoulder of Moel Lefn. Whilst much of the cliff is broken it is very large and there are substantial areas of rock amongst the vegetation. Several excellent climbs exist which deserve to become well known.

Unfortunately for climbers there is a very long-established breeding pair of peregrines on the cliff, which are in year-long residence at the cliff, under the watchful eye of the RSPB and NCC. To avoid confrontations with these powerful groups PLEASE DO NOT CLIMB AT ANY TIME between Helix and Second Coming.

The crag is most easily approached by driving to the head of Cwm Pennant and following the Bwlch-y-ddwy-elor track to beneath the cliff. Alternatively (a shorter drive and an easier walk) drive into Beddgelert Forest at Pont Caer's Cross, between Beddgelert and Rhyd Ddu, park near Hafod Ruffyd, and then walk up the Bwlch Cwm Trwsgl path.

The cliff is made up of three sections. To the north, hidden from the usual approach, is an excellent diamond-shaped slab. Left of the main part of the cliff is a large section of rock characterised by massive overhangs, ribs and grooves. The Widening Gyre and Mere Anarchy can be found here. The central section is composed of two long ribs bounding a heathery recess and running up to a large overhang with a cleaner area of rock above. The ribs are taken by Helix and The Second Coming.

A steep red tower, farther right just before a heathery gully, is taken by The Ceremony of Innocence. Well to the right again, across several hundred yards of broken ground and higher up, is a short and very steep outcrop which gives a couple of routes, the best of which is an E3, 5c groove up the prominent groove in the right wall of a deep gully. Unfortunately this is much shorter than it first appears.

The best descent from the routes is well to the left of the cliff.

Tu Tin Tut   320 feet   Severe   (1954)
The route lies up the rib rising from the wall at the north-west corner of the cliff, opposite Prince of Wales quarry. Start above the wall, below the rib.
The slabby rib with occasional stances is followed to a grassy terrace below an overhanging wall. Traverse right across slabs below overhangs for 20 feet. Climb a corner then move right to a recess from which the foot of a large slab to the right can be gained. Climb the slab and take the top overhang on the left. Finish easily up grassy slabs.

★ **The Exterminating Angel**   180 feet   E3   (1974)
This fine route follows the diamond-shaped slab at the north end of the cliff. The first pitch is not only technical but serious as well. Start below a fluted tongue of rock, directly beneath the ledge and tree belay at half-height.
1   60 feet 6a. Take the V-chimney to the right of the tongue of rock to gain a foot-ledge on the left. Climb up to a thin traverse line going left then follow this until it is possible to move up to a fragile spike beneath an overlap. Step left under the overlap then pull over it via a small corner to gain a slab above. Climb this then move right to reach the halfway ledge and holly tree belay.
2   120 feet 5a. Traverse left to gain, and climb, a slanting crack with an awkward finish. Possible belay. Continue up a grassy slab behind to a peg belay at foot level. It is possible to gain the crack from the ground at E1, 5b but this rather misses the point of the route.

Variation
★★ The Exterminating Angel – The Iconoclastic Exit   120 feet   E1
(1987)
2a. 120 feet. 5b. Climb a short corner crack directly above the
belay niche to a flake. Traverse left onto the wall to gain a
sloping shelf. Climb the centre of the slab above, passing a
diamond-shaped niche until a delicate pull into a shallow scoop
is made. Step right and follow the crack to the top. Peg belays
farther back.

★★ The Seraphic Sanction   160 feet   E2   (1987)
The vague groove line to the right of 'The Angel' provides an
enjoyable climb. Start as for 'The Angel'.
1 115 feet. 5b. Follow 'The Angel' for 15 feet then trend
rightwards to a vague groove. Climb this to a short impending
wall, pull over this and bear slightly right to join an easy crack
which leads leftwards to a block belay.
2 45 feet. 5a. Climb the innocuous-looking scoop behind to
reach easy ground, climb left and reach the peg belays on 'The
Angel'.

The Killing Fields   185 feet   E4   (1987)
The striking arête right of the previous route provides a
memorable outing devoid of the comfort of protection. Start at
the foot of a dirty groove, just left of the rib.
1 75 feet. 5c. A few feet of wet rock lead up the slab left of the
rib. Climb this to a thin horizontal break and some protection –
the last! Climb the slab above, passing a difficult overlap and
finish with a worrying mantelshelf onto a rounded ledge. Belay.
2 110 feet. 5b. Step right, round the corner, to enter a fine
overhanging crack which is followed until it joins the rib proper.
Follow this to a ledge, then finish up a higher rib above.

50 yards to the right again is a superb wall; the inviting crack
snaking up the wall provides the substance of the next route.

★★★ Day of Reckoning   185 feet   E3   (1987)
A tremendous route with superb climbing in a fine position.
1 70 feet. 5b. Directly below the wall is an easy looking rib of
clean rock on the right. Climb the rib to a surprisingly difficult
exit and move up left to belay below the cracks.
2 115 feet. 5c. Climb the right-slanting crack until good holds
lead back left to the centre of the wall. Climb the crack above to
a tiny niche and move right with difficulty to gain a layaway
edge. Move back left and up to enter a shallow groove and then
the top.

The Widening Gyre   250 feet   E1   (1975)
This route is up the central section of the cliff via the
aforementioned rib and grooves. Prominent features are an

immense overhang low down on the left, and a short bottomless chimney high up on the right. The climb follows the corner and crackline between these, taking a direct line up the crag at its highest point. Scramble up steep heathery grooves to reach the right-hand corner of the slab beneath the huge overhang.

1 150 feet. 5b. Follow a heathery ramp rightwards until directly below a corner. Climb a mossy slab into the corner and then climb it to a small overhang. Layback up to a larger overhang and pull over this with difficulty to gain better holds. The groove above leads to a grassy bay, then a short crack on the right leads to another higher bay. Belay left of the prominent chimney.

2 100 feet. 4a. Move left onto a ledge and climb a crack in the slab above to finish.

Mere Anarchy 150 feet   Hard Very Severe   (1976)

Start at the base of the rib which bounds the slab on the left of the start of The Widening Gyre.

1 70 feet 5a. Climb the rib until a difficult move at its top can be made up and right into a groove above an overhang. Climb this groove for a few feet until it is possible to move back left and continue up to a small stance and nut belays.

2 60 feet 4a. A groove on the right leads to a ledge with loose blocks. Continue up the wall behind to a heathery rake and go left to the base of a crack.

3 70 feet 4c. Climb the crack to finish.

Helix 360 feet   Hard Very Severe   (2 pts. aid)   (1966)

In the very centre of the crag are two prominent ribs. The route follows the left-hand rib and then forces a way through the top wall via a groove system which gives the meat of the climb after an easy and rather artificial lower section. Start by scrambling up heather to the base of a very short layback corner at the foot of the left-hand rib.

1 40 feet. Climb the corner to gain a slab, follow this, move left at the top and belay on a grassy ledge.

2 70 feet. Climb a little wall on the left on good holds, then ascend a small slab. Move left onto a rib and continue left into a corner. Climb this to a large ledge and peg belays.

3 50 feet. The corner crack on the right leads to a hand-traverse right. Continue straight up to a ledge and belays.

4 100 feet. Pull round the corner on the right and go over a small overhang, peg and sling for aid, into an obvious groove. Ascend this to a roof, then go left and up to a slab. Climb this to a corner and follow this to finish.

The Second Coming 380 feet   E1   (1975)

Start just to the left of the base of the right-hand rib, right of a prominent overhang.

1 150 feet. Climb a groove on the left for a few feet, then move up and right to gain the narrow crest of a rib. Follow this rib to its top and traverse right to a grassy bay and belays.

2 60 feet. A short corner behind the belay leads to steep heather. Struggle up this to a block belay beneath an overhanging corner.
3 120 feet. 5a. Go strenuously up the corner into a niche. Climb a groove rightwards to a rib, ascend this for a few feet until a traverse left can be made across a groove to a good flake. An open groove above leads to a grassy ledge and spike belays on the left.
4 50 feet. 5c. Move back right and go up to a good spike. Move across the wall on the left with difficulty to gain a shallow groove, which leads to the top.

The Ceremony of Innocence   200 feet   Very Severe   (1975)
A line up the steep red pillar at the right end of the main cliff. Start below and right of the pillar at a little rib standing out from the heather and reached by gripping heathery climbing.
1 110 feet. 5a. Take the rib to a heathery landing and move left into a scooped groove. Climb this to a ledge on the left. Go up the wall on good holds until a foot-ledge on the left is gained with difficulty. Climb leftwards up the slab into its left-bounding groove, and ascend this to a poor stance and belay.
2 90 feet. 4b. Traverse into the centre of the slab, and climb it, anticlimatically, to a niche. Move left to finish up a slab and a steeper groove above.

High on Moel Lefn are some easy-angled quartz-speckled slabs (clearly visible from Bwlch-y-ddwy-elor) which give a pleasant diversion whilst walking along the ridge.

THE TREMADOG CLIFFS

Tremadog Rocks – Access and Use by Climbers

In order to maintain good relations with local farmers and the Nature Conservancy Council it is hoped that climbers will take note of the following directions.

Craig y Gesail
Do not drive up to Tyddyn Deucwm Isaf. The farm track is private.

Craig Pant Ifan
Craig Pant Ifan lies within the Coed Tremadoc National Nature Reserve. The Nature Conservancy Council (NCC) leases the Reserve and is responsible for the management of the Reserve.

Since the access ban following the Fandango rockfall, restrictions have been lifted provided climbers approach the crag either from the stile below Vulcan or from the path behind Tremadoc Autospares. On no account should climbers approach (or descend) through the woods between these two points.

The crag and the hillside below it are of outstanding scientific interest and should be treated as such – go easy on cleaning and avoid leaving the obvious footpaths as much as possible – it's for your own good.

If the following code is adhered to no further access problems should arise.

Climbers' Code
(a) Keep to the made paths when approaching the base of the cliffs.
(b) Do not extend the clearances in the undergrowth at the foot of the climbs.
(c) Confine climbs to clean rock faces and avoid using vegetated gullies or opening up new climbs on rock faces with much vegetation on them.
(d) Do not use nailed boots.
(e) After completing a route use ONLY the made paths.
(f) Observe the Country Code.

The NCC is the government body which promotes a national policy for nature conservation. To this end it selects, establishes and manages a series of National Nature Reserves and gives advice about nature conservation based on detailed ecological research and survey. The NCC's North Wales Regional Office is at Ffordd Penrhos, Bangor, Gwynedd, LL57 2LQ ('phone 0248 (Bangor) 355141).

The NCC's Warden for Coed Tremadog is Mr F.L. Taylor, whose address is 34 Oberon Wood, Beddgelert, Gwynedd ('phone 076686 (Beddgelert) 250). He is a British Mountain Guide. The BMC is the body responsible for negotiating and maintaining access and is always keen to hear of access problems, both here, and in other areas. The BMC can be reached at: BMC, Crawford House, Precinct Centre, Booth Street East, Manchester M13 9RZ, Tel. 061 273 5835.

Craig Bwlch y Moch

In 1979 ownership of Bwlch y Moch passed to the BMC, thus ensuring future access. The BMC took over responsibility for maintaining the property although they were ably helped by the Snowdonia National Park Authority in erecting stiles and fences, for which the BMC is most grateful.

Approach:- Several small footbridges cross the ditch between the new and old roads. Ensure that no blockage of the ditch occurs that could impede the drainage. Do not enter the fields on the opposite side of the road.

Descent:- Use one of the well-worn, easy descent paths – Belshazzar Gully or the very steep path at the left-hand end of the crag above Bwlch y Moch farm.

These are reached by following the path along the top of the cliff. When following this path keep to the cliff side of the fence. On no account should this fence be crossed, or a descent made through the field or orchard of Portreuddyn Farm, nor through the grounds of Portreuddyn Castle. This is private land, there is no right of way, and climbers on this land in recent years have given rise to serious complaints.

Craig y Gesail (Crag of the Crook of the Arm)

O.S. ref. 545 411

This is the most westerly of the Tremadog crags, and it is reached from Penmorfa on the A487. Opposite the Post Office is a lane; follow this for a quarter of a mile to the gate of Tyddyn Deucwm Isaf. There is room opposite the gate for two or three cars but PLEASE do not block access to the fields. A faint path from the farm leads to a scree slope then continue up the left-hand side of this to gain the crag.

The crag consists of a number of buttresses, the lower parts of which are heavily vegetated with steep unpleasant gullies in between. The steep and impressive Castle, on the extreme left, is the first notable buttress. To the right is the prominent rib of Bramble Buttress forming the left edge of Sheerline Buttress. Backstairs Gully separates Sheerline from Princess Buttress, whose large area of slabs is a prominent landmark. To the right of the dividing gully is Midas Buttress, which has several pleasant climbs in its left half. Farther right again is a short steep wall.

There are two easy descents, one to the right of Midas Buttress, the other to the left by a fairly long walk. Descending by Backstairs Gully is steep and unpleasant and is thus not recommended.

Although not as good as the other routes at Tremadog they are nevertheless extremely pleasant and for those who wish to escape from the crowds at the other crags it is a perfect choice.

The first route is to the left of the summit of The Castle and takes a line left of The Chateau up a slab, wall and small overhang giving **Perilous Journey** 160 feet E2 4c 5c.

The Chateau 170 feet Very Severe (1966)
An almost direct ascent of The Castle giving pleasant climbing. Start directly below the summit a few feet left of a broken arête.
1 100 feet. 4b. Climb the arête until a traverse left is possible to another arête. Follow this to a large ledge below the overhanging final wall.
2 70 feet. 4c. Move right into a scoop in the overhanging wall, swing out right to the arête, climb it and the steep wall direct to the top.

Variation.
2a 60 feet. At the left-hand end of the ledge climb over a block and go up into a short groove. Traverse below the obvious smooth ramp until it is possible to pull up onto a large ledge. Finish easily up steep rock.

The Castle   90 feet   Very Severe   (1954)
Another pleasant route taking a line up the right flank of The
Castle with an exciting finish. Start by scrambling up a grassy
wall and ledges to a stance in a small bay about 20 feet below
an obvious pinnacle in a niche on the right-hand side of the
buttress.
1   90 feet. 4c. Climb the right-hand groove to the top of the
pinnacle. The corner above leads into a niche on the left. Swing
leftwards and climb an exposed wall to finish.

★ **Astonall**   95 feet   Very Severe   (1966)
A gymnastic climb giving entertaining climbing right of The
Castle. Start as for The Castle.
1   70 feet. 4c. Climb a line of flakes up the wall on the right to
gain a slight niche below a steep wall. A thin crack on the right
leads to a comfortable stance at the base of a steep crack.
2   25 feet. 4c. The steep crack and wall above lead to the top.
(An abseil descent to the base of the first pitch may be preferred
to avoid the horrors of the initial scramble.)

★ **Bramble Buttress**   190 feet   Very Difficult   (1953)
A pleasing route which improves steadily to give an excellent
finish. Start at the foot of the rib.
1   70 feet. Climb a series of little walls just to the left of the rib
to the foot of a small corner at 30 feet. Climb the corner then
move right onto the crest of the rib and go up this to the top of
a pinnacle. Belay in the gap behind the pinnacle.
2   60 feet. Move left into a groove, then go back right and up
the edge. Continue easily through the trees to the foot of the
final tower. (Care is necessary when wet.)
3   60 feet. Climb the final tower from left to right to finish.

The Jewel in the Crown   110 feet   E1   (1987)
A good climb taking the wall to the left of Clutch and starting
from the same ledge.
1   110 feet. 5b. From the left-hand end of the ledge climb onto
a small niche and step left into the obvious groove. Climb this
until forced to traverse left over a large detached block. Finish
up the left-hand edge of the buttress.

The Shining   100 feet   E4   (1 pt. aid)   (1988)
Start as for The Jewel in the Crown.
1   100 feet. 6a. Climb the obvious groove as for The Jewel in
the Crown but, instead of traversing left, move up right to gain
the crack in the head-wall which is followed with difficulty past
the aid peg. Move slightly left and finish up the centre of the wall.

★ **Clutch**   100 feet   Very Severe   (1953)
Another enjoyable pitch up the obvious groove in the centre of
Sheerline Buttress. A steep and unpleasant scramble to reach a

grassy ledge below and to the right of the groove is necessary to start.

1   100 feet. 4c. Move up left to reach the groove and climb it direct until forced onto the right rib about 10 feet below the top of the groove. Continue up to a flake and finish up a short wall.

Non Stop   80 feet   E2   (1982)
A short steep route with one hard move.

1   80 feet. 6a. Start as for Clutch, move left into a groove and go up it to an exit beneath the final headwall. Climb the crack in this to a niche, step left and follow a flake to the top.

Plumbline   100 feet   Very Severe   (1965)
Excellent climbing on steep rock taking the obvious sentry-box and wall above. Start by scrambling up steep and unpleasant vegetation to reach the start of Clutch.

1   100 feet. 4c. Climb a short wall and move right to the sentry-box, climb this until it is possible to pull left into a crack. Move back right above the sentry-box then climb straight up to finish as for Clutch.

★ **Sheerline**   100 feet   Hard Severe   (1953)
A pleasant route taking the steep wall right of Plumbline. Start from a grassy ledge below an obvious flake, which is reached by an evil vegetated scramble (right of the approach to Clutch and Plumbline).

1   30 feet. Climb onto the top of the flake then move left under a small overhang and go up into the sentry-box of Plumbline.

2   80 feet. Move up onto the large flake on the right. Step off the top of the flake onto a steep wall and ascend this to the top. A harder variation (Very Severe 4c) goes direct, instead of traversing left, till a junction with the normal route is made.

Caravansoreye   180 feet   Hard Severe   (1974)
"A climb which given regular traffic should prove worthwhile." Start in trees just right of the foot of Backstairs Gully.

1   120 feet. Traverse out across an awkward wall to reach a groove; this is climbed, with a step right to avoid a bulge, to a flat-topped pinnacle. Step onto a slab, and go up to a ledge and block belay.

2   60 feet. Move up behind the belay, move out right then go awkwardly rightwards over a bulge to good holds and an easy finish.

Ace High   150 feet   E1   (1980)
A reasonable route up the buttress left of Javelin. Start at the bottom left-hand end of the buttress.

1   90 feet. 5b. Climb up rightwards to reach some slabs. Follow these over two overlaps until below a steep wall. Climb up to easy ground and move right to a tree below the top pitch of Javelin.

Craig y Gesail

1	Acropolis	HS
2	Tachyphouse	E1
3	Avalon	HS
4	Touch and Go	VS
5	Touch Up	E1
6	Touchstone	HVS
7	Kitten Buttress	

2 60 feet. 5a. Climb the wall immediately behind the tree to a V-shaped overhang. Go over this then move rightwards to finish up some cracks.

Food for Thought   165 feet   E2   (1988)
Start 20 feet right of Ace High.
1 90 feet. 6a. Climb the leaning block to a grassy ledge. Continue up the slab until it steepens then make some difficult moves to gain the small arête (peg). Continue in the same line to a tree and a large ledge (junction with Javelin).
2 75 feet. 4c. Climb Javelin and move right after 10 feet into the next corner then go right again to a ledge. Move right over a flake to gain a blunt rib then follow this and the wall above.

★ **Javelin**   210 feet   Hard Very Severe   (1956)
A worthwhile climb at the lower end of the grade with some bold climbing on the first pitch. Start at the left-hand side of the Princess Buttress slabs, above a small tree.
1 100 feet. 5a. Climb slabs just left of a small overlap moving left to reach a large block under an overhang. Pull off the block (not literally) and climb a wall to reach a sharp rib. Climb this (crux) then follow a horizontal knife-edge to belay in a gap at the foot of the wall.
2 40 feet. 4a. Climb the wall then trend left up grass to a ledge below the final wall.
3 70 feet. 4c. The left-hand groove in the wall is climbed followed by a pleasant open crack above to finish.

Muscles   120 feet   E1   (1981)
A line to the right of the tower right of the final pitch of Javelin. It is best approached by abseil from the top. Start at the bottom right-hand side of the tower.
1 120 feet. 5b. Pull up through some overhangs and climb the crack above. Climb into, and then up, the right-hand of two grooves. At the top make a hard move right round the arête to a flake. Move up and go back left to an arête then layback up this to finish.

Princess   240 feet   Hard Severe   (1953)
At the lowest point of the right-hand side of the slab is a rib, about 25 feet left of an ivy-covered pinnacle.
1 130 feet. Climb up the rib for 35 feet to a ledge and groove. Move up then traverse right, using holds on the lip of an overhang, to reach an obvious slabby groove. Ascend this to a ledge then make steep moves left to a vegetated bay and belay.
2 30 feet. Follow slabs and a rib on the left to a big ledge on the very edge of the buttress.
3 80 feet. Ascend to a spike on the rib, move right and climb a crack to a ledge. Further cracks lead to another ledge. Either continue direct up a steep crack, or take the original and

marginally harder finish out right, onto the edge finishing up a small corner.

Variation
A more direct, though easier, line follows the slabs just left of the ivy-filled bay at the base of Princess Buttress. Climb the slabs for 35 feet, step right to a corner, ascend this then go leftwards to a weakness in the wall, which leads to the top of the second pitch.

★ **Acropolis**   210 feet   Hard Severe   (1960)
Worth doing for the top pitch. Start as for Princess.
1 70 feet. Go up the rib for 35 feet to a ledge and groove, move up and then right to reach a large slabby groove. Climb this to a ledge and belay.
2 60 feet. The wall on the right is climbed to a ledge. Moves up a grassy diagonal crack then lead to a leftward-sloping ramp, which is taken to a tree belay.
3 80 feet. Go up onto the wall on the right to gain an earthy ledge and continue up a small groove. Go delicately right descending slightly to the edge of the buttress and ascend this to a ledge. Move left then climb direct into a tiny V-groove to finish.

Sphincter   110 feet   Very Severe   (1961)
An entertaining route up the right-bounding wall of Princess Buttress giving climbing at the upper end of the grade. Start by gaining the bottom of a leftward leading gangway in the gully right of Princess Buttress.
1 60 feet. 4b. Climb the wall just left of a groove until a traverse right is possible (and necessary!) into a groove below a cracked overhang. Pull over this to a stance.
2 50 feet. 4c. Climb to the top of a huge leaning spike behind the belay. Move left to the base of steep diagonal cracks and climb these, finishing up large detached blocks.

Variation
Sphinx
2a 50 feet. 4b. Climb up leftwards to a block on the edge of the buttress, which is followed to the top to finish.

Wild Horses   120 feet   E3   (1988)
Start at the foot of a gangway as for Sphincter.
1 80 feet. 5c. Go easily up the gangway for 20 feet to a leftward-facing corner. Climb this and the overhang above. Move diagonally right to cross the overlap via a small niche. Continue in the same line to belay on a small ledge on the edge of the buttress.
2 40 feet. 4c. Climb the awkward crack behind the belay and continue up the arête to the top.

Tachyphouse   120 feet   E1   (1977)
Technically quite interesting but an artificial line. Start in the
groove just right of Sphincter
1   80 feet. 5b. Climb the groove till a step left across Sphincter
is possible. A further awkward move left is taken to a flake crack
which leads to a sloping ledge underneath a prominent roof. A
leftwards traverse leads to a thin diagonal crack which is
climbed, with difficulty, to a small stance and thread belay (in
the groove of Pitch 3 of Acropolis).
2   40 feet. 4b. Climb up behind the belay to reach a large
vegetated ledge. Move left and go up easy rock to finish.

Tumbledown   80 feet   E1   (1988)
Start 10 feet right of the gully which separates Princess Buttress
from Midas Buttress.
1   80 feet. 5b. Climb the rib and move left to gain the obvious
corner which is followed with interest to the top.

Jumble Tumble   75 feet   Hard Very Severe   (1987)
Start 20 feet right of the gully which separates Princess Buttress
from Midas Buttress at the left-hand end of a small overhang.
1   75 feet. 5a. Climb diagonally right below the overhang to the
corner. Pull through to a ledge on the right. Climb the wall to a
large detached block and pass this by its right-hand edge.
Continue in the same line to the top.

Golfball   80 feet   E3   (1988)
Start as for Jumble Tumble.
1   40 feet. 5a. Traverse right to a short crack. Climb this then
move right below the obvious block in the centre of the wall.
Continue to the ledge (poor belay).
2   40 feet. 5c. Climb the left side of the wall for a few feet and
make a difficult step right to gain the flaky crack. Climb this
moving left at the top.

Turn Terror   100 feet   Hard Very Severe
A line of chimneys up the far left-hand side of Midas Buttress.

Foul Touch   90 feet   Very Severe   (1957)
One of the main features of Midas Buttress is a central V-groove
capped by a roof. About 30 feet left of this groove is another
overhang-capped groove. Start below this.
1   40 feet. 4a. Climb the groove and pull over the overhang on
the right and follow the wall above to a good ledge below a
recessed slab.
2   50 feet. 4c. Climb a corner on the right-hand side of the slab.

Poison Ivy   120 feet   Very Severe   (1987)
Start at the foot of the groove of Foul Touch.
1   30 feet. 4c. Move left immediately to gain the slab and climb
the left edge to belay below the sloping roof.

Paul Williams soloing Silly Arete, Craig Pant Ifan.
Photo: Dave Lawson/Williams collection

Graham Parkes on Peuterey Girdle, Craig Pant Ifan.

Photo: Chris Craggs

2 60 feet. 4c. Move up left from the belay onto the wall. Climb this moving towards the right edge at the top then climb the front of the large block. Belay.

Variation
2a 60 feet. 5a. Having moved left from the belay and gained the wall above move right immediately below a small overhang. Climb this and continue up the arête to the same belay.

Touch Up   100 feet   E1   (1970)
A poorly protected and quite difficult route up the wall between the two grooves. Start by a flake.
1 40 feet. 5a. Climb the wall to a short groove. Awkward moves up this lead to diagonal moves leftwards to reach a steep gangway. Step left round the corner and ascend a short wall to a ledge on the right.
2 60 feet. 5b. A delicate traverse right along an obvious ledge (the traverse of Touch and Go in reverse) leads to below a small niche. Go straight up the wall into a shallow groove which is followed with difficulty to the top.

Avalon   120 feet   Very Severe   (1960)
A teasing top pitch. Start below the central groove.
1 50 feet. Climb up into the groove and immediately move left to a diagonal crack. Ascend this with an awkward finish.
2 20 feet. A short corner above leads to a ledge at the foot of the recessed slab.
3 50 feet. 4c. A difficult thin crack is climbed, up the centre of the slab, to an easier finish after a tiny ledge.

★ **Touch and Go**   120 feet   Very Severe   (1957)
This popular route gives excellent climbing with a gymnastic top pitch. Start as for Avalon at the foot of the central groove.
1 70 feet. 4c. Climb the groove to an overhang. A delicate traverse left leads to a good ledge. Continue easily up to another ledge a little higher.
2 50 feet. 4c. Up and right is a short groove between a wall and a flake. Pull into this groove with difficulty or, traverse across the bottom of the flake until its right edge can be reached. Either way leads to the top of the flake and then the finish via a steep wall.

Right Touch   120 feet   Very Severe
A poor route which follows the groove as for Touch and Go till a traverse right is possible to gain and climb a crack on the right edge of the wall.

Soft Touch   100 feet   Hard Very Severe   (1963/1976)
Just right of Touch and Go is, inevitably, another groove capped by an overhang.

1   100 feet. 5a. Climb the tricky groove and overhang to gain a small ledge below an obvious overlap. Climb up to and then go left under this with difficulty to gain a groove, which is taken to the top. This groove can be reached direct from the V-groove of Touch and Go.

Touchstone   100 feet   Hard Very Severe   (1977)
Interesting climbing up the centre of the wall. Start by a tree below a short groove.
1   100 feet. 5a. Move up into the groove then follow it to a steep little wall, just to the left of the crack on Right Touch. Continue up the wall above direct to finish up a short crack.

The Kitten   60 feet   Hard Very Severe
30 yards right of Midas Buttress is a short wall.
The smooth left-hand side of the wall is climbed taking an overhang to the left.

Overcome   60 feet   Very Severe
Climb the corner crack to the right finishing through a roof.

Puki   100 feet   Severe
Right again is a rib rising out of the trees giving the substance of the route.

Craig y Castell (Crag of the Castle)   O.S. Ref. 557 403

Near the junction of the A4085 and A498 there is a short lane which leads to a school. The crag can be reached easily from here though care must be taken to avoid blocking the lane with cars. Alternatively park in Tremadog village square.

The crag has a slabby left-hand flank capped by overhangs. The main buttress is bounded on the right by a prominent groove whilst right again are prominent overhangs capping a fine slab. Right again are smaller buttresses before the cliff fades into vegetation. A steep path on the right-hand side of the cliff gives the safest descent.

The cliff gives some superb classics on perfect rock including one of the best Severes in Wales, the quieter nature of the cliff is an added attraction.

150 yards left of the main crag is an isolated buttress giving a couple of worthwhile routes while left again is a prow with three groove lines to the right. These give the first routes.

Jill the Thrill   Hard Very Severe   (1982)
Start below the central groove.
1   5a. Climb shaly rock to a ledge, go up the groove above moving left round small overhangs till an easier section is reached. Continue directly up the groove splitting the headwall above.

Variation
Holly Tree Variation   E1   (1982)
1   5b. From the ledge at 10 feet move round left into a short groove. Ascend this for a few feet then move round into the left-hand groove. Go up this (crux) until easier climbing leads leftwards below a holly tree on the prow. Climb up to the left of the holly to finish up slabs and a bulge.

Brass   Hard Very Severe   (1982)
1   5a. Climb the obvious right-hand groove.

To the right is a smooth-looking buttress.

Rowland Rat   120 feet   E2   (1988)
Start at the cleaned ledge of Cheap Trick below the overhang.
1   120 feet. 5c. Traverse left and climb a series of overlaps to gain a shallow groove up the front of the buttress. The groove becomes a shattered crack leading to a horizontal break below the steep headwall. Climb this via a small corner to the top.

Cheap Trick   130 feet   E2   (1980)
Takes the centre of the buttress. Start below a large overhang at a 'cleaned' area.
1   90 feet. 5b. Go up to the overhang, pull through it and continue up the wall towards a small overhang. Move up and then go rightwards to a belay at the base of a corner.
2   40 feet. 5a. Climb the corner to finish.

Lonely Edge   100 feet   E2   (1981)
An excellent pitch giving some bold climbing. Start 20 yards right of Cheap Trick, below an arête.
1   100 feet. 5c. Climb the arête till a spike is reached (peg up and right). Continue up the arête to reach an overhang, pull over this then go up and right to a gripping finish up the top arête.

The next routes will be found on the main cliff.

Iolyn   180 feet   Hard Severe   (1964)
Not really worthwhile when compared to the finer routes to the right. Start at the left-hand side of the crag, just to the right of vegetation.
1   70 feet. Move up to an overhang and pull over this on the left to gain a slab. Move back right then go straight up the slab to a small stance.

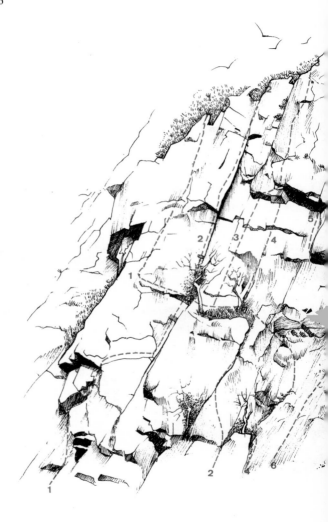

Craig y Castell

1	Creagh Dhu Wall	HS
2	The Wasp	E2
3	Bigger Bug	E4
4	Pellagra	E3
5	Tensor	E2
6	Tantalus	VS
7	Mensor	VS

2   60 feet. Climb up then traverse right to reach a tree belay.
3   50 feet. Climb the tree and fall into the left-hand of two grooves. Ascend this stepping left to finish at a large ledge.

Pulsar   180 feet   Hard Very Severe   (1979)
Start as for Iolyn.
1   70 feet. 5a. As for Iolyn to the overhang then move right under the overhang to gain the arête. Pull over the overhang onto a slab above and climb it via the right-hand edge to a tree belay.
2   110 feet. 4c. Ascend an easy slab in the left, move under a roof then go left to a small holly tree. Move up right via a loose spike onto the wall and climb this and a steep slab to finish.

Tiercel   180 feet   Hard Severe   (1958)
Again not a particularly worthwhile route. Start about 5 yards right of Iolyn, below a square-cut overhang.
1   110 feet. Climb up slabs to the overhang. Go left and then up to a small ledge. Pull through the overhang to a ledge, continue up the slab and on to the inevitable tree belay.
2   20 feet. Inspect trees until the belay on Iolyn is reached.
3   50 feet. Continue as for Iolyn.

★ **Salix**   160 feet   Hard Very Severe   (1964)
An excellent and technical first pitch with a final pitch which is serious for the grade with virtually no protection. Start at a steep cracked wall beneath and right of a steep rib.
1   90 feet. 5a. Move diagonally right to a thin crack. Climb this with difficulty and go over a bulge, then go left to a rib. Ascend this for a few feet, then go left and diagonally back right to a small stance.
2   30 feet. 4a. Climb up, yet again, to the tree belay of Iolyn.
3   40 feet. 4c. Ascend the tree (last runner), then step right onto rock. Go right again to gain the nose which gives an entertaining finish.

Jackdaw on the Edge of Time   170 feet   E1   (1981)
Some good climbing though rather disjointed. Start below Creagh Dhu Wall.
1   70 feet. 5c. An easy open groove leads to an overhang. Move left across a slab to join Salix at its crux. Pull out left and continue up a steep groove to reach a roof. Pull out left and go up to a small stance.
2   100 feet. 4c. Traverse right to gain and climb a fine flaky groove to finish up Creagh Dhu Wall.

Iron in the Soul   70 feet   E3
1   70 feet. 6a. Climb an obvious thin crack left of Creagh Dhu Wall to a square roof. Pull over this and climb a groove above into One Step in the Crowds. Finish up this.

★ One Step in the Crowds   170 feet   E1   (1979)
A good, enjoyable route just left of Creagh Dhu Wall, starting as
for that route.
1   50 feet. 5b. Climb up a tree (as for Creagh Dhu Wall) then
step left into a steep groove. Ascend this via a dubious flake till
below an overhang. Step right onto a rib then make difficult
moves to gain a sloping ledge. Belay out right on Creagh Ddu
Wall.
2   120 feet. 5b. A diagonal crack splits the overhang; this is used
to gain a jutting rib on the left. Pull up to another crack, follow
this round the roof moving right to better holds. Step back left
into a shallow groove/crackline and follow this and then a flake
crack on the right to gain a large overhang. Go over this and pull
round the arête on the left where an awkward move gives an
exciting finish.

★★ Creagh Dhu Wall   200 feet   Hard Severe   (1951)
An all-time classic which is a must for any visitor to Tremadog,
giving varied climbing on superb rock. Start below the large
corner at a large block.
1   90 feet. Scramble up to a tree at the foot of the corner. Climb
this and the corner to reach a tricky slanting crack (good runner).
Carefully foot-traverse right till a crack is reached which leads to
a large ledge and belay.
2   80 feet. Traverse out left along a horizontal crack to gain the
crest of the buttress. Savour the position then continue to a
belay on a good ledge.
3   30 feet. 4b. Move up left to make a difficult entry into a
sloping, polished groove (crux). Finish to the left or right of a
small overhang.

Variations
1a   110 feet. 5a. Very Severe. Climb the corner to a bulge and
make an awkward move left across the steep wall to reach a
diagonal crack. Ascend this joining the ordinary route on the
slabby nose then climb this to the stance.
★★ 3a   25 feet. 4c. Climb the slabby groove directly behind the
stance.
A fine pitch.

Bigger Bug   160 feet   E4   (1981)
A difficult eliminate giving some worthwhile climbing. Start 15
feet right of Creagh Dhu Wall.
1   70 feet. Move right around the corner and pull over the roof
via a short ramp to the base of a wide groove. Step out right
onto the arête and climb it to the belay terrace.
2   90 feet. 6a. Climb a thin crack in the slab between The Wasp
and Pellagra (peg) to a large roof. Climb this and finish direct.

Just to the right is the fine Tantalus slab.

Sisyphus   180 feet   E2   (1965)
Though an eliminate this route offers some interesting and quite
difficult climbing in an airy position. Start below a large corner
at the bottom left-hand corner of the Tantalus slab.
1   90 feet. 5b. Climb the corner till a traverse left can be made
to a large ash tree. Go left again with difficulty to a groove.
Ascend this to a stance at the left end of a large ledge.
2   90 feet. 5c. Go up the obvious corner for 15 feet (as for The
Wasp). Pull out left to a good hold on the arête. Continue left
with difficulty to a resting place. Finish up the slabby buttress
and a short groove.

** **The Wasp**   170 feet   E2   (1960)
A really enjoyable route with two excellent and contrasting
pitches. Start as for Sisyphus.
1   90 feet. 5c. Go up the corner for 30 feet till a tree is reached.
Traverse left to a pinnacle below an overhanging crack. Climb
this with difficulty (unless you're a gritstone addict) to a large
ledge.
2   80 feet. 5c. The superb corner at the left-hand edge of the
ledge is climbed direct moving left at the top.

Variation Start   E2   (1985)
1a   5b. From the foot of the crack of The Wasp move left onto
the wall and mantel onto a sloping ledge. Continue up to the
large ledge below the start of the second pitch.

** **Pellagra**   180 feet   E3   (1964)
A really excellent route giving technical climbing with a
particularly awkward first pitch. Start as for The Wasp.
1   90 feet. 6a. Ascend the corner, past the tree, to a bulge. Pull
over this to the right then make a difficult traverse on layaways
underneath a big roof (peg) to emerge onto the big ledge of The
Wasp.
2   90 feet. 5c. Above the right-hand end of the ledge is a bulge.
Pull over this and another bulge to reach the large roof. Traverse
left under the roof to join The Wasp or finish direct over the roof.
An excellent sustained pitch.

*** **Tensor**   220 feet   E2   (1964)
A brilliant pitch through the overhangs above the Tantalus slab.
Start at the foot of the Tantalus slab.
1   90 feet. 4b. Climb the slab in a direct line until a step right
into a short groove is possible. Ascend this to reach a belay on
a small ledge. (Tantalus pitch 1).
2   100 feet. 6a. Move down then traverse left across a slab
below the overhang until it is possible to move up to the
overhang. Move left and pull into a shallow corner, climb this to

a niche. Step right (peg) and make difficult moves over an overhang to a monster 'jug'. Pull up into a groove and go up to a belay. A heart-stopping pitch.
3 30 feet. Climb up into an easy groove to finish.

Cruel Tone 80 feet E3 (1979)
1 80 feet. 5c. The slab left of Tantalus leads past a tiny overlap to the roof. Traverse right to belay.

★ **Tantalus** 220 feet Hard Very Severe (1955)
A good route at the upper end of the grade. Start as for Tensor.
1 90 feet. 4b. As for Tensor.
2 100 feet. 5a. Climb up ribs and grooves on the right till it is possible to clip a peg in the wall to the left. A difficult move to reach the arête then thin moves across a slab bring better holds and a stance above the roof of Tensor.
3 30 feet. Finish as for Tensor.

Walk on By 80 feet E2 (1979)
1 80 feet. 5b. A faint brown streak right of Tantalus leads to the belay ledge. A good start to the next route.

Titanium Man 100 feet E3 (1978)
Start at the top of the first pitch of Tantalus.
1 100 feet. 5c. Behind the stance is a corner. Ascend this then pull left (peg) through an overhang. Continue up a steep groove to a junction with Tantalus. Finish direct up an arête and groove.

Tarantula 180 feet E1 (1966)
The right edge of the Tantalus slab gives some bold climbing. Start below an overhang on the right-hand side of the slab.
1 90 feet. 5b. Go up to the overhang and make a difficult step onto the slab above. Move across to the right edge and follow this to the Tantalus belay.
2 90 feet. 4c. To the right is a groove capped by a triangular overhang. Go up towards the overhang then move left onto a rib; follow this moving right to finish.

The pitches of Tantalus and Tarantula can be interchanged at will giving routes of a more sustained standard.

Niobe 150 feet Very Severe (1955)
The corner right of Tantalus gives a tricky pitch which can provide problems for the unwary. Start below the corner.
1 100 feet. 4c. Move rightwards onto the rib then move back left into the corner. Climb this, awkward, with a move left near the top to reach a tree belay.
2 50 feet. Continue up broken ground to the top.

★★ **Mensor**   160 feet   Very Severe   (1964)
A really delightful route giving superb, satisfying climbing. Start
just right of Niobe, below an obvious pinnacle.
1   70 feet.   4b.   Climb the left side of the pinnacle to below an
overhang. Step left and go up a steep wall moving right to a
sloping stance.
2   90 feet.   4c.   Pull up into a shallow groove and continue
rightwards to the rib. Climb a steep wall, with difficulty, then
continue more easily to the top.

Sorry Sally   150 feet   E1   (1979)
15 feet right of Mensor is a wide crack splitting the flake.
1   95 feet.   5a.   Climb the crack to a ledge then move up right to
the top of the flake. Step down then go across an easy ledge on
the right to a smaller flake pinnacle. Ascend this and bulges
above to a steep corner. Go left and up to join the traverse of
the second pitch of Mensor. Traverse 15 feet right to a belay.
2   55 feet.   5b.   Move up left from the ledge, then go back right
to the foot of a steep crack. Pull into it with difficulty and
continue up it, past a good resting ledge, with moves left at the
top to finish.

★ **Castell Girdle**   350 feet   E2   (1966)
An excellent right-to-left girdle giving good, exposed climbing.
Start as for Tarantula.
1   90 feet.   5b.   Pitch 1 of Tarantula.
2   90 feet.   5c.   The sandwich slab to the left has a niche at its
bottom right-hand corner. Ascend this to gain the slab then
traverse along this into the groove of Tensor. A difficult move
up leads to a roof (peg). Traverse left along a slab to join
Pellagra. Follow Pellagra to a tiny belay under the roof.
3   70 feet.   5c.   Continue into The Wasp. Reverse·this until the
good hold on Sisyphus can be reached. Continue as for Sisyphus
then continue into Creagh Dhu Wall.
4   40 feet.   Go down a little, then across to the tree of Salix.
5   60 feet.   5b.   Go left into a bottomless chimney, ascend this
then move right at the top to finish.

Craig Pant Ifan (Crag of Evan's Hollow)   O.S. ref. 569 406

This excellent crag rises from trees above the A498 one mile east
of Tremadog and a quarter of a mile west of Craig Bwlch y Moch.
The main section of the cliff lies at the end nearest to Bwlch y
Moch but isolated buttresses extend till almost above Tremadog
village culminating in the fine Two Face Buttress. For routes
right of this buttress the best approach is to park at Bwlch y
Moch Filling Station and then to walk up the road towards
Tremadog village for 150 yards. A stile on the right is crossed

and a steep walk up a scree slope leads to the cliffs. A variety of approaches lead to different sections of the cliff while the isolated buttresses farther left are reached by scrambles of varying unpleasantness. For Two Face Buttress park near Tremadog Autospares (on the A498 on the eastern side of Tremadog village) and through fields behind to the crag.

The main descent is by steps at the left-hand end of the main crag though a descent is possible though not advisable at the extreme right-hand side of the cliff. For Two Face Buttress a gully at the left-hand side (Helsinki Gully) forms a convenient and easy descent.

This is one of the finest cliffs in the area offering classic routes at all grades on incredibly good rock. The price you have to pay is the enormous popularity of the cliff, particularly at weekends.

Drug Test   120 feet   E1   (1988)
Start at the foot of Helsinki Gully.
1   40 feet. 4c. Climb the slabby wall moving left to gain a small ledge and stance at the left-hand end of the overhangs below a corner groove.
2   80 feet. 5b. Climb the groove, peg runner on the left, then make some difficult moves to gain a ledge on the left. Step back right and follow the weakness in the wall above to the top.

Ringwraith   130 feet   E3   (1981)
An excellent and difficult pitch. Start 15 feet left of Helsinki Wall.
1   60 feet. 6a. Climb the slab and make difficult moves through the roof (Friend and peg) to emerge gibbering at the second stance of Helsinki Wall.
2   70 feet. 5b. Ascend Helsinki Wall to the roof, step right under it and finish direct.

★ **Helsinki Wall**   140 feet   Hard Very Severe   (1955)
A popular route with enjoyable and interesting climbing. Start at the steepening of Helsinki Gully where an obvious traverse leads out right.
1   60 feet. 5a. Traverse right onto a yellow slab. Cross this to a ledge then go back left and up to a niche. Move right (peg) to a diagonal crack. Ascend this to a belay.
2   25 feet. Go back left below a small overhang. Move up through an obvious break, then go left to reach a stance below the upper wall.
3   55 feet. Ascend the wall and a groove above (peg) to an overhang. Move left and climb the crack to a step left and the top.

Variation   50 feet   Very Severe
1   50 feet. As for the normal route to the peg. Move left and go over a small overlap. The slab above leads to a roof. Go right below this until a pull over a small overhang leads to the second pitch of the normal route. Follow this to the belay.

★ **Olympic Slab**   155 feet   Very Severe   (1954)
A good route with an excellent top pitch. Start at the bottom left-hand corner of the buttress, beneath a groove capped by a roof.
1   90 feet. 4b. Traverse into the groove, go up it and then move right onto a rib. Traverse right again until it is possible to move up to a tree belay.
2   65 feet. 4c. Go easily left to a small ledge below the final slab. Climb a thin crack in the slab with difficulty to reach a better crack followed by a short groove which leads to the top.

The next three routes all start as for pitch two of Olympic Slab.

★ **Blade Runner**   50 feet   E3   (1982)
A little gem taking the left arête of Olympic Slab.
1   50 feet. 6a. Climb the front face of the slab till a swing left is possible. After a couple of moves up pull back right again (peg). Continue up the slabby arête of the slab to the top.

The Olympiad   70 feet   E2   (1977)
Not much point now with the creation of Blade Runner.
1   70 feet. 5c. Follow Olympic Slab to the final slab. Traverse left to the arête. Climb this to a wide crack and finish up this.

Orodruin   65 feet   E2   (1956)
A problematic and worthwhile pitch.
1   65 feet. 6a. Climb up to a large flake then move right into a groove. Climb this to a ledge then step delicately left onto a slab. A vicious pull through the roof (peg) leads to a groove. Ascend this to another slab and then the top.

★ **Surreal**   100 feet   E5   (1982)
A strange line but some good bold climbing. Start at the tree on Stromboli.
1   100 feet. 6b. Step left onto the slab and cross this leftwards to a thin crack (Plastic Nerve). Climb this into a corner, then go out left onto the arête. Stride left into a bottomless corner and then gibber out along the roof on the left till a quick pull over gains a small ledge on the slab above. Collapse off left to easy ground.

★ **Surreal – The Unreal Finish**   100 feet   E5   (1982)
An improvement on the original route with a very technical couple of moves.

1 100 feet. 6c. Follow Surreal to where it escapes left, then step back into the bottomless corner and climb it with difficulty to a peg below the roof. Go over the roof (crux) to another roof and cross this more easily to finish.

** **Surreal McCoy** 90 feet E5 (1984)
A fine route taking the bold right arête of the Unreal Finish. Start as for Surreal.
1 100 feet. 6c. Climb up into the bottomless groove then go right onto the arête. Climb this with trepidation to the top.

* **Plastic Nerve** 65 feet E3 (1980)
A good pitch left of pitch 2 of Stromboli. A long reach helps (otherwise it's 6a!). Start just left of the stance on Stromboli.
1 65 feet. 5c. Climb the slab on the left via a thin crack to a small ledge (old peg just to the right). Gain the quartz crack in the roof above and swing up right into a groove and climb this to another roof. Layback around this and finish either leftwards or direct.

** **Stromboli** 170 feet Hard Very Severe (1956)
An amazing top pitch more than compensates for the appalling approach. Start as for Olympic Slab.
1 100 feet. Traverse right along ledges till it is possible to pull over two overhangs onto vegetation. Grovel up to a tree belay below an impressive final buttress.
2 70 feet. 5a. Move up towards a wide capped chimney for 15 feet. Move left under the overhang on undercuts to a good hold. Pull over onto a slab and go up to another roof. Yawn over this by the V-chimney on the right to another slab capped by the inevitable roof (peg). Grope expectantly though unsuccessfully for a jug, recoup one's strength, then stretch a little farther to the elusive jug and then move out and up to the top.

The next three routes are reached by traversing right from the top of Pitch 1 of Stromboli to a ledge and tree belay (or by abseiling direct to the ledge).

** **Hitlers Buttock** 60 feet E5 (1981)
A brilliant route covering some unlikely ground. RPs essential for protection. Start 10 feet left of the tree belay.
1 60 feet. 6b. Ascend a short groove through an overhang to exit onto a slab. Go right to good nut runners then improvise out leftwards to a roof. Pull over this on 'tinies' (crux) then ascend the slab above to a finish over the final roof.

*** **Sexual Salami** 60 feet E4 (1980)
A truly magnificent pitch which gives superb intricate climbing on marvellous rock. Start at the tree belay.

Craig Pant Ifan
Stromboli Buttress

1	Bladerunner	E3
2	Olympic Slab	VS
3	Plastic Nerve	E3
4	Surreal	E5
5	Surreal McCoy	E5
6	Stromboli	HVS
7	Sexual Salami	E4
8	Cardiac Arête	E4

G.GRIFFITH.

1 60 feet. 6b. Go up an open groove till it is possible to move left and climb up to the first overlap (peg). A weird swing out left leads onto a slab. Ascend this to another overlap. (Poor peg and good wire). A sneaky sequence (or blind thuggery) leads over this into an easier finishing groove.

** **Cardiac Arête** 60 feet   E3   (1980)
An excellent complement to the other routes on this buttress. Check that the pegs are in before you start as they have a habit of disappearing! E4 without the pegs.
1 60 feet. 6a. As for Sexual Salami to the first peg then step right to a ledge on the arête (peg). Pull over the overhang and swing left onto the arête (two pegs on the right) and make heart-stopping moves up the arête to finish.

* **The Pain and the Ecstasy** X feet   E5   (1987)
A high girdle of Stromboli Buttress. A serious expedition. Start at the foot of Sexual Salami.
1 N feet. 6a. Follow Sexual Salami to the second overlap then make tenuous moves across to Hitler's Buttock. Swing round into Stromboli.
2 N feet. 6b. Traverse out left, at a slightly lower level to join Surreal. Finish along this.

Mention should also be made of the small cliff above Two Face Buttress which gives several good pitches in pleasant surroundings.

Well to the right of Two Face Buttress is a large scree fan with a tree-filled gully above it. There are three groove/crack lines on the buttress to the left of this gully which can be reached by climbing over vegetated rock from the largest tree in the gully. Right of the gully is a short wall.

Eifionydd Wall 110 feet   Hard Very Severe   (1956)
The top is quite strenuous and technically interesting. Start at the largest tree in the gully.
1 50 feet. Climb up to a large ledge overlooking the gully.
2 60 feet. 5b. Just to the right are two V-grooves. Climb the right-hand one for a few feet, then go right and climb up to a small ledge. Go diagonally left for 15 feet over a small bulge to another ledge then continue up a chimney to finish.

To the right a large overhang can be seen; this gives three routes.

Harvey Proctor's Spanking Groove 60 feet   Hard Very Severe
                                                                    (1987)
The bottomless V-groove to the left of Fear. Start 20 feet left of Fear at the foot of a rib.

Pete Crew on the second crux of Pellagra, Craig y Castell.
Photo: John Cleare

Joe Brown and Julie Collins on Tensor, Craig y Castell.

Photo: John Cleare

Joe Brown on Tensor, Craig y Castell.
Photo: John Cleare

Simon Horrox on Vulcan, Craig Pant Ifan.

Photo: Bernard Newman

1 60 feet. 5b. Climb rightwards onto the rib and move up to a groove, climb this and the continuation above.

Saffron Sunset   60 feet   E1   (1985)
Start just left of Fear.
1 60 feet. 6a. Climb up into an undercut groove left of Fear. Ascend this for a few feet then move right onto an arête and climb this to the top.

Fear   110 feet   E3   (1979)
Start below the huge roof.
1 60 feet. 6a. Move up onto a ledge below the right-hand side of the overhang. Pull over, with difficulty, and climb the edge to a belay ledge.
2 50 feet. 4c. Go left and climb an obvious short corner crack left of the arête to finish.

Tamlin   85 feet   E2   (1985)
Takes the left edge of the slab up and right of Fear. Start below the edge.
1 20 feet. 4b. Go up right to a short crack, and climb it to a tree belay.
2 65 feet. 5c. Climb the left edge to the top. Small wires required.

Right again is a clean arête reached by a vegetated scramble.

★ **Electric Edge**   90 feet   E2   (1978)
After a disgusting approach this route improves to give some excellent climbing up a steep groove. Start at the right-hand side of the arête after a 50-foot wallow through thorn bushes.
1 90 feet. 5c. 'Up the right backside' of the arête for 10 feet then move onto the front face. A difficult move leads to the arête proper. Ascend this to a recess below an overhang (peg) then go left and straight up to finish.

To the right of the next gully are the remains of Hound's Head Buttress. These give three routes.

R.I.P.   140 feet   Very Severe
Long may it remain so. Start below a thin crack in the front of the buttress.
1 140 feet. 4c. The thin crack proves awkward till a ledge is reached (possible belay).

★★ **Curved Air**   120 feet   E4   (1978)
A bold and precarious route – don't blow this one!
1 50 feet. 5a. Climb the first crack on the right side of the buttress till easier ground and a belay below the groove on R.I.P. is reached.

2 70 feet. 5c. Climb up to the overhang, step right and make difficult moves over it. Continue to the top with trepidation leaving all protection a long way below.

Pengo's Eliminate 70 feet E3   (1981)
Start at the top of Curved Air's first pitch.
1 70 feet. 6a. Climb up to a groove right of Curved Air via a crack. A difficult move to enter the groove leads to somewhat easier climbing above.

To the right are two small climbs. The obvious lines have been climbed but do not warrant descriptions.

Krakatoa 270 feet Severe   (1956)
Napalm may make this route enjoyable but otherwise is lost forever. The odd bit of rock that does exist is quite pleasant. Start in the descent gully for the main crag (Porker's Gully) below a cave.
1 80 feet. Ascend to the cave and pull through the roof on the left to reach a grassy ledge. Move diagonally right across a slab to reach a crack which is climbed to the crest of the rib.
2 80 feet. Traverse horizontally right across a slab (if it's still there!) to a short rib. Round the rib and go right again across another slab, then climb up to an oak tree belay.
3 30 feet. Ascend straight up to another tree.
4 80 feet. Go horizontally left for 30 feet under an overhang. Move up into a short groove then carry on up a rib to a tree belay. Continue through vegetation to the top.

Several worthless routes have been climbed in this area. One route however is worthwhile.

Etna 210 feet Severe
A line up vegetated slabs right of Krakatoa gives a surprisingly enjoyable route. Start at the foot of a vegetated groove, on the right side of the rib at the foot of the buttress.
1 40 feet. Go up the rock on the right side of the groove to a tree belay at the base of a slab.
2 60 feet. Move diagonally up right to a small niche. A traverse line leads back left to below a large tree. Go up to this and belay.
3 60 feet. Climb up and a little left to yet another tree. Roll up over some blocks to reach a tree belay below the top pitch of Krakatoa.
4 50 feet. Move up into a niche at the foot of a groove (Pear Tree Variation). Stride left across the base of the slab on the left to reach a steep wall. Ascend this on seemingly loose holds then move left to easier ground and a tree belay. Alternatively finish up the top pitch of Krakatoa.

Just to the right of Porker's Gully is a small isolated rib and slab.

Terraqua   50 feet   E3   (1976)
1   50 feet. 6a. Climb up to a bulging wall (peg), step left below the peg, then go up and rightwards to finish.

Pear Tree Variation   170 feet   Very Severe   (1955)
This route, up the left flank of the main crag, gives interesting climbing with a good top pitch. Start at a groove on the left of the break in the lower slabs directly below the obvious deep chimney (Strapiombo).
1   70 feet. 4c. Ascend the groove for a few feet then go left into an obvious crack. Climb this and go over a large block to a tree belay.
2   30 feet. 4a. Climb vegetated slabs on the left to reach a short steep corner and climb it to another tree belay (no pears).
3   70 feet. 4c. Climb left into a recess at the base of a groove, and ascend it to reach a short crack. Climb this, then step right and go back left into another groove to finish.

Silver Crow   70 feet   Hard Very Severe   (1980)
A line to the left of The Struggler. Start at the final belay of Pear Tree Variation.
1   70 feet. 5b. Move up into a recess above the tree and swing out right. Move up then go back left to reach an arête; climb this then do the crux of Pear Tree Variation to reach a large block. Step off this and finish up a short wall and groove.

★ **The Struggler**   70 feet   E2   (1964)
Aptly named, the initial moves being both technical and strenuous with an easier groove above. Start at the first belay of Pear Tree Variation.
1   70 feet. 5c. A vicious pull through a bulge above the belay brings better holds in a large groove. Continue up this and a roof above to finish. It is possible to reach this pitch from the final stance of Strapiombo.

Borchgrevinck   220 feet   Severe   (1957)
A damp and rather dingy start leads to an enjoyable finish. Choose a dry day after a heatwave! Start just left of the obvious break which leads up to the deep chimney of Strapiombo.
1   50 feet. Ascend the groove for a few feet, then make awkward moves out right onto a rib. Climb this to a tree belay.
2   40 feet. Continue up damp cracks to another tree.
3   30 feet. Go horizontally right to a ledge below a wide crack in the slab.
4   50 feet. Climb the vegetated crack then continue up a corner above to reach a ledge. Alternatively the diagonal crack on Great Western, to the right, can be used.
5   50 feet. Traverse left moving over some blocks till a wide ledge can be reached. Continue left then climb the front of the buttress to finish.

Craig Pant Ifa

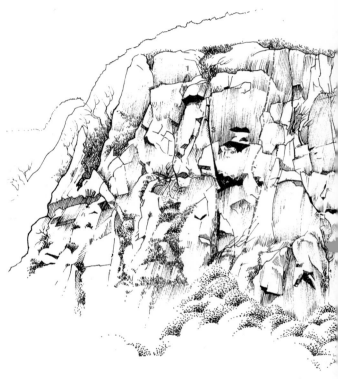

Central Section

GREG GRIFFITH.

The next three routes start from the top of pitch 2 of Borchgrevinck.

★★ Groove of Horror   120 feet   E5   (1978)
A route of blatant thuggery; if this doesn't tire you nothing will.
1   40 feet. As for Strapiombo pitch 1.
2   80 feet. 6a. Go left across a slab to a niche below an overhanging crack. A committing swing left gains the crack (peg). Climb it with difficulty (peg) to a poor rest in a short groove. Swing out left onto a slabby wall then go up and back right to finish up Strapiombo.

Strapiombo   100 feet   (HVS - E3!)   (1955)
A frightening experience taking the large chimney. (Older climbers however will be able to rest on most moves of the big pitch, and will probably find much of the route to be VD.)
1   40 feet. Climb direct to the tree at the base of the chimney.
2   60 feet. Gibber up the chimney to the top. A nightmare.

★★ Erebus   120 feet   E3   (1966)
An excellent route with some exposed and technical climbing.
1   40 feet. As for Strapiombo pitch 1.
2   80 feet. 5c. Finger-traverse out right across the wall to an arête (peg). Pull round the arête (peg) and go up, with difficulty, to reach a roof. Pull out right and climb a slab, trending left at first, to finish.

★ Tall Dwarfs   110 feet   E3   (1977)
A desperate little pitch – long arms and short legs help. Start from the big ledge below the last pitch of Poor Man's Peuterey.
1   110 feet. 6a. Climb the slab 5 feet left of the crack on Borchgrevinck towards an obvious groove. A wild undercut/layback leftwards (crux) gains the groove, then continue up it to a large ledge. Ascend an easier groove above exiting left at the top.

★★ Poor Man's Peuterey   230 feet   Severe   (1953)
An excellent classic giving varied climbing with an exposed and exciting finale. Start at an earthy ledge at the lower left-hand end of the large overlapping slabs (about 50 feet right of Borchgrevinck).
1   40 feet. Ascend the wall on the left to reach a sloping ledge below a triangular overhang.
2   40 feet. Climb up to the overhang then swing rightwards round a rib to gain a cracked groove. At the top of this hand-traverse left and move up to a tree belay.
3   30 feet. Scramble easily rightwards to a stance on the edge of a slab.
4   100 feet. Move up right (peg) then traverse out right to an exposed position on the nose of the buttress. Climb this to a

small ledge. Continue in a superb position up cracks in the slab till a long step right brings a belay ledge within reach.
5 20 feet. Pull over a block and finish up a short chimney.

★ **Great Western** 220 feet Very Severe   (1957)
A long and interesting route giving good climbing. The route starts at the left-hand corner of the large slab to the right of Poor Man's Peuterey below a shallow groove.
1 50 feet. 4b. Go across right into another shallow groove and climb it for a few feet. Move left and go over a bulge to a ledge and a large tree. Traverse right and go up to a tree at the foot of a large chimney.
2 40 feet. 4b. Move left and climb a thin diagonal crack in the slab to another tree in a groove.
3 20 feet. 4c. Ascend to an overhang and pull into a short but difficult corner; follow this to the belay on Poor Man's Peuterey.
4 60 feet. Climb a crack, moving left to a good ledge below the corner of Borchgrevinck. Ascend this to a tree at the foot of the final corner.
5 50 feet. 4b. Pull up right into a wide chimney. Struggle up this to a small ledge then enjoy a final thrash up a narrower chimney above to finish.

Quakerman 160 feet E2   (1979)
1 160 feet. 5c. Climb thin cracks leading up to the stance of Great Western (pitch 2), and move out right as for Monkey Puzzle. Difficult moves through the roofs between Monkey Puzzle and Pincushion lead to a finish up the steep arête overlooking the top groove of Silly Billy. A stretchy rope helps.

Monkey Puzzle 160 feet Hard Very Severe
Good, intricate climbing which is bold on the second pitch. Start at the top of the second pitch of Great Western.
1 50 feet. 5a. Climb to the top of the belay tree until the slab above the overhang can be reached. Climb this up to a roof then step right into a bottomless groove, which is followed to another roof. Move left to a small ledge below the final slab of Poor Man's Peuterey.
2 60 feet. 5a. Traverse delicately right, in a fine position on the lip of the overhang, to reach an obvious wide crack. Climb this to the top.

★★ **Pincushion** 200 feet E2   (1956)
A difficult roof leads to a superb slab. One of the most popular pitches at Tremadog and deservedly so.
1 50 feet. 4b. As for Great Western Pitch 1.
2 150 feet. 5c. Climb the hideous-looking chimney to a large roof. Traverse left with difficulty (peg) then make more difficult moves over the roof to gain better holds on the slab. Go up, via a thin crack, until about 10 feet below another overhang. Move

right to reach another crack and climb this to some trees under a third overhang. Step right and make an awkward move up a crack to finish.

Silly Billy   140 feet   E2   (1979)
A rather silly route! Start as for Pincushion.
1   140 feet. 5c. Ascend the chimney and go over the overhang as for Silly Arête. Follow cracks between Pincushion and the arête finishing up a tricky groove.

★★★ **Silly Arête**   130 feet   E3   (1971)
The best! Superlatives are inadequate – just do it.
1   130 feet. 5c. From the belay on Pincushion step right and climb the awkward arête moving slightly left at 15 feet then go back right and up the arête to the overhang. (A high nut runner in Pincushion is usually used to protect the first 15 feet.) Committing moves through the overhang above the Pincushion chimney lead to a move right onto the arête immediately above the overhang. Climb this carefully (some good nuts) to a small, but excellent, resting foothold. (The cunning will clip a peg round to the right on Fingerlicker Direct.) Tricky moves up the arête lead to a short finger-crack and a ledge before easier climbing leads to the top.

Around to the right is the huge corner of Barbarian.

★★ **Fingerlicker**   170 feet   E4   (1975)
Yosemite comes to Tremadog! An excellent crack (usually with an in situ hangdogger) leads to some steep wall climbing until an escape can be made onto Silly Arête. Start by scrambling up vegetated ground to the foot of the large corner.
1   65 feet. 5.10d/5c. Climb up an awkward pod in the left wall of the corner then go up a superb finger crack to an awkward exit left up to a roof. Move back right and climb the corner above till a belay in Barbarian can be reached.
2   105 feet. 5c. Follow Barbarian for 10 feet then make a difficult diagonal traverse left (peg) onto the arête to finish as for Silly Arête.

★★ Variation. **Direct Finish**   90 feet   E5   (1982)
An excellent finish with some long, long reaches.
2a   90 feet. 6b. Follow Pitch 2 to the peg then pull out right to another peg. A hard move gains a big jug and a rather poor peg. Another difficult move leads to the crack at the top of Silly Arête for a finish.

★★ **Barbarian**   160 feet   E1   (1958)
A tremendous route of great character. The main pitch is strenuous and seems never ending when on it. Scramble up to the foot of the corner to start.

1 50 feet. 4a. Climb the wall just right of the corner till it is possible to move into the corner.
2 110 feet. 5b. A difficult move is made to pull over an overhang then continue up the corner above till a step right to some cracks can be made. Ascend these to a niche under the large final overhangs. Pull up on to the left wall then make a difficult sequence back right to attain a layback position in the crack above. Ascend this to a ledge on the left (peg) then pull back right into an easier finishing groove.

★ **Scratch** 170 feet Very Severe (1953)
Some excellent climbing up a steep corner crack. Start as for Barbarian.
1 70 feet. 4b. Take the slabby wall on the right for a few feet then make a slightly rising traverse right to a tree belay at the base of a corner.
2 100 feet. 4b. Go straight up the awkward corner till a traverse right to a crack can be made. Finish up the crack.

★★ **Mangoletsi** 180 feet E3 (1964/1977)
A fine roof gives the meat of the route. Start by a step in the path right of the start of Barbarian.
1 90 feet. 5b. Ascend the left-side of a pinnacle then go left to reach a grassy ledge. Go back right and climb a short groove, moving left at the top and then straight up to a good tree belay (junction with Scratch).
2 90 feet. 6a. Pull into the corner of Scratch then move left onto a slab and ascend a thin crack to an overhang. Move left to a roof crack and make an exciting sequence over the roof (crux) into a groove above. Finish up the still difficult groove.

Variation
The Original Way 130 feet E1
An inferior, though still pleasant, version of the above.
2a 90 feet. 5b. Follow the route to the roof crack then continue into Barbarian. Belay on the peg runner of Barbarian (pitch 2)
3a 40 feet. 5b. A difficult traverse left leads to an arête; finish up this.

★★ **Spare Rib** 170 feet E4 (1977/1979)
Basically an eliminate but with some fine climbing on the top pitch and a bold bottom pitch.
1 90 feet. 6a. Ascend Mangoletsi until, about 5 feet right of the groove, a line of holds leads out right below a clean-cut overhang to a difficult move onto the rib on the right. Move up and then left to join Mangoletsi.
2 80 feet. 6a. As for Mangoletsi onto the arête, then go straight up this to an overhang. Step right onto the steep wall then go back left onto the lip of the roof. Continue up, first on the front then just right of the arête.

★ Itch   200 feet   E2   (1966)
A really excellent top pitch with a problematic sequence of moves on the bottom pitch. Start just right of Mangoletsi, by a large oak.
1   90 feet. 6a. Go straight up slabby rock to a bulge. Climb this with difficulty (peg) to vegetated ledges. Follow these to a big ledge.
2   110 feet. 5b. Start 10 feet right of the corner. Ascend the slab above to below a corner formed by the left end of an overhang. Climb the corner to join Scratch. Step left and swing over a bulge then finish by a small overlap high up.

Rhych y Din   80 feet   E2   (1984)
1   80 feet. 5b. Take the slab between pitch two of Scratch Arête and Itch pulling through the roof via a thin crack on the steepest part of the wall. Alternatively, take the overhang on the right at about the same grade.

★★ Scratch Arête   200 feet   Hard Very Severe   (1962)
A superb route with one of the most fallen off moves at Tremadog! Start at the foot of a rib about 7 yards right of Mangoletsi.
1   100 feet. 4c. Ascend the rib and a shallow groove to a ledge at the base of a crack. Climb the crack then move right at its top and make some difficult gropes over a bulge to gain a tree belay. An interesting variation is to climb an obvious T-shaped crack then move left to join the groove.
2   100 feet. 5a. Climb the awkward slab, first on the left then back right to join the arête just below the overhang. (Peg round to the right). Make some committing moves over the roof to better holds. Continue staying on the left of the arête, in a fine position, to finish.

Ivy Crack   80 feet   E1   (1973)
A steep gritstone-like crack gives a worthwhile pitch. Start by scrambling right from the tree belay on Scratch Arête to a belay beneath a crack in the right wall of the arête.
1   80 feet. 5b. Hard starting moves lead to a ledge then pull over a bulge (leaving the backs of your hands behind) to finish up loose flakes.

Slabby Flues   120 feet   Severe   (1973)
A short route up the steep wall at the very eastern end of Peuterey Buttress. A revolting scramble (at least E2) gains a ledge 7 yards right of the first belay of Scratch Arête. Belay by a slabby, rightwards-leaning chimney.
1   120 feet. Ascend the chimney to an overhang then go right to a loose flake in a niche. Step back into the chimney and go up to an oak branch, which enables a move left to be made into

a cave. Climb an easier chimney above to join and finish up Scratch Arête.

Girdle of Peuterey Buttress 400 feet E1 (1975)
An excellent girdle, to be avoided on Bank Holidays!
1 100 feet. 4c. As for Scratch Arête Pitch 1.
2 150 feet. 5b. Climb the slab moving leftwards to reach the left end of the overhang. Continue up and left to join Scratch (possible belay). Move left onto the slab and traverse left under the roof to Barbarian. Go over the roof as for Barbarian then step left to a stance.
3 80 feet. 5b. A strenuous traverse left leads to the arête and round into Pincushion. Step down to a stance by a tree under a roof. Swing left and along into Poor Man's Peuterey.
4 70 feet. Finish as for Poor Man's Peuterey.

The next seven routes are best approached by climbing a dirty, vegetated gully directly below a roof-plastered buttress right of Scratch Arête or by traversing right from the top of the first pitch of Scratch Arête.

Laser Crack 150 feet E1 (1979)
Two steep cracks give the substance of this worthwhile route. Start just left of the second pitch of Integral.
1 70 feet. 5b. Climb a small roof and steep cracks to a tree belay.
2 80 feet. 5b. Ascend a bulging crack above, with difficulty, to finish up a short chimney.

★ Integral 240 feet E2 (1965)
The obvious left arête of the buttress gives a bold but enjoyable route.
1 30 feet. Climb the gully to a detached block below the steep part of the wall.
2 60 feet. 5c. Step left off the block onto the wall, moving right to the arête. Some bold moves up lead to a swing right across a steep wall to reach a tree belay.
3 80 feet. 5b. Climb the wall to a good hold then step back left onto the arête. Ascend this, then traverse left to a short crack. Follow this to a swing right, another crack and a tree belay.
4 70 feet. Step left and go up a grooved slab to the top. Or, more conveniently, abseil from the tree belay.

★★ Integral Direct 220 feet E3 (1979)
A gem of a route taking a bold line just left of the arête. Start as for Integral.
1 30 feet. As for Integral pitch one.
2 120 feet. 5c. Step off the block and go up the wall trending rightwards to the arête. Go straight up this to an overhang,

1	Holloway	HVS
2	Psyche 'n Burn	E6
3	Vulcan	E3
4	Falcon	E2

5	Scarecrow	E3
6	Steelfingers	E2
7	Raven's Nest Wall	E1
8	Gothic Grooves	HVS
9	Hogmanay Hangover	
		HS
9a	Direct Finish	HVS

Craig Pant Ifan
Right-hand Section

traverse 12 feet left, then pull over. Go up to a short crack and finish as for Integral.
3 70 feet. As for Integral Pitch 4 or abseil off.

Limited Edition   120 feet   E5   (1984)
Start as for Integral Direct.
1 120 feet. 6b. Climb the arête to the spike runner, step onto the right wall and climb a line of thin cracks to a junction with the normal route.

The Toit   140 feet   E4   (1961)
A disgusting approach leads to a hard roof. Start from the top of Integral's second pitch.
1 70 feet. 6b. Struggle through brambles to reach the roof. A hard pull over leads into a bottomless groove. Move to a crack on the right and ascend this to a tree belay.
2 70 feet. Step left and follow slabs to the top.

The next two routes are best approached by abseil.

The Sandbagger   120 feet   E5   (1984)
Start at the large tree, as for Dune Child.
1 120 feet. 6b. Climb the steep groove behind the tree until a step left to the cracks of Dune Child is possible. Ascend these to the roof (peg), pull straight over and continue up the wall above, trending right, for 35 feet. Finish up a flake crack.
A bold pitch.

Dune Child   150 feet   E4   (1980)
Some good climbing up the edge of the roofs. Start 30 feet right of The Toit, at a large tree.
1 65 feet. 6a. Ascend an overhanging groove to reach large roofs. Traverse right to a thin crack in the wall overlooking the gully. Climb this to another roof (peg). Move left to a ledge and belay.
2 85 feet. 5c. Make a quick move up the arête then swing onto the wall. Climb the wall and a thin crack to finish.

To the right is the vegetated Avalanche Buttress which gives a variety of appalling routes which, for obvious reasons, have not been included in this guide. Right again is a steep slab formerly taken by the excellent Fandango, now alas, gone.

Technical Master   140 feet   E3   (1981)
With the demise of Fandango this route gained some point. Start below the thin crack in the slab.
1 80 feet. 6a. Climb the crack with hard moves up and right to reach a peg. Go over the bulge and then move left to a belay.
2 60 feet. 5c. Move back right to an arête and ascend this, over an overlap to a crack finish.

Wanda   180 feet   Very Severe   (1977)
A vegetated approach leads to an 'interesting' upper pitch up
the cracked tower high up on Avalanche Buttress. Start direct
beneath the rock scar (the remains of Fandango).
1   80 feet. Ascend vegetated rock, trending rightwards, to a
good tree belay.
2   100 feet. 4b. Climb up behind the tree belay to another tree.
Move up to the base of a groove then move round the arête to
a tree below a wide crack. Climb this, with detachment, to a
ledge and then on to the top.

To the right the rock improves giving the steep Strangeways
Buttress. The routes can be reached either by traversing
rightwards from below Technical Master or by climbing the first
pitch of Holloway. A large flake, Strangeways Pinnacle, situated
in the centre of the buttress, is an obvious feature.

★★ Alcatraz   100 feet   Very Severe   (1961)
A very fine route indeed giving steep climbing up the prominent
crack on the left of Strangeways Buttress. Start below the crack.
1   100 feet. 4c. Move up to the crack and follow it to a bulge.
Pull over this into a niche then go up the wall on the left to a
tree belay just below the top. Sustained.

Bucket Rider   100 feet   Hard Very Severe
1   100 feet. 5a. Climb a groove and crackline to the left of
Alcatraz.

Hey!   100 feet   E1   (1981)
1   100 feet. 5b. Take the wall 15 feet right of Alcatraz until a
finish can be squeezed between Alcatraz and Holloway.

Holloway   210 feet   Hard Very Severe   (1961)
A good route with an excellent top pitch. Start at a rib which
leads up to Strangeways Pinnacle.
1   60 feet. 4c. Climb the rib to the base of the pinnacle.
2   40 feet. 4c. Traverse right to a steep chimney and climb this
to a belay on the pinnacle.
3   110 feet. 5a. Climb up into a niche above the belay, move out
left onto the wall and move up to another niche below a steep
crack. Move diagonally across the wall to a resting place, then
go straight up to a tree. Continue to another tree and a belay
just below the top.

Back to Nature   110 feet   E4   (1979)
Some interesting climbing in a good position. Start just left of
the foot of the top pitch of Holloway.
1   110 feet. 6a. Climb diagonally up flakes on the wall to reach
the diagonal traverse on Holloway. Move across this to reach
and finish up the thin crack between Holloway and Crocadillo.

★ Crocadillo   200 feet   E1   (1974)
An excellent and varied route which is quite bold. Start as for
Holloway.
1   100 feet. 5b. Climb the rib till below the pinnacle. Ascend the
steep face above to a good hold on the left edge. Climb up till a
traverse right is possible just below the top of the pinnacle.
2   100 feet. 5b. Move right into the bottom of a red-coloured
groove. Precarious and rather scary moves up this lead to a step
left to join Holloway at the second niche. A steep, but safe crack
leads to an awkward exit onto a grassy ledge just below the top.

Strangeways   130 feet   Very Severe   (1955)
Not particularly worthwhile except as the easiest way up the
buttress. Start from below Alcatraz.
1   40 feet. 4a. Traverse diagonally rightwards to reach Strangeways Pinnacle. Continue rightwards across the top of a groove
to a small stance.
2   60 feet. 4b. Ascend a slab then pull through overhangs on
the right to a perched block in a groove. Pass this carefully then
go up the groove to a belay at the foot of a vegetated gully.
3   30 feet. Finish up the gully.

Agoraphobia   120 feet   Hard Very Severe   (1967)
A reasonable route with some interesting climbing. Start above
pitch 1 of Strangeways.
1   120 feet. Climb the slab to a small overlap then step left into
a groove. Go left again onto the front face of the buttress. A
teasing traverse left for 20 feet is taken till it is possible to move
up to an oak tree. Go left again to another oak, step right and
climb a short crack to finish.

Right again is a steep, smooth wall with a superb corner farther
right. Two of the finest routes at Tremadog can be found here.
First however are:

Broadmoor   100 feet   E1   (1972)
Start at the bottom of Pitch 3 of Hogmanay Girdle.
1   100 feet. 5b. Climb up to gain the obvious ramp. Follow this
out left to the top.

Life in a Day   90 feet   E3   (1981)
Start at the tree at the foot of Broadmoor/Pitch 3 of Hogmanay
Girdle.
1   90 feet. 5c. Move right and layback a big flake to a peg on
Broadmoor. Move up and step left onto a ramp. Traverse the
ramp (poor peg) till a hard move leads to easy ground. Follow
obvious flakes trending right to the top.

Andy Pollitt going for it on Strawberries, Craig Bwlch y Moch.
Photo: Glenn Robbins

Sean Myles in the groove of Zukator, Craig Bwlch y Moch.
Photo: Glenn Robbins

★ **Psyche 'n Burn**   140 feet   E6   (1981)
Finger-ripping, tendon-snapping, arm-pulling, heart-racing . . .
'nuff said! Belay at the top of pitch 1 of Vulcan.
1   140 feet.   6b.   A vicious piece of vegetation on the left is
overcome to reach the base of a pencil-thin crack in the wall.
Either climb the wall on the left, bold, or, technically harder (6c)
but safer, the crack itself. Anyway a peg is reached and passed
with difficulty to some good holds. Continue rather more easily
past another peg to a ledge. On the left is a thin crack; climb this
and get onto a ramp leading left. Go along it then go back right
to finish. Turbo charger essential.

★ **Vulcan**   180 feet   E3   (1962/1977)
The outstanding line at Tremadog which lives up to its
reputation. Not quite as hard as first appearances suggest. Start
by scrambling up to the foot of a slab in the vegetation below
and right of the corner.
1   60 feet.   Move up the slab, step right and ascend a short
groove to a nut belay on a grass ledge. Beware of the huge loose
flakes at the start of pitch 2.
2   120 feet.   6a.   Traverse left and climb a steep crackline to the
base of a smooth groove capped by an overhang. Pull left and
make a frantic layback up to the overhang. Hard moves up and
over this (crux) lead to a reasonable resting place. Climb the
corner above, still quite difficult, to the top.

★ **Falcon**   120 feet   E2   (1962)
A popular route, deservedly so, up the steep crackline right of
Vulcan. Start from the nut belay at the top of pitch 1 of Vulcan.
1   120 feet.   5c.   Climb up to the base of the smooth groove (as
for Vulcan). A tricky sequence out right leads to the base of the
crack. Ascend this in a great position to finish.

★ **Pippikin**   120 feet   E3   (1977)
A great route up the intimidating flakes and groove right of
Vulcan. Start at the nut belay at the top of Pitch 1 of Vulcan.
1   120 feet.   6a.   Climb a difficult overhanging crack just to the
right (poor peg) to join Falcon below the top crack. Pull up and
left to reach some undercut flakes then gibber up these, to reach
a small ledge (peg). Compose yourself then pull into a slim
groove with difficulty and follow it to the top.

Sonic Sinbin   120 feet   E4   (1980)
A strange line but some good climbing. Start at the top of pitch
1 of Vulcan.
1   120 feet.   6a.   As for Falcon along the traverse right then
continue right to make a long reach into the bottom of a groove.
Ascend the groove till beneath an overhang and go over this
rightwards (crux) to reach another overhang. Climb the wall
above to finish up a groove on the left.

★ Scarecrow   170 feet   E3   (1977)
An interesting route giving steep, sustained climbing. Start from
the top of Pitch 1 of Vulcan.
1   30 feet. Walk along the ledge and go up to a tree belay under
the roof.
2   140 feet. 5c. Traverse awkwardly left till an awkward pull
leads into an overhanging groove. Climb it (two pegs) to a good
resting place (possible belay). Continue with difficulty up the
continuation crack to an easier finish.

Variation. Direct Start   50 feet   E4
1a   50 feet. 6a. Climb directly into the overhanging groove,
scary.

Steelfingers   170 feet   E2   (1977)
A tricky start then easier climbing in a good position. Start from
the nut belay at the top of pitch 1 of Vulcan.
1   30 feet. As for Scarecrow.
2   140 feet. 5c. Move out right and go up a short wall to a steep
groove. Climb the groove (peg) to a move right (crux) onto a rib.
Ascend the rib to a traverse-line left which leads to two pegs.
Follow the thin crack above to finish up a groove right of an
obvious pillar.

The Steal   80 feet   E4   (1984)
A technical pitch. Start as for Steelfingers.
1   80 feet. 6b. Climb the left side of the roof left of Steelfingers
to a groove which leads to the upper section of that route. Finish
as for Steelfingers.

The path continues rightwards till an overhung bay with a
prominent tree above is reached; a slaty pillar on the right is
another landmark. The slaty nature of the lower section of the
crag gives steep exciting climbing on good holds with rather
rambling climbing above.

Raven's Nest Wall   170 feet   E2   (1956)
Quite a good route. Start by scrambling through vegetation to a
ledge in the overhung bay.
1   50 feet. 5c. Climb a bulging wall left of a narrow slaty slab
then step right with difficulty. Ascend the steep rib to a ledge
then go left to a tree belay.
2   60 feet. 4c. Move up behind the tree then step round the
corner on the left. Move up into a groove above and climb it to
a fine stance.
3   60 feet. 4c. Climb the groove to the top.

Gothic Grooves   180 feet   Hard Very Severe   (1967)
An intricate route. Start as for Raven's Nest Wall.
1   60 feet. 5a. Climb the wall on the left for 10 feet till a small

but well-defined rib is reached then traverse left to a black recess. Move up and slightly right (peg) then step right onto the lip of an overhang. Move up to the tree on Raven's Nest Wall.
2 70 feet. 5a. Traverse right from the tree to a V-groove; this is climbed to an exit left at the top to a ledge.
3 50 feet. 4c. Finish up the groove above.

Variation
Rookery Nook   100 feet   Hard Very Severe   (1977)
2a 100 feet. 5a. Step right from the tree and pull through an overhang. Move left to an old peg then go back right to gain a steep wall. Follow this and a thin crack to finish.

W.O.B.   160 feet   Hard Very Severe   (1956)
A rather dingy start leads to good climbing on the upper wall. Start as for Raven's Nest Wall.
1 90 feet. 4c. Step up and right around the rib to an awkward pull onto a small sandwich-slab. Move right then go up into a niche under an overhang (the niche is on the left wall of another overhung bay). Step left on doubtful rock to a ledge and go left again to a hanging flake. Ascend this to gain the wall above, from which a shallow groove leads to a small stance.
2 70 feet. 4b. Climb diagonally leftwards to gain the foot of a groove. Ascend the right wall of this to a niche then move right to finish. A direct finish up the groove is also possible.

Stormy Weather   130 feet   E3   (1984)
1 130 feet. 6a. Climb the thin cracks and wall right of W.O.B.

∗∗ Hogmanay Hangover   160 feet   Hard Severe   (1954)
An exciting route at the grade through some unlikely ground. Start at a slaty overhang on the right-hand side of a recess just above the path.
1 70 feet. 4b. Climb up left to a corner in the right-hand side of the recess. Move up over a tricky bulge then go up to a ledge on the rib. The left-hand side of the bulge leads to a step right almost to the edge of the buttress. Move back left to the foot of a tree-filled groove.
2 30 feet. Climb the tree-filled groove moving left to a tree at the foot of the final imposing corner.
3 60 feet. Ascend the corner till a delicate traverse right along a sloping slab leads to the arête, which in turn leads to the top.

Variation. **The Direct Finish**   50 feet   Hard Very Severe
3a 50 feet. 5b. Climb the steep and interesting corner direct. A good pitch.

To the right of Hogmanay Hangover is a steep descent gully. In the descent gully is a steep overhanging wall.

Omerta Crack   80 feet   E2   (1985)
1   80 feet. 5c. Climb the fine crack splitting the overhanging wall.

★ **Hogmanay Girdle**   570 feet   E3   (1973/1984)
Some good climbing, particularly the section to gain Vulcan. Start from below the crack of Alcatraz.
1   40 feet. 4a. As for Strangeways Pitch 1.
2   60 feet. 4b. As for Strangeways Pitch 2.
3   40 feet. Scramble right to an oak tree belay.
4   80 feet. 6a. Go up to a small tree and holly roots. Move up to a peg then make an increasingly difficult and technical traverse right into Vulcan with the last moves the crux – the pendulums are long!
5   50 feet. 5c. Pull around the arête into Falcon, go down a few feet then traverse right to reach Scarecrow below the final crack.
6   50 feet. 5b. Carry on rightwards, go under a bulge then round the corner to an obvious nose. Continue right to a ledge.
7   50 feet. 4c. Descend the obvious groove then traverse right under an overhang to a tree belay (pitch 2 of Raven's Nest Wall in reverse).
8   100 feet. 4c. Continue right on an obvious line till below the second pitch of Hogmanay Hangover. Continue rightwards to a sloping stance and a peg belay on the edge.
9   90 feet. 5a. Climb a left-slanting groove to a tricky move at 20 feet. Pull up into a shallow groove and ascend this to the finishing rib.

Valerian   320 feet   E1   (1965)
The route takes the first pitch of Hogmanay Hangover, reverses the girdle to Falcon and finishes up that route. Belays can be taken as necessary.

Craig Bwlch y Moch (Crag of the Pass of the Pigs)

O.S. ref. 577 406

The crag lies just above the A498 between Bwlch y Moch cafe and Portreuddyn Castle. Limited car parking is available at the old filling station along with an excellent 'climbers' cafe. The crag is split into several distinct buttresses divided by deep vegetated gullies. Different tracks lead up from the road to the base of the various buttresses. In summer finding these paths can be a problem, as several parties have found to their misfortune. The easiest way to find a route is to identify the upper section of the route from the road then cross the closest of the small footbridges over the stream and then go up the nearest path to the route. There are two descent paths: Belshazzar Gully near the right-hand end of the crag and a very steep path at the left-hand end above Bwlch y Moch farm – this gives an exciting 'no-hands' problem for those interested! On NO account should the fence at the top of the crag be crossed, or a descent made through the field or orchard of Portreuddyn Farm, nor through the grounds of Portreuddyn Castle. This land is private and should be treated as such. Please give the owners no further cause for complaint. The crag gives much brilliant climbing, the best section being, undoubtedly, Vector Buttress with excellent routes on perfect rock.

The first buttress to be seen, when looking from the car-park, is Grasper Buttress. This gives a selection of superb routes up fine lines.

★ Valerie's Rib   230 feet   Hard Severe   (1951)
A really enjoyable first pitch leads to a disappointing finish. Start just above and left of the lowest point of Grasper Buttress, level with the overhangs at the left extremity of the crag.
1   140 feet. A difficult traverse diagonally right leads to a ledge on the very edge of the rib (possible belay). Continue up steep slabby ribs and grooves to a large grassy ledge. A fine but bold pitch.
2   90 feet. Scramble up to the right to a ledge and an obvious rock scar. Moves lead round to the left and then up to gain a broken crack. Finish up this.

★ Valour   250 feet   E1   (1964)
A good route giving some exposed and technical climbing. Start at the bottom of slabs beneath the prominent overhang at the foot of Valerie's Rib.
1   65 feet. 5a. Ascend the slabs and go over a little overlap to reach the overhang. Move right and go up around the right-hand side of it to the stance on Valerie's Rib, or, climb the roof by a crack on the left.
2   110 feet. 4c. Move up rightwards to a short groove capped by a small triangular overhang. Pull over this and climb a short ramp, then move diagonally right to a tree at the base of a chimney (possible belay). Climb this then move left to belay below the rock scar on pitch 2 of Valerie's Rib.
3   75 feet. 5c. Climb the crack then go up the smooth slab on the right to a very exposed position on a small ledge. A quick pull gains some good holds in a slanting groove which leads to a good ledge. Finish up an easy wall on the left.

★★ The Grasper   160 feet   E2   (1961)
One of the best E2s at Tremadog giving a varied route with a trouser-splitting top groove. Start on a clean sloping ledge at the foot of the steep wall round to the right of Valerie's Rib.
1   90 feet. 5c. A shallow groove leads to a narrow ledge then move left across a rib to an overhanging niche. Move left again

onto another rib and go up a groove to a small roof (peg). A bold layback round this leads to a good foothold on the right, then move left to gain a thin crack which leads to a large spike just right of Valerie's Rib, Step right to an exposed stance with peg and high nut belays below the top groove.

2 70 feet. 5c. A steep little wall gives access to the groove. Wide, wide bridging up the groove (3 pegs) leads to an overhang. A difficult pull over this (crux) leads to a step left onto the arête. A quick move up this leads to the top.

New Management   140 feet   E2
A poor eliminate. Start just right of Grasper.

1 140 feet. 5c. Go up for a few feet till a diagonal crack crossing The Grasper is reached. Follow this out left till below a groove between Valour and The Grasper. Follow this till a move right into The Grasper at the crux. Ascend The Grasper to finish.

★★ Zukator   180 feet   E4   (1964/1976)
A deceptive bottom pitch leads to a tremendous top groove in an exposed position. As a famous book once said "The ascent of this groove is akin to bridging up a groove in the bottom of an egg – with about as many holds!" One of the few routes where being short is an advantage. Start at the foot of an obvious corner right of The Grasper (Clapton's Crack).

1 90 feet. 5c. Move left into a niche then pull leftwards onto a small ledge. Some difficult moves up lead to a square-cut ledge in the middle of the wall (peg). Further difficult moves lead up to some overhangs level with the stance of The Grasper. Traverse left to the stance and belay.

2 90 feet. 6a. Follow The Grasper to the first peg then make some committing moves down and right to the foot of an overhanging groove. Ascend this, with difficulty, winklepickers essential, past 3 pegs to easier ground and a rightward exit at the top.

★ Quite Easy for Big Heads   150 feet   E6   (1986)
A good eliminate with some bold climbing. Start as for Zukator.

1 150 feet. 6b. As for Zukator to the traverse left into The Grasper. Hard moves (peg) then lead to the ledge below the groove of Zukator. Step out right onto the arête and go up it, in a wild position, to join Marathon Man near the top.

★★ Marathon Man   170 feet   E5   (1977)
A technical top pitch which requires careful nut-placements. Micro-wires useful!

1 80 feet. 5c. As for Zukator to the traverse left, then traverse right to a good stance and tree belay (top of pitch 1 of Clapton's Crack).

2 90 feet. 6a. Move left along a vegetated ledge to the foot of an obvious groove. Ascend this with difficulty to large sloping ledges and a small spike up and right. Move left and make difficult moves to reach a large undercut (good Friend placement). Pull over this to better holds and an easy finish.

Variation
2a 90 feet. 6a. From the small spike step right and up another little groove to some bulges then go through these to the top.

★ **Clapton's Crack** 175 feet   Very Severe   (1961)
An excellent first pitch. Start as for Zukator at the base of an obvious corner crack.
1 75 feet. 4c. A steep layback up the polished corner leads to easier ground and a large stance on the right.
2 100 feet. 4b. Climb a steep wall to reach a rightwards-sloping ramp which in turn leads, via broken slabs, to the foot of a chimney. Move onto a slab on the left then thrutch up a deep crack above to the top.

Broken Edge 190 feet   E2   (1979)
A rambling route but some good individual pitches. Start at the bottom of Clapton's Crack.
1 120 feet. 5a. Traverse right till below an obvious slabby arête. Ascend this, at a surprisingly easy grade, till it is possible to plunge rightwards through the vegetation to belay below the third pitch of The Neb.
2 20 feet. 5b. Climb the left arête of the third pitch of The Neb.
3 50 feet. 5c. Climb the left arête of Neb Direct.

Clean Edge 100 feet   E2   (1980)
A fine pitch giving safe, technical climbing. Start 50 feet left of, and below, the start of Kestrel Cracks, at a large tree below an overhang.
1 100 feet. 6a. Ascend a crack, then move right to spikes. Climb a broken groove to reach a good foothold on the right. Go up a thin crack in the middle of the wall (crux) to reach a large ledge. Belay on the tree well back. Finish up The Neb.

To the right of Grasper Buttress is Neb Buttress which has an obvious roof crack in its upper section.

Kestrel Cracks 200 feet   Hard Very Severe   (1961)
Start at the foot of a prominent overhang-capped groove at the base of the buttress.
1 85 feet. 4c. Climb direct to the overhang and pull over it on the right to reach a steep crack, which leads to a stance.
2 35 feet. Ascend the rib on the right to the foot of a leaning corner.
3 80 feet. 5a. Climb an awkward corner for 20 feet to a large spike. Move left to a small crack then follow this and a deeper continuation crack on the left to finish.

Craig Bwlch y Moch
Left-hand Section

GREG. GRIFFITH.

1	Valour	E2
2	The Grasper	E2
3	Zukator	E4
4	Marathon Man	E5

5	The Neb	E1
5a	Neb Direct	E3
6	The Plum	E1
7	The Fang	HVS
8	Extraction	E2

★ The Neb   220 feet   E1   (1961)
Two problematic pitches make this a must for gritstone crack
addicts. Start just right of Kestrel Cracks.
1   90 feet. 5b. Climb the right wall of the corner, moving right
to a small ledge, then go up and round the arête. A steep wall
leads, with difficulty, to a large ledge and a short groove. This
in turn leads to the stance at the top of the first pitch of Kestrel
Cracks.
2   50 feet. Follow a rib on the right then traverse into a grassy
bay to reach the foot of a thin overhanging crack.
3   20 feet. 5c. The hideous crack is climbed to a tree belay.
4   60 feet. 5c. Another nasty crack leads to a slab below a large
roof. A delicate traverse right leads to a short groove. A final
awkward pull and the top is reached.

★★ Neb Direct   50 feet   E3   (1960s)
A terrifyingly-positioned route. More 'out there' than Little Plum!
Start at the belay at the end of Pitch 3 of The Neb.
1   50 feet. 6a. As for The Neb to the roof. Yawn out over the lip
via a crack then make a difficult move to better jams and the top.

★ Anagram   100 feet   E1   (1978)
Some good steep climbing. Start about 100 feet up the gully
between Neb Buttress and Grotto, below an obvious groove.
1   100 feet. 5c. Ascend the groove to a ledge. Move right to a
steep crack and climb it past a ledge to join The Neb to finish.

Final Exam   110 feet   E1   (1978)
Start below the corner of Anagram.
1   110 feet. 5b. Climb a short overhanging crack to an easier
chimney, and ascend this to a good ledge. A steep crack and
niche above lead, past a hard exit, to easier ground.

To the right is Plum Buttress with a slabby left flank and a steep
right edge.

Magic Mushroom   100 feet   E3   (1979)
Start just left of Grotto.
1   100 feet. 6a. Climb the wall leftwards on spaced holds for 35
feet then step right to place protection in Grotto. Continue
straight up the wall above to finish.

★ Grotto   150 feet   Very Severe   (1964)
Some good climbing which is better than it looks. Start by
climbing the first two pitches of Christmas Curry and then
traversing left to an obvious flake belay.
1   45 feet. 4c. Climb straight up the wall to a step left into a
shallow corner. Ascend this for a few feet then move left across
a steep slab to the bottom of an obvious groove.

2 45 feet. 4c. Pull round the roof at the foot of the groove then go up to another roof. Climb this on the right and ascend a short corner to a spike belay, or climb the crack on the left, harder and often wet.

3 60 feet. 4c. Go up for 10 feet then diagonally left to a sloping ledge. Climb straight up a steep rib to the top of the crag.

★ **Direct Variation**   150 feet   Very Severe
A good line. Start as for the original route.
1 90 feet. 5a. Go straight up the wall above the flake to join the steep crack just right of the arête. Follow this to a small ledge, move left below an overhang and climb a short slab to join the parent route just below the short corner on its second pitch. Climb this to the spike belay.
2 60 feet. 4b. Climb the steep slab and rib above the belay to the top (just left of the final pitch of Christmas Curry).

Vindaloo   150 feet   Hard Very Severe   (1968)
Not particularly worthwhile. Start as for Grotto.
1 90 feet. 5b. Climb a diagonal crack on the right and then the steep wall above to a small ledge. Step left to a crack on the arête and climb it to the belay on Grotto.
2 60 feet. 4c. Ascend an obvious groove, moving left at the top.

★ **Christmas Curry**   250 feet   Severe   (1953)
Some good climbing ideal for the 'experienced' beginner. Start at the bottom right-hand side of the buttress, at the foot of a short slab beneath an obvious chimney.
1 40 feet. Climb the slab and chimney to a tree belay.
2 90 feet. Move up leftwards to reach sloping ledges. The steep wall above is climbed to a recess. Go up right on good holds till a move back left onto the slab above is possible. A crack then leads to a large ledge.
3 60 feet. Climb the slab behind the tree then step onto the wall to the left above a sharp-edged overhang. A steep wall is climbed on good holds to another large ledge.
4 60 feet. Move into a prominent corner on the left, then pull left across a rib to reach a cluster of spikes. Continue up the wall above into a groove and a rightwards finish.

Variations

★★ **Micah Eliminate**   120 feet   Hard Severe   (1954)
A tremendous finish giving bold, exposed climbing.
3a 120 feet. From the stance step right and go up a short groove. Climb another groove to a ledge right of the last stance on the ordinary route. Continue up a thin crack then step right onto the arête, which is followed to the top.

GREG GRIFFITH.

1	Grim Wall	VS
2	Meshach	HVS
3	Shadrach	VS
4	Venom	E3
5	Leg Slip	HVS
6	First Slip	E1

Craig Bwlch y Moch
Central Section

Treemudrock Finish   50 feet   Very Severe   (1968)
4a   50 feet. 4c. Climb the prominent corner direct to the top.
Unfortunately rather vegetated.

Finish of Moments   50 feet   E3   (1978)
A frightening experience.
4b   50 feet. 5b. Climb the left arête of Treemudrock Finish.

★★★ **The Plum**   145 feet   E1   (1961)
Varied and sustained; one of the finest routes at Tremadog. At
the foot of the right edge of the buttress is a shallow corner
capped by a roof. Start below this.
1   65 feet. 5b. Climb direct up the corner and go over the roof
(or step in from the right at half-height to reach the roof). Step
left onto the rib and climb this with difficulty to a small ledge
below a V-groove. Ascend the groove, awkward, to a small
stance and flake belays.
2   80 feet. 5b. A steep crack leads to a small ledge, step right
and climb a rib, gradually easing to the top.

Bombshell   150 feet   Hard Very Severe   (1979)
1   30 feet. 5a. Climb the variation pitch 1 of The Plum.
2   40 feet. 5a. The groove line right of The Plum is followed
awkwardly.
3   80 feet. 5a. Take grooves above until a move left into The
Plum is possible. Finish up this. (The groove can be climbed all
the way at E2 5c.)

Molar   90 feet   Hard Very Severe   (1964)
A poor route. If you can be bothered it is reached by scrambling
up steep vegetation right of The Plum, or from the end of the
traverse of pitch 2 of The Fang. Start at a tree belay at the foot
of a small buttress high up and left of The Fang.
1   90 feet. 5b. Climb up to a small overhang then pull into a
short chimney which leads to a ledge. Fight through a holly tree
to a crack, which leads to the top.

Footless Frenzy   200 feet   E1   (1981)
Start by the path up to The Fang below some obvious corners.
1   100 feet. 5b. Climb the corners moving slightly right near the
top. Belay on the spikes of The Fang then stroll up to the Molar
belay.
2   100 feet. 5a. Go up as for Molar then go right up obvious
corners and grooves to finish up a small wall. Belay as for Molar.

★★ **The Fang**   200 feet   Hard Very Severe   (1961)
A fine route with two totally contrasting pitches. The buttress
between The Plum and Vector Buttress contains a large roof with
an inverted rock spike – The Fang. Start at the foot of the gully
on the right.

1 80 feet. 5a. Climb the thin crack just left of a leaning pinnacle, to the left of the gully. Step left into a short overhanging groove, and climb this to a ledge where a step right brings a crack to hand. Follow this to a stance and peg belay.

2 120 feet. 5a. Move up and left and make a difficult couple of moves down left onto a sloping ledge on the arête. Traverse left then move up, and back right, into the centre of the final slab. Continue direct up the fine slab, with poor protection, to finish. Care is needed on this pitch to avoid rope drag.

Variations

Quimbo 60 feet E1   (1981)
1a 60 feet. 6a. A very thin crack on the left edge of the buttress is climbed, with a hard start, to the belay on the ordinary route. Nearly always dry.

2a 80 feet. 5b. Ascend the corner behind the stance to the overhang then step left with difficulty to join the normal route.
2b 110 feet. 5a. As for the normal route to the end of the traverse. A tricky groove above leads to the top.

★★ **Extraction** 160 feet E2   (1975)
An enjoyable route. Start just right of The Fang below a thin crack.
1 60 feet. 5c. Gain and climb the thin crack direct to the first stance of The Fang.
2 100 feet. 5c. Move across the wall till a bold move enables a small ledge on the arête to be gained. Climb the sloping rib to where the wall starts to overhang. Pull round the arête via a hidden hold (crux) and move onto the slab of The Fang. Ascend the right-hand side of this to the top, or more logically, go up the final slab of The Fang. An exciting pitch.

★★ **Striptease** 160 feet Very Severe   (1961)
Just right of The Fang is a gully which gives a steep and interesting route that often stays dry in the rain. Start at the bottom of the gully.
1 120 feet. 5a. Climb up the chimney over two overhangs, stepping right at the second one to go up to a good tree belay.
2 40 feet. 4b. Move left onto the arête, and go up this to finish.

Burlesque 120 feet E2   (1966)
Surprisingly good though the top is contrived. Start up and right from Striptease, beneath an overhang.
1 90 feet. 6a. Ascend to the overhang and pull round it on the left to reach a slab. Precarious moves up and right (peg) lead to a groove. Climb the groove to reach slabs right of Striptease. Move right and climb, directly, up little slabs and overhangs till forced right onto easier ground (G String). Continue up to a tree belay above and right of the big tree of Striptease.
2 30 feet. 4c. Climb the steep wall above to the top.

The Singer/High Kicks   130 feet   E2   (1978)
Some good climbing, particularly on the second pitch.
1   50 feet. 5b. Start up G String then traverse left into a groove
and go up to a belay on Burlesque.
2   40 feet. 5c. Ascend the obvious groove above and right of
the belay.
3   40 feet. 4c. Finish up the wall above.

G String   130 feet   Hard Very Severe   (1964)
1   130 feet. 5a. Climb the large corner right of High Kicks, exiting
right and go up to a tree. Abseil off or continue (4c) to the top.
A pleasant route.

Farther right is an obvious large buttress – this is Vector
Buttress.

Vector Buttress
The pride of Tremadog, this single buttress is one of the finest
pieces of rock in Wales. From the classic One Step in the Clouds
to the ferocious Dream Topping it offers a collection of stunning
routes to suit all varieties of tastes.

Hail Bebe   225 feet   Very Difficult   (1954)
The exception that proves the rule! A scrappy and rather
vegetated climb which is however useful for beginners as the
pitches are short and the stances large. Start at the foot of Vector
Buttress.
1   30 feet. Gain a large tree via steep blocks.
2   45 feet. Traverse left to a large patch of vegetation and then
ascend to a forest belay.
3   40 feet. Awkward moves entering the crack above which
leads to the inevitable tree belay.
4   50 feet. Climb a short crack above to guess what sort of
belay?
5   45 feet. Move right to a slab then traverse diagonally right to
a ledge and belay. No tree.
6   15 feet. Climb another short crack to finish.

Variation
1a.   Start at the foot of the corner of G String then climb steeply
up right to a belay tree on the normal route.

★★ One Step in the Clouds   230 feet   Very Severe   (1958)
An extremely pleasant route; an early start is essential to avoid
the crowds. The exposed final section up the slabby left flank of
the buttress must rank as some of the finest climbing at the
grade at Tremadog. Start as for Hail Bebe.
1   90 feet. 4b. As for Hail Bebe to the blocks. Climb up behind
the tree into a V-groove. This leads to a large stance beneath
some depressingly large overhangs.

Vector Buttress

GGRIFFITH.

1	Diadic	E1			
2	Nimbus	E2			
3	Cream	E3	8	Strawberries	E7
4	Vector	E2	9	Dream Topping	E7
5	Croaker	E3	10	Void	E3
6	Bananas	E4	11	The Snake	E2
7	Llanberries	E7	12	Mongoose	E5

2 90 feet. 4c. Sneak off left and climb a shallow crack to a sloping ledge. Move diagonally right off the end of the ledge to a spike runner. Difficult moves lead via a little groove to a good stance and belay.
3 50 feet. 4b. Step right a few feet and go up to a block. A series of difficult moves first left then right lead to an awkward mantel and an easier finish. A bold pitch.

The next routes are up the true Vector Buttress, an intimidating and usually overhanging section of rock – for 'men only'.

Dark Side/A Vengeance   80 feet   E3   (1972/1978)
Start at the belay at the end of pitch 2 of One Step in the Clouds.
1 80 feet. 6a. Move right a few feet then go up to a thread runner. Move left and enter an overhanging chimney/groove via a vicious move. Continue up the groove till it eases then with difficulty ascend another groove leftwards followed by a V-flake to finish on the crux of One Step in the Clouds.

★★★ **Sultans of Swing**   180 feet   E4   (1980)
'The' girdle. A masterpiece of route-finding with an incredible finale on the Vector Headwall. Care must be taken with ropework on pitch 2. Start as for Dark Side – at the belay at the end of pitch 2 of One Step.
1 40 feet. 6a. As for Dark Side to where the angle eases. Hanging belay. Alternatively, and better, move right to belay beneath the top groove of Diadic.
2 140 feet. 6a. Traverse right beneath a wide crack (Croaker) and make awkward moves round right onto the edge of the foreboding headwall. Mentally cross your fingers and set off rightwards to a good spike. Climb straight up onto a detached flake and a resting place on Cream. Move out right to a good hold on Void and climb this, peg, until about 15 feet from the top of the crack. Follow good holds out right to join and finish up Mongoose. A pitch to set the heart racing and the blood pumping (and the cameras clicking!).

★★ **Diadic**   220 feet   E1   (1964)
An indifferent start leads to an extremely enjoyable third pitch in an impressive position.
1 30 feet. As for Hail Bebe.
2 60 feet. 4b. As for One Step in the Clouds.
3 80 feet. 5b. Move right a few feet and go up to a thread runner. Move right around a fang of rock with difficulty and then pull over the bulge above (large thread placement). The groove above is then climbed to a short slab and junction with Vector. Climb the top crack on Vector (of which more later) to gain easier ground on One Step.
4 50 feet. Easy climbing leads rightwards to finish.

★ **Nimbus**   220 feet   E2   (1961)
A left-to-right girdle of the buttress giving some difficult (and nearly always dry) climbing.
1   30 feet. As for Hail Bebe.
2   60 feet. 4b. As for One Step in the Clouds.
3   90 feet. 5c. Move across right to a tree, step down and traverse with trepidation to a sloping ledge at the base of a groove. Climb this with difficulty to a flat-topped spike then move diagonally right to belay in the Vector Cave.
4   40 feet. 4b. An obvious diagonal line rightwards is followed to a large stance overlooking the gully. From here an easy traverse leads across the gully to the tree on Grim Wall. Either abseil from here or continue up Grim Wall or Meshach – to complete the longest route at Tremadog!

Variation
1a   90 feet. 5a. A shallow groove right of One Step can be followed till it is possible to step left to the good stance.

★★ **The Weaver**   210 feet   E2   (1980)
Although an eliminate this route offers brilliant climbing through unlikely ground. Start just right of One Step in the Clouds.
1   40 feet. 5b. Climb an awkward faint groove then move right and climb a short wall to the first belay on Vector.
2   120 feet. 5c. A great pitch. Step up then go left for 10 feet. Climb a steep wall, peg, to join Nimbus at a triangular overhang. Move right and go up to a groove then move back left to reach good footholds. Continue up a crack to join Diadic. Climb this to gain easier ground and the belay of One Step.
3   50 feet. As for Diadic.

★★★ **Bananas**   220 feet   E4   (1980)
A route on the very edge of nowhere giving powerful and terrifying climbing. Needless to say it is a memorable experience.
1   40 feet. 5b. As for The Weaver.
2   100 feet. 5c. As for The Weaver to the large thread on Diadic. Move right and go over a roof to a hanging belay beneath the overhanging chimney of Croaker.
3   80 feet. 6b. This is it! Climb the steep crack above (Croaker), peg, then move out right with difficulty to a flake crack in the arête. Either find the knee-lock rest and sort your brain out or battle on up the crack to a final nervewracking mantelshelf onto easy ground.

★ **Llanberries**   65 feet   E7   (1987)
A surprisingly fine pitch squeezed up the wall left of Strawberries. Start 20 feet below the spike on Cream using that as a belay.

Craig Bwlch y Moch
Right-hand Section

1	Daddy Cool	E2
2	Merlin	VS
2a	Merlin Direct Finish	
		HVS
3	Geireagle	E2
4	Vulture	E4
5	Oberon	VD

GREG GRIFFITH.

1 65 feet. 6c. Climb the slab left of Cream, to the crack of Strawberries. Layback the footholds of Strawberries to a jug (peg, Rock 1, RP3). Make difficult moves up and then left; a difficult move up (crux) then leads to the arête. Finish up this in a fine position.

★★★ **Strawberries** 60 feet E7   (1980)
A contender for the most coveted pitch in Wales. This stunning route captured the imagination of the climbing world and lives up to its reputation. Start at the spike belay on Cream – below its top pitch.
1 60 feet. 6b. Step up to the base of Cream's top crack then move left again to the base of a thin crack. Start the crack with difficulty and race up to its end. Pull out left to a second crack which leads with difficulty to better holds and the top. Shout with delight then abseil for the gear and rescue your belayer.

★★★ **Dream Topping** 60 feet E7   (1984)
The climax to development at Tremadog. This brilliant pitch is essentially Strawberries Direct.
1 60 feet. 6c. As for Strawberries to the top of the first crack. A desperate sequence then leads to and hopefully up the continuation crack above. Easy ground at the top leads to the large ledge and a welcome relief.

★★★ **Cream** 220 feet E3   (1976)
A great route giving a lot of hard climbing in some outrageous positions. Start just right of One Step.
1 40 feet. 4c. Climb a groove moving left to a spike belay (as for Vector).
2 80 feet. 5c. Climb up above the spike to cracked blocks. Pull around and down to the left and climb an awkward short groove to join Nimbus. Follow this to the belay in the Vector cave.
3 50 feet. 5c. Step left as for Vector and pull up to below Croaker. Traverse wildly right, around the prow, to a spike belay below the top crack. This last section is shared with Sultans.
4 50 feet. 6a. Climb the crack to a small ledge. Difficult moves lead to good holds leading left to the top. An exhilarating pitch in a tremendous position.

Variations
2a 70 feet. 6a. As normal to the cracked blocks then step left and layback with difficulty to join Nimbus. Continue as for this route to the Vector cave stance.
3a 40 feet. 4b. It is possible to follow Nimbus moving left to the spike belay. This gives inferior climbing.

★★★ **Vector** 250 feet E2   (1960)
The ultimate classic which gives complex and brilliant climbing, albeit somewhat polished, with a steep finish. A must for any aspirant.

1 60 feet. 4c. Climb a short groove then step right onto a slab. Move delicately left to a short groove which leads to a small stance and spike belay on the left.
2 80 feet. 5c. Move awkwardly right to the start of a diagonal crack. Climb this to a large spike runner on the right. Difficult moves up left and back right lead to the foot of an ochre-coloured hanging slab. Climb this, peg, and pull over the bulge at its top to enter a groove and climb this to the large roof. Traverse left to a cave with peg belays. A pitch to tire the legs at an alarming rate.
3 60 feet. 5b. Move down left then go awkwardly over a bulge. Continue left onto a slab below an overhanging crack. This is the scene of many epic retreats so 'psyche and burn' to the top where easy ground is reached.
4 50 feet. Climb diagonally right to the top.

★★ **The Croaker** 70 feet   E3   (1964)
Starting from the Vector cave this pitch gives steep and powerful climbing in an 'out there' position.
1 70 feet. 5c. Move left from the cave and go up onto the slab (as for Vector). Climb the wide crack in the overhang above and move left, peg, to a second overhang. A nose-grinding mantel over this leads to easier ground and the belay on One Step, up which it finishes.

★★ **The Atomic Finger Flake** 150 feet   E3   (1980)
Brute force pays dividends on this route which essentially follows the hideously overhanging flake on the underside of the ochre slab. Start just right of Vector.
1 60 feet. 5b. Climb the slab between Vector and Void until forced into the latter at the belay.
2 90 feet. 6a. Take the tricky shallow groove on the right to a vegetated ledge. Climb up to a bulge, peg, then make a difficult traverse left on undercuts to gain the overhanging flake crack. Power up this to a peg and pull over a small bulge on the right into a groove. Continue up this to emerge gasping at the belay of Void.
3 Either finish up Void or cross right to the tree on Grim Wall.

Variation
2a 90 feet. 6b. A trivial though harder alternative is to traverse left below the first peg and make a couple of desperate moves up to join the normal route on the overhanging flake.

★★ **Void** 200 feet   E3   (1975)
A route ahead of its time with a stunning finish on the right edge of the Vector Headwall. Start at the foot of the groove directly beneath the ochre slab.
1 45 feet. 5b. Climb the groove to a large spike belay.

2   85 feet. 5c. As for Vector to the final traverse left to the cave. Instead, move up rightwards onto a ledge in an overhanging wall. Go right again to find a hidden crack (hopefully!). This leads to a large sloping stance overlooking the gully.
3   70 feet. 6a. Above the belay is a superb hanging pod. Enter this with difficulty and move up to its top. Swing out left to a large hold. A hard move past the peg above leads to good holds in the crack. Continue up this to the top.

The next two routes start from the stance overlooking the gully. Either do Void or Grim Wall to reach this stance.

★★ **The Mongoose**   80 feet   E5   (1977)
1   80 feet. 6a. Climb an easy slab in the gully till level with a hanging pod on the left. Swing out and pull into this with difficulty. Move up then go out left onto the front face of the buttress. Arrange protection then wobble your way up the wall above to good holds. Pull up to an easier crack to finish. A bold pitch – not to be undertaken lightly.

★ **The Snake**   90 feet   E2   (1975)
1   90 feet. 5c. As for The Mongoose to the front face of the buttress. Continue left along the obvious traverse line, crossing Void, to finish.

Right of Vector Buttress is a steep wall which contains several fine climbs. An obvious chimney low down (the first pitch of Shadrach) is an obvious landmark.

★ **Grim Wall Direct**   180 feet   E1
Some good steep climbing. Start immediately right of the vegetated gully before a step in the path.
1   100 feet. 5b. Climb a striated crack onto a slab then move diagonally left to a bulge. Go over this to a slab, which leads with difficulty to a large stance and tree belay.
2   80 feet. 5a. Climb straight up to an overhang, step right then go direct to the top. A good pitch.

★ **Leg Break**   170 feet   E4   (1978)
Aptly named – a good but poorly protected route. Start at a shallow groove 20 feet right of Grim Wall
Direct, at a tree.
1   95 feet. 5b. Climb the shallow groove then move up into another shallow groove. Move right and go up the front face of a flake to the Grim Wall hand-traverse. Bold moves up the slab above lead to an easier slab. Traverse left to a belay on Meshach.
2   75 feet. 6a. Pull onto the block above then move diagonally up with difficulty, to a break in the overhang (long reach useful). Pull over the overhang then shake leftwards across Meshach to finish up a leftwards-leaning crackline.

** **Grim Wall**   180 feet   Very Severe   (1957)
A classic route with a superb top pitch. Start below the obvious chimney of Shadrach.
1   100 feet. 4b. Climb up then slightly left to reach a scoop and go left again to a sharp flake. Hand-traverse energetically left to a corner. Awkward moves up this and a rib on the left to gain a ledge below the final wall.
2   80 feet. 4c. Climb up and right then pull over a small overhang to reach a small ledge on the left. Traverse left to a rib and climb this steeply to the top.

** **Meshach**   190 feet   Very Severe   (1962)
An indifferent start but a superb finale up the headwall. Start below the chimney of Shadrach.
1   110 feet. 4c. Climb up a slabby rake which leads left to gain a ledge. Go up a scoop above, followed by a shallow groove on the right. Step right to a good ledge. Ascend the wall for a few feet to join Shadrach, follow this for a few feet, then step down left to a good niche. Move straight up the wall on the left to a good spike and traverse left to the stance at the top of pitch 1 of Grim Wall.
2   80 feet. 5a. Climb straight through the overhang just to the right. Move right along the lip then go up the wall above, past a peg, with difficulty. Trend left then right to finish.

Variation
Rattlesnake Finish   70 feet   E1   (1978)
2a   70 feet. 5c. The flake and thin crack from just before the crux of Meshach. Crux at the top.

Blinkers   160 feet   E2   (1978)
A poor eliminate. Start as for Shadrach.
1   85 feet. 5b. Go straight up to a prominent overhang just left of the Shadrach chimney. Pull over this roof to join Shadrach and follow this to a belay by two small trees.
2   75 feet. 5b. Go diagonally left for a few feet to a poor flake at the start of Meshach's traverse. Climb straight up the wall above to the widest point of the roof. Go over this via a flake crack, then ascend diagonally left to cross Meshach and go up the final wall finishing at its highest point.

Variation
2a   70 feet. 5a. From the belay climb a shallow groove on the left finishing up twin cracks.

* **Shadrach**   170 feet   Very Severe   (1951)
The classic of the wall, direct up the centre. Start below the chimney.
1   60 feet. 4b. Climb up the inside, very strenuous, or preferably the outside (poor protection), of the chimney.

2   50 feet. 4b. Step left onto a flake then go up the wall above to a belay at a huge block.
3   60 feet. 4c. From the top of the block, make the famous stride into a shallow groove above. Ascend this for a few feet then step right finishing up the wall.

The Brothers   190 feet   Very Severe   (1957)
Some good climbing right of Shadrach. Start as for Shadrach.
1   90 feet. 4b. Climb the wide crack right of the chimney then move down right before climbing diagonally rightwards to a ledge and belay.
2   50 feet. 4b. Move left under an overhang and cross a short groove to reach the huge block on Shadrach. Belay as for Shadrach pitch 2.
3   50 feet. 4c. Finish as for Shadrach pitch 3.

Variation **Direct Finish**   60 feet   Hard Very Severe
2a   60 feet. 5a. Ascend straight up the wall then go over an overhang to a ledge. Easily to the top to finish.

Oblatron   160 feet   E3   (1979)
1   80 feet. 5a. The arête left of The Brothers.
2   80 feet. 5c. Go up right on a flake, pull over an overhang, then ascend a crack. Step left and finish direct over an overhang to finish up a tiny flake.

Emily Street   130 feet   E2   (1980)
Worthwhile and quite bold on the first pitch. Start as for Shadrach.
1   80 feet. 5c. Climb up onto the slab right of The Brothers, then move up into a slim groove. Climb it to an overlap, move rightwards and gain a slabby groove. Ascend this to a belay above the first pitch of The Brothers.
2   50 feet. 5a. As for the Direct Finish to The Brothers.

Sometimes   160 feet   E3   (1979)
A right-to-left girdle of Meshach Wall in two pitches (5a, 5c). The intricacies of the route-finding are left for those sufficiently desperate to do the route.

Nifl-Heim   200 feet   Very Severe   (1955)
The difficult sections are short. Start at an obvious chimney below and right of the start to Shadrach.
1   40 feet. 4a. Climb the chimney to a large flat ledge with a large flake belay under an overhang.
2   60 feet. 4c. Walk left then climb a shallow corner followed by a narrow ramp which leads to easier ground on the right. Move right to a tree belay (junction with Leg Slip).

3 80 feet. 4c. Go straight up for 15 feet to a horizontal crack. A difficult horizontal traverse left leads to a tree followed by easier climbing to another tree and a belay below a crack.
4 20 feet. 4c. Ascend the crack and an easy slab to finish.

Variation   40 feet   Very Severe
2a 40 feet. 4c. Climb the overhang right of the flake belay and continue to the tree belay.

Pretzel Logic   170 feet   E1   (1974)
Not a bad route with a good finishing pitch. Start at a small groove 15 feet left of the start of Venom.
1 55 feet. 5b. Ascend the groove then go up and left to the tree belay of Leg Slip.
2 70 feet. 5a. Climb a steep V-chimney on the left then go up to a belay below the crack of Nifl-Heim.
3 45 feet. 5c. Step left and move into a steep corner-crack. Climb this and go through the overhang above to a steep finishing crack.

★ **Venom**   180 feet   E3   (1976)
Often done for the first pitch alone which gives a classic little bridging problem. Start below a smooth groove right of the chimney of Nifl-Heim.
1 50 feet. 6a. Climb the excellent groove (peg) by calf-pumping bridging to an exit left onto a slab under a roof (junction with Leg Slip). Either abseil off or:
2 85 feet. 5b. Move left and climb the steep, awkward wall till a bold move left below an overhang leads to easier ground. Continue up till below the crack on Nifl-Heim.
3 45 feet. 5c. As for Pretzel Logic pitch 3.

★★ **Leg Slip**   200 feet   Hard Very Severe   (1960)
A good sustained route. Start at an obvious groove capped by a roof, just right of Venom.
1 50 feet. 5a. Climb the groove till a leftwards escape can be made to reach the top right-hand end of a sloping ramp and a small stance under a roof.
2 65 feet. 5a. Ascend through the overhang to reach an obvious groove. Climb this until a move right onto a rib becomes necessary, if not essential! Trend left to a tree belay.
3 35 feet. 5a. The groove behind the tree is climbed to an overhang. Step left with difficulty to reach easy ground and a tree belay.
4 50 feet. Scramble up to a grass ledge then go up an easy-angled slab to the top.

★★ **First Slip**   160 feet   E1   (1960)
A really fine bridging problem, thin and precarious. Start as for Leg Slip.

1   110 feet. 5c. Go up the groove to the roof then traverse right to reach a foot-ledge below the right-hand groove. Climb this with increasing difficulty till the crux last move brings a good ledge to hand.
2   50 feet. 4b. The flake above and then a series of ribs to finish. Scrambling to the top remains.

Freudian Slip   190 feet   E2   (1978)
Start below the arête right of the first groove on Leg Slip.
1   80 feet. 5c. Ascend the arête till below the groove on First Slip. Tree belay on the right.
2   110 feet. 5b. Climb the slab behind the belay till a groove on the right wall can be reached. Ascend this (peg) to an easier crack and finally the top.

Routes have been climbed in the jungle to the right – take a machete! Higher up in the trees right of the Slip climbs is a small tower split by a groove. There are two good routes on this buttress, best reached by abseil.

Slipway   100 feet   Hard Very Severe   (1970)
A good groove pitch.
1   100 feet. 5a. The groove is taken direct to the top.

The Jackal   100 feet   E1   (1979)
1   100 feet. 5b. Climb the crack and groove system right of Slipway, up the centre of the buttress.

Low down and to the right is a light-coloured buttress with a scree-fan below it. This is Gladeways Buttress which suffered a rock fall some years ago. Two routes have been climbed since. Neither is safe and they are only recommended for Japanese Kamikaze pilots who failed.

Crazy Diamond   100 feet   E1   (1979)
1   100 feet. 5b. The shallow groove in the centre of the buttress.

Solitaire   100 feet   E1   (1979)
1   100 feet. 5b. The groove and buttress left of Crazy Diamond.

Right again, hidden in the trees, and just left of the Belshazzar Gully descent path is a large slab (Oakover Slab).

Knell for a Jackdaw   150 feet   Severe   (1955)
A good first pitch with a poor upper section. Start at the left end of a ledge below the small buttress left of Oakover Slab, overlooking a huge rock fall.
1   60 feet. Go up a groove, moving rightwards in the upper part, to make an awkward bulging layback to finish.

2   30 feet. Step up and left into a corner with large blocks, then climb to the trees above (an escape is possible and, advisable, here).
3   20 feet. Follow the buttress edge on the right to a tree belay.
4   40 feet. Finish up a crack.

⭐ **Hedera**   130 feet   Very Severe   (1964)
A very pleasant route. Start at the foot of a curving corner on the left of the slab.
1   40 feet. 4b. Ascend the corner to a tree belay.
2   90 feet. 4c. Continue up the corner, past a small tree, to an overhang. A difficult traverse right leads to a crack which is followed, trending left, to the top.

Oakover   140 feet   Very Severe   (1955)
A really enjoyable route up the slab. Start as for Hedera.
1   40 feet. 4b. Hedera pitch 1 (or the slab just to the right).
2   60 feet. 4c. Traverse right onto the slab and go up awkwardly to a ledge. Move out right again then climb up with difficulty to a ledge below a large oak tree. Step into the groove on the right and go up through trees to a belay.
3   40 feet. 4b. Ascend a short slab and a crack to the top.

Heartline   120 feet   E3   (1978)
A bold eliminate line. Start at the base of Oakover Slab.
1   120 feet. 5c. Go up the right-hand edge of the slab and move diagonally leftwards, on small flakes, to an obvious groove. Ascend the groove, moving either left or right at the top.

Bloodsucker   130 feet   E2
1   130 feet. 5c. Go up Heartline till a rampline on the left can be reached then climb this to the top.

Axeminster   120 feet   Hard Severe   (1968)
Not a very good route up the right-hand edge of the slab. Start at the base of a flake-crack below a leaning corner.
1   30 feet. Ascend the flake-crack for 15 feet to a tree, traverse right and go up a crack to a ledge on the edge of Belshazzar Gully.
2   60 feet. Follow the slab above to an awkward move into a groove. Climb the crack to the right until a move left to a tree belay.
3   30 feet. Ascend the groove easily to the top.

Variation   Severe
1a   90 feet. The leaning corner can be climbed to link with Oakover or trend rightwards back into Axeminster.

The next routes can be found on the right of Belshazzar Gully.

Re-entry   100 feet   E2   (1981)
1   30 feet. 5c. Climb the steep wall to the left of Belshazzar to the tree belay on that route.
2   70 feet. 5a. Above is a small overhang; climb this moving right to a ledge. Trend left to reach and climb a short curving corner crack. Ascend this onto the arête and finish as for Daddy Cool.

Belshazzar   200 feet   Hard Very Severe   (1951)
Worth doing for the upper section. Start at the foot of a crack in the secluded bay just right of the foot of Belshazzar Gully.
1   30 feet. 4c. Climb a crack and go over a bulge to a ledge and tree belay.
2   120 feet. 5a. Traverse right a little then climb a wall to a ledge. From the right-hand end of the ledge take a slab till a move round a rib into a groove is possible. Ascend the groove to a ledge on the rib. Step right onto the wall on the right and make a delicate traverse along this to a corner (Rienetta).
3   50 feet. 4b. Climb the corner and crack, stepping left to finish.

Right of Belshazzar is a big recess. The left wall has several interconnecting pitches on it. The following routes probably offer the most rational lines but they can be varied at will. An obvious feature is the slabby ramp which cuts the wall diagonally from left to right.

Earthsea   140 feet   Hard Very Severe   (1978)
A contrived route. Start below the slabby ramp at a large tree.
1   80 feet. 5a. Scramble up to the ramp. In the steep wall to the left are two grooves, the second containing a tree. Ascend the first groove stepping first left then right to easier ground. Move up and right to reach a diagonal crack in a steep wall. Follow this, in a good position, to a large ledge and belays well back.
2   60 feet. 4a. Step right and go up the edge of the steep wall, or scramble up easy slabs.

★ **Daddy Cool**   130 feet   E2   (1978)
The best route in the bay giving good steep climbing. Scramble up the ramp to the tree in the second groove.
1   65 feet. 5c. Follow the ramp for a few feet then move back left onto a pedestal below a diagonal crack. Move boldly up the crack to an overhang and pull over this into a left-sloping groove. Climb this to a sloping ledge where a move right and up leads to a belay on Earthsea (an escape up Earthsea is possible but it is better to continue).
2   35 feet. 5a. Move up and right onto the steep wall making a delicate traverse into the corner (as for Belshazzar).
3   30 feet. 5c. As for The Sting Pitch 2.

Salamanda   160 feet   Hard Very Severe   (1978)
Start at the bottom of the blunt rib which leads up to the ramp.
1   90 feet. 4c. Climb the rib then the ramp to a tower and block belays. A bold pitch.
2   70 feet. 5a. Move straight up above the block, over a small overhang, to a narrow ledge. Go straight up the wall above to finish up a steep crack.

The Sting   140 feet   E2   (1978)
Rarely done for itself but still worthwhile. Start beneath the slabby ramp.
1   75 feet. 4a. Climb the corner crack of the slabby ramp to the block belay on Salamanda, or climb pitch 1 of Salamanda.
2   65 feet. 5c. Across on the right is a smooth corner; traverse into it then climb it, with difficulty, to the top. An excellent pitch.

Heartbreak Hotel   150 feet   Hard Severe   (1978)
1   75 feet. As for The Sting to below a large blocky corner.
2   75 feet. Climb a crack to a tree then follow the corner and crack above, moving left to finish (as for Rienetta pitches 3 and 4).

Rienetta   200 feet   Hard Severe   (1952)
Quite worthwhile with some tricky moves. Start at a chimney just right of the foot of the spur which comes down close to the road.
1   40 feet. Climb the chimney to a recess and continue to a tree belay.
2   80 feet. Ascend the slabs above moving right to a good ledge and another tree belay.
3   30 feet. Traverse left to a corner, then move out to a crack which leads to a large, woody, perennial plant belay. (Care is required with loose rock on this pitch.)
4   50 feet. Continue up the corner and crack above moving left to finish.

Dragon   170 feet   E2   (1974)
A vicious move. Start 10 feet left of and below the broken blocks at the start of Merlin.
1   90 feet. 4b. Move diagonally left over the arête into a bottomless chimney. Ascend the chimney to a roof, step left then climb easily up to a tree belay.
2   80 feet. 6b. Move up left to a steep crack. A hard move leads to a ledge, step up and left then go straight up the wall to finish.

Merlin   180 feet   Very Severe   (1956)
A popular route. Much of the first pitch has been destroyed by a recent rockfall and the route is now started to the left. Start as for Rienetta. (Alternatively climb the original route at 6a)

1 80 feet. 4c. Go up a few feet then rightwards along a thin crack to reach an overhang above the rock scar. Pull over this (crux) then go left up easy slabs to a tree belay below a steep wall.

2 80 feet. 4b. Climb a crack above a short slab then step down right onto a wall and go up this to a ledge. Traverse right along a slab into a groove and ascend this to tree belay.

3 20 feet. 4a. Finish up the steep corner behind the tree.

★★ Variation. **The Direct Finish** 80 feet Hard Very Severe   (1959)
A brilliant pitch, one of the best of its grade at Tremadog.

2a 80 feet 5a. As for pitch 2 to the ledge then go left and up and left to gain a steep wall. Climb this in a superb position.

★★ **Vulture**   120 feet   E4   (1975)
A cracking pitch suitable for short-legged orang-utans. Start below the crux overhang of Merlin.

1 100 feet. 6a. Climb a shallow groove up on the right then climb the steep layback crack above the first ramp of Geireagle by precarious, 'barndoor' laybacking to a junction with Geir-eagle. Either finish up this or better, climb the continuation crack till a junction with the final groove of Merlin.

2 20 feet. Ascend the corner to finish.

★★ **Geireagle**   150 feet   E3   (1966)
I hope the name is spelt correctly! A strange route with precarious yet quite strenuous climbing. Start as for Vulture.

1 130 feet. 5c. Climb the shallow groove as for Vulture then balance along the ramp to its end. Some hard moves then lead to a good ledge. A long reach left gains the arête (peg). Continue up the slab above to the corner of Merlin.

2 20 feet. 4a. Finish as for Merlin up the corner.

★ **Y Broga**   140 feet   Hard Very Severe   (1962)
A route for the vain as the first pitch is so polished you can see your face in it! Start right of Merlin at the corner bounding a large slab.

1 50 feet. 5a. Climb the difficult corner to a big ledge.

2 60 feet. 4b. Ascend a steep crack on the left to a small ledge then go up to another ledge. A groove above leads to a tree belay.

3 30 feet. 4c. Climb the slab above for 10 feet till a difficult step left gains an arête. Climb this to the top.

What's its Name?   145 feet   E3

1 50 feet. 5a. As for Y Broga Pitch 1.

2 60 feet. 5c. Go up a few feet till a swing left into Geireagle at the ledge is possible. Ascend the groove above to rejoin Y Broga. Belay on this.

3 30 feet. As for Y Broga Pitch 3 to finish.

Geraldine Taylor, the Vulture, Craig Bwlch y Moch.
Photo: Glenn Robbins

Traffic jam on Vector, Weaver and Diadic, Craig Bwlch y Moch.
Photo: Paul Williams

Oberon   170 feet   Very Difficult   (1955)
Although scrappy this is a popular and worthwhile route. Start
at the foot of the slab, on the left.
1 50 feet. Climb up and right to the edge of the slab, then step
leftwards to reach the top of the slab.
2 60 feet. Climb into and up a chimney on the right, to an easy
slab and tree belay.
3 60 feet. Climb a corner behind a tree to a steep crack. Ascend
this awkwardly to finish.

Emotional Crisis   60 feet   E4   (1983)
A superb and bold arête, not for the faint-hearted. Start at the
top of Oberon's second pitch below an obvious sharp arête.
1 60 feet. 5c. Climb the arête – once you go, don't come back!

Boo-Boo   200 feet   Hard Very Difficult   (1961)
Right of Merlin Buttress is an area of vegetated slabs. Start at
the foot of the arête on the right-hand side of the slabs.
1 50 feet. Climb rightwards to the foot of a steep corner. Climb
the right-hand side to a tree belay (or the slightly harder crack
on the left).
2 50 feet. The corner behind the tree leads to an overhang. Pull
right onto slabs above. Ascend these to a large ledge.
3 100 feet. Climb a crack behind a large detached pinnacle. A
tricky step left onto slabs can be made. Go up these to finish.

Up and right of Boo-Boo is a ridge running up the hillside.
Scramble up the gully for a little till a chimney just above the
ground can be seen with an obvious little corner just to its left.

Tweek   100 feet   E3
Start 10 feet left of Rock on Tommy.
1 100 feet. 6a. Climb the little corner with difficulty till a traverse
can be made into Starship Trooper. Finish up this.

Rock on Tommy   100 feet   E3
1 100 feet. 6a. Start 10 feet left of Starship Trooper. Take the
obvious ramp moving left to a good flake layaway. Ascend this
to a junction with Tweek and finish up this.

Starship Trooper   90 feet   E4   (1978)
A fine bold route. Easy for the grade. Start below the chimney.
1 90 feet. 5c. Ascend into the chimney until an exit left onto a
small ledge. Continue direct till a rather loose flake on the left
can be reached. A poor peg can sometimes be clipped out right,
then make some scary moves up the shallow groove above the
flake to reach sloping ledges. Move up and right to another
groove and ascend this to emerge in a state of shock on the final
easy slab.

Hot Rats   100 feet   E3   (1978)
Interesting climbing right of Starship Trooper. Start as for
Starship Trooper.
1   100 feet. 6a. Climb a crack and overhanging groove just left
of ivy to a resting ledge (peg). Ascend the steep wall above for
10 feet then traverse right on good holds to another resting
ledge below an overhang. Swing round to the right of the
overhang (poor peg) then climb the wall and arête with difficulty
to a large ledge. Step left and climb a thin crack and overhanging
corner to finish.

Down right and just above the road is a huge boulder; above
this is the obvious arête of Chwys. Before the boulder is reached
a white triangular wall up on the left can be seen. This can be
reached by bush-whacking or, better, by abseil.

Savage Man   60 feet   E3   (1979)
Start on an ivy-covered ledge at the base of the white wall. A
good pitch.
1   60 feet. 6a. Go straight up via small cracks to a peg. Hard
moves up and left (crux) lead to a crack running left-to-right. A
difficult move leads into a niche then go up blocks to finish.

Cnychwyr   140 feet   Very Severe   (1985)
Start about 60 feet left of Chwys at thin cracks in a slab.
1   70 feet. 4c. Climb the thin cracks past an oak tree to a stance
and belay.
2   70 feet. 4c. Continue up to a rightward-slanting crack. Above
is a steep wall with a small groove; climb these to finish.

Gwaed   130 feet   Hard Very Severe   (1981)
A worthwhile route. Start at a tree 20 feet left of Chwys below a
corner.
1   80 feet. 5b. Climb the corner and a crack to a roof. Pull over
the obvious overlap (crux) onto a rib on the left. Gain a slab and
climb to a belay on Chwys.
2   50 feet. 4c. The overlapping flake on the left part of the slab
is followed to finish.

Penicillin   100 feet   E4   (1980)
A difficult problem. Also known as Big Bug. Start just left of
Chwys.
1   100 feet. 6b. Climb the arête just left of Chwys then cross that
route and climb an overhanging groove to an awkward exit.
Finish more easily.

★★ **Chwys**   140 feet   Hard Very Severe   (1967)
A fine sustained route, hard for the grade. Start by scrambling
up to a tree at the foot of a groove on the right-hand side of the
buttress.

1 90 feet. 5b. Go up easily to the base of a smooth groove. Ascend the groove and go over a bulge at its top, moving left onto a steep wall. Go up, then diagonally left, along a steep ramp and over an overhang at its end. Continue to a grass ledge and belay.
2 50 feet. Easy slabs to finish.

Twelve yards right of Chwys is a clean arête (Yogi). Just left is a deep corner.

Sheer Khan   80 feet   Hard Very Severe   (1980)
1 80 feet. 5a. Climb up to the foot of the corner. Follow the corner direct to the top.

Sheer Resist   70 feet   E4   (1982)
The left wall of Sheer Khan gives a difficult and worthwhile pitch. Start at the foot of the corner.
1 70 feet. 6b. Traverse left onto the wall then climb rightwards to reach a steep crack. This is taken to a hard exit left at the top.

Yogi   120 feet   Very Severe   (1961)
A really pleasant route. Start at the foot of the clean arête.
1 50 feet. 4b. Climb the steep lower part of the arête on the right for 15 feet then pull out left onto slabs. Continue straight up the rib to a large ledge.
2 70 feet. Ascend the rib for 30 feet, till a step left onto a small grassy ledge below the final slab. The right-hand side of the slab leads to the top.

Smarter than the Average Bear   120 feet   Hard Very Severe
                                                            (1988)
1 50 feet. 5a. Pull round the undercut base of the slab then follow the thin crackline to a bulge. This is climbed direct to the belay on Yogi. A bold pitch.
2 70 feet. 5a. Follow Yogi for 20 feet then trend left to reach a grassy ledge below the final slab. The slab is climbed left of a crystal-filled fissure, on small holds to the top.

A corner and crack just to the right give a Hard Severe route which has been claimed by many parties.

Moel y Gest Quarry   O.S. ref. 555 390

The cliff is situated high on Moel y Gest on the opposite side of the road to Craig y Castell, about half a mile from Porthmadog along the Criccieth road.

The best approaches are from the cemetery (no comment!) adjacent to the refuse tip, then go straight up a ramp to the foot of the cliff or, less strenuously, go up a path behind the cemetery (difficult to find).

Long out of fashion Moel y Gest may yet prove to be a popular crag; with the present explosion in the slate quarries of Llanberis it can only be a matter of time before some inquisitive soul strays down 'just for a look'.

The climbing lies, at present, on the left-hand cliff which is about 200 yards long and 120 feet high. Though clean there are many patches of loose rock and care should be taken on all the routes (pre-cleaning by abseil may be essential). As on all slate care must always be taken with the ropes as sharp edges abound. Finally, remember that on the first ascents all peg runners and belays were removed so again an abseil is recommended to replace the gear (please give generously).

The routes are described from left to right.

Inferior Grooves   95 feet   Very Severe   (1967)

Short Wall   95 feet   Very Severe   (1967)

Chough   100 feet   Hard Very Severe   (1 pt. aid)   (1967)
An old peg is used on pitch 2.

Blogg's Route   100 feet   Very Severe   (2 pts. aid)   (1968)
An old peg at the start and one at the top.

The Prow   125 feet   Hard Very Severe   (1967)

Eclipse   120 feet   Hard Severe   (1 pt. aid)   (1967)
An aid sling on the top wall.

Penumbria   120 feet   Hard Severe   (1967)
The easiest route on the cliff with some nice climbing but be careful of loose rock.

Oblique   140 feet   Very Severe   (1 pt. aid)   (1967)
A peg is used to leave Penumbria but afterwards the route is easy.

Damocles   150 feet   Extremely Severe   (2 pts. aid) (1967)
A good route. One old peg is used halfway up pitch 1 and another aid peg at the start of the second pitch.

Irony   150 feet   Extremely Severe   (2 pts. aid)   (1967)
Two aid pegs in the groove on pitch 1.

Fracture   125 feet   Very Severe   (1 pt. aid)   (1967)
An aid peg is required to move up and left from the ledges 30 feet up the first pitch.

Scorpion   130 feet   Very Severe   (1967)
A difficult route with a final sting.

Oughtogo   130 feet   Hard Very Severe   (1 pt. aid)   (1967)
Very loose. An aid peg assists the move right on pitch 1.

Cut-throat   130 feet   Extremely Severe   (1967)
A good route.

Knife Edge   140 feet   Hard Very Severe   (1 pt. aid)   (1967)
A peg for aid on the final overhang.

The Milky Way   130 feet   Very Severe   (1967)
The obvious Quartz Vein.

The Swinger   130 feet   Extremely Severe   (2 pts. aid)   (1967)
One of the better routes in the quarry. On pitch 1 a small nut is used to move right from a groove and then a peg to move left from the top of the pillar.

Contrast   150 feet   Extremely Severe   (2 pts. aid)   "(1967)
Some good, varied climbing. Two aid pegs are used at the top of pitch one.

Joe Soap's Route   125 feet   Hard Very Severe   (aid)   (1968)
Aid nuts are used in the groove.

Deception   130 feet   Hard Very Severe   (3 pts. aid)   (1967)
A peg and two aid nuts are used to climb the groove on the first pitch.

The following is a more recent route.

Space Panic   100 feet   Hard Very Severe   (1981)
Scramble 50 feet over big blocks in the right-hand bay to a large ledge below an enormous corner.
1   100 feet. 5a. Jam the corner to a roof, traverse left (peg) into a groove and go up this to the top.

Carreg Hyll-Drem (Ugly Rocks)   O.S. ref. 614 432

The cliff lies immediately above the Aberglaslyn – Penrhyndeudraeth road about a mile north of the village of Carreg. The crag is the termination of a small spur of Cnicht and gives incredibly steep climbing on strange, rather smooth, rock.

Carreg Hyll-Drem

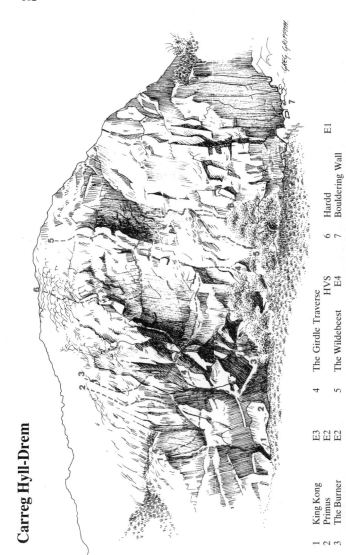

1	King Kong	E3
2	Primus	E2
3	The Burner	E2
4	The Girdle Traverse	
5	The Wildebeest	HVS / E4
6	Hardd	
7	Bouldering Wall	E1

Strength and boldness are essential for success on the routes here – the master of slab climbing would do well to leave this crag alone! One particularly useful aspect of the crag is that it rarely gets wet so climbing can be had when the nearby Tremadog cliffs are out of condition.

At the left-hand end of the cliff, low down, are some large roofs while up and right are a series of overhanging grooves, roof-cracks and one particularly hideous overhanging chimney. Right again is a rightward-sloping gangway with a concave wall above it. Farther right just past a fence is a short steep wall – The Hyll-Drem Bouldering Wall.

The best descent is to the right of the crag.

The first route is reached by scrambling up vegetation at the left-hand side of the crag to a small slab.

Troubador 130 feet E2 (1973)
A short but excellent hard section through a spectacular overhang.
1 90 feet. 5c. From the slab step down right onto a ramp about 30 feet off the ground. Go along this till beneath a flake in the roof. Swing up over this into a chimney and ascend this to a poor stance.
2 40 feet. 4b. Climb a groove to finish up easy slabs.

King Kong 120 feet E3 (1974)
A wild and worrying pitch. Will the flake stay on or won't it? Start at the left-hand side of the crag, below an obvious flake-crack splitting the lower roof.
1 30 feet. 5c. Power out along the roof to an awkward move on the lip, above which is a stance and peg belay.
2 50 feet. Go right for 20 feet to a slab which leads back left to a stance and peg belay.
3 40 feet. 5a. Stroll right 10 feet then ascend an overhanging chimney to the top.

King Kong-Troubador Connection 135 feet E3
The best combination – very very steep.
1 30 feet. 5c. As for King-Kong pitch 1.
2 25 feet. 5b. A tricky traverse left leads to the base of the roof on Troubador.
3 40 feet. 5c. The roof on Troubador pitch 1.
4 40 feet. 4b. Finish as for Troubador pitch 2.

Compromising Positions 40 feet E4 (1983)
Bigger, badder, bolder and butcher! Start right of King Kong below a faint weakness in the roof.

1 40 feet. 6b. Climb the line of least resistance through the roof (peg) to reach a stance and belay on Troubador. Escape any which way you can.

★ Primus   180 feet   E2   (1960)

A very steep route with a sharp, but short, crux. The lower section of the main crag is split by a prominent groove. Start at slabby rock just to the left of the groove.

1 75 feet. 4c. Climb up the slabby rock until an awkward traverse right leads into the groove. Ascend this easily to a stance and peg belay beneath the overhangs (junction with The Girdle).

2 55 feet. 5c. Move across the slab on the left to a rib. Climb this for a few feet then move back right across a steep wall until an overhanging groove above (peg) can be reached. Ascend the awkward groove to reach easier ground and a good spike belay with an exposed stance on the right.

3 50 feet. 4c. Move up above the spike then move left to finish.

Sunset Traverse   200 feet   Hard Very Severe   (1977)

A low-level traverse following slabs between the roofs at the left-hand side of the crag. Start below twin grooves about 30 feet right of the groove of Primus.

1 50 feet. 5a. Climb the right-hand groove, then traverse left (tricky) onto a slab. Continue left to a stance in the groove of Primus.

2 50 feet. 5a. Move down then go left across a slab to a tree (stump) belay (junction with The Girdle).

3 100 feet. 5a. Go easily along the slab then up steeply to finish.

★★ The Burner   180 feet   E2   (1966)

A great pitch crossing unlikely ground on (relatively) large holds. Very, very exposed. Start as for Sunset Traverse.

1 60 feet. 5a. Climb the right-hand groove to a junction with The Girdle. Follow this leftwards to a stance and peg belay on a rib.

2 70 feet. 5b. Ascend the rib on the left to a small platform then launch out left across an overhanging wall until a small niche straight above can be reached. Swing left round an arête to the stance and belay on Primus.

3 50 feet. 4c. As for Primus Pitch 3.

★★ Burner Direct Finish   110 feet   E5   (1986)

A route to stimulate the fast twitch muscle fibres! Start at the top of the first pitch of Burner.

1 110 feet. 6a'ish. Follow the second pitch till it escapes left then blast up and onwards to reach better holds.

★★ Raving Lunatic feet   E5   (1984)
An inviting prospect through the 'gash' right of The Burner. The
Separate Reality of Wales. Start at the top of the first pitch of
The Burner.
1 110 feet. 6b. Move up to the evil roof-crack then swing out
on arm-bars etc. till a final struggle on the lip brings sanctuary
within reach.

★★ Raging Bull 110 feet   E5   (1983)
Another stunning and equally hideous line up a shallow
overhanging chimney. Suitable for dwarfs. Start at the top of
pitch 1 of The Burner.
1 70 feet. 6b. Ascend Samurai Groove till below the open
chimney then swarm up it (3 pegs), by overhanging back-and-
footing, till the lip is reached. Continue up steep rock till the
belay on the top of the second pitch of Samurai Groove is
reached.
2 40 feet. As for pitch 3 of Samurai Groove.

Total Bull 110 feet   E4   (1987)
A steep route – spacewalking practice on Skylab essential!
1 70 feet. 6a. Ascend Samurai Groove to the open chimney of
Raging Bull, swing out right and go up an exposed scoop until
the belay on Samurai Groove is reached.
2 40 feet. Pitch 3 of Samurai Groove.

★ Flare Up 140 feet   E6   (1988)
A strenuous and impressive route. Start down and left from
Samurai Groove in a small alcove.
1 50 feet. 6a. Rock up into the obvious left-slanting gangway
and follow it for 10 feet until a move into an easy groove can be
made.
2 90 feet. 6c. The slab on the right is followed for a few feet
until is is possible to launch boldly up the overhanging wall
above an undercut to reach a hidden peg runner in a niche. Hard
moves past the peg lead to a good jug. An even bigger jug above
leads to a swing up left into a slanting chimney then follow
easier rocks to the top.

★★ Samurai Groove 180 feet   E3   (1971)
"There exists no pitch more out there!" This sums up well a
totally mind-blowing route which gives one of the best pitches
of its grade in Wales. Care is needed to avoid rope drag on the
second pitch.
1 60 feet. 5a. Pitch 1 of The Burner.
2 80 feet. 5c. Climb a short groove above the belay till a
traverse line leads right below an overhanging nose (Raging
Bull) to a saddle. A terrifying move down and right leads to a
good jug (the infamous 'mother'). Pull up and round to the right
into a steep groove. Ascend this until a difficult exit left from an
overhung niche leads to a belay on easier ground.

3   40 feet. Finish up broken rocks.
(N.B. On pitch 2 the original route exited direct from the groove
with one point of aid).

Going for Gold   130 feet   E6   (1988)
A direct line up to the blank overhanging groove right of the top
of Samurai Groove. Start as for Samurai Groove.
1   130 feet. 6c. Move up and right onto a steep wall next to some
ivy. Move up left to an easier groove leading to a short chimney.
Climb this to a smooth overhanging wall where hard moves up
past a roof lead to a slab below the overhanging groove. Go up
past a poor peg to clip the 'golden peg' then blast the groove
above to gain a big flake above it. Finish as for Samurai Groove.

★★ **Gwyddbwyll**   100 feet   E5   (1987)
The name means 'chess' – an accurate description of the
subtleties required to beat this fine route.
1   100 feet. 6b. Go 15 feet along the Girdle Traverse to an
obvious crack (Friends), ascend the crack to a peg then traverse
right for 10 feet to another peg. Move straight up to 2 pegs
together then go left and up a groove to join Hardd at the stance.
Either abseil off or continue up Hardd Direct.

★★ **The Wildebeest**   150 feet   E4   (1981)
A direct start to a direct finish! Although the new climbing on
the first pitch only takes you to the start of Hardd it is still very
worthwhile, while the top pitch – the old direct finish to Hardd,
is superb. Start by scrambling behind a large oak tree to reach
the rightwards-leading gangway at the base of a sharp rib.
1   100 feet. 5c. Climb the rib to a large undercut. Pull out left
then go up to a block roof. Awkward moves out right lead to the
foot of the short crack on Hardd. Continue up as for Hardd.
2   50 feet. 5c. Move right again onto a smooth little wall then
make a difficult move up to gain an awkward position on the left
side of an overhanging groove. Move straight up on very steep
rock to a niche beneath an overhang. Swing left to easy ground
and the top.

Rain Shadow   120 feet   E5   (1988)
A spectacular traverse which seems to stay dry in all weather.
Start as for Hardd.
1   120 feet. From the start of Hardd move left to the flakes
above the roof of Wildebeest and traverse left with these at foot
level until thin climbing up and across the slab gains the break
of Gwyddbwyll. Continue leftwards past the pegs below the top
groove of that route to the bay before an overhanging nose.
Climb round the nose with difficulty into Samurai Groove and
finish up this.

Dion 100 feet E4 (1988)

Start at the stance of Harold.

1 100 feet. 6b. Climb up to and clip the peg on Hardd then step down and left to a point above The Wildebeest. Make hard moves left to clip a peg on Gwyddbwyll. Reverse this past its first peg to a good ledge before the obvious ramp. Traverse this to below Raging Bull. Step down to the Girdle stance to finish.

** Hardd 160 feet E2 (1960)

A tremendous classic with a 'big cliff' feel about it. Start by scrambling up behind the oak to reach a large ledge some way up the gangway.

1 80 feet. 5c. Step left onto the steep wall and climb it leftwards to the foot of a short crack. Ascend this to a bulge then make a difficult and very delicate traverse left to a good resting spot. Move onto the smooth slab on the left and continue up in the same line over some bulges to reach a small exposed stance.

2 40 feet. 4b. Step down the steep groove below until an escape out left on good holds is possible to reach easier ground. Ascend this to a good stance.

3 40 feet. Climb easy broken rocks to the top.

Variations

** The Original Way 80 feet E1 (1960)

1a 60 feet. 5c. As for the normal route to the good resting spot. Instead of stepping left pull straight over bulges to reach a small stance.

2a 20 feet. 4b. Move left into a groove and climb it for a few feet until a step left to reach the small stance at the end of pitch 1 of the Ordinary route is possible.

For those wishing for harder things the old direct finish (now the second pitch of The Wildebeest) can be followed making the route E3.

Poker 140 feet E3 (1966)

Strenuous and poorly protected with some loose rock – classic! Start as for Hardd.

1 70 feet. 5c. An overhanging groove above the stance is climbed (peg) to a step right. Move up into an overhung niche and a peg belay.

2 70 feet. 5c. The smooth groove on the left leads to an obvious spike runner. Move awkwardly onto a slab, step right and then back left around a bulge. A diagonal traverse left across a steep wall remains.

The Spook 140 feet E1 (1966)

An unpleasant route. Start as for Hardd.

1 70 feet. 5a. Go up the gangway then step left onto the wall. Ascend this trending left to belay in the niche of Poker.

2 70 feet. 5c. Difficult moves lead out of the right-hand side of the niche then trend left across the upper wall to the top.

Biggles   140 feet   Hard Very Severe   (1979)
An enjoyable pitch. Start as for Hardd.
1 140 feet. 5a. As for The Spook but keep moving right to reach another rightwards-sloping ramp. Climb this delicately to the top.

★ **The Girdle Traverse**   220 feet   Hard Very Severe   (1960)
A great route for a wet day. Easy for the grade. Start at the large oak at the foot of the gangway.
1 65 feet. 5a. Climb leftwards along an obvious break to reach a short groove. Ascend this then make a difficult move left onto a rib (crux). Peg belay.
2 35 feet. 4b. Move across a slab on the left to another rib, then go down a groove on the other side for 20 feet to a small stance.
3 40 feet. 4b. The slab on the left is traversed after which a descent down a broken groove leads to a good ledge and tree belay. (Many parties abseil off but be warned, the tree has a very short life expectancy.)
4 80 feet. 4c. Climb a slab to a tree belay. Alternatively, climb the groove until forced onto the slab.

Variation
Maybelline Finish   100 feet   Hard Very Severe   (1965)
4a 100 feet. 5a. Climb the groove to the overhang, pull over this into a rightward-slanting groove then follow this to the top.

Nightmare of Black Donkeys   350 feet   E3
This is an exposed but rather pointless high-level girdle of the crag. The route starts up Primus to the junction with The Burner. A rising traverse right leads to the last stance of Hardd. Reverse pitch 2 of Hardd to the exposed stance where a fine final pitch across the wall to the right is climbed to finish.

To the right just past a small fence is a short overhanging wall. This gives some excellent, powerful bouldering plus a few mean routes.

Bay of Pigs   30 feet   E5   (1988)
1 30 feet. 6b. The overhanging pod left of Weirpig is gained by a boulder problem and climbed, past a poor peg, using holds on the right arête. Lower off the belay of Weirpig.

★★ **The Weirpig**   80 feet   E5   (1981)
A nasty piece of work with poor protection. Start below the obvious niche in the centre of the wall.
1 80 feet. 6b. A boulder problem start gains the niche (poor Friend placement). Make a difficult sequence of moves to stand

in the niche (crux) then swing out left and back right leading to an easier finish up a broken groove.

★ **First Blood**   40 feet   E4   (1983)
A poky start with hard moves past a sling. Start 3 yards right of The Weirpig below a groove with a sling and a peg.
1 40 feet. 6a. Shake your way up to the sling, make a difficult move past it then continue more easily to reach fixed slings (abseil off).

Tarzan   40 feet   E3   (1973)
Needs constant reclimbing to avoid becoming overgrown again. A pleasant and quite difficult pitch. Start at a pointed boulder just right of First Blood.
1 40 feet. 5c. Step off the boulder and move up to a peg (awkward to clip). Move leftwards to reach an in situ thread, pull out left (crux) and go up into a slabby grove. This is climbed to some fixed slings. Abseil off.

Ryan's – Son   50 feet   E4   (1983)
1 50 feet. 6b. Climb up to, and through, the obvious large roof right of Tarzan. (2 pegs).

Craig y Gelli (Crag of the Grove)   O.S. ref. 591 436

Craig y Gelli lies on the lower slopes of Moel Ddu, overlooking the A498, two miles south of Aberglaslyn Bridge, towards the end of a straight stretch of road and just before a cottage on the left. Just before the bend there is a small lay-by on the right with room for three cars (DO NOT park opposite the cottage). A faint path leads from the lay-by up to the right of the crag.

The main feature is a line of slabs topped by an overhang, with smaller buttresses to the right and left. The easiest descent is on the left, down a grassy slope with a short steep scramble down to the start of Via Gellia. A descent to the right of the crag, starting at a short tree-filled gully is also possible.

Although little frequented Craig y Gelli is well worth a visit, especially for those in search of peace and quiet on a busy day at nearby Tremadog.

★ **Via Gellia**   120 feet   Very Severe   (1956)
The left subsidiary buttress forms a steep slab divided from the main crag by a vegetated gully. This route takes the left edge of the slab giving a fine little route. Start just below and left of a little overhang at the foot of the buttress.

1 60 feet. 4b. Go up to a detached flake then move right across a rib onto the edge of the slab. Climb the slab to a ledge and belay.
2 60 feet. 4b. Step onto a block out right then go up the wall above, awkward to start, to another ledge. Continue over a thin detached flake and a slab to easy ground and the top.

Hindleberg   80 feet   Hard Very Severe   (1973)
Another interesting route. Start right of the detached flake of Via Gellia, below a corner.
1 80 feet. 5b. Climb the corner then step right to a crack in the slab. Climb the slab to a horizontal break then step left to a steep slab which is climbed direct, past another horizontal break, to the top.

A steep groove just left of the gully has also been climbed.

Tornado   150 feet   Very Severe   (1962)
Not really worth the effort though there are some good moves. Start at trees below the left side of the main cliff, 15 yards right of the vegetated gully. Scramble up behind the trees then go right behind a block to the base of a short steep corner below a small overhang.
1 40 feet. 5a. Climb the corner to the overhang, then a difficult couple of moves right lead to a ledge and tree belay.
2 30 feet. 5a. Step left and go over an overhang to reach a ledge. Ascend the wall above to a ledge and another tree belay.
3 50 feet. 4b. Cracks and ribs lead to a large heathery ledge and a tree below a chimney.
4 30 feet. 4a. Finish up the chimney.

★ **Cursor**   160 feet   E1   (1964)
A fine top pitch gives the meat of the route. Start just left of an obvious tree-filled gully.
1 70 feet. 4c. Go diagonally left to a fault in the slab and climb it to a tricky step left to a small ledge and peg belay.
2 30 feet. 4c. Climb back right and go up an overhanging groove; this leads to a large ledge and tree belay.
3 60 feet. 5b. Traverse left along a big flake till below an obvious break in the overhangs. Climb the break till a traverse left, below the final roof, to easier ground is possible. An exposed and exciting pitch.

Tumbleweed   150 feet   Very Difficult   (1955)
The revolting gully to the right is taken, belays where required.

Hurricane   150 feet   Hard Very Severe   (1979)
A fine route up the far right-hand edge of the cliff. Start by some
slabby grooves.
1   100 feet. 5a. Ascend an easy-angled groove to an overhang.
Move right then go back left on the lip of the overhang (crux).
Climb up and right to reach a crack on the right-hand side of the
buttress. Ascend this, then go up the edge of the buttress for a
few feet to a stance and tree belay.
2   50 feet. 4c. Move back right onto the arête and climb this
direct to the top. Rotten tree belay – good luck!

Pothook   145 feet   Hard Severe   (1955)
Bold for the grade. Start at a groove on the right of a tree-filled
chimney, seven yards right of the edge of the buttress.
1   45 feet. Climb a groove then traverse right under an overhang
to an awkward move which leads to a ledge on the edge of the
buttress. Alternatively, climb the less obvious groove just to the
right.
2   50 feet. Step up and left to reach a ledge. Some difficult
moves lead left then climb the right wall of a groove to a large
ledge and tree belay.
3   50 feet. Climb easily to the top.

ABERGLASLYN AND NANTMOR

A rarely frequented area by the climber and although there is much rock most of it is unsuitable. Having said that there is much for the connoisseur to delight in. The following routes have been recorded and are worthwhile.

ABERGLASLYN PASS   O.S. ref. 596 463
The east side of the Pass is very steep giving one particularly enjoyable route.

Canyon Rib   235 feet   Difficult   (1951)
Well worth doing – the nearest thing to Verdon in Wales! Start well above the path, at a small oak 200 yards up-stream from the bridge.
1   35 feet. Climb the clean sharp rib to a stance below a large block.
2   15 feet. Pull onto the block and stroll back to the bottom of an excellent wall.
3   35 feet. Ascend the wall to a stance on the right edge.
4   45 feet. Move out right to the edge of the next rib. Climb the steep sharp edge to a small stance.
5   30 feet. Go up easily till beneath the final wall.
6   50 feet. The wall above is vertical, forming the left side of the rib. Start on the left and move back right, following an obvious line of holds to a stance and belay.
7   25 feet. Broken rock leads to the top.

CRAIG Y DYNIEWYD   O.S. ref. 612 475
The only really worthwhile crag in the Nantmor Valley. The cliff lies on the south side of Moel y Dyniewyd, just below the top. The main point of interest is a large imposing buttress of good rock with short gullies on either side. A loose wall, with a pinnacle at its base, lies past the right-hand gully.

The crag can be approached from Clogwyn Farm in Nantmor itself or from the village of Nantmor.

Christmas Climb   110 feet   Difficult   (1947)
A pleasant route, well worth the trek. Start at the toe of the main buttress.
1   30 feet. Move onto the wall and climb a right-slanting groove to a bollard.
2   30 feet. A steep rib above the belay leads to another bollard under a roof. Step left across the wall to the far side of a hanging slab.

Paul Clarke on Fingerlicker, Craig Pant Ifan.
Photo: Bernard Newman

Neil Foster on Silly Arete, Craig Pant Ifan.
Photo: Bernard Newman

Doing it the old way on Pincushion, Craig Pant Ifan.
Photo: John Cleare

Dave Alcock leading Scratch Arete, Craig Pant Ifan.
Photo: John Cleare

3 50 feet. Steep cracks lead up for 30 feet till the steep sidewall is reached. This is followed awkwardly to a final pull over the crest of the ridge to finish.

Gash Wall 150 feet   Hard Very Severe   (1950)
A fine route, quite hard for the grade. Start just left of Christmas Climb at the left-edge of the buttress.
1 70 feet. Climb straight up the edge of the buttress to the overhang. Pull over this then go out right to a ledge. A difficult move over an overhang then up a groove above leads to a mantelshelf to the right. Easier climbing leads to the second stance of Christmas Climb.
2 25 feet. A descending traverse right leads to the bollard under the roof.
3 55 feet. Move diagonally right across a steep and slightly unstable wall. Ascend a crack for a few feet then traverse left to finish.

Chimney and Face Climb 120 feet   Severe   (1948)
Follow the gully right of the buttress until it starts to overhang, then move onto the right wall and climb it to the top.

CRAIG Y LLAN (Crag of the Church)   O.S. ref. 594 477
The ridge bounding the Aberglaslyn Pass on the east gives a couple of routes on its west flank. The nearest and best crag being Gravestone Buttress, the main buttress of which faces Gelert's Grave in Beddgelert. It can be reached in a little over 10 minutes from Beddgelert via the Fisherman's Path which is followed to a point just beyond the last barn. The crag is then directly above.

The Ordinary Route 250 feet   Difficult
This takes the easiest line up the front of the slabs, traverses left onto the main rib and goes up this and the wall above to finish. Belay at will.

The Direct Route 245 feet   Very Difficult
Takes a direct line to the top starting at the toe of the buttress.

NANT GWYNANT

Craig y Llyn (Crag of the Lake)   O.S. ref. 619 502

Craig y Llyn rises out of woods above the A498 at the head of Llyn Dinas. The crag is best seen from the foot of its right-hand side.

The most obvious feature is a steep tower split by a crack in its top section and separated from a lower wall by a grassy gangway. The right-hand side of the cliff is rather unattractive and eventually fades into the hillside. The Sanctuary, a large grassy ledge beneath the upper section of the crag provides the starting point for Aquila and Thirty-Nine Steps and is reached via an awkward wall near the foot of the grassy gangway in the left wall.

100 yards left of the left-hand wall is an open gully which is the safest descent for all the routes.

The crag gives superb, and invariably bold, wall climbing with the occasional brilliant crack pitch. Unfortunately due to lack of traffic many of the routes have become very lichenous. Only increased traffic will remove it – so get going!

Down and left of the main crag is a small domed buttress.

★ **Beyond the Cosmos**   70 feet   E3   (1984)
A fine bold pitch. Start at a faint arête in the centre of the crag left of a tree.
1 70 feet. 5b. Strike diagonally right till beneath an overlap. Take this leftwards then climb on to a ledge reached from the left. Finish up an obvious slim crack.

★ **Honorary Grit**   20 feet   E5   (1986)
A superb problem with the most technical of sequences. Start at the ledge below the top crack of Beyond the Cosmos.
1 20 feet. 6c. A thin crack left of Beyond the Cosmos is climbed with subtle moves on directional holds to a final dyno (one peg low down in the crack).

Erotickos   140 feet   Hard Very Severe   (1979)
1 140 feet. 5a. Ascend slabs on a small overhanging buttress to the left of the main crag.

Honeysuckle Wall   160 feet   Severe   (1953)
The first route on the main crag has a good start then a swim up heather to finish. Start at the left edge of the left-hand wall below a crack left of a large flake leaning against the wall.

1 80 feet. Climb the flake then step left onto the wall. Move up slightly left, then move right and go straight up to ledges. Step up right then move around the wall above onto the right-hand face of the buttress. Move diagonally right to reach an ash tree belay below a slanting rake.
2 40 feet. Move out left across an exposed wall left of the rake, past a ledge, to two wedged flakes at the top of the rake.
3 40 feet. Step left a few feet then go straight up to a flake belay. Breast-stroke remains.

Clonus 120 feet   Very Severe   (1969)
At the foot of the crag is a dead tree; start above and to its left.
1 60 feet. 4b. Go up steeply for 20 feet to a small ledge. Move left then wade back right through vegetation to a sloping heathery ledge.
2 60 feet. 4b. Move left a few feet then go up an obvious groove to the top.

Split Finger 150 feet   Very Severe   (1969)
Right of the dead tree is a large perched block.
1 30 feet. Climb an easy diagonal crack to the top of a large pinnacle.
2 120 feet. 4b. Step onto the slabby wall above with difficulty then climb up to a good spike near a ledge. Move left from the ledge into a groove and ascend this to a small overhang. Step right to another groove which leads to easy ground. A pleasant pitch.

★ **Death Can Be Fatal** 120 feet   E5   (1982)
Well named! A frightening experience up the wall left of The Moon. Start at a pointed flake left of the start of The Moon.
1 120 feet. 6a. Step right off the block then go direct up the wall above for 30 feet to good holds below a very steep wall. A difficult traverse left for ten feet gains a good slot and, thankfully, a good wire. Move straight up on huge flakes to reach a long horizontal flake. Step up and right till better holds lead up leftwards to the base of a thin crack. Follow this to the top.

★ **Perdido Street** 150 feet   E3   (1979)
Good steep climbing providing a first pitch to the routes on the upper wall. Start as for The Moon at a large rib.
1 40 feet. Scramble up and left to a tree below a steep wall.
2 110 feet. 5c. Behind the belay is a rib, which is climbed direct to a spike. Move right to reach a V-pod, then go up and out of this onto the wall above. Traverse right to a good spike, then go up to reach flakes that lead to a ramp and corner. Ascend the corner to finish.

Craig y Llyn

1	Perdido Street	E3	4	Wailing Wall	E4
2	Death Can Be Fatal	E5	5	Sybilla the Pun	E4
3	The Moon	E4			

★ **The Moon**   200 feet   E4   (1977)
A fine varied route, serious on the first pitch whilst technical but
safe on the second. Start at a square-cut block below a steep
wall with a slim groove in its upper half.
1   120 feet. 6a. Climb the steep wall past a poor peg to reach
the slim groove; this is followed to a difficult exit out right. Belay
on the big grass ledge above.
2   80 feet. 6a. An easy slab leads to the foot of a hideously
overhanging crack. Flail up this and a groove above to reach
easy ground and the top.

Terra Nova   200 feet   Hard Very Severe   (1966)
The groove is excellent but the lower section is so disgusting
that the effort is hardly worthwhile. Start at a tree below a
groove which leads to a grassy gangway crossing the left-hand
buttress.
1   150 feet. 5a. The wall behind the tree leads to a vegetated
ledge. Move left then go up a difficult moss-filled crack until a
step left onto the grassy gangway is possible. Grovel up the
gangway to belay below an obvious groove.
2   50 feet. 5a. The fine groove leads to the top. Worth the effort?

Marshall Hearts   145 feet   E4   (1981)
A serious route. Start 15 feet below and right of the groove on
pitch 2 of Terra Nova.
1   75 feet. 5c. Go diagonally right to a spike (peg on the right)
then hand-traverse left on the slab below the ramp of Wailing
Wall to reach a small niche. Climb up to a peg in a corner to
belay.
2   80 feet. 5b. Traverse right below a blunt arête then move up
and right under a square overhang into a corner. Follow this with
a difficult exit left at the top.

★ **Danger Days**   120 feet   E4   (1981)
F . . . F . . . F . . . Frightening climbing but well worth it. Start as
for Marshall Hearts.
1   120 feet. 6a. Ascend Marshall Hearts to the peg then climb
up to join Wailing Wall at the ramp. Climb this rightwards for a
few feet then wobble out left across a steep slabby wall to the
foot of a corner. Pull left over a square overhang and follow a
superbly positioned crack (peg) and wall to the top.

★★ **Wailing Wall**   160 feet   E4   (1978)
A tremendous route giving steep and bold climbing – a stretchy
rope is very useful! Start by climbing the first pitch of Peachpla
then scrambling up left for 15 feet onto the grassy gangway and
a peg belay.
1   160 feet. 6a. Step right onto the wall to a flake then go straight
up to the foot of a groove (The Deceiver). Go left to reach a ramp
and follow this for 40 feet to where it widens. Climb another

ramp leading right until it turns into a steep rib. Climb the rib (peg runner way out right – hard luck if you're short!) to better holds about 20 feet above the peg. A little higher is a groove, go up a little then move round left to a flake crack, which takes you to the top.

Chance Encounter   155 feet   E2   (1978)
Similar to, but easier than, Wailing Wall. Unfortunately rather loose and grassy. Start as for Wailing Wall.
1   155 feet. 5b. Step right to the flake then go up to the groove on The Deceiver (as for Wailing Wall). Climb the groove then step left to a flake crack, which leads to a ledge. Climb the wall above to the foot of a huge flake. This leads to the top. A worrying pitch.

Peachpla   230 feet   Very Severe   (1962)
A worthwhile route. Start at the left-hand end of the wall barring entry to The Sanctuary and below the grassy gangway.
1   30 feet. Take the wall to a grassy ledge below a rightwards-trending ramp.
2   80 feet. 4c. Step right and climb the ramp, delicate, until a step left is possible to reach a crack forming the right side of a large flake. Climb this then a short wall above which leads, in turn, to a small ledge and belay.
3   120 feet. The wall behind the stance leads to a steep and awkward crack; then carry on to shattered blocks (possible stance and belay). Step left onto a ledge then go up to a niche. After an awkward move left finish direct.

The Deceiver   240 feet   E2   (1971)
Yet another serious route. Start at the left-hand end of the wall guarding entry to The Sanctuary (as for Peachpla).
1   30 feet. Climb the wall to a grassy ledge below the ramp of Peachpla.
2   70 feet. 5c. Move right and climb the ramp until a difficult move left is possible onto a steep wall under a roof. Climb up to a fang then go round it into a groove, which is climbed (2 pegs) to a poor ledge and peg belays.
3   100 feet. 5b. Traverse left delicately for 10 feet to gain a groove, which is followed (peg) to a hanging flake. Ascend the flake then move left into another groove (peg) which leads to a belay on the gangway above.
4   40 feet. 5a. Climb the corner and cracks above to finish.

Aquila   200 feet   Hard Very Severe   (1955)
Some quite enjoyable climbing. Start from The Sanctuary at a rib left of a shallow corner.
1   100 feet. 5a. Climb the rib to reach the upper section of a shallow corner. Ascend an easy crack in the left side of this to a block belay below a steep wall (the stance is round to the left behind the block).

2   35 feet. 4b. Move right along technical grass to a huge block overlooking the gully.
3   25 feet. 5a. Climb a short wall to the base of a shallow groove then move right around the corner. A crack then leads to a good ledge.
4   40 feet. 4c. Ascend a corner to another good ledge and finish up a crack on the left.

Variation
1a   90 feet. 5a. The shallow (and usually wet) corner is climbed for a few feet then climb the left wall until the corner is regained via a small bulge. Go over the bulge then step left to join the first pitch at the easy crack.

** **Sybilla the Pun**   150 feet   E4   (1978)
A humourless first pitch leads to a stunning crack. Start at the foot of a diamond-shaped wall 30 feet higher up The Sanctuary from Aquila.
1   70 feet. 5c. Climb faint grooves, moving left halfway up the wall to a better defined groove. Climb this to the block belay at the second pitch of Aquila. Remember to tell your second where the car keys are!
2   80 feet. 5c. Move down left along a quartzy break to reach a groove. Climb this to a square-cut roof then go over this on the right to reach and climb a sensationally positioned crack which leads to the top.

The large recess right of Aquila has been climbed but is not worth the effort.

Bychan   135 feet   E2   (1983)
Takes the left arête of Thirty-Nine Steps.
1   35 feet. Climb a corner and step right onto a ledge and belay.
2   100 feet. 5c. Follow a cracked arête above to the top.

Cunnyson   E4   6b   (1987) is the groove left of Thirty-Nine Steps.

Thirty-Nine Steps   130 feet   E1   (1969)
Yes! You've guessed it, another bold pitch. Start by scrambling up to the foot of twin cracks beneath the right-hand wall of the crag (right of the large recess).
1   20 feet. Climb the left-hand crack to a stance and belay.
2   110 feet. 5a. Go diagonally left, round a flake at the base of a corner crack. Climb the crack to an awkward move right to the foot of a shallow chimney. At its top traverse right to a left-trending crack; this is taken to a niche. Step up and right to finish. A very bold and impressive pitch.

Clogwyn y Wenallt (Crag on the White Hillside)

O.S. ref. 647 528

This is the dome-shaped crag, about 200 feet high, set in the hillside just north-east of Llyn Gwynant. It can be reached in about ten minutes from the gate by the side of Hafod y Rhisgl on the old road (50 yards from the main A498 road). Cross the river by the foot-bridge about 300 yards above the lake.

The cliff gives some superb climbing in a lovely setting; the rock is good with steep 'juggy' wall-climbing being the norm.

A stone wall and a large boulder meet the foot of the crag at its centre, while a broad grassy ledge cuts the cliff on the left at one-third height, getting smaller towards the right.

Bovril 100 feet   Very Severe   (1954)
A beefy route giving some good climbing despite the adjacent jungle. Start at the first corner on the left-hand side of the lower tier.
1   25 feet. 4b. Climb diagonally left until a traverse right to a tree is possible. Move up to the large terrace and a tree belay in a corner.
2   45 feet. 5a. Climb the wall just left of the tree, with a move left into a niche above a small holly. A delicate traverse left leads to a small tree below a steep crack.
3   30 feet. 4c. Ascend the difficult and strenuous crack to finish.

The Gamekeeper 80 feet   Hard Very Severe   (1979)
A line up the steep left edge of the buttress at the beginning of the terrace containing Ferdinand.
1   80 feet. 5a. Climb a leftward-slanting V-groove to a small ledge and some flakes. Bridge up slightly and swing out right to finish directly up the wall.

Caligula 110 feet   Hard Very Severe   (1979)
Some good climbing. Start 40 feet left of pitch 2 of Ferdinand beneath an arête.
1   60 feet. 5a. Climb the arête, past a large tree, then move slightly right and go up a groove right of the arête to a stance.
2   50 feet. 5b. Step left, climb an overhanging groove past a spike to a delicate mantelshelf exit. Finish up the arête in a good position.

★★ **Ferdinand** 140 feet   E2   (1959)
A steep and strenuous crack on the second pitch makes up for a scrappy first pitch. Start at a shallow corner about 6 yards right of Bovril.

Clogwyn y Wenallt

1	Ferdinand	E1
2	Oxo	VS
3	Poacher	E4
4	Bovine	HVS
5	The Death Wisher	E2
6	Shake	VS

1   60 feet. 5a. Climb a short wall into an overhanging niche. Step right on good holds to a tree and then cross to a grassy ledge. Stroll along this to an easy crack which is climbed to belay below a corner (or better, avoid this pitch by walking in from the left).
2   80 feet. 5b. Ascend the corner for 20 feet until a tricky move into an overhanging crack on the right wall is possible. Climb this to an overhang, pull over it on the left and finish up another crack. Belay well back. A direct start up the crack is possible, but harder.

Picador   150 feet   Hard Very Severe   (1979)
Start as for Carol Crack.
1   50 feet. 4b. As for Carol Crack.
2   40 feet. 5b. Climb the leftward-slanting crack above to reach a series of ledges. Wander rightwards to more ledges. Go up these to a belay below the final pitch of Carol Crack.
3   60 feet. 5a. The wide and slightly overhanging crack is climbed followed by a rib on the right to finish.

Carol Crack   140 feet   Hard Very Severe   (1953)
Some good climbing but a rather disjointed route. Start at a corner crack containing a tree, about 10 yards right of Ferdinand.
1   50 feet. 4b. Climb the cracks, moving right through jungle (machete useful) to reach a short rib which leads to the grassy ledge.
2   40 feet. 4b. An easy sloping crack is climbed followed by an awkward little wall to reach a niche below the final wall.
3   50 feet. 4c. The wall above the niche, moving right to finish. A poorly protected pitch.

Torero   140 feet   E1   (1959)
A bold and difficult second pitch. Start left of a prominent corner 7 yards right of Carol Crack.
1   50 feet. 5a. Move into the corner and climb it to a small ledge. Move diagonally right across a short wall to a grassy ledge below an easy groove.
2   90 feet. 5b. Stand on a flake and pull up into a scoop then step up and back right onto a flake. Move left into a corner to finish.

Toreador   150 feet   E1   (1964)
A fine route. Start below the prominent corner of Torero.
1   70 feet. 5a. The corner is climbed, virtually direct, then cross a grassy ledge to the foot of an easy groove on the right.
2   25 feet. Ascend the easy groove to belay at the foot of a corner.
3   55 feet. 5c. Climb the corner, as for the start of Ferdinand's final pitch, but continue till the right wall starts to overhang. A difficult move right leads to a finishing slab.

★★ Oxo   220 feet   Very Severe   (1953)
A highly enjoyable route, the easiest on the crag. Start at the left
end of the lowest bulge, by a black recess about 10 yards left of
the stone wall.
1   100 feet. 4b. A horizontal traverse right leads to a black ledge.
Keep going right past a detached pinnacle, to a short wall. Climb
this, then go up to a gangway. Continue along the gangway to
a tree on the grassy ledge on the right.
2   30 feet. An easy slab on the left leads to a tall tree below a
crack.
3   90 feet. 4c. Ascend the crack then move round the rib to a
ledge on the right. Continue right, across the wall to finish
straight up on good holds. Alternatively, instead of crossing the
wall, climb a difficult corner above the ledge then swing right to
finish.

★★ Fishbox   45 feet   E4   (1984)
1   45 feet. 6b. Climb the obvious thin overhanging crack just left
of Death Wisher. At 35 feet where the crack steepens, cop out
right onto the arête and easy ground (or try the unclimbed direct
finish).

The Death Wisher   170 feet   E2   (1979)
A fine top pitch left of Bovine. Start a few feet left of Bovine.
1   80 feet. 4c. Move up to the traverse of Oxo then follow Oxo
to the stance and belay on Bovine.
2   90 feet. 5b. Climb Bovine for 10 feet then move left to a steep
crack. Ascend this past a wafer-thin flake (precarious) then carry
on up the crack above to the top. A direct entry into the crack is
possible but harder.

★★ Poacher   180 feet   E4   (1978)
A tremendous and powerful line blasting up the centre of the
cliff. Start a few feet left of Bovine.
1   90 feet. 5c. Go over a bulge then up to the traverse of Oxo.
Step left and climb the wall left of the corner of the first pitch of
Bovine to a ledge. Move a little right and climb a shallow groove
to the terrace. A bold pitch.
2   45 feet. 5b. Move out right into a groove and climb it to a
good ledge and belay (junction with Oxo).
3   45 feet. 6b. The overhanging groove is climbed direct past 2
pegs. As the previous guide said 'Bold, technical and spectacular'.

The Matador   180 feet   Hard Very Severe   (1977)
Although the climbing is good very little of it is new.
1   90 feet. 5a. As for Bovine pitch one.
2   50 feet. 5a. Climb Oxo for a few feet then move left onto the
wall to reach a scoop. The wall above leads to a stance and peg
belay on Torero.

3   40 feet. 4c. Climb the crack on the left as for Torero.

★★ **Bovine**   200 feet   Hard Very Severe   (1957)
After a wandering start the route waltzes up a very steep top
wall on amazing holds. Start midway between Oxo and the stone
wall.
1   90 feet. 5b. Climb the impending wall above, from right to
left, to a detached flake on the Oxo traverse. Ascend the corner
(peg) to a gangway then go up a tricky corner on the right to
reach the terrace.
2   20 feet. Move down the slab on the right till below a steep
wall.
3   90 feet. 4c. Move up a groove for a few feet then swing right
onto the wall, which is full of nice surprises all the way to the top.

★★ **Oxine**   190 feet   Very Severe
The first pitch of Oxo followed by the top pitch of Bovine gives
a superb combination.

Shake   170 feet   Very Severe   (1954)
Short, but sharp. Start 7 yards right of the stone wall.
1   90 feet. 4b. Scramble up to an ash tree then climb the steep
wall above till a traverse left and an ascent up to a small slab is
possible. Step back right to a crack and climb it to a large ledge.
2   30 feet. 4a. Ascend the fault to a tree.
3   50 feet. 4b. Step onto and up the rib on the right, stepping
left into a groove for a few feet till a move back right across the
rib is possible. The slab, so gained, is taken to the top.

The Fugitive   170 feet   E3   (1980)
An eliminate but good climbing.
1   50 feet. Scramble up to a tree belay on Shake, pitch 1.
2   40 feet. 5c. The corner crack on the left of the stance is
climbed to a belay on a big grassy ledge.
3   20 feet. Walk right to a tree below the top pitch of Shake.
4   60 feet. 5c. Climb the overhanging groove on the left past
some loose flakes until a step right to a tree is possible. Finish
up the arête behind the tree.

Psychedelic Cult   250 feet   E2   (1984)
A high-level left-to-right girdle. The exact line is left for the
curious to discover.

Clogwyn y Bustach (Cliff of the Ox)   O.S. ref. 625 535

An unfrequented cliff containing some good routes – perhaps
most visited for that all-time classic Lockwood's Chimney. The
cliff is best reached from the Cwm Dyli power station. Don't park
within the gates. A foot-bridge across the river leads to a path

which, after a few yards rises diagonally up the hillside over a small col. The cliff appears suddenly. A path running under the big overhangs of the North Buttress gives access to the routes. There are four distinct walls or buttresses; from the left these are a small clean wall, followed by a black-streaked wall taken by The Maelstrom. To the right is an obvious natural arch, The Marble Arch, while right again is a large vegetated buttress containing Lockwood's Chimney. The vegetated gully on the right is North Gully with the impressive sweep of North Buttress beyond. However, the first route is to be found on a huge overhanging boulder down by the river.

★★ **(The Tawg) In Homage to a Hound**   30 feet   (1986)
1   30 feet. 6a. A crack/layaway in the roof is climbed – it overhangs 45 degrees in the first 25 feet!

Kellogg Crack   100 feet   Hard Very Severe   (1961)
A rather loose route requiring the gentle touch. Start below the centre of the small wall on the left of the crag.
1   40 feet. 4c. Climb a steep crack in the centre of the wall for 20 feet (peg) then traverse right to a steep groove and climb this to a tree.
2   40 feet. 4c. The groove above leads to an overhang and a step right onto the wall. Move leftwards to a grassy ledge and tree belay.
3   20 feet. 4b. The corner at the left end of the ledge leads to the top.

The Tenth Rib   220 feet   Very Difficult   (1952)
An Amazonian approach leads to some clean climbing above. Start at the foot of the left-hand rib of the steep messy corner left of The Maelstrom Wall.
1   30 feet. Emerge from trees onto rock for a fleeting moment. Move left over vegetation to a tree at the base of a steep wall.
2   60 feet. Ascend diagonally right up a wall to the crest of the rib. Climb this then go left through jungle to a tree.
3   40 feet. Move back to the crest then climb onto grassy ledges. Pass a gorse bush on the right to reach a large grassy ledge.
4   20 feet. The crack just left of a nose leads to a ledge below a large tree.
5   40 feet. A crack above leads to an oak tree belay.
6   30 feet. Move left from the tree and go up the edge leftwards to finish.

A truly disgusting route has been climbed up the corner to the right.

Femaelstrom   200 feet   E1   (1966)
Some reasonable climbing but the rock is rather friable. Start at the base of the steep wall between The Maelstrom and the

messy corner at a line of weakness going left, below a bottomless corner.

1   120 feet. 5a. Move left a little then go diagonally back right for about 60 feet to just below, and 6 feet right of, the bottomless corner. Go up left into the corner then climb it until a swing out left at the top leads to a good resting place. Go straight over the bulge above on worrying holds then traverse right a little and move up to a tree belay.

2   40 feet. Ascend the wall behind the belay till a traverse right into a groove and another tree belay.

3   40 feet. Go diagonally left and up easily on good flakes.

Paranoia   200 feet   Hard Very Severe   (1970)
Steep and serious. Start at a large tree on the left of the black-streaked wall.

1   120 feet. 5a. Climb straight up for 30 feet then move right with difficulty to a small ledge in the centre of the wall. Move diagonally right crossing The Maelstrom then go straight up to a small holly tree. The wall above is climbed, stepping right to an arête and a peg belay (junction with Side Entry).

2   80 feet. Climb the arête then step off the pinnacle onto a steep wall. Climb the wall, past a small tree, and move left to finish.

The Maelstrom   205 feet   Hard Very Severe   (1958)
A serious route, protection is poor and the rock friable. Other than that it is an excellent route! Start at the right-hand end of the wall.

1   60 feet. 4c. Climb a corner for 10 feet to a big tree. Go left with difficulty and climb a steep wall till a horizontal traverse left to a shallow scoop and a peg belay.

2   90 feet. 4c. Move left for a few feet then go up to a high-level traverse line. Go left to a small tree then climb the wall above to another tree on the right. Ascend steep vegetation to a large tree.

3   55 feet. 4b. Climb a little wall on the right to a large flake then finish up the wall above.

Side Entry   200 feet   Severe   (1952)
Start at a corner on the right of The Maelstrom Wall.

1   40 feet. Ascend the corner to a tree then climb a small chimney to a stance on a broad rib.

2   50 feet. A little crack leads to a leftward-trending gangway. Go up this and a slab above to a tree belay.

3   60 feet. The slab behind the tree leads to a horizontal traverse left round a corner to a large grassy ledge and tree belay.

4   50 feet. Climb the wall trending right to a big holly tree.

Forest Wall   110 feet   Severe   (1934)
Worth doing for the excellent top pitch. Start 10 yards right of The Marble Arch.

1 60 feet. Climb an awkward little wall to a broad ledge, then go easily up a slab to a tree belay.
2 50 feet. Steep ivy-covered slabs are climbed to a terrace and a detached flake. An exhilaratingly steep wall is climbed on large holds, a small tree, to finish by a holly tree.

Variation. **Direct Finish** 30 feet   Hard Severe
Start at a cave above the ivy-covered slabs of pitch 2.
3a 30 feet. The crack above the cave is climbed followed by moves rightwards to trees. Continue up a break to finish. Alternatively, climb direct to the top from the cave.

Forte Strapiombo 130 feet   Very Severe   (1961)
A loose climb up the arête on the vegetated buttress containing Lockwood's Chimney. Start at the end of pitch 1 of Lockwood's Chimney.
1 50 feet. Traverse left for 20 feet on grassy ledges. A short wall leads to a small slab below huge overhangs then go back left again to a small tree belay.
2 80 feet. Move right across a steep wall below the overhang then go diagonally right on loose flakes to a small ledge on the skyline (peg). Finish up the steep arête.

Lockwood's Chimney 200 feet(ish)   Difficult   (1909)
The most traditional of routes. To gain full satisfaction it is best to do the route by moonlight; the party should 'preferably be large and of large men' (preferably drunk!). Start at The Marble Arch (200 feet of vegetation up an arête below is also possible).
1 60 feet. Go down a few feet and move right along ledges to the base of a prominent block-crack with a birch tree at its top.
2 20 feet. Struggle up the crack or climb round to the right.
3 40-100 feet. (Depending on finding the short cut.) A massive flake has split from the main cliff leaving a superb chimney. Enter it from the front or by walking round the rib to the right. Once inside climb up to a chockstone at 20 feet. Struggle along (hard for the 'larger' person) then climb up at the end to pop out of the other side of the cliff, or back up from the depths to reach an outer window. Alternatively, but harder, it is possible to emerge at the chockstone through a small window and then to climb up the outside of the chimney and thus miss out all the caving.
4 40 feet. Scramble to the top in a fine position.

Variation
Great Chimney Wall 80 feet   Very Severe   (1951)
2a 80 feet. Climb the wall left of the ordinary route more or less direct.

★ **Gallop Step**   165 feet   Hard Very Severe   (1956)
A fine route, unusual in that it starts and finishes on the ground
(ideal for the lazy). Start from a block beneath the left-hand end
of the big overhang of North Buttress.
1   65 feet. 4c. A diagonal traverse right under the overhang is
taken till a strenuous pull at 50 feet round an edge leads to a
niche and peg belay.
2   100 feet. 4c. Continue along the line of weakness, loose and
tricky, to some vegetation. Continue easily till the hillside can be
regained.

Anniversary Waltz   120 feet   Hard Very Severe   (1956)
Some good climbing in an exposed position. Start directly below
the large overhangs at the lowest point of North Buttress, about
10 feet right of a detached flake.
1   45 feet. 4c. The smooth wall is climbed, on small holds, to
an open groove. An easy slab above leads to a stance and peg
belay.
2   40 feet. 5a. Climb a corner, on large holds, to an overhang
then traverse left in a fine position to reach a comfortable stance.
3   35 feet. Traverse 10 feet left and ascend a wall to a tree belay
at the top.

The Ox Bow Incident   200 feet   E2   (1 pt. aid)   (1972)
Some difficult climbing. Start below a shallow groove in the
white wall of Anniversary Waltz.
1   90 feet. 5c. Move up to the groove and follow it to a peg. Gain
a leftward traverse line and follow it until it is possible to climb
direct to reach Gallop Step. Traverse right along this to reach a
tree belay.
2   90 feet. 4c. Go right 15 feet to the top of a black pinnacle then
ascend steeply to two small trees and a move left onto a narrow
gangway; this leads awkwardly onto a steep slab below the final
roof. Belay at a poor tree.
3   20 feet. 5a. Finish to the right with a sling for aid.

Variation
An easier start to the route. Start at a block 15 yards right of
Anniversary Waltz.
1a   70 feet. Climb a leftward-sloping ramp, normally wet, then
ascend to a spike on Gallop Step. Pull over the overhang to reach
the two small trees on the second pitch of the ordinary route.

Below and to the right of the main crag is an isolated buttress
about 30 yards above the river. Ironically this gives the best
route 'on' the crag.

★ **Sleeping Beauty**   120 feet   E4   (1981)
A spectacular route giving bold and exciting climbing. Start at a
layback flake on the right-hand side of the cliff.

Fred Crook on the flake of The Plum, Craig Bwlch Moch.
Photo: Paul Williams

The crux of Atomic Finger Flake, Craig Bwlch y Moch.
Photo: Paul Williams

1 120 feet. 5c. Ascend the flake for 15 feet till a hand-traverse left to a peg. Climb the overhanging wall above to a roof, pull over this on the right via jugs, then go up a slab for 20 feet to a tree belay. Abseil descent.

Direct Start – The Witching Stick   (1987)
1 120 feet. 6b. Climb direct up the wall to join the original route at the end of the traverse left.

Minor Crags in and Around Nant Gwynant

CWM Y LLAN   O.S. ref. 615 525

The Gladstone Slab
A fine 200-foot high slab lies right of the Watkin Path up Snowdon at the Adwy Bwlch Du just beyond the Gladstone Rock. It gives several easy routes.

CRAIG DDU
Is a broken and vegetated crag higher up the back of Lliwedd above the Gladstone Slab.

CLOGWYN DU   O.S. ref. 605 530
Along the flank of the south ridge of Snowdon is an extensive line of broken cliffs, with Snowdon itself forming the head of the cwm. Clogwyn Du is the highest and least broken of these cliffs about half a mile north of Bwlch Cwmllen above the disused reservoirs in the cwm. The only value the crag has is as a playground in winter – the big gully in the centre, in particular can give a fine route.

CLOGWYN PENMAEN (Elephant Rock)   O.S. ref. 643 522
The obvious little cliff above Llyn Gwynant has not yet been girdled without some swimming – or has it?

The Gwynant Crack   O.S. ref. 648 528
This lies on a small vertical wall on the east side of the main road just before the side of Llyn Gwynant. The main crack gives a very 'traditional' (i.e. hideous) problem, unless anorexic when a through exit can be made.

The wall just to the left gives a fine micro-route:-

Bleed for the Dancer   30 feet   E5   (1987)
1 30 feet. 6a. Solo the gnarly wall. Good luck!

THE CRAG ABOVE THE POWER STATION   O.S. ref. 650 538
High above Cwm Dyli Power Station is a large but broken crag.
The front face consists of two large, very broken ribs with a gully
between. Round the edge to the left is a smaller, but better, face.
A number of routes have been recorded, the best being:

Gwastadanas   260 feet   Very Severe   (1968)
Takes the cleanest stretch of rock available. Start at a small cairn
below a very obvious thin crack-line running up to an
overhanging reddish wall.
1   90 feet. 4c. Climb a groove to a small tree, move right into
the crack and go up it to a strenuous exit onto a good ledge.
Step right to a tree belay.
2   80 feet. 4c. Move right below a vegetated chimney then climb
steeply up a rib to a small overhang. Step left (awkward) into a
clean chimney, and ascend this to a broad ledge.
3   90 feet. 4b. Follow steep slabs to a grassy area. Descend to
the left.

THE MOELWYNS

The Moelwyns are a range of hills, dotted with crags, on the eastern side of the Moelwyn ridge, which runs roughly south-to-north in the rugged country between Beddgelert and Blaenau Ffestiniog. Despite the intrusion of a hydro-electric power scheme, the ravages of the slate quarries and the extension of the Ffestiniog Miniature Railway the Moelwyns still retain a considerable charm of their own; to the seeker of solitude in the mountains they are ideal.

From the town of Blaenau Ffestiniog, head for the small village of Tan y Grisiau. From there, go up the hill on the right, across the miniature railway. Eventually a gate is reached and a bridge across the river on the right (Cwm Orthin track). (The service road continues on past the usually locked gate). Go over the bridge then go left to a small car-park beneath a quarry tip. The crags can all be reached from this point by a short walk.

The Moelwyn crags offer a wide variety of fine routes on rough pockety rock with routes of all grades except the very highest.

CRAIG STWLAN   O.S. ref. 667 446
Although small this attractive crag has two facets – one looking south-west over the northern shores of Llyn Stwlan and one looking south-west over the lower reservoir.

Birthday Route   155 feet   Very Difficult   (1967)
Start in a corner left of a nose and just left of the prominent steep face of Pocked Wall.
1   30 feet. Ascend the corner to a traverse right round an arête, to a stance in a corner on a grassy ledge.
2   90 feet. The wall left of the corner is climbed till level with an overhang on the left. Traverse right a little then go left over a bulge to easy rock, which is climbed direct to a large ledge.
3   35 feet. Climb the wall above to the top.

Pocked Wall   105 feet   Very Difficult   (1953)
A steep and pleasant route. Start at a little corner left of a quartz rib by the steep face right of the chimney.
1   15 feet. Ascend the corner.
2   30 feet. Step left onto the main face, move right and go up to a large heathery ledge.
3   60 feet. Climb leftwards up a gangway on the edge of the steep face then traverse right onto the edge and ascend this to the top.

The Moelwyns
As seen from the South-East

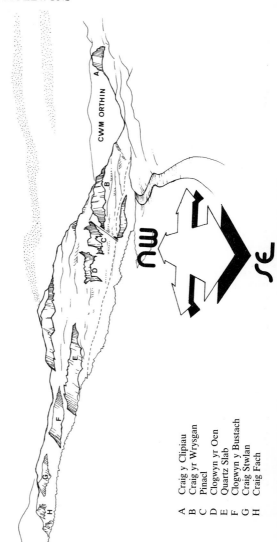

A   Craig y Clipiau
B   Craig yr Wrysgan
C   Pinacl
D   Clogwyn yr Oen
E   Quartz Slab
F   Clogwyn y Bustach
G   Craig Stwlan
H   Craig Fach

Easter Parade   Moderate   (1951)
Start at a big square block at the northern end of the south-east facet. There are three pitches: the crack on the left of the block, an arête and a slab.

CRAIG FACH (Little Crag)   O.S. ref. 669 444
This is a small slabby crag, about 200 feet high, standing above the third hairpin bend of the upper part of the service road. A boulder field-cum-gully marks the left-hand side of the crag while a break runs back down right across an overhanging wall. The nature of the cliff means that one can climb almost anywhere at about Very Difficult standard. However the following routes have been described as they are perhaps the most logical lines. It is particularly recommended for beginners.

Top Plate   Moderate   (1950s)
An easy slab on the left of the buttress is climbed followed by a chimney up and right to finish.

Milky Way   220 feet   Difficult   (1932)
Start under the overhanging left edge of the slab, near its foot.
1   55 feet. Pull up onto the slab edge then go up a crack moving right, to belay on the edge of the slab.
2   65 feet. The knife-edge above is climbed, then continue up the slab to a grassy ledge. A belay can be found in a niche round the corner on the left.
3   35 feet. Walk round the corner and climb a small chimney.
4   65 feet. Ascend a pocketed slab heading towards a notch on the summit dome.

Variation
3a   70 feet. Move right from the niche and climb slabs and a nose on the right to the top.

Mars   180 feet   Very Difficult   (1957)
This gives some pleasant climbing. Start 40 feet right of Mars at a flake cairn.
1   70 feet. Climb a purple slab to a long grassy ledge. Belay by a crack in the bulge above.
2   60 feet. Step left a little then climb slabs diagonally left to a heathery groove, which is taken to another ledge.
3   50 feet. A wall just left of the belay leads to the top.

Orion   320 feet   Difficult   (1960)
A fine traverse of the cliff. Start at two cairns on a ledge 20 feet below and right of Top Plate.
1   55 feet. Swing out and climb on to a rib, ascend this to a good ledge then take an obvious line right across to a quartz slab till a descent onto a knife-edge and a good stance is possible (top of pitch 1 of Milky Way).

2   40 feet. Climb down a little crack behind the stance, then cross the next slab to a detached flake (top of pitch 1 of Mars).
3   70 feet. Move right across the flake to a thread on the edge of a shallow gully. Step across this then climb the slab on its far side, ascending slightly to a stance in a corner.
4   55 feet. Step below a nose and cross the next slab to reach a grassy corner. Move across the right wall and go up to easy ground on a rib.
5   100 feet. Climb down the easy rib by a diagonal line to the right-hand end of the crag.

Clogwyn y Bustach (Cliff of the Ox)   O.S. ref. 672 448

A short but steep crag just beyond and a little higher up the hillside than Clogwyn yr Oen. The main face is very steep and is split by several cracks, with a line of chimneys on the left-hand side. At the bottom of the centre of the crag is a large detached flake.

Floating Rib   145 feet   Difficult   (1952)
This route takes the rib running up the crag left of the line of chimneys.

Fork   145 feet   Difficult   (1955)
Climb the chimney grooves between Floating Rib and South Chimneys.

South Chimneys   140 feet   Very Difficult   (1951)
Start below the chimneys.
1   20 feet. Climb shattered rock to a ledge at the foot of a chimney.
2   120 feet. Climb the chimney, past a projecting block, and continue to the top over another block. Belays can be taken on this pitch if required.

Southern Cross   200 feet   Very Severe   (1974)
Takes a line up the arête right of South Chimneys gained by a traverse from that route.

Dal-y-Twrch   90 feet   E3   (1983)
1   90 feet. Climb the left arête of Groan to a flake and peg. Finish straight up above this.

Groan   90 feet   E2   (1970)
Steep, strenuous crack climbing. Start 15 feet right of South Chimneys.
1   90 feet. 5b. The wall is climbed to a thin, rightward-trending crack. From this, move to a jamming crack which leads to the large stance of Flake Wall. Ascend the short wall above to finish.

★ Titus   100 feet   E2   (1969)
An excellent steep pitch up the cracked wall 15 feet right of
Groan.
1   100 feet. 5b. Climb the cracked wall for 25 feet to a
rightward-sloping, thin crack. A flake above leads into a small
niche. Move left into a square bottomless chimney, and finish
up a short wall.

Gormenghast   100 feet   E2   (1980)
Another steep enjoyable pitch. Start just left of the large
detached flake (start of Flake Wall), beneath a ramp-line.
1   100 feet. 5b. Climb leftwards up a ramp-line, across Titus to
reach a bulging crack. The crack and wall above lead to a short
jamming crack just left of an open chimney. Ascend a short wall
to finish.

Acoustic Flake   110 feet   E1   (1981)
Start as for Gormenghast.
1   110 feet. 5b. Ascend the ramp for a few feet then go straight
up the wall to the 'acoustic' flake. Beat it up to the traverse of
Flake Wall. Climb the wall to finish up a groove splitting the
bulge.

★ Flake Wall   125 feet   Hard Very Severe   (1955)
A fine classic giving steep climbing. Starts at the large detached
flake.
1   105 feet. 5a. Ascend the left edge of the flake to its top, step
left and go up on good holds to an obvious foot-traverse leading
leftwards. Go along the traverse to a short crack and a good
ledge.
2   20 feet. Follow a short wall above to finish.

Going Straight   90 feet   E1   (1978)
Interesting climbing. Start behind the large flake.
1   40 feet. 5b. Emerge from the depths then move diagonally
leftwards on hollow-sounding flakes to reach a groove. Climb
this to belay before the foot-traverse of Flake Wall.
2   50 feet. 5b. Move diagonally rightwards to reach a sloping
ledge (peg). Step right, then go straight up the bulging wall to
finish.

Mr Flibbertigibbert   100 feet   E2   (1981)
A scary start and an interesting finish.
1   100 feet. 5b. The wall behind the large flake leads to a small
ledge below a shallow leftward-slanting groove (poor peg).
Ascend this (bold) then trend leftwards to reach a curving line
of flakes. Traverse along these to finish over the final bulge of
Acoustic Flake.

Fiddler on the Dole   100 feet   Hard Very Severe   (1978)
Start 20 feet right of Flake Wall, below an obvious triangular
overhang.
1   100 feet. 5b. Climb up to the overhang and traverse left to a
foot-ledge below a cracked groove. Ascend this with a difficult
exit left at the top.

Creeper   100 feet   Very Difficult   (1953)
Start below a crack just to the right.
1   70 feet. Scramble up to the wide crack and climb it to a ledge.
2   30 feet. Climb the continuation crack to finish.

North Chimney   75 feet   Difficult   (1951)
1   75 feet. The short chimney to the right is climbed direct.
Easier to descend than to climb!

★ **The Ebb Tide**   120 feet   E2   (1981)
An excellent girdle. Start by climbing South Chimneys to the first
of the ledges.
1   70 feet. 5b. Bridge out right to a large foothold then traverse
right and go up to the jamming crack on Groan (crux). Ascend
this then make a slightly rising traverse to a position above the
groove of Flake Wall.
2   50 feet. 5a. Step diagonally right to a sloping ledge (peg),
then continue rightwards to the finish of Creeper.

Barbarillo   Hard Very Severe
This is a high-level girdle of the crag but it is not as worthwhile
as the above.

Clogwyn yr Oen (Cliff of the Lamb)   O.S. ref. 673 449

This is the largest of the Moelwyn crags and it is also the most
easily accessible. The cliff has two facets. The left-hand side is
the South-West Face, split by a terrace at half-height with the
headwall above. Just to the right of the bottom half of the face
is a large perched boulder. The main face of the crag is the
South-East Face and is more broken.

The left-hand side of the crag gives a quick and easy descent.
The first routes described are those on the South-West Face.

Crossover   170 feet   Hard Severe   (1968)
A very pleasant route on good rock. Start below a short white
groove and to the left of the patch of orange-coloured rock.
1   30 feet. Ascend a short wall to a large ledge.
2   50 feet. Climb the white groove then continue up to a niche
belay.

3 90 feet. Move right then go up a steep wall direct avoiding easy ground on the left. Easy scrambling to finish.

★ **Orange Outang**   250 feet   Hard Severe   (1953)
An enjoyable route on steep rock. Start by scrambling up to the foot of the orange patch.
1 70 feet. Move onto the orange wall, then traverse to its centre. Continue straight up to a niche belay (junction with Crossover).
2 60 feet. The wall above is climbed until one is forced to move left then pull over a little overhang to a ledge and block.
3 120 feet. A pleasant walk leads to a rib on the right and follow it to the top. (Or scramble off left to join the descent route.)

★★ **Pinky**   250 feet   Very Severe   (1953)
Another excellent route. Start at the foot of a recessed wall, 6 yards right of Orange Outang.
1 80 feet. 4b. Move up the wall, past a bulge at 25 feet. Climb up to the left of a mossy scoop then go up a steep rib above on good pockets, moving right to a stance.
2 90 feet. 4c. Move back left and carry on, passing a steep little wall to reach a terrace. Scramble across the terrace to the base of a grassy corner in the steep upper wall.
3 50 feet. 4b. The corner leads past two trees to another ledge.
4 30 feet. 4c. Above the ledge are three cracks, the right-hand one is the most interesting.

Skerryvore   80 feet   E1   (1979)
A pleasant crack pitch. Start beneath a blunt arête a few feet right of the corner of Pinky.
1 80 feet. 5b, Climb steeply up the undercut arête to a good resting place below the thin crack; this is followed to the top.

Ectoplasm   80 feet   Hard Very Severe   (1964)
A good jamming exercise. Start below a spike 10 feet right of the start of Skerryvore.
1 80 feet. 5b. The spike is reached with difficulty, follow the crack above to the top.

Plasma   85 feet   Hard Very Severe   (1964)
Start as for Ectoplasm.
1 85 feet. 5a. Climb to the spike then step down and around a nose. Step up to reach a block then move left via a horizontal break to a jamming crack. Finish by climbing a rightward-leaning ramp.

★★ **Remembrance**   85 feet   E2   (1972)
A fine steep route, quite bold. Start at an overhanging V-groove right of Plasma.

1 85 feet. 5b. Climb the V-groove, past a poor peg, with a hard move to leave it. The wall above is climbed to a block then move up and right to finish up a blind crack.

★★ **The Widowmaker**   80 feet   E4   (1981)
A brilliant steep pitch giving bold and technical climbing. For bachelors only. Start just right of the V-groove of Remembrance.
1 80 feet. 6a. Move right onto the wall then climb direct up the wall to a bulge (rurp runner – snigger). Move out left to a layaway, then move rightwards up the wall to a horizontal break. Finish up an obvious groove.

Badger by Owl-light   85 feet   E3   (1982)
Start at a prominent groove right of The Widowmaker.
1 85 feet. 5c. The groove is climbed to a small ledge, move left over a bulge and finish directly up the obvious final groove.

Erewhon   150 feet   Hard Very Severe   (1978)
An excellent girdle of the Headwall. Start just left of the tree-filled corner (pitch 2 of Pinky).
1 45 feet. 5b. Climb the front face of the large flake, move left and then back right; to belay on the top of a large boulder.
2 25 feet. 5b. Pull across the wall on small pockets to reach a hanging belay in the crack of Ectoplasm.
3 80 feet. 5a. Move down and traverse across to the block on Plasma. A thin crack in the green wall leads to a difficult finish up an undercut groove.

Hole and Corner Climb   220 feet   Difficult
This route goes behind the left side of the huge boulder and then follows the huge terrace to finish.

Slate   120 feet   Very Severe   (1962)
Start at the front face of a large perched boulder on the South-East Face.
1 60 feet. 4c. A short wall is climbed, followed by a crack and the continuation face on the left-hand side of the boulder.
2 60 feet. 4c. A scramble rightwards leads to a corner, beneath a flake below a corner groove. Climb the side of the flake then pull into a prominent groove. Climb the groove to the top.

The next two routes are based on the rib that divides the two facets of the cliff.

★ **Kirkus's Climb**   210 feet   Very Difficult   (1928)
A pleasant route overshadowed by its neighbour. Start by a stone wall of the buttress.
1 50 feet. A chimney just left of a stone wall leads to a pillar. Move down and right into a deep-cut chimney, then climb this using large flakes, to a cave-like belay.

2 35 feet. Climb the left-hand crack above then the slab on its left with a move right at the top to belay at the base of a steep arête split by a groove.
3 80 feet. Ascend the arête and step left after a few feet into a large groove round the corner. Climb the groove then move leftwards along slabs, moving back to the crest and a short crack to reach a triangular stance.
4 45 feet. Climb rightwards till an obvious leftward line up the slab leads to a ledge and block belay. Scrambling leads to the top.

** Kirkus's Climb Direct   210 feet   Severe
A lovely route, steep and interesting. Start by the stone wall at the foot of the buttress.
1 60 feet. Climb a steep wall which then turns into a slab. This leads to a pillar; step from the pillar to a slab and climb this to its top. Step right to a cave-like belay.
2 35 feet. The right-hand crack above is climbed till a swing out onto the front face is possible. Slabs then lead to a belay at the foot of a steep arête split by a groove.
3 75 feet. The arête above is climbed, via the groove, to a ledge. A hard move from the right-hand end of this leads to easier slabs and a triangular stance.
4 40 feet. Ascend the right-hand groove above the belay to a ledge and block belay. Scrambling remains.

Cuckoo Waltz   360 feet   Very Severe   (1988)
Start at the undercut pillar between Kirkus's Direct and Block.
1 120 feet. 5a. Climb the overhung pillar on its right-hand side. Climb the slabby wall above by its left arête over an overhang to the belay of Kirkus's Direct and Block.
2 180 feet. 4b. Walk up a grassy ramp to the headwall on the right. Climb this direct, right of a corner, followed by grass to a thread belay. Stretchy rope helps!
3 60 feet. 4b. On the back of the grass bay is a steep wall split by two horizontal breaks and a crackline. The first half of the crack is climbed to a step right and a finish up a pocketed crack. Thread belay 40 feet up and back.

Variation
Flyover Finish   60 feet   Hard Very Severe   (1988)
3a 60 feet. 5a. This takes the wall direct on small pockets through the two breaks just left of a cream-coloured patch of rock.

Block   230 feet   Severe   (1953)
Start just right of Kirkus's Direct, below a jutting block 60 feet up.
1 120 feet. A variety of climbing leads to the block; a groove and steep slab above then lead to a belay on a sloping break. Stroll over to another belay on the left beneath a corner.

2   50 feet. The corner leads to a ledge and bollard belay.
3   60 feet. A short steep crack in the left wall leads to a sloping ledge. A continuation crack with a leftward exit leads to the top.

Thumbelina   280 feet   Severe   (1967)
A pleasant route. Start 10 yards right of Kirkus's Climb Direct at the foot of easy slabs.
1   80 feet. The slabs lead to a shallow corner and onto a belay on the right.
2   80 feet. Move onto the rib above and go up it to reach a good ledge.
3   40 feet. A corner left of the chimney is climbed.
4   80 feet. A short steep crack leads to a large sloping ledge. Along this to another crack. Finish up this.

In Memoriam   190 feet   Very Severe   (1976)
A steep, direct line up the crag. Start 3 yards left of Chic.
1   95 feet. 5a. Move up leftwards till below the short rib on Thumbelina. A move left, followed by direct climbing to a bulge near the top leads to a large break.
2   70 feet. 4c. The wall left of the corner above is climbed direct up its middle to a sloping ledge. A bold pitch (be warned by the name!)
3   25 feet. At the right-hand end of the ledge is a leftward-slanting chimney with a groove to the left. Climb the groove, overhung at the top, or grovel up the chimney.

Chic   225 feet   Very Difficult   (1952)
A pleasant route up the left edge of the large quartzy slab. Start at a broad rib just left of a heathery gully.
1   85 feet. The easy rib is climbed followed by a harder continuation above to a ledge below a steep wall.
2   80 feet. Ascend the steep wall to a ledge and corner, move left, then go up and left to the left edge of the large slab. Continue to reach some large perched blocks on a long grassy ledge.
3   60 feet. A rightward-slanting crack leads to an easy slab. This is followed to another grassy ledge. The short corner above leads to the top.

★ **Bent**   245 feet   Severe   (1953)
A nice route. Start at a flat slab midway between Chic and the pillar leaning against the face on the right.
1   70 feet. The slab is climbed, finishing just left of a crack.
2   70 feet. Continue up in the same line to the base of a short wall, which is climbed rightwards to the foot of the big slab.
3   65 feet. Move up the slab a little then move into a corner on the right. The corner is climbed past a shallow cave at half-height, to reach a steep crack splitting the right wall. This is followed to the foot of a very large pinnacle.

4 40 feet. Climb the chimney behind the pinnacle, finishing up the left edge of a steep rib.

Slick   220 feet   Very Difficult   (1953)
Yet another enjoyable route up the big slab. Start at a pillar leaning against the face forming a sort of rib.
1 60 feet. The rib is climbed to a ledge with a flake on the left.
2 80 feet. Move off the flake then go up a little wall to reach an easy scoop. Traverse left 15 feet, then go up again to the base of another short wall, which is climbed rightwards to the foot of the big slab.
3 50 feet. Climb to the top of the blocks, then climb the slab past a wobbly spike to a grassy rake.
4 30 feet. Ascend a steep crack on the left to an easier continuation which leads to the top.

Variations   Severe
3a 50 feet. Climb the slab via a thin crack up its centre to a horizontal break then continue just right of the 'wobbly' spike to the rake.
4a 30 feet. The steep wall to the right leads to good holds and a short steep crack to finish.

★ **Slack**   235 feet   Severe   (1960/66)
A great route – the best on the wall. Start below a two-tier slab below a large detached flake on the ledge.
1 70 feet. The slab leads to the flake.
2 65 feet. Climb the right edge of the flake, move onto the wall, moving left at the top to a short crack. Ascend this to a belay below some overhangs.
3 40 feet. Traverse left below the nose overlooking the big slab. This leads to a good thread belay.
4 60 feet. Climb a corner, moving left to another corner to finish.

Variation   Hard Very Severe
3a 35 feet. 5a. Straight above the belay is a weakness in the overhangs. Climb up to this then swing left to reach a steep slab which is followed to a large belay.

Tight   220 feet   Severe   (1968)
A taut route next to Slack. Start as for Slack.
1 70 feet. Climb the slab to the flake.
2 60 feet. Move right onto a steep wall and climb it, moving right where it steepens then step back left to reach a small tree. Block belay on the left.
3 90 feet. Step onto the slab above the block and climb it to a crack just right of an overhang. Climb the crack up to a ledge and finish up the short walls above.

Pied Piper   190 feet   Severe   (1953)
An excellent route. Start at the foot of the quartz-streaked slab
below a broad rib on the right-hand side of the face behind a
queue of cragrats.
1   50 feet. Climb the slab to a bay following a crack rightwards
onto the face.
2   70 feet. Climb a crack and step right at its top. Ascend direct
up the rib and a slab on the right until a step left at the top leads
to a good ledge
3   70 feet. Cracked blocks and mossy slabs lead to a terrace.
Move across this, then go straight up to reach the quartz-covered
face of a huge block. Traverse left finishing up the crack behind.

Variation
3a   40 feet. From the terrace, go up right of the huge block to
climb a tricky quartzy slab to the base of chockstone-filled crack.
Pull up this to finish.

One for the Road   330 feet   Difficult   (1953)
An 'expedition' but it has its moments. Start beneath a left-facing
corner, 6 yards right of Pied Piper.
1   50 feet. An easy slab leads up to a corner.
2   45 feet. Climb the corner and the right-hand rib above.
Scramble up to a cave below a crack.
3   85 feet. The crack and slab above lead to a belay on the
terrace.
4   50 feet. Take the cleanest quartz slab above, finishing to the
right of the spiky rocks on the skyline. Finish here, or if a glutton
for punishment, walk right to the foot of the final face.
5   20 feet. Ascend a left-sloping gangway to a stance beneath
a crack formed by a flake slanting up left.
6   80 feet. Climb the crack then step right finishing up the centre
of the face.

Waspie   385 feet   Very Difficult   (1959)
The best of several lines – surprisingly worthwhile. Start at a
large grassy corner above the perched boulder on the South-
West Face.
1   50 feet. Step up onto the top of a large flake, move across a
mossy wall and then go up to a triangular stance (top of pitch 5
of Kirkus's Climb Direct).
2   60 feet. Climb down diagonally rightwards to the top of a big
flake; this is followed to a large grassy bay (junction with
Thumbelina).
3   50 feet. Cross the right wall of the bay, then go over the top
of a flake and down its right edge to reach a little edge in a corner
(top of pitch 3 of Chic).
4   50 feet. Move rightwards then go up a rounded nose to some
large blocks.

5 65 feet. Move right to some blocks and traverse the big slab to the cave stance of Bent.
6 30 feet. Pull out round the rib then go down a little to a small ledge.
7 80 feet. Move right to easy ground.

Pinacl   O.S. ref. 678 453
This is a small buttress high on the hillside just before the waterfall on the way to Clogwyn yr Oen.

The Tumor   70 feet   E2   (1981)
Start below a thin crack in the left wall of an obvious corner.
1   70 feet. 5b. Climb the awkward crack using fragile holds to finish direct.

Cancer   70 feet   Very Severe   (1963)
1   70 feet. 4c. Ascend straight up the corner.

Craig yr Wrysgan (Crag of the Scrubby Growth)
O.S. ref. 679 454

This crag is easily identified by a prominent incline which begins at the service road and passes the left-hand side of the crag to enter a short tunnel (one of the descents). The easiest line of approach is to follow the Cwm Orthin track till just below the first ruined building, cross the stream and follow grassy terraces up leftwards to the boulder-field below the crag.

A prominent feature of the crag is a large quartz-streaked slab with a short tower above. Below is a large grassy ledge, Y Borfa. Towards the centre of the crag is a prominent V-corner, while right again and higher up is a large enclosed area, The Green Wall.

The cliff gives several superb routes on excellent rock in fine positions.

Descent is either down the aforementioned incline or down the right-hand side of the crag.

Y Taith   200 feet   Hard Severe   (1978)
Start at a leftward-facing corner on the left-hand side of the crag.
1   70 feet. Climb the corner, past two rowan trees then go rightwards to a ledge and stance overlooking the grassy gully.
2   70 feet. Move across the funnel to reach the quartzy slab then move right to a horizontal traverse line. This leads to a grassy ramp below the steep tower. Move onto the narrow slab below the tower and go along this to Y Borfa.

3 60 feet. Move diagonally right across the right wall of Y Borfa to finish up a steep little groove (The Black Corner).

Y Drafel   110 feet   Very Difficult   (1953)
Start 25 feet right of Y Taith, at a large pointed spike.
1 80 feet. Go rightwards, then back left using an undercut flake to a slab. Climb this past a perched block and continue to a belay overlooking a grassy gully.
2 30 feet. Ascend the arête (Y Drafel) then scramble off to finish.

Agog   130 feet   Very Difficult   (1958)
Its only use is as an approach to the Tower Finish. Start between the easy way to the grassy bay and Y Drafel.
1 20 feet. A short wall and crack lead to a perched block and large ledge.
2 60 feet. Move leftwards to a belay beneath a narrow gangway just left of the grassy gully. Step across the short gully and climb a slab and shallow chimney.
3 50 feet. Climb easily to the base of the steep tower, pass it on the left then go up a steep wall to the arête. Climb this to the top.

Variation. **Tower Finish**   50 feet   Hard Severe   (1961)
3a 50 feet. Easy rocks lead to the top and a finish up the steep front face.

Daufaen   160 feet   Severe   (1958)
A good route overshadowed by its neighbour. Start at a short vertical corner in the grassy bay.
1 50 feet. A crack is climbed followed by a slab which leads to a ledge with blocks on it.
2 50 feet. Step out right onto the slab and go up pockets to Y Borfa.
3 60 feet. Traverse right along Y Borfa to escape, or better, go up Honeysuckle Corner.

★★ The White Streak and **Honeysuckle Corner**   160 feet
    Hard Severe   (1958)
A tremendous route giving varied climbing, one of the best routes of its grade in the Moelwyns. Start in a recess below the large slab, at a large spike.
1 50 feet. Climb up leftwards then move diagonally right to reach a triangular corner breaking the right edge of the slab.
2 50 feet. Step left and climb the bold slab to Y Borfa.
3 60 feet. The obvious corner in the tower above gives a brilliant finishing pitch.

★★ Y Gelynen   250 feet   Very Difficult   (1953)
A delightful route – the Crackstone Rib of the Moelwyns. Start
just left of the V-groove of Dorcon.
1   80 feet. Traverse left and climb a blunt rib to a holly tree.
2   50 feet. Move left and ascend the rib above till below a steep
wall.
3   50 feet. Step left and go up to and over an overhang, then
climb the slab above to Y Borfa.
4   70 feet. Go diagonally up the right wall of Y Borfa, passing a
steep groove on the left.

Variation Finish   Severe
The steep corner on the left.

Bad Reputation   120 feet   Very Severe   (1985)
Start 15 feet left of Condor.
1   120 feet. 4c. Climb direct up to an overhang, step left, then
go back right and continue more easily straight up to belays.

★ Condor   140 feet   E1   (1978)
A lovely little pitch in the left wall of Dorcon's V-groove. Start
below the V-groove.
1   140 feet. 5b. A difficult start up the centre of the wall left of
the groove leads to a crack. This is climbed awkwardly followed
by a rib above to a stance and nut belays. Scramble off to finish.

Conrod   100 feet   E3   (1985)
1   100 feet. 5c. Climb the thin crack between Condor and Dorcon
with a bold start.

★ Dorcon   155 feet   Hard Severe   (1960)
Good climbing up three almost separate pitches. Start below the
V-groove.
1   45 feet. Climb the V-groove to an exit right, then go up to a
grassy ledge below overhangs.
2   50 feet. Step left and climb a rib left of the overhangs. Move
right to a large grassy bay.
3   60 feet. A corner and crack above give difficult climbing (crux)
to another ledge. The short wall above leads to the top.

Taith y Pererin   335 feet   Difficult   (1953)
A long and rather tedious route. Start as for Dorcon
1   85 feet. Traverse right along a ledge into a large corner.
2   80 feet. Move diagonally left, past a ledge, then carry on
leftwards to a nose above a V-groove. Move up into a corner.
3   40 feet. Traverse right along a ledge and round a rib into a
niche.
4   50 feet. Climb a corner-crack then scramble up a groove to a
good ledge.
5   80 feet. A slab on the right leads to easy ledges, then a short
wall above leads to the top.

146

Craig yr Wrysgan

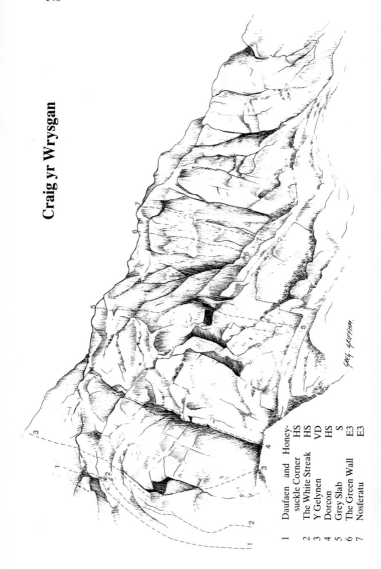

1	Daufaen and Honey-suckle Corner	HS
2	The White Streak	HS
3	Y Gelynen	VD
4	Dorcon	HS
5	Grey Slab	S
6	The Green Wall	E3
7	Nosferatu	E3

Grey Slab   135 feet   Severe   (1953)
Start in the corner at the end of pitch 1 of Taith y Pererin.
1   60 feet. The rib on the left is climbed direct, then cross a
gangway and go up a short wall to a sloping stance.
2   75 feet. Climb above the stance then go up a groove until a
traverse leftwards to the crest of the buttress. This is followed
to the top.

Mistral   125 feet   Very Severe   (1964)
A harder version of Grey Slab. Start at the lowest point of the
crag at a huge overhanging boulder.
1   25 feet. 4b. From the nose of the boulder pull up steeply using
flakes till it is possible to climb rightwards up the slab. Continue
easily to a belay.
2   100 feet. 4b. The wall left of the stance is climbed to a
gangway. Cross this and climb a steep slab above to an
overhang. A difficult move leads onto a slab. Go straight up the
middle of the slab, step left at the top, then ascend a rib and a
short crack to finish.

Hot Pants   140 feet   Very Severe   (1971)
1   25 feet. 4b. As for Mistral.
2   70 feet. 4b. Climb a faint depression in the slab moving left
to a corner and make a move up to a small ledge. Pull over a
block overhang to another ledge and belay.
3   45 feet. 4b. Move right and finish direct up the slab.

The next routes can be found in the recess dominated by the
overhanging Green Wall.

★★ **The Green Wall**   85 feet   E3   (1972)
A stunning pitch giving steep and strenuous climbing. Start
below a short corner.
1   85 feet. 5c. From a ramp climb the short leftward-facing
corner, then make bold moves up the wall above to reach a
scoop below a thin crack. Ascend this moving slightly left to a
steep finish.

★★ **Nosferatu**   85 feet   E3   (1980)
A superb complement to The Green Wall giving another
spectacular pitch. Start below a shallow groove just right of the
start of The Green Wall.
1   85 feet. 5c. Climb the shallow groove then go straight up to
an obvious crack (peg). Strenuous climbing up the crack leads
to the top.

Gethsemane   80 feet   Hard Very Severe   (1972)
A good line but unfortunately dirty. Start below the large corner
right of The Green Wall.
1   80 feet. 5a. Ascend the corner to the second overlap; difficult
moves right then lead to easier ground and the top.

Scallywag   80 feet   E4   (1984)
An eliminate between Bing the Budgie and Gethsemane.
1   80 feet. 6a. Climb the crack in the wall left of Bing the Budgie,
then move left to a good hold. Move right to above the overlap
of Bing the Budgie, then go straight up to the obvious overhang.
Pull over this and exit right to finish.

★ **Bing the Budgie**   80 feet   E4   (1977)
A great pitch giving steep and serious climbing. Start 10 feet
right of the corner. Easy for its grade.
1   80 feet. 6a. Climb a crack then foot-traverse left until it is
possible to move up to an overlap. Step slightly right then go
straight up to an exit right at the top.

Variation   80 feet   E2   (1981)
1a   80 feet. 5c. As for the normal route but continue up the crack
to the overlap. Step right to the arête or pull over the overlap
(harder) then go up the arête to finish.

The Wanderer   110 feet   Hard Very Severe   (1972)
A pleasant traverse. Start at the foot of Gethsemane.
1   40 feet. 4c. Ascend the corner to a ledge.
2   70 feet. 5a. Move up and left to reach a traverse line leading
across The Green Wall. Move down slightly to the foot of a
gangway, which leads to the top.

Variation
1a   60 feet. 5c. Ascend Space Below My Feet to the arête then
move onto the wall of Bing the Budgie just above the overlap.
A horizontal traverse left across the wall leads to the ledge on
Gethsemane.

★ **Space Below My Feet**   100 feet   Hard Very Severe   (1961)
A lovely route with steep airy climbing. Start at a boulder
beneath an overhanging groove right of Bing the Budgie.
1   100 feet. 5a. Ascend the strenuous groove to a ledge then go
up a wall onto the arête. Climb this, savouring the position till it
eases and the top is reached.

Variation   100 feet   Hard Very Severe   (1972)
1a   100 feet. 5a. Start as for Bing the Budgie then toe-traverse
right onto the arête. Finish up this.

Babylon   100 feet   Very Difficult   (1958)
Start by an easy scramble up to a large block beneath the nose
of the buttress.
1   30 feet. Move right and ascend a slab, stepping leftwards to
an earthy ledge.
2   70 feet. Climb the corner behind a sapling then step right
onto a rib, follow this to the top.

Y Lloer   80 feet   Very Severe   (1981)
Start just left of Y Gilfach.
1   80 feet. 4c. Climb the left wall of Y Gilfach on small pockets finishing direct.

★ **Y Gilfach**   80 feet. Very Difficult   (1958)
A little gem! Start below the right-hand side of the crag.
1   80 feet. Climb a V-groove direct to the top.

Stained Class   80 feet   Hard Very Severe   (1985)
Start on a large ledge below the groove of Y Gilfach.
1   80 feet. 5a. Step right from the ledge and go up to good holds, then move up towards a rightward-slanting crack. Climb this and step left to finish.

Upper Wrysgan   O.S. ref. 676 455

The Upper Cliff lies beyond the quarry buildings and behind the Main Cliff. It is reached from the top of the Main Cliff or, by walking up the track from the car-park, then breaking left from the first level and up an obvious path through the slate tips. Although short the crag gives several excellent routes on perfect rock and gives an ideal finish to a route on the Main Cliff.

The crag is split into two wings with the easier routes on the left. These are described first.

Cat Walk   100 feet   Severe   (1964)
Start below a triangular overhang 30 feet left of a square cave.
1   70 feet. Ascend a groove and flake cracks to a ledge.
Finish up a wide crack going right at the top.

★★★ **Peachstone**   80 feet   E4   (1988)
A superb pitch traversing above the cave. Start at the saplings above the right-hand end of the cave (gained by scrambling from the right, or by abseil).
1   80 feet. 6a. Climb the corner for a few feet then swing left and traverse the very lip of the cave to a peg. Make a hard move up past this to good pockets. The bulge above is passed by a long reach to more good holds and a peg above. Climb the wall left of the peg to a vague break and a third peg. Finish straight up or off left to the top (small hex's useful on this pitch).

Yoghurt Miscellaneous   70 feet   Very Difficult   (1968)
Start below some overhangs right of the square cave.
1   30 feet. Climb a groove to a large ledge with a perched block.
2   20 feet. Go straight up the shallow chimney above.
3   20 feet. A short wall leads to the top.

Ash Tree Slabs   85 feet   Very Difficult   (1964)
Start at a short wall just right of the cavern.
1   30 feet. Climb the short wall to a ledge; a slab above leads
to an ash tree belay.
2   25 feet. Ascend the slab above scrambling left to a good
belay.
3   30 feet. Go up a slab on the right, then a crack to reach a
grassy ledge. Easy scrambling leads to the finish.

Dentist's Debut   80 feet   Very Severe   (1966)
Start at an obvious flake crack 30 feet left of the gully separating
the two wings.
1   80 feet. Climb the crack, step right and go up a short slab to
reach a sloping grassy gangway. Ascend this and a groove
above to the top.

Llaregub   80 feet   Very Severe   (1970)
This poor route takes the dirty slabs left of Dentist's Debut.

Central Gully   70 feet   Very Difficult   (1966)
Start below the gully separating the two wings.
1   70 feet. Climb the gully and a slab on the right to an exit
through a hole.

The right wing gives steep, uncompromising climbing.

Buzby   70 feet   Hard Very Severe   (1978)
Start below the right wall of the gully, at a large flake.
1   70 feet. 5a. Ascend the flake then pull into a groove. Move
left to a small sapling and finish up a short groove above.

Chim Chu Roo   70 feet   Hard Very Severe   (1978)
Care is needed with some of the holds. Start below a wide
chimney 15 yards right of Buzby.
1   70 feet. 4c. Follow the chimney to the top.

★ **Neusk Prospect**   25 feet   E4   (1988)
Short but quite pleasant.
1   25 feet. 6a. Climb the centre of the pocketed wall left of
Sasquatch.

Sasquatch   75 feet   E3   (1978)
At the right-hand side of the crag is an obvious V-groove
(Gremlin Groove). Start 10 yards left of this at the second thin
crack left of a square-topped boulder.
1   75 feet. 5c. Climb the crack and its continuation to reach a
sloping ledge. The wall above leads to a series of converging
short cracks. Move right to a horizontal break, then finish direct.

★ Dislocation   75 feet   E1   (1967)
Start at the square-topped boulder.
1   75 feet. 5b. Ascend a flake and thin crack to a ramp. Go up
the continuation crack to finish.

Louis Wilder   75 feet   E4   (1981)
A fine bold pitch. Start between Wall of Ghouls and Dislocation
below a very shallow groove.
1   75 feet. 6a. Hard moves lead into the shallow groove. Climb
the groove and the wall above to the top.

Wall of Ghouls   75 feet   E1   (1980)
Start 6 feet left of the groove. A technical pitch.
1   75 feet. 5c. The wall just left of the groove is climbed trending
leftwards (crux). Step right finishing up a thin crack straight
above the groove.

Gremlin Groove   75 feet   E2   (1974)
Start below the V-groove. Loose flakes and poor pro!
1   75 feet. 5b. Ascend the groove to a short crack, step right and
go up a short wall and slab to finish.

Craig y Clipiau (Crag of the Buttress)   O.S. ref. 683 458

The cliff is best approached by going directly up the Cwm Orthin
track from the car-park. Go right from the dilapidated buildings
on the first level section above the steep rise from the car-park.
At the top of a steep incline walk rightwards until the first part
of the crag is reached. This is the South-West spur, with a short
pockety wall (Johnson's Wall). The next buttress along is Vestix
Buttress and around again is the Main Face – the South-East
Wall. The obvious large quartzy slab on this face is the White
Slab. Right again at one-third height, starting from a grass funnel
is the line of Mean Feat. Right of the funnel is a steep and narrow
wall, the line of Double Criss. Descents can be made on either
side of the crag.

The cliff gives some stunning routes, particularly in the upper
grades, on good rock and in spectacular positions. The first four
routes described lie on the South-West spur.

Johnson's Wall   70 feet   E2   (1980)
Steep and technical. Start at the base of the aforementioned,
steep pocketed wall. Beware! See appendix.
1   70 feet. 6a. Climb the centre of the wall, using layaways and
pockets (peg), then move right at the top of the wall onto a
hollow-sounding jug. Climb straight up a steep slab above to
finish.

152

Craig y Clipiau

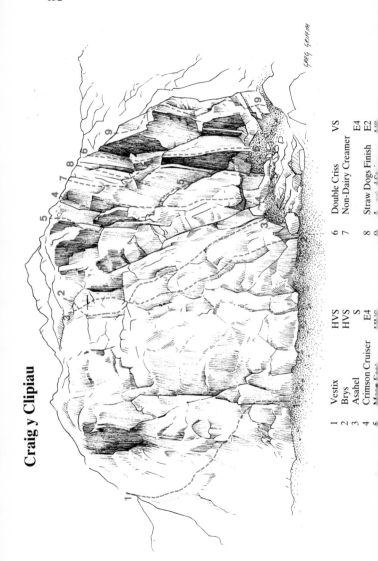

GREG GRIFFITH

1	Vestix	HVS
2	Brys	HVS
3	Asahel	S
4	Crimson Cruiser	E4
5	Mean Feat	HVS

6	Double Criss	VS
7	Non-Dairy Creamer	E4
8	Straw Dogs Finish	E2
9		HS

Jones's Crack   70 feet   Very Severe   (1959)
1   70 feet.   4c. Ascend the first crack, then the continuation above, to finish up a blunt nose.

Trick of the Tail   120 feet   Hard Very Severe   (1980)
Start at a short corner left of Betimes.
1   120 feet.   5a. Climb the corner then ascend the crack on the right to a slab. Step left and go up a prominent crack (crux) to finish up an arête.

Betimes   155 feet   Difficult   (1934)
A worthwhile route. Start below the depression to the right.
1   20 feet. Scramble up to a crack forming the left side of the depression.
2   45 feet. Follow some flakes on the left of the crack to a belay.
3   35 feet. Continue to a large block and pull over this to reach a platform.
4   55 feet. Traverse left from the depression and climb a rib to finish.

Depression Direct   95 feet   Hard Severe   (1953)
Start below the crack starting the depression.
1   65 feet. Take the crack then continue up the depression to a stance on large blocks.
2   30 feet. Move right onto the pointed block and go up a strenuous crack to finish.

The next three routes take lines up Vestix Buttress.

★ **Thin Wall Special**   115 feet   Very Severe   (1953)
A fine steep route. Start as for Depression Direct.
1   100 feet.   4c. Climb the crack then move out right to some flakes. Go up a thin crack (crux), then climb rightwards onto a nose. Climb this to a good stance.
2   15 feet. Step right, then go straight up to finish.

★ **The Emerald**   100 feet   E4   (1980)
A steep line with some difficult climbing. Start 10 yards left of the arête of Vestix.
1   100 feet.   6b. Hard moves from a loose spike on the left lead up a groove (peg). Step right onto a ramp then move up to an obvious undercut (peg) finishing up a groove just left of a nose.

★ **Vestix**   105 feet   Hard Very Severe   (1965)
A steep, strenuous pitch with good climbing. Start below a prominent diagonal crack on the right of the buttress.
1   105 feet.   5a. Climb the crack to the arête then follow it to the top. Alternatively go up the arête finishing on the blunt nose.

The remaining routes are on the impressive main face.

★★ **Africa Rib**   120 feet   Very Difficult   (1953)
A delectable route up the left edge of the White Slab. Many
variations are possible on the existing route. Start below two
parallel chimneys formed by a block pinnacle, at two iron stakes.
1   40 feet. Climb either of the chimneys, or the face of the
pinnacle to reach a ledge with a rowan tree.
2   65 feet. Move left then go straight up the edge of the quartzy
slab onto a large block, a move right to a large stance is then
possible. Alternatively, move left from the block and ascend a
layback crack.
3   15 feet. Climb a corner groove on the right to finish.

★ **Usher's Dilemma**   120 feet   Hard Severe   (1953)
A fine variant on White Slab giving good climbing. Start at the
slab just right of the chimneys of Africa Rib.
1   40 feet. The slab leads to a small sentry box then continue
up to the stance of Africa Rib.
2   65 feet. Step right and climb the thin slab to a junction with
Africa Rib at the block. Move right and go up to some overhangs
then move back left to a rib and heathery ledges.
3   15 feet. Finish up the corner groove on the right.

Variation. **Eagle Finish**   60 feet   Very Severe   (1961)
3a   60 feet. 4b. Traverse right from the block beneath the
overhangs to the corner of the slab. Step right onto a block (The
Eagle) and move onto a slab, which leads to the top. A better
finish is to move right across the exposed nose.

Brys   135 feet   Hard Very Severe   (1978)
A pleasant route. Start beneath the middle of the slab.
1   70 feet. 4b. Climb direct up the centre of the slab, then step
right to a stance (on Asahel).
2   65 feet. 5a. Continue up the slab till beneath a groove in the
overhangs. Climb the groove, finishing left on a good hold.

★ **Asahel**   140 feet   Severe   (1955)
A fine technical pitch. Start at the extreme right-hand side of the
slab.
1   75 feet. The slab is climbed close to the corner of the slab,
past a good quartz thread, to a small stance.
2   50 feet. Continue to the overhang; a traverse is then made
into Usher's Dilemma at the large stance above the overhangs.
3   15 feet. Ascend the corner above or use the Eagle Finish to
Usher's Dilemma.

Great Feat   110 feet   Hard Very Severe   (1967)
A steep, worthwhile pitch. Start behind a sapling in a grassy bay
below and right of the V-groove of Mean Feat.

1 110 feet. 5b. From behind the sapling pull over a bulge (peg on the right). Move diagonally left then climb a groove, step left and make some hard moves into a grassy funnel. Continue over some blocks to finish.

⋆ Crimson Cruiser   120 feet   E4   (1980)
The best route in The Moelwyns. Big, bad, bold and butch! Start as for Great Feat.
1 120 feet. 6a. Follow Great Feat to the protection peg. Carry on straight up, move slightly right and go up to a ledge below a steep groove. Move up to a green ledge just right of the groove. Step left and climb the groove (crux) to a ledge on Mean Feat. Step right and finish in a ridiculous position up the final overhanging prow.

⋆ Mean Feat   110 feet   Hard Very Severe   (1957)
Another brilliant route. Start at the top of the grassy funnel beneath the right-hand side of the headwall.
1 50 feet. 4b. An obvious diagonal traverse leftwards leads to a stance beneath a V-groove.
2 60 feet. 5a. The V-groove is climbed with difficulty (crux) to a good ledge. A high step right leads to another good ledge. Finish up a short awkward wall.

⋆⋆ Non Dairy Creamer (with the **Non-creaming Dairy Start**)
110 feet   E4   (1980/1981)
A tremendous route – as good as the Cruiser, giving bold sustained climbing in a wild position. Start as for Mean Feat.
1 110 feet. 5c. Follow the traverse of Mean Feat to the first spike. A steep shallow groove and wall above lead to some ledges. (It is possible to traverse into this point from a ledge on the right.) Climb an overhanging pocketed wall past a good flake-hold, to finish up a crack.

The next two routes girdle the headwall in opposite direction.

⋆⋆ Return of the Horsemen   160 feet   E2   (1981)
An exciting girdle in an 'out-there' position. Start at the bottom of Asahel.
1 70 feet. 5b. Climb to the thread on Asahel, then step right to the second of two holly trees. Move right onto a steep slab and continue up to the bottom of the V-chimney of Mean Feat.
2 90 feet. 5c. Climb the V-chimney and traverse right along the wall to a sloping foothold. Some difficult moves lead to another traverse right to a diagonal flake jug. Pull up this to its end (junction with Non Dairy Creamer) finishing up a crack as for that route.

★ **The Muleman**   110 feet   E2   (1981)
Fine, exposed climbing. Start at the corner of The Liquidator.
1   90 feet. 5b. Climb the corner and step left into an open
square-cut chimney. Move slightly up and leftwards to the final
ledge on Mean Feat.
2   20 feet. 4b. Ascend a short wall to finish.

The Liquidator   70 feet   Very Severe   (1978)
A good way to get to the large ledge and the various finishes
above. Start as for Mean Feat.
1   70 feet. 4c. Climb the corner past a holly tree and some blocks
to the ledge.

★ **Straw Dogs Finish**   40 feet   E2   (1977)
A steep crack pitch. Start on the large ledge.
1   40 feet. 5c. From the ledge move left to below the left-hand
of the two overhanging cracks. Pull over a small roof and ascend
the crack to the top. Mean!

★ **Double Criss**   110 feet   Very Severe   (1953)
A good route with an evil finish. Start below the left edge of the
wall.
1   90 feet. 4b. Climb virtually direct up the left edge of the wall
to the ledge.
2   20 feet. 5a. Fight up a brutal corner crack to the top.

Variation   80 feet   Very Severe
1a   80 feet. 4b. The crack in the right wall of The Liquidator is
climbed to a swing round onto the main face of the slab.
Continue up to the ledge.

★ **Overhanging Cracks**   110 feet   E2   (1961)
A difficult top pitch. Start just right of Double Criss, below the
middle of the slabby wall.
1   80 feet. 4b. Climb the wall till a traverse left leads to the edge.
Ascend this to the ledge.
2   30 feet. 5c. Steam up the overhanging crack above to a niche
and then the top.

Phidl   120 feet   Hard Very Severe   (1973)
Some bold climbing on the top pitch. Start below the right-hand
corner of the slab.
1   85 feet. 5a. Move into the corner, using the right wall and
continue up to the ledge.
2   35 feet. 5a. An obvious traverse line leads across the right
wall to an arête; swing right onto a slab and climb this to finish.

Inverted Staircase   110 feet   Very Severe   (1958)
A pleasant route. Start below an inverted staircase (surprise,
surprise!) in the buttress right of Double Criss.

1   45 feet. 4a. Climb a groove to a stance.
2   65 feet. 4b. The steep left wall of the groove leads to an easy slab to finish.

★ **Special K**   75 feet   E3   (1984)
The overhanging arête left of Inverted Staircase. Start at the groove just right of Phidl.
1   75 feet. 6a. Climb the groove to a bulging wall and step up to a traverse right which leads to some creaking flakes. Climb the arête (2 poor pegs) until a move right under a boulder gains the top.

The Mole   70 feet   Hard Severe   (1961)
Start just left of a large boulder 7 yards right of Inverted Staircase.
1   70 feet. Move up to a flake then traverse right to a short crack. Climb this and finish up a slab.

Peth Bras   70 feet   Hard Very Severe   (1981)
Start as for The Mole.
1   70 feet. 5b. Climb a corner on the left to a short steep crack. Ascend this to a diagonal crack which leads onto a final easy slab.

Clogwyn Holland (Cliff of Holland)   O.S. ref. 689 461

A very broken crag which can be seen from Blaenau Ffestiniog. The cliff has the dubious distinction of lying above the bacon slicer factory in the village of Tan y Grisiau. The crag is reached by crossing the Miniature Railway then scrambling steeply up to the crag. The descent is by a large grassy gully on the right.

Septentrionale   230 feet   Very Difficult   (1932)
Start at the base of the left-hand buttress.
1   30 feet. Climb the front of the buttress to a grassy ledge.
2   50 feet. Ascend cracks to a groove, move right and go up a short corner to another ledge.
3   60 feet. A chimney leads, past ledges, to a blocked groove. The groove is climbed to a terrace.
4   20 feet. A steep slab right of a heathery corner leads to a long ledge.
5   70 feet. Step onto a perched block from the right-hand side of the ledge then climb up an exposed rib. Easy rock leads to the top.

Raspberry   200 feet   Very Severe   (1973)
Start at the lowest point of the right-hand buttress.
1   40 feet. 4a. A short crack is climbed till a step left leads past a tree. Scrambling leads to a belay among boulders.

2   40 feet. 4a. A short wall behind the belay is taken to a horizontal break and the foot of the buttress proper. Step left to a poor stance.
3   90 feet. 4c. Climb a short overhanging groove on good holds then climb the tower above to a large terrace.
4   30 feet. 4b. From the right-hand side of the final tower climb an obvious crack which is gained from the right.

Strawberry   200 feet   Very Severe   (1978)
Start at vegetated slabs below a prominent left-facing corner on the right-hand buttress.
1   60 feet. The slabs lead to the foot of the corner.
2   100 feet. 4c. Climb the corner, past horizontal spikes low down and a niche at three-quarter height.
3   40 feet. 4b. Scramble across to a forked crack. Ascend this to finish.

The Hump   140 feet   Hard Severe   (1967)
A good top pitch but hardly worth the start. Start by a scramble up a grassy gully on the right-hand side of the crag till beneath a vegetated crack.
1   60 feet. A crack leads to a ledge (The Crow's Nest), then follow a crack in a short wall to a grassy terrace.
2   40 feet. A slab below a steep wall behind the terrace to a grassy groove on the left.
3   40 feet. Scramble up to twin-forked cracks in the final tower. Climb the wider of the cracks, with a tricky finish.

Busby   100 feet   Hard Very Severe   (1978)
1   100 feet. 5a. Cracks and a groove in the right wall of the gully.

Minor Crags in the Moelwyns

CARREG BLAEN-LLYM   O.S. ref. 666 440
A heathery crag on the flanks of Moelwyn Bach. The rock is terrible with climbing to match.

MOELWYN BACH — SUMMIT CLIFFS   O.S. ref. 663 438
On the east side, beneath the summit, is a 150-foot high crag. This gives a few routes of Difficult to Very Difficult Standard.

MOELWYN BACH — SUMMIT NOSE   O.S. ref. 660 440
The prominent nose seen on the Moelwyn ridge is about 90 feet high. It can be climbed almost anywhere at Difficult standard. An overhanging section gives a harder and more strenuous problem.

CRAIG YSGAFN   O.S. ref. 657 443
A small crag on the connecting ridge between Moelwyn Bach and
Moelwyn Mawr offers short routes on fragile rock.

MOEL YR HYDD — SUMMIT CLIFFS   O.S. ref. 672 453
The south-eastern face of the mountain has a band of rock broken by
heathery terraces and various gullies, one with a pointed pinnacle,
The Huntinghorn.

QUARTZ SLAB   O.S. ref. 672 449
Lots of easy climbing suitable for soloing as there are few belays.

MOORS NORTH-EAST OF FFESTINIOG

Carreg y Fran (Rock of the Crow)   O.S. ref. 735 449

Carreg y Fran lies south-east of Blaenau Ffestiniog and faces south. It is most easily approached by following a well-surfaced road from Ffestiniog leading up Cwm Teigl to Manod Quarry. Although in a pleasant situation the rock is poor, and only a few of the many recorded routes merit detailed description.

The westerly buttresses are vegetated and bounded on the right by a deep gully, Gashed Gully. This has a steep right wall in its upper reaches.

Tykes Wall   120 feet   Very Severe   (1967)
A good route up the steep right wall of Gashed Gully. Start at the foot of the gully.
1 40 feet. Scramble up mixed rock and grass in the gully to a peg belay on the left.
2 50 feet. 4c. Step down slightly and climb the wall on its left side to a sloping slab. Step up left to an overhanging crack, which leads to a sloping ledge at the foot of a leaning corner. Peg belay.
3 30 feet. 4c. The overhanging corner is climbed to a good ledge. Go straight up the short wall above to finish.

Nazgul   120 feet   Very Severe   (1966)
A pleasant route. Start in a corner between the arête right of Gashed Gully and a red wall.
1 60 feet. 4a. Step onto the top of a large block then move left into a corner groove. Ascend this to a leftwards exit then go up a short wall to a stance on an arête.
2 60 feet. 4c. Climb the arête by a shallow groove on the left then continue up the steep final section of the gully wall. An exposed pitch.

Red Wall Crack   140 feet   Hard Very Severe   (1969)
A difficult crack provides the meat of the route. Start at the foot of a crack splitting the red wall.
1 60 feet. 5a. Go straight up the crack to a large ledge.
2 80 feet. 4c. A short wall and a corner lead to another short wall and the top.

Two mediocre routes have been climbed up the broken rock right of the red wall and are a waste of time – do not climb!

A superb feeling of the Void, Craig Bwlch y Moch.
Photo: Chris Craggs

Nearing the finish of Meshach, Craig Bwlch y Moch.

Photo: Paul Williams

Twr   125 feet   Very Difficult   (1957)
A fine little route. Start at the foot of an arête composed of blocks.
1   65 feet. The arête is followed to a stance.
2   30 feet. The corner above leads to a grass ledge.
3   30 feet. Ascend the wall above to finish.

Little Plum   110 feet   Very Severe   (1969)
A great route at the top end of the grade. Start right of Twr at the foot of a clean corner at the left-hand side of a steep smooth wall.
1   50 feet. 4c. The corner is followed to a stance below the upper section.
2   60 feet. 5a. Some difficult moves are encountered up the final clean-cut corner.

Psycho   100 feet   E4   (1967)
Another good route giving very steep climbing. Start at a short wall beneath a crack splitting the steep wall.
1   30 feet. Climb the short wall to the foot of the thin crack with a small overlap at half-height.
2   70 feet. 6a. Climb the strenuous crack as quickly as possible.

The Corner   105 feet   Hard Very Severe
Start at the foot of a system of grooves left of an overhanging nose in the centre of the crag.
1   30 feet. Ascend grooves for 10 feet then move left to the foot of a corner.
2   75 feet. 5a. The overhanging corner crack leads with difficulty to better holds at 25 feet. Continue more easily up the corner above until the final overhang is reached then traverse left under this to finish.

Pigtail Grooves   100 feet   Severe   (1958)
An enjoyable pitch. Start as for The Corner.
1   100 feet. Climb the system of grooves to the top.

The Nose   125 feet   Hard Very Severe
A frightening experience up the overhanging nose of rock. For the suicidal only.

Chamber of Horrors   115 feet   Very Severe
A similar route to The Nose up the steep undercut rock to the right.

Strider   100 feet   Very Severe   (1966)
Start by a cairn beneath an obvious groove right of the steep undercut wall.
1   80 feet. 4b. The groove is climbed to grassy ledges. Continue up a vegetated crack to another grassy ledge.
2   20 feet. 4b. A short slab above leads to the top.

A few short routes start from the grassy bay on the right before the final buttress, which gives two pleasant routes.

Gay   100 feet   Severe   (1967)
Start at the foot of the arête forming the left edge of the buttress.
1   40 feet. A shallow groove just right of a crack leads to a stance.
2   60 feet. Go straight up the wall above, move right across it then follow a steep groove to the top.

Deceiver   100 feet   Severe   (1966)
Start directly below a large pinnacle, below a shallow groove.
1   40 feet. The groove is climbed to an awkward exit onto a stance and belay at the foot of the pinnacle.
2   60 feet. The right-hand side of the pinnacle is climbed followed by the wall above to the top.

CRAIG GOCH (Red Crag)   O.S. ref. 752 441
This is a half-mile long line of broken crags east-south-east of Blaenau Ffestiniog. Although many routes have been climbed they are of poor quality on unsound rock and therefore have not been recorded.

CARREG Y FOEL GRON (Rock of the Bald Hill)   O.S. ref. 745 427
A small crag visible from the Ffestiniog – Penmachno road. There are a number of routes varying from 50 to 100 feet in height. It is particularly useful as a training ground for novices.

THE LLEDR VALLEY

Carreg Alltrem (Steep-looking Rock)   O.S. ref. 739 507

A small crag situated on the eastern side of Cwm Penamnen, the valley which runs due south from Dolwyddelan. Turn off the A496 and take the road to the railway station. Turn right immediately after the railway bridge then continue past some houses to a narrow gated road, which leads to a parking place opposite the crag. A rickety bridge and a short path through the woods just left of a fire-break lead easily to the crag.

This is one of the most beautifully situated crags in the area, with climbing to match. The rock is good, the routes are exposed and very quick-drying. Climbing here is a delight.

The groove starting from a sort of cave on the left of the crag is taken by Whale; a deep groove to the right is taken by Leviathan Direct. For the next 30 yards the wall is split by a series of grooves with the V-chimney of Lightning Visit at the extreme right and the large corner of Penamnen Groove marking the end of the wall. Civetta follows the steep tower, the right edge of which is taken by Lavaredo. The tower on the right is defined by a rough slab cut off below by a steep bay of greenish rock, the back wall of which is taken by Green Wall. The bay ends with a steep broken arête, Rib and Groove, and farther right Pinnacle Gully, an easy descent. A descent at the far left of the crag is also possible.

Whale   180 feet   Hard Severe   (1964)
Quite a good route, spoilt somewhat by a break near the top of the first pitch. Start at the groove which starts from the shallow cave.
1   70 feet. An overhanging start leads into a V-chimney which is ascended to a grassy ledge on the left. Move right onto an arête and climb it to a large ledge.
2   110 feet. Move left and climb awkwardly to a crack. The crack is followed to the top to finish.

Leviathan Direct   170 feet   Very Severe   (1964)
A very pleasant route. Start below the deep groove right of Whale at a boulder.
1   70 feet. 4b. Move off the boulder into the groove and ascend it to gain a thin curving crack. Climb this and grass above to the base of a steep crack.
2   100 feet. 4b. The strenuous crack is climbed to some loose flakes. Stride out right into a slim groove and climb it to the top.

Carreg Alltrem

REG GRIFFITH

1	Leviathan Direct	VS
2	Fratricide Wall	HVS
3	Lightning Visit	VS
4	Penamnen Groove	E1
5	Civetta	E2
6	Lavaredo	VS

The Last Post   160 feet   Very Severe   (1962)
A steep strenuous route. Start just right of a boulder, at the foot
of a short steep wall guarding entry to a square-cut corner.
1   80 feet. 4c. The wall is climbed followed by the difficult corner
to an exit left. Continue up to the highest grass ledge.
2   50 feet. 4b. Ascend a steep groove on the left to flake belays.
3   30 feet. 4b. A shallow crack leads to the top.

Leviathan   175 feet   Hard Severe   (1961)
Not very satisfying. Start below the groove right of The Last
Post.
1   65 feet. The groove is steep but easy and leads to the foot of
an open chimney. Climb this, steeply, and on somewhat loose
holds then step onto a rib on the left. Ascend this to a good
ledge.
2   110 feet. Climb up to the next ledge and traverse it to its
left-hand end. Climb up some large loose spikes then move left
to a steep but easy groove, which leads to the top.

★★ **Fratricide Wall**   145 feet   Hard Very Severe   (1960)
A brilliant route giving steep varied climbing in a good position
and at the top end of its grade. Start at a short groove leading
to the right end of a grass ledge.
1   70 feet. 5a. The groove is climbed to the ledge. Move onto
the wall above and climb a smooth groove. Step round a bulge
to the right then go back left. Continue left easily to a good
stance beneath a steep wall.
2   75 feet. 5a. A short thin crack leads to a sloping ledge.
Traverse along this and round a nose until it is possible to move
up to another ledge below a steep corner. The corner is climbed
until heart-stopping moves out right (crux) lead to an arête.
Ascend this to finish.

Greenpeace   120 feet   E1   (1978)
Some good climbing up an obvious arête. Start at the foot of
Penamnen Groove.
1   30 feet. 4c. The left wall of the corner leads to a ledge and
belay left of Lightning Visit.
2   90 feet. 5b. Go up to another ledge. The hanging arête on the
left is climbed until a move right is possible just below the top.

★★ **Lightning Visit**   130 feet   Very Severe   (1959)
A delectable route up an obvious line. Start at a groove just left
of the obvious corner of Penamnen Groove.
1   55 feet. 4a. Climb the groove and the wall above to belay on
a boulder. Alternatively, climb the more difficult arête on the
right.
2   75 feet. 4c. Climb up to a good ledge. Step right to a pinnacle
then step awkwardly into a prominent V-groove which leads to
the top.

Penamnen Groove 120 feet E1 (1956)
A fine line which proves disappointing on closer inspection; still, a fine thrutch for those in the mood. Start below the obvious groove of a square corner.
1 45 feet. 4c. The left wall of the corner is climbed, with a long reach to finish. Scramble up to a pinnacle belay on the right. The corner can be climbed direct but is often wet.
2 75 feet. 5b. Struggle up the corner to the roof with a difficult exit left around it. A harder exit right is also possible.

Civetta 115 feet E3 (1964)
Some good, difficult climbing. Start at the foot of a steep crack 6 yards right of Penamnen Groove.
1 50 feet. 4b. The crack leads to a belay above a pinnacle.
2 65 feet. 6a. Move up to a small niche then go up again to reach an uncomfortable ledge beneath a large overhang. Step right and ascend thin strenuous cracks to the top.

Pin Up 130 feet E1 (1982)
Some excellent crack climbing.
1 50 feet. 5a. The shallow groove in the left arête of Civetta.
2 80 feet. 5b. Follow Civetta but continue up leftwards to below a roof. Pull over this and up an excellent jam crack to the top.

Original Route 165 feet Hard Very Difficult (1953)
A pleasant route in a good position. Start just left of the edge of the buttress, where a spike is jammed in a groove.
1 50 feet. Climb onto the spike then follow holds up left to the top of the crack of Civetta. Continue in its line, more of a chimney really, to the pinnacle.
2 30 feet. A diagonal traverse right over detached-looking blocks leads to a ledge on an arête.
3 60 feet. Cracks in the slab above lead to a spike belay.
4 25 feet. A tricky slab in the corner above is followed to finish.

Lavrol 120 feet E2 (1977)
An eliminate with some difficult moves. Start as for Original Route.
1 120 feet. 5c. Start up Original Route then continue up the crack to a large ledge. Move up detached blocks then get into a rightward-slanting groove gained from the right. The groove is climbed to an exit left. Continue into Civetta, and ascend this until a crack, on the left of the finish of that route, can be climbed.

Lavaredo Variations 140 feet Hard Severe
A poor man's Lavaredo. Start as for Original Route.
1 70 feet. Ascend the groove on the left of the almost detached pillar forming the nose of the buttress. Carry on to the block belays of Lavaredo.

2   70 feet. Climb the gully for a few feet then move into a groove on the edge of the wall. Step onto the face above its steepest part then go up to a shallow groove and the top.

★★★ **Lavaredo**   140 feet   Very Severe   (1961)
A mouth-watering route worth savouring. Start in the groove on the right of the almost detached pillar.
1   70 feet. 4b. The groove leads to a flake on the right. Step left onto a ledge, or go straight up, then follow a rib to a good stance and block belay.
2   70 feet. 4b. From the large block pull onto a bulging wall with difficulty. A stretch leads to good holds and climb steeply to a step left into a final groove. A sensationally positioned pitch.

Route II   110 feet   Severe   (1953)
A poor route. Start at a thin crack running down to the right from a large holly.
1   35 feet. The steep wall is climbed to the holly. Continue more easily to the stance on Lavaredo.
2   75 feet. Thrutch into the crack betwixt the slab and the wall above, and climb it to perched blocks. Finish up any of several available cracks.

The Falconer   120 feet   Hard Very Severe   (1982)
Start between Route II and Bay Groove.
1   45 feet. 5a. Climb the wall and thin cracks to belay on the slab overlooking the top pitch of Lavaredo.
2   75 feet. 5a. Climb up to the base of the arête right of Lavaredo. Ascend it in a fine position to the top.

Bay Groove   125 feet   Very Difficult   (1953)
Start at the apex of a grass tongue below a groove.
1   50 feet. Move past a small holly and go up the left wall of a steep open chimney to belays on the edge of a slab.
2   75 feet. Move onto the belay and step across a groove onto another slab. Ascend this to finish.

Bavarian Dream   100 feet   E3
1   100 feet. 5c. The crack left of the arête of Green Wall is followed to the top.

Green Wall   120 feet   Very Severe   (1967)
A steep route and an exposed top pitch. Start at a narrow slab which runs up under the steep back wall of the bay.
1   35 feet. 4a. A groove and slab lead to the foot of an impending wall. Traverse right to belays on a good ledge.
2   55 feet. 4c. Move left onto a ledge, continue up a groove then go round left into another groove with a boulder-filled ledge at its base. Steep moves lead onto a white pedestal on the left. Climb the overhanging wall on the left, via an awkward crack. Belay on a slab.

3   30 feet. The easy slab leads to the top.

Rib and Groove   120 feet   Severe   (1966)
Worth doing for the top pitch. Start at the foot of the ridge on
the right of the green bay.
1   70 feet. Start up the right side of the rib, but step left at 10
feet. Continue up to a ledge with many spikes beneath a
prominent V-chimney and go up to a belay.
2   50 feet. The groove in the green wall is followed diagonally
left until a strenuous move gives access to a slab and the top.

Craig Rhiw Goch (Crag of the Red Hill)   O.S. ref.767 541

A fine little crag, pleasantly situated, Rhiw Goch is a National
Trust property facing south on the bank of the River Lledr, just
below the A496 Betws y Coed to Dolwyddelan road. The crag is
easily reached directly from the road in less than five minutes.
The iron ladders in the river bank are private property and are
used for fishing. Parking is very limited here, so be prepared to
walk a little!

Reign   80 feet   Severe
1   80 feet. The left side of the crag is taken with a steep finish.

Megalomania   80 feet   E2   (1986)
1   80 feet. 5c. Follow Reign for a little, then step up to a spike.
Move right then climb the bulge, peg, via a crack, then the steep
wall above.

Congl   105 feet   Very Severe   (1965)
An obvious groove line.
1   105 feet. 4c. Move into the groove and go up it until a delicate
move left leads onto an obvious traverse. Finish on good holds.
A much harder alternative is to continue up the groove to the
top (HVS, 5b).

Endgame   100 feet   E2   (1972)
A poky route giving strenuous climbing on poor rock. Start as
for Congl.
1   100 feet. 5c. Follow Congl for a few feet until a step left into
an overhanging groove is possible. Ascend this and the
V-groove above, with a move left to finish.

★★ The Riparian   100 feet   E2   (1972)
An excellent route with a serious top section. Start by a large
embedded flake beneath a steep slab right of Congl.
1   100 feet. 5c. Climb the wall and a narrow groove above,
avoiding the cop-out to the left, then step right onto a steep wall.

Ascend this to a short groove at the foot of a gangway then climb the groove and a steep wall (crux) to a good spike. A further short groove leads to the top.

The Anvil   80 feet   E2   (1982)
Start at the foot of a short overhanging groove behind the large flake at the foot of The Riparian.
1   80 feet. 5c. The groove is climbed with an awkward exit at its top. A thin crack and face above lead to good holds and the top.

Mur Dena   100 feet   E1   (1965)
Start on a ledge to the right of the pinnacle flake.
1   40 feet. 4c. The right edge of the slab above leads to a break in some overhangs. Pull through them and ascend to a stance amongst large blocks. Alternatively climb the left edge of the slab.
2   60 feet. 5b. Traverse left across a steep wall to a crack, then follow this to a good spike on the right. Move onto the spike, step delicately right to the edge and climb this to the top.

Smiler's Route   80 feet   Hard Very Severe
Start beneath an obvious flake round to the right of Mur Dena.
1   80 feet. 5a. Climb the steep wall above the flake.

Clogwyn y Gigfran (The Giant's Head)

O.S. ref. 793 542

Pleasantly situated overlooking the Lledr Valley above the A496, about two miles out of Betws y Coed towards Dolwyddelan. Access to the crag is not defined, the most direct approach being rather brambly. A longer but more pleasant approach is to strike south-west through the pine woods above the Conway-Lledr river junction to the railway line. This is crossed immediately, followed by a diagonal ascent to the foot of the crag, 20 minutes from the road. The crag is 150 feet at its steep central section, reducing to 100 feet at the slabby left-hand end. To the right the crag degenerates into broken vegetated rock. The climbing is rather scrappy and vegetated; this combined with the friable nature of the rock demands care, particularly on the steeper routes.

Black Arrow   100 feet   Very Difficult
1   100 feet. Takes the slabs at the left-hand end of the crag.

The left-hand end of the central section is split by three grooves above a grassy bay. All three grooves have been climbed, the right-hand being the hardest, whilst the central one is the best, and gives the following route.

Titan   150 feet   Very Severe   (1962)
Start below the right-hand groove.
1 50 feet. 4c. Step onto a slab and make an awkward swing left
into the groove. Step left again into the central groove and climb
it to a narrow grassy ledge.
2 100 feet. 4b. A thin crack in the steep slab above is climbed
to a corner. Ascend this to the top.

Several other pitches are available and may be combined with
the other grooves.

The Ent   160 feet   E1   (1967)
A steep and intimidating first pitch. Start at the left end of the
rocky ledge beneath the large roof right of the start of Titan.
1 80 feet. 5b. Go easily along the ledge to an obvious narrow
rib. This leads to a junction with the end of the roof followed by
a steep vegetated crack above.
2 30 feet. 4c. Step left into the foot of an overhanging corner;
this is climbed to a grassy ledge.
3 50 feet. 4c. Ascend a corner crack for a few feet then step
right onto a rib and climb it to the top.

Shelob   150 feet   Hard Very Severe   (1967)
A steep and bold first pitch but a poor finish. Start by scrambling
up unpleasant vegetated rock to the lower left corner of the
grassy recess in the centre of the crag.
1 80 feet. 5a. Traverse left and go up to the foot of a steep
groove just right of The Ent. Pull over the bulge in the groove
(bold), then follow a line of holds out right until it is possible to
climb direct to a grassy ledge.
2 70 feet. 5a. A rib on the left of the corner behind the stance
is climbed to a small ledge. Traverse right onto overhanging rock
then climb the wall above with difficulty, past a small tree on
the left, to exit onto an easy-angled slab. Finish easily up this.

Cyclops   160 feet   Hard Severe   (1962)
A good route with some steep climbing. Start at the right-hand
end of the crag, beneath a steep wall formed by a flake, with a
prominent impending narrow crack leading from a niche above.
1 50 feet. The steep wall is climbed, moving left into the niche.
The crack is climbed strenuously to a grassy ledge and a tree
belay beneath a recess.
2 40 feet. The steep right wall of the recess is climbed, on big
flake holds, to a ledge under an overhang. Traverse left to a good
ledge on The Ent and Shelob.
3 70 feet. The corner behind the stance is climbed until it
overhangs. Step right into an exposed position above a large
roof then continue up slabs above to the top.

Variations   Very Severe
2a. 30 feet. The steep left arête of the recess.

A number of routes are reputed to have been climbed to the right of Cyclops, but the climbs are still trapped under the vegetation.

LONE BUTTRESS   O.S. ref. 708 548
Lying above Llyn y Foel on the eastern slopes of Moel Siabod is a solitary buttress, cleft by a gully in the centre. Right again is a steep section of rock, with an easy gully (Embryo Gully) on the right. The following route follows the line of the rib forming a ridge up the steep section.

Lone Buttress   200 feet   Difficult (1939)
A nice route though it has some loose rock. Start at the foot of the rib, right of a pinnacle with an overhang.
1   100 feet. Gain the rib from the left and go up its edge pleasantly to a grassy stance.
2   100 feet. Follow the line of the rib to the top.

Flanking the cwm right of Embryo Gully is a ridge of easy-angled slabs, which give easy scrambling at Easy standard. On the left end of the cwm is another rocky ridge (Daear Ddu), which gives some interesting problems on the side facing Llyn y Foel.

CWM SILYN AREA

by Dave Farrant

Historical by Geoff Milburn

In recent times the Snowdonia mountains and the surrounding valleys have been a hive of human activity and since the early 1900s a constant stream of travellers has passed along the main highways: the coastal road from Chester to Bangor and Anglesey, and from Caernarfon to Porthmadog; and the road down the Gwynant valley leading through Beddgelert to centres such as Harlech, Barmouth and Dolgellau. Within this region, to the south of Snowdon, there is a relatively secluded tract of countryside which has remained unspoiled to the present day.

The history of this area goes back at least to the early Celtic tribes who fought to obtain a foothold and there are various hill-forts remaining which serve to remind us of the fighting which undoubtedly took place to defend the high places against marauding invaders.

One legend from Roman times relates how the warrior queen Elen Lueddog was following in the steps of her youngest son who was on his way to Caernarfon. While her son was passing along the southern shore of Llyn Cwellyn his brother Cidwm killed him with an arrow – shot from the rocky ramparts of what was to become known as Castell Cidwm.

Little else is known about this hill area, but there is one surviving story about Owain Glyndwr who, about the year 1400, was on one occasion running away from his armed pursuers. In desperation he climbed Simnai Foel Hebog (the chimney of Moel Hebog) to reach the summit of Moel Hebog. He then fled to a cave on Moel yr Ogof where he hid for six months. Whilst in hiding he was sent provisions by the Prior of Beddgelert and his lonely refuge must have been both cold and damp for much of the time (take note those who moan about the length of time that they spend on stances!).

Early mountaineers approached Snowdon from the southern side and stayed at the small inn, Snowdon Ranger. Craddock in 1770 referred to it as 'a small thatched hut at the foot of the mountain' and there he was entertained by 'blooming country girls' who danced and rendered their own brand of local music. The early accounts of Snowdon refer to Hamer's 'personally conducted' ascents which occurred weekly starting from Caernarfon. Later Beddgelert became the main centre for walkers.

Moel Hebog was soon recognized as a prominent peak and according to Haskett Smith (1895) was ascended 'last century by

Lord Lyttelton, by the Ordnance surveyors, and in August 1857 by J H Cliffe. In Cliffe's 1860 book he comments that the summit cairns were very ancient.

Haskett Smith reckoned that a man in the pink of condition could top Moel Hebog from Beddgelert in three-quarters of an hour.

W.P. Haskett Smith is regarded as the first true rock-climber to explore the cliffs of the Nantlle/Cwellyn/Pennant area but as early records have been lost it is not known whether or not he was preceded.

Smith's article 'Twixt Snowdon and the Sea' published in the 1905 Climbers' Club Journal gives a wonderful insight into the early days. The approach to the area was via the London and North-Western Railways through Caernarfon to Dinas Junction which is to the west of the mountains. A change had then to be made to the North Wales Narrow Gauge Railway, which was described as 'a string of medieval trucks, which seem to have been left in a siding many years ago and allowed to drop to pieces'.

The windows were mostly broken or artfully mended with rough board, so that travellers had to peep through chinks wherever they could. The line passed down the Cwellyn valley to drop passengers for Snowdon Ranger while at the terminus simpler board and lodging could be found.

Later, in 1913, George Mallory summarized the pros and cons of staying locally:

> 'The migration of a few nomads from Gorphwysfa to Snowdon Ranger must not be reckoned as the concerted movement of a party, but rather as the aggregation of a few flecks of foam after the great Easter fermentation. It is worthy of remark that we left the first inn with no hurry after one o'clock lunch, and ate proper half-past four tea at the other; and I wouldn't like to say how many times we halted on the zig-zags. For those who are still unacquainted with Cwellyn, I have drawn up such remarks about the hotel and the locality as readily occur for praise or criticism.'

For:
(1) The beer is good. The porritch is particularly good. In short one feeds well.
(2) The beds are comfortable, and large enough to accommodate a climbing dream of the first order of sensations.

(3)   One may obtain the use of a private sitting room (i.e. a place of refuge from other parties, but not from his own).

(4)   An absolutely first-class playground with granite cracks and caves can be reached in ten minutes from the further side of the lake.

(5)   The inhabitants have no objection to bathing parties in the lake, and a good place presents itself after three minutes walk from the Hotel.

Against:

(1)   The usual indifference of those who live in remote places to the prime comfort – hot water.

(2)   The furniture was depreciated by our visit; but the springs must be remarkably good since they withstood shocks that shattered legs and castors.

(3)   To walk round the end of the lake is to violate the primary instincts of the true mountaineer, and to cross it in Mr Harrison's boat pre-supposes an act of faith.

(4)   The party bathed on the first morning but not again.

Mr Harrison, the proprietor, makes special terms for climbers; we paid 6s a day, the extras were insignificant.'

Thus did the pioneers base themselves and spread out from Cwellyn to the adjacent crags. It is little wonder that *Castell Cidwm Gully* was the first gully to be recorded, although who made the first ascent is not known. W.P. Haskett Smith must certainly be a strong contender for that honour as in 1905 he not only led a party up the *Eastern Arête* of Y Garn, but also did the *Pinnacle Ridge* of Craig y Bera with G. Hastings as well as returning to Castell Cidwm for *Wolf's Buttress*.

With a guidebook to the area in mind Climbers' Club parties began to visit the area from 1910 and at the forefront was J.M. Archer Thomson who opened his account with *Sentries Ridge* on Craig y Bera before recording in the December 1910 Climbers' Club Journal:

'Several interesting discoveries, including an arête with thirteen gendarmes, were made on the west side of Snowdon . . . we found the *East ridge of Y Garn* a charming climb well scored by a will-o'-the-wisp trail of scratches, which constantly disappeared at the foot of the harder obstacles. These were virgins and proved very difficult to surmount.'

Thomson finished his day by cycling to the station. A year later, at Easter, Thomson discovered Llechog on the slopes of Snowdon and in addition to climbing the first few routes he directed others to begin the assault. He also wrote enthusiastically of the development:

> ' . . . it may be said of Llechog that the several gullies are good, that many of the ribs are delightful, but better than all are the magnificent stretches of unsheltered slabs, which provide climbing of the highest order and quality. In a word, with the exception of Lliwedd, I am inclined to think no face in Wales offers to strong parties a wider or more varied field for excellent climbing.'

Thomson recorded that the Llechog routes had been done 'straight-forwardly, without preparation by descents and emasculating experiments with the human windlass.' It is surprising however that he did not record two very hard routes that were done in September of 1911. George Mallory and Harold Porter succeeded in climbing *Eastern Gutter*, a Very Severe, on Llechog and also climbed *Mallory's Ridge*, on Y Garn. Thomson had tried the latter in 1910 but had backed off from the crux. Shortly afterwards, the fine climber Anton Stoop was killed while attempting the ascent. It was thus a tremendous step forward when Porter made the first successful ascent. Both Eastern Gutter and Mallory's Ridge were amongst the hardest of Welsh climbs and the latter was unrepeated for many years.

Another major discovery was made by Thomson in 1911. Under the summit of Mynydd Mawr a large north-facing cliff had remained hidden from the eyes of the early climbers although it could easily be seen from the west in the dying embers of the day. Thomson enthusiastically threw himself at Craig Cwm Du on several occasions during a year which he described as the best of his life. Some years later, in 1926, Herbert Carr assessed the development:

> 'The discovery of Cwm Du was made by J.M.A. Thomson in 1911. Most of the pioneer work was done by him with the assistance of H.O. Jones, G.H.L. Mallory, L. Noon, K.J.P.Orton and R. Todhunter. In recent years the discovery has been practically ignored. In general, the climbing is of a high standard of difficulty and it is suitable only to strong and experienced parties. The rock is treacherous and the leader has always to exercise extreme caution. Despite their unsound character these climbs possess a distinct charm, and they cannot be neglected by competent climbers who desire to widen their experience on all types of rock.'

Pete Crew on the 1st ascent of Zukator, Craig Bwlch y Moch.

Photo: Ken Wilson

The immaculate Vector Buttress, Craig Bwlch y Moch.

Photo: Ken Wilson

Dave Alcock high on Vector, Craig Bwlch y Moch.

Photo: John Cleare

Keith Sharples on Neb Direct, Craig Bwlch y Moch.
Photo: Ian Smith

In the Climbers' Club Journal Thomson did let it be known that some of the details of new routes had been suppressed as there was an opinion at the time that articles and books were unnecessary – their very existence removed the sense of the unknown when climbing. We do know however that Thomson did make the first ascent of the fine *Adam Rib* which Mallory was to straighten out a year later.

At Easter 1912 a large party gathered at Cwellyn to repeat the new climbs on Llechog, Craig y Bera and Craig Cwm Du. The party consisted of Miss Andrew, A.W. Andrews, Miss Benecke, Miss Chapman, H.M.F. Dodd, Miss Jones, H.O. Jones, K.J.P. Orton, M.K. Smith, R. Todhunter and of course Thomson. In addition to repeating Adam Rib and Green Pitch Gully they also added a new face climb and a gully with seven pitches. No details are however now known. What is more surprising is that a visit was paid to Clogwyn du'r Arddu and the cliff was ascended by grassy ledges and traverses.

The same year Mallory and Todhunter went up into Cwm Silyn but they did not attempt the Great Slab, instead they went for *Four Pitch Gully* on Clogwyn y Cysgod. Todhunter returned later for *Sunset Rib*, the first route to be done on Craig yr Ogof.

Tragedy was to strike for some years starting with the untimely deaths of both Thomson and H.O. Jones in 1912. The first World War then claimed many more lives and not only a generation of climbers was lost but also many of the precious records of new climbs which had been collected for a proposed guidebook. Even worse was to follow. Mallory, one of climbing's best known names, disappeared on Everest in 1924 and this was followed by Todhunter's death on the Rosetta in 1926. Amidst this confusion Herbert Carr a young Oxford graduate spent much of the early 1920s preparing his 'Climbers' Guide to Snowdon and the Beddgelert District.' This third pocket guide, published in 1926, followed 'The Climbs on Lliwedd' by Archer Thomson and A.W. Andrews in 1909 and 'Climbing in the Ogwen District' by Archer Thomson in 1910. Carr was on several first ascents in the Cwm Silyn area and *Overhanging Chimneys* on Trwyn y Graig, on which he accompanied Downes and McNaught, was undoubtedly one of the better routes done at that time.

The stage was set for an assault on the Great Slab of Craig yr Ogof and in retrospect it is hard to understand why the *Ordinary Route* had to wait until 1926 before it was completed by a strong team made up of David Pye, W.R. Reade, C.A. Elliot and N.E. Odell. Another generation of climbers then made an appearance and after Kirkus had led his fine route on the Great Slab Menlove Edwards established the superb *Outside Edge Route*. Also in 1931 another strong team comprising Kirkus, A.B. Hargreaves and Alf Bridge made a successful ascent of the *Upper Slab Climb*. Kirkus and Edwards then went on to greater things in the Llanberis Pass and up on the black cliff of Clogwyn du'r Arddu. For the next twenty years little of note was to happen in the area and there were certainly no major innovatory developments.

The Second World War saw the death of Kirkus who was killed in action and it also scarred Edwards despite the fact that he was not directly involved.

In the post-war period routes appeared steadily and one of the better ones was *Angel Pavement* on Craig y Bera by C.P. Brown and Tony Moulam. One of the factors which affected the development of the area was the fact that the Manchester University Mountaineering Club acquired a hut near Llyn Cwellyn in 1945, and it was from Tyn y Weirglodd that the club began work on an interim guidebook. G. Eglinton began the task and finally E.W. (Ted) Dance joined in to complete the task. During the work they discovered that Paul Work was exploring from Beddgelert and had completed many climbs on Moel Hebog. He was also preparing a guidebook to the Moel Hebog cliffs but he readily divulged the relevant information to allow Ted Dance to complete 'The Cwellyn Area' interim guidebook which appeared as a reprint from the 1954 M.U.M.C. Journal. This coincided with plans made by the Climbers' Club for a guidebook to the cliffs of Cwm Silyn and Tremadoc and John Neill's supplement was reprinted from the 1955 Climbers' Club Journal.

One hard route which had seen several failures was the 'awe-inspiring face' of *The Ogof Direct*. Eventually Tony Moulam fresh from his recent success on Mur y Niwl in the Carneddau proved that the route was possible with some aid, a trend that became fashionable for a while in the 1950s before a bolder style of climbing restored earlier ethical standards. Moulam used eight pitons, several were thought to be essential, but only three were mentioned in the Supplement. What is more fascinating is that he started the day with a party of some 17 people at the cave but somehow managed to 'lose' most of them before the successful ascent. Another climber who was prepared to use artificial aids was Tom Bourdillon – probably because of his interest in the Alps. He had already failed on *Anniversary Waltz*, Clogwyn y Bustach, at his first attempt in 1954 but had succeeded on Dover Road another A2 on Craig yr Ysfa.

During March 1956 D.H. Briggs and D.P. Davis got a long way up the groove to the left of Great Slab, but were finally defeated before they reached the top. Owing to loose rock and insecure pegs the climbing was thought to be A3 and this was confirmed two months later when Bourdillon and Hamish Nicol completed the route. Nicol completed the hard top pitch and to acknowledge the considerable effort of the previous team the route was called *Briggs' Climb*. In another seven years Peter Crew would point the finger at pegging activities in the hills but for the present there would be more pegging seen in Wales but mainly on the Tremadog cliffs. Bourdillon an accomplished Alpinist, who had been on both Cho Oyu and Everest expeditions, had clearly set his sights beyond 'trivial' ethical matters on 'small' British crags. Sadly however, two months after completing Briggs' Climb, he died with Dick Viney in an accident on the Jägihorn.

By 1959 climbing in Snowdonia was ready for a major change. Joe Brown went south first to the Gwynant crags and then in 1960 to Tremadog. Rumours of secret crags have always captured the imagination of climbers and Brown was intrigued to hear of one such possible monster which supposedly Hugh Banner had discovered. It was also rumoured that a well-known climber had fallen off while exploring. Luckily Claude Davies remembered seeing a crag in a gorge when he was only fourteen. Near the crag Brown was grumbling as he wandered through heather:

> 'Our eyes went up and were transfixed by a fantastic
> wall overlooking the stream. It had breadth and
> verticality and was bristling with a fringe of over-
> hangs . . . The steepness of the face was awe-inspiring
> and we were at a bit of a loss where to look for a breach
> in the defences . . . We got up 60 feet then none of us
> could climb higher . . . the cliff had an unnerving
> character.'

Later Brown returned to complete *Dwm* with Harry Smith leading the top pitch. Unfortunately the slab under the overhang was running with water and Smith had to use three pegs for aid – nevertheless the route was a tremendous achievement. It was certainly the route of the crag as far as other climbers were concerned but Brown's other two routes of that year, *Vertigo* and *The Curver* also became highly popular in the following years. With no real competition Brown left the crag for the time being and resumed his onslaught on the Tremadog cliffs, putting up a large number of hard and high-quality routes. Two years later, however, he returned to Cidwm for a mind-bending roof-crack that no-one else would have considered at that time. Although *Tramgo* required some aid it was nevertheless a savage and demanding pitch which top climbers were to keep away from for many years.

Strangely it was not Brown who grabbed the top line of the Cwm Silyn cliffs, but Baz Ingle who was Pete Crew's regular climbing partner. The route, *Crucible*, was a stunning line through the steep parts of Craig yr Ogof where Hugh Banner had been defeated and several other confident leaders had taken flight when they ran out of steam. Ingle with Richard McHardy also grabbed *Desifinado* another fine line which crosses the face above the cave.

During 1964 tales began to circulate about some spectacular antics which were taking place on Castell Cidwm. John Clements, mainly accompanied by Alan Bell, stole a march on the other top climbers operating in Snowdonia. Several hard steep lines were climbed sometimes with spectacular falls into space in the process. *Glwm* was the starting point, but *Central Wall* gave one of the best routes in Wales and breached a very improbable-looking section of rock. *The Erg* followed and finally, in October 1965, the *Cidwm Girdle* which Clements tenaciously worked on with Dave Potts until they ultimately succeeded to give one of the most intimidating routes in Wales. Yet again, with success came tragedy, and the genius of Clements came to an abrupt stop when he was killed while climbing in Glencoe.

In the latter half of the 1960s development slowed down to a trickle with only a few memorable routes in the area. On Craig yr Ogof two worthwhile routes appeared: *Brutus* by Baz Ingle and *Eureka* by the two Holliwell brothers who were about to make their presence felt all over Snowdonia. Another fine climber who saw remaining possibilities on Craig yr Ogof was Ray Evans who first worked out *Codswallop* in 1968 then returned two years later for the superb *Jabberwocky*. He also succeeded on a much-fancied line, *Dulyn Groove*, which sadly only yielded with aid. Evans's partner on Jabberwocky, Mike Yates, was involved in writing the long-awaited Cwm Silyn guidebook and with co-author Jim Perrin they had a lot of work in front of them to sort out the scattered details of routes done over many years. While enthusiastically checking the obscure crags they went up to Llechog where Perrin identified and led Thomson's gaunt red crag to produce *Resurrection* one of the best routes of its grade in Snowdonia.

When the Cwm Silyn and Cwellyn guidebook came out (1971) it stimulated people to go up to Cwm Silyn for the classic routes but there was no rush to the outlying cliffs and even Castell Cidwm did not prove to be popular for the mainstream crowds of climbers. Strangely it did not even trigger off a search for new routes and in the next ten years only six new routes were to appear. Yates was still keenly interested in Llechog and was to return for four new routes. After completing *Redog* on Moel Hebog *Blood on the Tracks* was the first offering and on the latter

Hugh Banner was introduced to the possibilities of the cliff. They returned and with Banner in the lead *Slopey* a sustained E3 was produced. Not surprisingly they were drawn back to a stiff problem up the true line of the gaunt red crag to give Banner the superb *Erection* that he richly deserved, but route naming at that time did not come as easily to him.

Of all the major crags in Snowdonia few with great potential have been left untouched for long by the jackals in the 1980s. Hard new lines are at a premium and usually need a critical eye of faith. On Castell Cidwm however there were quite a few glaringly obvious lines just crying out to be done.

Two Crooks stole *Zwm* in 1979 but left it at that. Then in 1980 Jim Moran who was putting up hard routes on several Welsh cliffs returned with Geoff Milburn for the big roof line that they had spotted while on Tramgo two years earlier. Early in the season *Hang 'em High* needed a big effort and they returned to the Peak District for milder weather. Like so many before them they vowed to return but time passed by until 1988 when Pat Littlejohn went to the cliff and couldn't believe his luck. That year he snatched no fewer than seven superb routes. Firstly with John de Montjoye he climbed what must be three of the hardest routes in the Cwm Silyn area: *Balance of Power* was a good start but *Potency* at E6 with two 6b pitches was a magnificent achievement by any standards. And that was just one day's climbing. Two weeks later they grabbed *Heading for Heights*, another spectacular line. Littlejohn was hooked and went back yet again with Steve Monks for *Dwmsday* and *Glasnost* two immaculate routes to the left of Dwm. *Light Years* through the roofs above The Curver must stand as one of the hardest lines in the South Snowdonia region if not North Wales and it is likely that this route alone will attract the leading climbers of the 1990s. Lastly *Equinox* a mere E4 was Littlejohn's final offering of the year, but it certainly won't be the last route to be done on Cidwm's ramparts.

Between Haskett Smith and Littlejohn there has been a gap of 84 years and in that time comparatively few climbers have made their mark in this region with new routes. This area may never appeal to the hardened cragrat who will have to make the effort to walk to the cliffs, but when the main Tremadog crags finally yield the last micro-routes there will still be a great deal of rock waiting to be explored. There are several chapters to be written in this story, but whatever happens in the future this area of wild cwms and secluded valleys is still likely to draw those who will appreciate what is one of the most beautiful parts of North Wales.

CWELLYN AREA

Llechog

O.S. ref. SH 597 537

Llechog is the large cliff bounding the southern rim of Cwm Clogwyn beneath the ridge taken by the Snowdon track from Beddgelert and Rhyd Ddu. It provides plenty of interesting climbing in fine mountain situations.

The cliff faces north-east and is about four hundred feet high. It is set at high slab angle and takes little drainage which is a welcome contrast to many of the climbs in this area. The quality of the rock is variable but on the best routes it is sound, rough and so compact that protection can be difficult to find.

The cliff is divided into two sections by a Central Couloir. The best of the climbing lies on the steeper section right of this couloir, the Western Cliff. The Eastern Cliff is easier-angled and more broken, trailing off to the left into scree. Distinctive features of the Eastern Cliff include the long narrow Arrow Slab high up to the left, and the steeper quartzy area taken by Central Rib.

The first feature of the Western Cliff, to the right of the Central Couloir, is a typical gutter, Mermaid Gully, which runs to slightly more than half the height of the cliff. A slabby area right of its base gives the start of The Mermaid Climb, which traverses rightwards across the terrace above to finish up a depression on the left of a prominent red slab.

The three-tiered buttress capped by the red slab is taken by Resurrection and Erection. Right again are vegetated slabs capped by a dark, diagonal rock-cornice. The Cloister Climb runs up to the left-hand end of this. The Black Rib, distinctly visible from the right, but less so from the left, runs up to the lower end of the cornice and is bounded on the right by Central Gully.

Immediately right of the gully is Central Ridge which bounds Trinity Buttress A on the left. Five Cave Gully, conspicuous by its cluster of four caves near the top, splits Trinity Buttresses A and B. Blood on the Tracks takes the left edge of Trinity Buttress B. To the right again is Grey Gully, then Trinity Buttress C with its obvious smooth lower wall taken centrally by Slopey. The climbing is bounded to the right by the deep cleft of North Gully.

The quickest approach to the cliff is to take the Snowdon Path from the Rhyd Ddu car park, or Ffridd Uchaf. This runs along the top of the cliff and allows access in about an hour. The other approach, via the Snowdon Ranger Track and Cwm Clogwyn, is significantly longer and wetter but it is the best way of reaching Llechog Facet.

The Central Couloir provides the best descent from all of the routes. The top of this can be recognised as a depression some 20 yards left, facing outwards, of a stone wall crossed by the Snowdon Track. Descend into the couloir via a left-hand branch, again facing outwards, which begins slightly to the left of the main depression.

EASTERN CLIFF

Arrow Slab   390 feet   Very Severe   (1955)
This rather artificial climb lies about one-third of the way along the Eastern Cliff from its left-hand end. Start at the back of a slight bay some 50 yards left of Central Rib. Arrows and the name may be discerned faintly scratched on the slab above the cairn.
1   60 feet. Climb up the slab for 25 feet, traverse right beneath grooves and ascend the rightmost one. Step left awkwardly after 20 feet to a poor stance in a niche.
2   55 feet. Traverse 10 feet right from the niche, and climb ribbed rock to a small overhang. Trend leftwards to a grass ledge beneath a slab.
3   115 feet. Continue up the slabs for about 100 feet, crossing a grassy rake on the way, then move left to a recess.
4   60 feet. Climb diagonally rightwards over ribs.
5   100 feet. Continue to the top.

⋆ **Central Rib**   410 feet   Very Difficult   (1911)
A good route with some delightful slab climbing. A prominent leftward-slanting rib, high up in the centre of the cliff, gives the climb its name. Start at the lowest point reached by the Eastern Cliff, in a little bay 70 feet left of a prominent quartz-speckled toe.
1   100 feet. Pleasant slab climbing 'with good holds economically supplied. Of great value, too, are sundry little round cavities into which the digits of a limb can be fitted to a nicety.'
2   90 feet. Easier slabs lead to a series of grassy terraces.
3   40 feet. Climb a crack to a pinnacle above and to the right. The main rib rises from a grassy terrace twenty feet to the right.
4   100 feet. Climb the rib direct on small holds near its left edge, to a ledge and small belay on the right.
5   80 feet. Continue easily past a quartz-spattered bay to the top.

An unidentifiable route, **Cross Slab and Arête**, 355 feet, Very Difficult, has been climbed between Central Rib and the next climb.

Torpedo Route   350 feet   Difficult   (1911)
From near the foot of the Central Couloir, a continuous narrow gutter runs nearly to the top of the cliff. This route follows the slab on the left of the gutter. Start to the left of the gutter's base. Easy climbing on sound rock, the holds 'a source of quiet

184

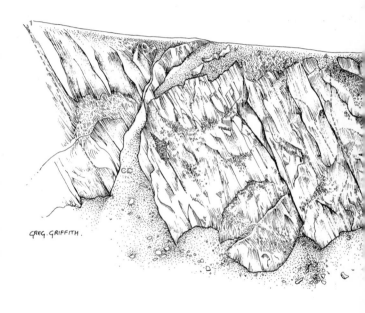

GREG. GRIFFITH.

Llechog
Western Cliff

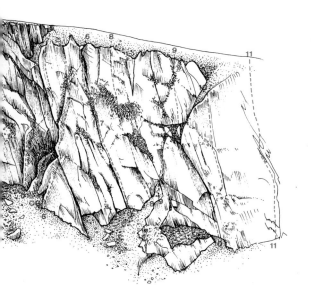

delight', leads up the slabs left of the gutter for 200 feet to a grass terrace. The 'Ribbed Wall' above is climbed with some interest, gradually easing after a steeper grooved section has been passed. Continue easily to the ridge.

Eastern Gutter   280 feet   Very Severe   (1911)
A mysterious, and for many years lost, route; one of the earliest of its grade in Wales. One of the more interesting lines on the Eastern Cliff. Start below the obvious gutter to the right of the broad area of slabs taken by Central Rib. The slabs just to the left of the gutter are conspicuously marked with black.
1   60 feet. Typical gully climbing until the bed steepens and becomes a groove curving up to the left. Poor belay.
2   100 feet. 4c. The groove gives sustained bridging increasing in difficulty to grassy ledges at 60 feet. Scramble up to belay.
3   120 feet. Continue up typical Llechog slabs and grass to the top.

The huge **Central Couloir** contains one pitch of Difficult standard, a slabby chimney-groove of 40 feet on loose rock, high up in the main branch. The normal way down from all the routes is to descend the right-hand branch of the main couloir, which comes in just below the pitch. This is easy, but care should be taken.

WESTERN CLIFF
The area of rock immediately to the right of the Central Couloir is very broken and the rock is poor towards the top. The next route lies to the right of another characteristic gutter, Mermaid Gully.

The Mermaid Climb   340 feet   Severe   (1911)
On the right of Mermaid Gully is an area of slabby ribs leading up to a heathery terrace. Start at the foot of these ribs.
1   110 feet. Climb the steep slabby ribs keeping to the right, and continue up slabs to the terrace.
2   110 feet. Traverse the terrace and go up easy rock to the base of a V-groove.
3   60 feet. Climb the smooth groove with difficulty to a stance.
4   70 feet. Continue up beside the red slab of Resurrection into a chimney on the left. Climb this to gain easier rock and thence the top.

To the right is a prominent buttress composed of three tiers of slabs. This buttress provides the best climbing on the cliff.

★★ **Resurrection**   410 feet   Hard Very Severe   (1970)
This fine near-classic route takes a direct line up the three smooth slabs of the buttress, the top slab being the 'gaunt red slab' described as 'quite impossible' by Archer Thomson.

Although it is possible to escape between pitches, this does not detract from the climbing which increases progressively in difficulty and quality. Start directly below the lower tier of the buttress, some 30 feet left of the shallow gully of the start of Cloister Climb.

1   80 feet. Scramble up heathery breaks to belay at the foot of the first wall.

2   100 feet. 4a. Move right into the gully on the right and climb it easily for a few feet. (The route can be gained from Zarquon here.) Traverse left across some perched blocks, then continue straight up into a shallow groove. Climb this and the short crack above to a large grassy ledge. Belay on the right.

3   100 feet. 4c. Climb the edge of the slab to gain and follow a short right-facing groove to a ledge on the left. Continue delicately up the open groove on the left into a shallow scoop. Step left round the rib and move up to easier climbing which leads to a belay in a minor gully on the left.

4   130 feet. 5a. Climb directly up the crack in the centre of the smooth final slab until a thin diagonal crack can be followed to the left-hand edge of the slab. Swing round the arête and cross the steep wall to gain a corner. Move left again into a crack and follow this over a bulge to a small ledge. Move back right across the groove onto the front face and follow this to the top.

** Erection   100 feet   E2   (1982)

The proper way up the 'gaunt red slab': a superb pitch, even better than the original finish. Start from the belay at the end of the third pitch of Resurrection.

1   100 feet. 5c. Follow pitch 4 of Resurrection to the left arête, then climb the thin crack just right of the edge to the top.

The Cloister Climb   360 feet   Severe   (1911)

An interesting route, up the vegetated slabs below the huge diagonal rock cornice, but it is rather spoilt by the vegetation. Start in the shallow gully right of Resurrection, to the right of the heathery area beneath the red slab.

1   90 feet. Climb easily up the groove for 30 feet, then take a right-hand branch until a traverse right leads to the edge and a grassy ledge.

2   80 feet. Step right and climb up onto the main slab. Follow this trending slightly left to a stance.

3   90 feet. Continue up the slabs in the same line, move left and go up a groove to another large grassy ledge.

4   100 feet. Climb a slim groove on the edge of the main slab into a recess, the Cloister, under the cornice. Follow this until a rough chimney leads suddenly to the top.

Zarquon   340 feet   Hard Very Severe   (1982)

A natural line up the left-hand edge of the slabs right of Resurrection which crosses then finishes up Cloister Climb. The first two pitches give a good alternative start for Resurrection or Erection. Start up to the right from the foot of the edge, in a bay left of a pillar.

1 60 feet. 5a. Go straight up thin cracks to the grassy ledge at the top of pitch 1 of Cloister Climb.

2 50 feet. 5a. Climb diagonally left across the pink slab into a recess. Continue leftwards up a groove to a stance right of the blocks on pitch 2 of Resurrection (which can be joined at this point).

3 70 feet. 4b. Climb the corner crack and the slab above to a large heathery ledge.

4 60 feet. Climb up right to a crack and groove, which are followed to another large ledge on Cloister Climb.

5 100 feet. As for Cloister Climb, climb a slim groove on the edge of the main slab into the Cloister under the cornice. Follow this until a rough chimney leads suddenly to the top.

★ **Black Rib**   260 feet   Difficult   (1911)
A pleasant route taking the dark-coloured rib, so obvious from the right, which runs up to the right of the lower end of the cornice. The rock is of a different texture to the rest of the cliff, steep, and with plenty of holds. Start at the foot of the rib.

1 150 feet. Climb the rib, past possible stances, to belay in a large bay.

2 110 feet. Climb the rightmost of the three ribs rising from Central Gully to the right, starting from a recess on its left side and moving onto the edge, which is followed to the top. Other lines have also been climbed.

To the right is **Central Gully**; the right-hand rib of this gives:

Central Ridge   400 feet   Difficult   (1911)
A pleasant climb on excellent rock. Start on the right near the foot of Central Gully.
Gain the crest of the rib and follow it for 200 feet to a grassy platform. From a grassy chimney to the right, traverse left to gain the edge again and follow it to another ledge. Pass a small overhang on the left and continue to the top.

Five Cave Gully   380 feet   Hard Severe   (1911)
The conspicuous gully with prominent caves. Start at the foot of the gully.

1 130 feet. Climb the bed of the gully to the first cave at 90 feet. Step left to a grassy ledge and climb the groove above to another groove which leads to a heather terrace.

2 150 feet. Scramble up the gully bed to the caves above.

3 100 feet. Start up the left wall of the first cave, then move right. Climb the second cave direct and evade the final two on the left.

Between Five Cave Gully and Grey Gully is Trinity Buttress B.

★ **Blood on the Tracks**   350 feet   Hard Very Severe   (1982)
A good natural line up the nose of the buttress, giving some fine
delicate climbing. Start at the foot of an obvious rib at the lowest
part of the buttress.
1 110 feet. 5b. Go straight up the rib by shallow grooves and
follow the single groove, which breaks through the smoothest
and steepest section, to ledges on the left. Continue up a final
short groove to a large grassy ledge on the right.
2 50 feet. 5a. Follow the central groove through the bulge
above, then move left and go steeply up a rib to more ledges.
3 100 feet. Follow easy ground to the final wall.
4 90 feet. 4c. Gain the ochre-coloured scoop slightly left of the
centre and follow it to easy ground and the top.

The vegetated central area of this buttress has been followed by
various routes. All of these take only vague lines with much
scope for variation.

Sunset Slabs   380 feet   Severe   (1956)
Start in the middle of the buttress.
Follow slabs for 100 feet to a vegetated ledge. Traverse left to
the base of another area of slab and climb this to more heather
(90 feet). Ascend a short steep wall to trees. Climb the wall on
the left, with difficulty at first, to reach a stance in a grassy
chimney. Follow chimneys and cracks to the ridge.

Trinity Buttress B   225 feet   Severe   (1911)
Another vague climb which starts a very short distance left of
Grey Gully and Wall and takes an indeterminate line to the top
of the cliff. Start at the foot of two slimy ribs.
Climb either rib, step left into a groove, and go up vegetation to
a terrace below an overhang (70 feet). Avoid this on the right
and follow a rib to a ledge. From the right-hand end of this follow
a shallow groove, bearing left to easier ground (100 feet). Climb
the upper wall, hard if taken direct, but avoidable by a grassy
chimney to the left. Start the steep wall above direct, then
traverse to the right, and finish up another shallow grassy
chimney.

Grey Gully and Wall   300 feet   Severe   (1911)
Vegetated gully climbing, leads to a fine finishing pitch. Start in
the gully bed.
1 90 feet. Climb the bed of the gully and the vegetation to its
right to a ledge.
2 70 feet. Continue up the gully to a large heathery ledge below
the final wall.
3 90 feet. Climb the shallow depression in the wall, to the left
of the grassy chimney-line of the gully to reach a ledge.

4   50 feet. Continue easily in the same line to the top.

The buttress to the right, Trinity Buttress C, has an impressively smooth lower section. Earlier routes outflanked this on either side but this defect has now been rectified with Slopey which forces its way up its centre.

Trinity Buttress C   260 feet   Severe   (1913)
Takes the left-hand side of the buttress by a series of grooves. Start at a conspicuous leaning block 30 feet from the lowest point of the buttress.
1   70 feet. Climb the groove to a scoop above a grassy ledge. From a higher ledge traverse right to a steep slanting groove, and go up over grassy ledges to a flat balanced block.
2   75 feet. Climb the wall above to a heathery ledge. Follow an awkward groove to easier climbing leading up to a steep wall.
3   75 feet. Climb the wall trending left, and traverse right to a small ledge. Ascend a steep corner to its right on small holds.
4   40 feet. Follow the arête above on its right edge, to finish up a short crack in the face.

★ **Slopey**   100 feet   E3   (1981)
A sustained and precarious pitch. It follows the obvious break slanting leftwards up the lower wall of the buttress. Start at the top of pitch 1 of Slab and Groove, on the narrow ledge below the main wall of the buttress.
1   100 feet. 5c. Climb the left-hand of the twin central cracks for about 40 feet to a horizontal break where the crack ends, then step up right to gain the right-hand of the cracks. Follow this then go up and slightly right to a horizontal crack near the top. Step back left and climb a short groove to finish on the terrace. Either descend one of the slanting gullies or follow one of the other buttress routes to the top.

Slab and Groove   380 feet   Very Severe   (1949)
The previous best attempt on the buttress. Start at the foot of the buttress, almost in North Gully.
1   50 feet. Climb the groove on the right to a grassy ledge.
2   100 feet. Go up to a crack near the right-hand edge of the slab and follow this for 70 feet, until a traverse left is possible along a slanting crack, to gain the top of the slab.
3   100 feet. Scramble up heather to a rib overlooking North Gully.
4   40 feet. Climb the groove until it becomes difficult, then continue up flakes on its left edge.
5   90 feet. Climb the steep wall above.

The **North Gully**, Very Difficult, (1911), gives broken climbing with two pitches; a 60-foot groove low down, and a 15-foot chimney. The rest is rather loose scrambling, with climbing available as desired.

Revised Access Notes

Prepared by Andy Newton for The Climbers' Club on behalf of the B.M.C. Committee for Wales, the Snowdonia National Park and the Nature Conservancy Council. These notes supersede or supplement the relevant sections in the 1989 edition of Tremadog and Cwm Silyn.

Craig y Gesail   page 23
Although the landowner does not wish climbers to approach the crag via the farmyard, the National Park Wardens and the B.M.C. have agreed a waymarked access path and a limited additional parking area just off the minor road. This arrangement is solely for the benefit of climbers as there is no right of way to the crag and the information is clearly displayed in Eric's Cafe, Bwlch y Moch.

Craig Pant Ifan   page 23
The access ban on the crag has not technically been lifted and the Nature Conservancy Council have not given permission for climbers to use the cliff. The wardening which took place some years ago to advise climbers to keep off the cliff was stopped, but this has been replaced by a number of fences and signs. In this way the N.C.C. have been advised that they are discharging their duty as regards land occupancy, but it should not be construed as a lifting of the access ban or implied permission to use the cliff for climbing.

The Warden for Tremadog is Mr. D. Oliver, telephone 0766 810235, not as stated in the guide.

The telephone number for the N.C.C. in Bangor is 0248 370 444, not as stated in the guide.

Craig Bwlch y Moch   page 24
Whilst Eric's Cafe does a great deal of trade with visiting climbers, it should be noted that the car park is not for the exclusive use of climbers. Climbers cars should be parked in accordance with the wishes of the owner, usually in the left-hand car park. It should be emphasised that the cafe is a business; not a public rubbish tip nor public toilets. The owner has every right to expect climbers parking here to use the cafe and not to consume their own food in the immediate vicinity of the cafe. The campsite behind the cafe continues to provide an excellent service to the itinerant climber.

The fence at the top of the crag was paid for by the B.M.C. and erected by the National Park on their behalf; damage to the fence should thus be avoided.

Craig yr Wrysgan   page 143
and Craig y Clipiau   page 151
The approaches to these crags may, from time to time, be affected by the working of the re-opened Cwmorthin Slate Quarry, particularly the temporary closure of paths during blasting!

The whole of the Cwellyn Area is beset by access problems that are rather sharper than in the more popular valleys of Snowdonia. It is vital that the work of the National Park Wardens, in securing the access routes that do exist, should not be placed in jepardy by climbers who might be trying to save a couple of minutes walking time.

Castell Cidwm   page 192
The cliff should not be approached via the *Castell Cidwm Hotel*, even though occasional trespass is tolerated; the landowner of the far bank of the river will not allow access to the crag. The correct approach is from Planwydd farm.

Craig Cwm Du   page 205
Cars should not be parked beyond the end of the road at Fron, to do so would be a Road Traffic Offence.

Craig Cwm Silyn   page 214
At the present time parking is tolerated in the field at the end of the tarmac road, although a number of cars were vandalised on one occasion. There is no guarantee that this situation is permanent and nothing should be done to disturb the status quo; in particular do not drive across the field nor camp in Cwm Silyn.

Clogwyn Yr Adar   page 313
The access position at this crag is precariously balanced after large numbers of climbers have visited the crag and ignored requests to ask permission of the landowner before climbing. The farmer and landowner, Mr. Noble, is willing to allow climbing if some respect is exhibited by visitors; the situation being made even more tenuous by the presence of Protected birds nesting in the *Cheshire Cat* area of the crag. It is also vital that climbers park as directed. Bearing in mind the fiasco at Craig Y Forwen, climbers will only have themselves to blame if access to this pretty little crag is lost.

Many of the crags in this area are subject to bylaws which preclude dogs at certain times of the year eg. lambing season. All dogs on public paths should be under close control and preferably on a lead at all times; in particular they should not be allowed to roam free at the base of crags.

The Climbers' Club   *July 1990*

LLECHOG FACET   O.S. ref. SH 592 545
This is the line of four small cliffs, which lie below the rim of
Cwm Clogwyn. They are of little climbing interest, being small,
north-facing, vegetated and usually wet. The Afon Treweneu-
nydd, flowing from Llyn Nadroedd, cascades between the Far
North Bluff and the North Bluff. A stone wall descends from the
South Bluff to join the wall dividing the cliff from the marshy
area in the valley bottom. The approach is as for Llechog from
Snowdon Ranger or Rhyd Ddu.

NORTH BLUFF
Although the largest cliff of the four, it is broken and vegetated
with a steep wall on its right-hand side, and a slabby area on
the left beneath a grassy terrace. The following routes are
scarcely worth recording.   **Batelion** (130 feet, Severe) starts at
the foot of the slabby area, follows the slab to grass and then
continues to the top. About 40 feet right of this **The Bar Steward**
(120 feet, Very Difficult, 1950) starts off a rocky table and follows
a shallow ridge to finish up the wall above. **The Greenhouse
Roof** (195 feet, Very Difficult, 1951) starts about 100 feet above
and to the right of the Bar Steward, follows a vague ridge
through vegetation and wanders on to the top. Finally, **Nadroedd**
(300 feet, Severe, 1949) lies up the heathery buttress bounding
the North Bluff on the right.

SOUTH BLUFF
This provides a little better climbing.

Residents' Wall   110 feet   Very Severe   (1949)
The route follows the obvious overhanging flake crack, starting
20 feet right of the stone wall. Climb a ramp to an overhang,
move left up a short crack then go back right to belay below the
flake. Climb the desperate overhanging crack and continue
easily up the crack to the top of the flake to finish delicately up
the wall above.

The Little Rocker   140 feet   Very Severe   (1966)
Start at the lowest point of the cliff.
1   30 feet. Climb the wall to a terrace.
2   110 feet. Follow a wide, slabby groove for 25 feet until forced
right onto the rib. Climb the groove above and gain a good ledge
on the left. Traverse up leftwards for a few feet, surmount a
block, and go left to climb the crack to the top.

Castell Cidwm (Castle of Cidwm – The Wolfish One)

O.S. ref. SH 550 554

This large crag lies at the north-west end of Llyn Cwellyn, low down on the slopes of Mynydd Mawr. There is a lot of rock, but much of it is broken by heathery ledges. By far the most significant climbing is concentrated on the South-East Face, overlooking the Afon Goch which bounds the cliff to the left.

The cliff has always had a reputation of providing only harder routes. This has been confirmed with the near doubling of the existing routes in a few weeks following years of unwarranted neglect of the cliff. The addition of these routes, very much in the modern vein, has only just started to fill the vast expanses of unclimbed steep walls.

The South-East Face is very steep and presents few obvious features beyond an instant impression of serried overhangs. The rock is smooth, having an almost glassy texture, and is generally very sound. The face takes no direct drainage but has a tendency to seep after heavy rain; this is particularly a problem on the last pitch of Dwm. The sunny aspect of the face quickly resolves this in good weather.

As the South-East Face is so featureless the following general indicators should help in locating the routes. Most of the routes start from the large grassy terrace which is most easily gained at its left-hand end. The left-hand side of the face is dominated by a line of large overhangs, which are side-stepped by The Curver in a long rightwards traverse. High in the smooth wall to the right of the overhangs is the prominent thin crack taken by the second pitch of The Erg, which reaches this point by a vague line up the wall below. Low in the centre of the face is a prominent V-groove used by Central Wall. Above this the face bulges out in a great prow; Glwm, after much wandering, finishes up the groove on the left of this. To the right again is the steep shadowy corner of Dwm capped by large overhangs. At this point the terrace at the base of the cliff turns uphill under the very steep walls and tiered overhangs through which Tramgo and Hang 'em High make their ways. One slight route has been climbed on the buttress below and right of the main face.

The North-East Buttress of the cliff which lies to the right of the South-East Face has produced a few routes of a mountaineering nature. Some poor routes have also been done on the small buttresses above the forestry track to Cidwm, on the South side of the Afon Goch.

The normal approach to the cliff follows the forestry track above Llyn Cwellyn beginning at Planwydd (O.S. ref. SH 568 539), the farm on the Rhyd Ddu-Caernarfon road. The track ends at a disused quarry; go through this almost at lake level and cross the wall at the far end to gain the Afon Goch gorge which is followed up to the crag. Orienteers might like to try to follow the old path which passes above the quarry but is now overgrown by the forestry plantations. Safe parking at Planwydd is impossible due to the narrowness of the road; unless the farmer gives permission for his farmyard to be used, the nearest parking places are at Rhyd Ddu or at the roadside on the north-east shore of Llyn Cwellyn. The direct approach to the cliff at the north-west end of Llyn Cwellyn, past the Castell Cidwm Hotel, also presently appears to be tolerated after many years of prohibition.

The best descent for the South-East face takes the grassy rake slanting down below Tramgo and Dwm. Castell Cidwm Gully can be descended from routes on the North-East Buttress.

SOUTH-EAST FACE

The Curver   180 feet   Hard Very Severe   (1960)
A good and popular route taking the easiest line on the face, following the obvious gangway under the overhangs on the left-hand side. Communication can be difficult between leader and second if the river is running high. Start in the corner below the start of the gangway under the large overhangs.
1   60 feet. 4c. Climb awkwardly onto the gangway and follow it rightwards to a niche. Peg belay.
2   120 feet. 4c. Traverse right again, moving round a steeper section, to continue on good holds in an airy situation. A more difficult move leads into a small corner; finish up this. Rope drag can be a problem on this pitch.

Light Years   120 feet   E6   (1988)
Wild, bold climbing through the middle of the big roofs above The Curver. Start about 20 feet right of The Curver.
1   120 feet. 6c. Climb rightwards up a ramp then slant back left to join The Curver at a smooth black slab. Climb to a small incut ledge directly above and continue to the crack beneath the roofs. Move left along this for 15 feet to a weakness in the roof. Powerful moves out and rightwards gain an undercut crack leading round into a corner. Climb this to the next roof and pull through this rightwards to easy ground and belays above.

Equinox   120 feet   E4   (1988)
Good varied climbing up the wall between The Straighter and The Erg. Take care with the rope drag. Start in the niche as for The Straighter.

1	The Curver	HVS
2	Central Wall	E3
3	Dwm	E3
4	Hang 'em High	E5

Castell Cidwm

1   120 feet. 6a. Climb straight up to a large pointed flake and continue direct to the traverse of The Erg. Move right for a few feet, then go up and left to some steep flakes leading up rightwards onto a slab. Trend up and leftwards to the old slings and karabiners on The Girdle Traverse, then follow an obvious break diagonally left through the overhangs to gain the traverse of The Curver. Move up, then leftwards on flakes to finish.

The Straighter   130 feet   Hard Very Severe   (1963)
A strenuous route taking the easiest line up the steep wall below the traverse line of The Curver. 100 feet right of the corner at the start of The Curver, a smooth gangway leads upwards and rightwards above the terrace. Start at a large ledge halfway up the gangway where a shattered blocky ramp-line runs back up and leftwards.
1   90 feet. 5b. From the top of the blocky ramp, climb the steep wall to a ledge system. Go right for a few feet then climb steeply up past a peg trending leftwards to a prominent black hole beneath the overhangs. Move round the overhang on the left and climb up right to the bottomless chimney which leads to the traverse of The Curver, belay 10 feet to the left.
2   40 feet. 4c. Follow The Curver to the top of the cliff.

★★ The Erg   150 feet   E5   (1965/1980)
This excellent steep route at last goes totally free and requires a considerably greater energy output than its name would imply. It takes a faint line of weakness right of The Straighter to reach the prominent crackline in the smooth wall right of the finish of The Curver. Start as for The Straighter.
1   90 feet. 5c. As for The Straighter, from the top of the blocky ramp, climb the steep wall to a ledge system. Locate a prominent ramp 30 feet horizontally to the right and make a precarious unprotected traverse to reach its sanctuary, old peg. Pull onto the ramp past another peg and launch boldly onto the wall above and climb this first direct then rightwards to a small stance, peg belay.
2   60 feet. 6b. Move up rightwards to beneath the daunting roof, pegs, and contort round the lip to a peg and good footholds, then follow the sustained seam direct with a step left just below the top.

★★★ Potency   210 feet   E6   (1988)
A very steep and bold route which takes in the crux of The Erg. Start from the terrace directly below the stance of Central Wall, at a good wire belay below a slabby wall undercut by a long roof.
1   90 feet. 6b. Climb the slabby wall and the short wall above, then move left past an ancient threaded tape and pull up left strenuously into a niche below a roof. Climb the wall above the niche, past a spike, to a shelf with good holds on the left, peg. Climb straight up above the peg to a line of holds leading left to the stance of The Erg.

2   120 feet. 6b. Traverse right and pull through the roof as for
The Erg then follow the crackline for 25 feet to the flake where
The Erg goes left. Step right and climb boldly up the middle of
the face to good finishing holds. Easier slabs lead to the top.

◦★ Balance of Power   200 feet   E5   (1988)
An excellent bold climb on perfect rock. It goes directly to the
stance of Central Wall via an overhanging groove, then breaks
left out of its second pitch. Start as for Potency.
1   80 feet. 6a. Climb straight up the middle of the slabby wall
to a large block on a ledge. Go up the short wall above to a
sloping ledge, peg. Move up and right with difficulty to a large
sloping foothold, then step back left and climb to the base of the
overhanging groove. Follow this, using a good crack on the left,
to the stance of Central Wall.
2   120 feet. 5c. Climb up and go over the first set of overhangs
as for Central Wall, then climb leftwards up the wall to an
obvious good hold at the left-hand end of the roof. Pull round
into a shallow groove which leads to slabbier rock. Bear left, still
interesting, to the top.

◦★ Central Wall   180 feet   E3   (1964/1977)
A modern classic. Start in the middle of the grassy terrace below
the obvious clean-cut V-groove.
1   80 feet. 5c. Climb easily to the groove and follow it to a tricky
leftwards exit at its top (peg) to gain a block. Ascend the
awkward wall above to reach the overhang, peg. Move left and
climb leftwards through this, pegs, to gain a ledge, peg and nut
belay.
2   100 feet. 5c. Move left for a few feet, then climb diagonally
back rightwards to the roof. Pull over this on good holds and
continue up a gangway, finishing boldly leftwards through the
capping roof.

◦★ Heading for Heights   160 feet   E5   (1988)
An excellent route with a strenuous crux which breaches the
great expanse of rock between Central Wall and Vertigo. Start
as for Vertigo.
1   90 feet. 6b. Climb straight up the flake cracks above the belay
until they end, then trend right up a ramp to join Vertigo at its
crux. From the flake above this, move up leftwards into a smooth
open groove and follow this to a diagonal break which leads up
leftwards beneath a bulge. Move up on the left side of the bulge
and use an undercut to make a long reach to a hidden slot in
the wall above. Go up the wall to better holds in a groove and
follow this up and left to a nut belay below the steep white final
wall.
2   70 feet. 5c. Move onto the wall and climb steeply up its
left-hand arête to easier-angled rock which is climbed, keeping
right on the best line, to the top.

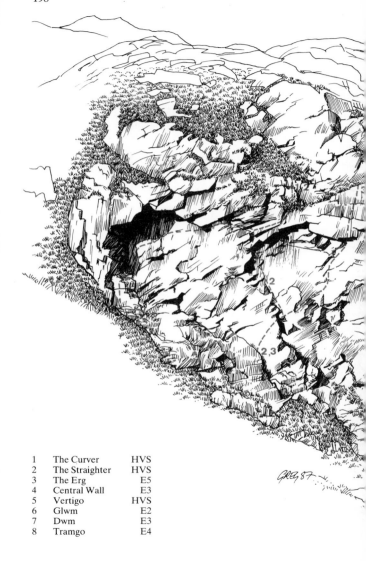

1	The Curver	HVS
2	The Straighter	HVS
3	The Erg	E5
4	Central Wall	E3
5	Vertigo	HVS
6	Glwm	E2
7	Dwm	E3
8	Tramgo	E4

Castell Cidwm

★★ **Vertigo**   130 feet   Hard Very Severe   (1960)
A fine steep and exposed route on good holds, taking a diagonal line below the steepest section of the main face, to an exposed finish above the diedre of Dwm. Start at the extreme right of the terrace, some 20 feet right of the start of Central Wall, below and to the left of black slabs leading up to a scoop.
1   60 feet. 5a. Climb diagonally right for 20 feet to the left-hand end of the long overhang. Move left to out-flank this and go back right into the scoop. Follow this, exiting right at the top, peg, to a good stance.
2   70 feet. 4c. Move right round the arête to gain the obvious flaky crack. Ascend this steeply to the final bulges, finishing either up the small chimney above, or, with maximum exposure and 'more charm', by traversing right until the top can be gained.

★ **Glwm**   270 feet   E2   (1964)
An exposed and tricky but wandering route which crosses the cliff searching for difficulties which it finds in two difficult, but now otherwise unconnected pitches; the freeing of the original, aided link pitch would give a much more impressive route of greater continuity. Start some 15 feet right of the start of Vertigo where a small groove leads up to slabs and a prominent black roof.
1   80 feet. 5b. Climb up to the roof, and traverse right beneath it for 20 feet, until it is possible to break through at the obvious weakness. Climb up leftwards past a pinnacle to join and follow the first pitch of Vertigo rightwards to the stance.
2   100 feet. 5a. Move right round the arête to gain the obvious flaky crack. Ascend this steeply to the final bulges, as for Vertigo, then traverse left to gain a stance in a corner.
3   40 feet. 5b. Move left to a spike and climb down to the lip of the overhangs beneath the Prow. Move round the bulge on the left and climb up to a stance in the corner, below a steep green groove.
4   50 feet. 5a. Follow the groove to the top.

Original Pitch 2: 100 feet. Using aid, follow the horizontal crack across the steep wall on the left of the stance, round the overhanging arête into a groove. Pull over the roof to gain the stance.

Zwm   E1 5b   (1979)
Starts as for Glwm to the roof, then continues right in a rising line to reach join Dwm in the middle of its second pitch and finishes as for Dwm.

★★ **Glasnost**   230 feet   E5   (1988)
A long and sustained route taking a leftward-trending line from the foot of Dwm to finish at the highest point of the crag near Heading for Heights. Start directly below the niche 20 feet up Dwm.

1 130 feet. 6a. Climb to the base of the niche then hand-traverse left for 5 feet and pull up into a groove which is followed to some huge blocks. Step off the highest block, move up and right and climb the steep wall to a resting place below another steep section. Go up in same line until forced left at some bulges (peg above on the girdle). Continue to join Glwm then go more or less direct to the stance of Vertigo.
2 100 feet. 5c. From the right-hand side of the stance climb straight up for 20 feet then follow a break leftwards to a shallow groove leading to small ledges beneath the final wall. Climb the deep groove directly above to some steep finishing moves and then easier ground leads to a large thread belay at the top.

⋆ Dwmsday 180 feet E5 (1988)
A forceful route taking the slim groove which cuts through the left side of the overhang above Dwm. Start as for Dwm.
1 70 feet. 6a. Climb into the niche and follow the crack up right for a few feet before moving up left to a steep groove. Climb this and the easier wall above to a small stance at a cluster of 3 pegs (on Dwm).
2 110 feet. 6b. Move right to a peg on Dwm then climb more or less straight up the wall to a good crack beside a huge block beneath the overhang. Move up right into the groove and gain a sharp flake high on the left. Make a hard move into the rightward-slanting groove above the roof and follow this for 20 feet in a fine position to better holds leading up leftwards to the top of Vertigo.

⋆⋆ Dwm 180 feet E3 (in a drought), or, Hard Very Severe/A1
(in a normal British summer) (1960)
A great route, the classic of the cliff, which follows the great overhung corner which is the most striking feature of the cliff. The final pitch is often wet and then usually requires some aid but it gives excellent and unusual climbing when dry. Start on the grassy rake on the right-hand side of the cliff, below the great corner.
1 60 feet. 5a. Climb onto a large block and move left across the steep wall into a niche or gain the niche direct with greater difficulty. Follow the crack rightwards out of the niche to reach a good ledge on the left.
2 60 feet. 5b. From the left-hand end of the ledge climb the steep wall to another ledge. Admire the line of the girdle which goes out left, then, with difficulty, gain the wall on the right above the overhangs, and teeter diagonally right to a tiny stance in the corner below the huge roof.
3 60 feet. 6a (or 4c/A1). Climb the corner crack to the overhang, and, cursing the drainage, fight rightwards across beneath this, plenty of pegs, to gain a short chimney which leads quickly to the top. Or more usually swing across to the chimney on aid. (You really wanted to do it free didn't you, but it was just too wet – honest!)

Alternative finish: 90 feet. A3/Very Severe. Follow pitch 3 to the roof then gain a line of rotting ironmongery leading straight across the roof. This leads to free climbing on the wall above the overhang.

★ **Tramgo**   135 feet   E4   (1962/1978)
This is the steep crack-line of legendary strenuosity which splits the roofs right of Dwm; at the time of writing it is very overgrown but when cleaned it gives a tremendous three-star pitch. Start farther up the grassy rake from the corner of Dwm, at the foot of the crack. Seconds standing below for long periods of time should try not to dwell on how much the route overhangs. Whatever the angle, it is considerable.
1   135 feet. 6a. Move left across the wall to gain the crack-line and follow it through two sets of overhangs. Climb the wall and groove above, then turn the next(!) overhang on the left to gain a resting place. Continue up the crack moving right, past a possible stance, to finish up an easier groove.

★ **Hang 'em High**   110 feet   E5   (1980)
The roof crack right of Tramgo is harder and more sustained than its partner. It is also very intimidating and makes one long for the vertical. Start 40 feet right of Tramgo at a slightly higher level.
1   110 feet. 6a. Move up on good footholds and trend diagonally up left, past an old peg in a roof, to another peg at a small ledge. Climb the crack above to a poor resting place at a small niche. Steeper and more precarious moves lead up leftwards to a wide crack where the angle eases. Finish easily.

★★★ **Cidwm Girdle**   600 feet   E3   (1965/1983)
An excellent expedition, very sustained and in a fine position, taking a high line across the cliff from right to left. Start as for Dwm, on the grassy rake on the right of the cliff, below the great corner.
1   60 feet. 5a. As for pitch 1 of Dwm. Climb onto a large block and move left across the steep wall into a niche. Follow the crack rightwards out of the niche to reach a good ledge on the left.
2   90 feet. 5b. From the left-hand end of the ledge climb the steep wall to another ledge. Follow the obvious leftwards traverse for 15 feet to join Glwm. Pull through the overhang at the obvious weakness. Climb up leftwards past a pinnacle to join and follow the first pitch of Vertigo rightwards to the stance.
3   100 feet. 5a. As for pitch 2 of Glwm. Move right round the arête to gain the obvious flaky crack. Ascend this steeply to the final bulges, as for Vertigo, then traverse left to gain a stance in a corner.
4   40 feet. 5b. As for pitch 3 of Glwm. Move left to a spike and climb down to the lip of the overhangs beneath the Prow. Move round the bulge on the left and climb up to a stance in the corner, below a steep green groove.

5   70 feet. 6a. Move left with difficulty and pull round into the final groove of Central Wall, peg. Reverse Central Wall to the belay ledge at the top of pitch 1.
6   30 feet. 5b. Move left round the arête and finger-traverse to a ledge beneath the roof, the second belay of The Erg.
7   90 feet. 6a. Semi-hand-traverse the crack which leads leftwards across the wall to a spike and continue with difficulty by blind moves to a niche in the roofs. Descend very steeply for 15 feet to a slab, and follow it to a junction with The Straighter. Climb steeply up leftwards to a prominent black hole beneath the overhangs. Move round the overhang on the left and climb up right to the bottomless chimney which leads to the traverse of The Curver, belay 10 feet to the left.
8   120 feet. 4c. Descend the leftward-sloping gangway to the grassy bay on the left of the cliff (pitch 1 of The Curver in reverse).

Hors d'Oeuvre   230 feet   Very Severe   (1962)
A rather scrappy route taking the obvious groove-lines in the more broken area of rock below and to the right of the main face. Not really what most people come here for. Start in the middle of the lower wall by a red slab below an obvious open groove.
1   100 feet. Climb a short wall right of the slab to a grassy ledge. Step left into the groove and climb it, moving left through a holly to gain a stance.
2   50 feet. Follow grass up leftwards to a stance below a groove.
3   80 feet. Traverse down right for 30 feet to gain the central groove and follow it to a small ledge. Move right awkwardly to another ledge and continue to the top.

NORTH-EAST BUTTRESS
The buttress is bounded by the easy **Castell Cidwm Gully** which contains one wet cave pitch of 15 feet. The first climb takes the wall overlooking the gully on the right.

Finale Wall   220 feet   Very Difficult   (1960)
A pleasant enough route, bearing in mind the material available. Start at the narrowing of Castell Cidwm Gully, some 100 feet above the cave pitch.
1   30 feet. From a few up the right wall, climb broken rock to a belay on the right edge of the gully.
2   60 feet. Ascend the wall above to the left-hand end of a heather ledge.
3   50 feet. Climb the bulge above and continue up cracks to a narrow ledge.
4   80 feet. Move round to the left of an overhang and continue more easily to the top.

Wolf's Buttress 400 feet Difficult (1905)
A vague climb taking the easiest line up the buttress. Start about 30 feet below the narrow entrance to Castell Cidwm Gully. Scramble steeply up to the foot of a heathery slab. Climb the slabs for 150 feet to a large grassy bay beneath an overhang. Escape leftwards and continue up for some 100 feet to the right-hand of two conspicuous chimneys splitting the upper part of the cliff, tree belay. Climb the chimney in two pitches to the top.

Variation. 160 feet Very Difficult. From the tree belay, trend left over loose vegetated rock to climb a steep striated wall and belay on the ledge above. Follow the ledge up rightwards and climb a steep crack to easy ground.

Lamb's Leap 370 feet Severe (1960)
A route which seeks out harder pitches on the main buttress but still manages to get its share of the vegetation. Start in the grassy bay above the first section of Wolf's Buttress.
1 80 feet. Climb the loose and awkward right-hand corner of the overhang and continue rightwards up the vegetated wall above to a stance.
2 80 feet. Go up the steepening slabs, moving leftwards near the top.
3 40 feet. Traverse 15 feet right and climb the steep corner to belay on the right of a rowan tree.
4 50 feet. Climb the small overhang and continue delicately to a narrow ledge.
5 60 feet. Continue straight up to a grassy terrace and belay at the foot of the final slabs.
6 60 feet. Start up the crack and finish steeply on good holds.

To the right of Castell Cidwm Gully the buttress is divided by a shallow gully line; the next two routes take the clean rock to the right of this.

The Mystery II 380 feet Hard Severe
This route had been cleaned and presumably climbed by an unknown party prior to the first recorded ascent. Start on a grassy ledge, above the left-hand end of small stone-walled enclosure, with a pile of blocks at its right-hand end, reached by scrambling up to the right of a tree.
1 120 feet. From the left-hand end of the ledge go awkwardly up to the left and move up over ledges to a groove-line. Follow a crack up this, passing a ledge and tree at 70 feet, to reach a slab and belay behind a bollard.
2 50 feet. Go easily up the slab to belay near the bottom of a rake.
3 60 feet. Gain the wall behind the belay and continue up rightwards on small holds to a horizontal break. Traverse right to belay on a block ledge.

4 150 feet. Reverse the traverse and climb a groove to an overhang. Turn this on the left using dubious blocks and continue steeply up shattered rock to reach easier-angled slabs. Pleasant climbing leads to the top.

Acrophily   330 feet   Very Severe   (1972)
An open line generally to the right of the previous route, with a delectable finish on the upper buttress. Start on the right-hand end of the same ledge as the previous route.
1 50 feet. From the blocks at the right-hand end of the ledge, step up left and climb a steep groove to a small square overhang. Turn this on the right by a difficult move and continue to a cave with a tree belay on the right.
2 80 feet. Step left from the cave and go up to ledge on the left. Continue direct to a niche and step right into a steep and undercut mossy groove. Follow this, finishing left with difficulty to reach the bollard belay of the previous route.
3 50 feet. Go easily up the slab to the rake, then walk a further 50 feet up the rake to belay beneath a rightwards-slanting ramp.
4 100 feet. Gain the ramp from the right and move up it past a doubtful block, then go up a short wall to the right on good holds to a niche. Step down and left from the niche and climb a steep crack to a small ledge. Move up leftwards on small holds in an exposed position to reach a flake hold below the final bulge. Step left again and up to a small ledge above the line of overhangs. Belay a few feet higher.
5 50 feet. Finish easily up slabs.

Craig Cwm Du (Crag of the Black Hollow)

O.S. ref. SH 537 551

This large shadowy cliff, so obvious from the road between Waunfawr and Betws Garmon, is strangely neglected. Although it gives little climbing of the highest quality it nevertheless offers a number of good long routes in the lower grades in often fine situations. There is only a little loose rock on the better routes and this is easily managed.

The cliff extends across the whole back wall of the cwm. On the left is the wide broken area of the Eastern Cliffs. Farther right is the more substantial Eden Buttress with its prominent right arête taken by Adam Rib. This is separated by Eden Gully from the wider Fluted Buttress which is split by a large heather terrace. Beyond another gully is the largest section, the Central Cliff, again divided into an upper and lower tier. Right again past two further gullies are the vegetated Western Slabs.

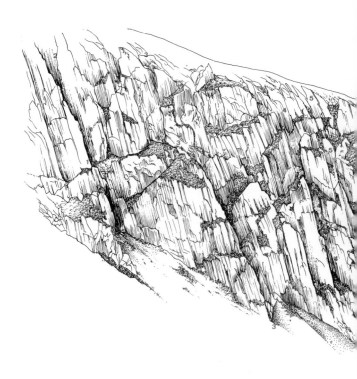

1	Adam Rib	HS
2	Eden Gully	
3	Saxifrage Gully	
4	Grass Pitch Gully	
5	Avalanche Gully	
6	Civil Servants Gully	
7	Raven Gully	
CR	Central Rake	

Craig Cwm Du

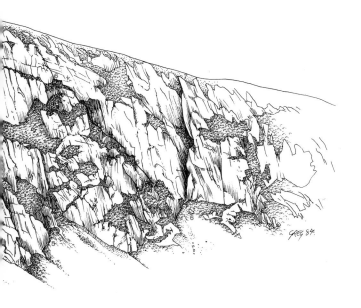

The modern climber is spoon-fed with a variety of comprehensive guidebooks which incorporate detailed diagrams. Here is a basic diagram drawn from a slightly unusual angle – with only the bare minimum of information – as one might have in the Gully Epoch. Explore this complex crag and draw in your own lines on the diagram – if you can!

The cliff can be quickly reached from the end of a narrow road leading from the village of Fron (park at O.S. ref. SH 522 554 or earlier if you aren't in a Landrover) and hence an easy walk across the moor (20 minutes). Alternatively a public footpath starting at Betws Garmon (O.S. ref. SH 546 563) leads to the cliff in about 50 minutes. All of the routes are easily accessible via the narrow path which traverses immediately below the cliff.

The summit of Mynydd Mawr is surprisingly close to the top of the cliff and some may wish to continue to it. Otherwise the grassy slopes to the west of the cliff provide an easy descent. For those of a masochistic temperament and with good navigational skills, two other descents are feasible. The first begins down Saxifrage Gully, gained by going down rightwards (facing out) from the broken area at the top of the Central Cliff, and then follows the grassy slopes of Central Rake leftwards at half height. The second follows the Central Rake in its entirety, reaching it by descending the top of Grass Pitch Gully.

THE EASTERN CLIFFS

This large but rather broken and vegetated area on the left side of the cliff has no recorded routes of sufficient continuity to merit recording in detail; its only value is for scrambling purposes, although the prominent Crazy Pinnacle is worthy of a visit. A loose route, **Jezebel**, 160 feet, Very Difficult, has been produced up the rib immediately left of the Pinnacle.

EDEN BUTTRESS

The cliff now asserts itself in this steep narrow buttress with a striking right arête which gives the best route on the cliff.

Eve's Folly   270 feet   Difficult   (1949)
A reasonable route which suffers from comparison with its neighbour. Start by scrambling up to the foot of the broad left-hand rib of the buttress.
1   40 feet. Move up to a ledge from the left, climb over the perched block above and follow a crack to a grassy ledge.
2   70 feet. Gain the grassy ledge on the left, then follow the rib on the right to a large grassy ledge.
3   90 feet. Scrambling leads to another grassy ledge beneath an overhang; belay by a small cave on the right.
4   70 feet. Climb the nose above the cave from the left, then go rightwards to a ledge. Step right round the rib and go diagonally right to finish.

★★ **Adam Rib**   400 feet   Hard Severe   (1911)
This route takes the right edge of Eden Buttress with an impressive and unusual final pitch. Well worth seeking out. Start at the foot of the right-hand rib, just left of Eden Gully.

Martin Crook in novel attire on the crux of First Slip, Craig Bwlch y Moch. *Photo: Paul Williams*

Typical Tremadog climbing on Shadrach, Craig Bwlch y Moch.
Photo: Richie Brooks

Chris Craggs on Hardd, Carreg Hyll-Drem.
Photo: Craggs collection

An airy position on Lavaredo, Carreg Alltrem.

Photo: M. Whittaker

1 150 feet. Easy climbing leads to a grassy ledge where the rib steepens.

2 90 feet. Move into the wide groove on the left and climb its left wall to gain the subsidiary rib on the left. Follow this to an obvious traverse back right onto the main rib at a grassy ledge. Alternatively the groove on the right of the stance can be followed to gain the main rib which is climbed with some interest to the same stance.

3 90 feet. Follow the cracks left of the edge to easier climbing and a small ledge; move left and go up to a small stance. The direction of the next pitch is uncomfortably obvious.

4 70 feet. Gain the exposed and narrow rib from the right, taking care with some wobbly holds, and follow it in a splendid position to the top.

Eden Gully is the well-developed gully to the right. Its dripping recesses do not warrant close examination.

FLUTED BUTTRESS
To the right is a wider buttress split at mid-height by a large heather terrace.

★ **Knight's Move Climb**   450 feet   Very Difficult   (1911)
A good route taking a zig-zag line up the cleanest part of the lower part of the buttress to finish up the obvious ridge on its right edge. Start at the foot of the slabs at the left edge of the buttress.

1 100 feet. Climb up leftwards to a ledge on the left edge, then follow the groove on the right to a grassy ledge on the left.

2 50 feet. Move back right and onto the arête, then follow ledges round a corner to the heather terrace.

3 100 feet. Go easily up right to the edge overlooking Saxifrage Gully and continue to a small stance just left of a minor gully.

4 100 feet. Follow the ridge above to a ledge, then move left round the corner, up a few feet and go back right to a grassy ledge (the Knight's Move). Climb a short wall to grass and follow this up to belay at some large spikes.

5 100 feet. Move up to a small bay on the right and climb another short wall; scrambling remains to the top.

An inferior direct start is possible following the right edge of the buttress more directly, but with more vegetation. This takes the obvious rib to a terrace below an overhang at 100 feet, then the groove on the right to the heather terrace.

An alternative to the pitch 4 described has also been climbed. This joins the minor gully (Kershaw's Gully) by a traverse right 10 feet above the stance and follows it until the parent route can be regained.

Saxifrage Gully is unattractive and wet but provides a possible descent route. About 100 feet up the right wall of the gully relents and the start of the Central Rake can easily be gained. This splits the Central Cliff to the right and provides access to the routes on its upper part.

UPPER CENTRAL CLIFF

Although this area of the cliff has many small overhangs, it is in fact mostly rather broken by ledges and grooves. It is more continuous on the left; this area is taken by the only two routes. Both routes start on a terrace which runs from the Central Rake into Saxifrage Gully some 200 feet up. A grassy recess some 40 feet up, reached by both routes, is another landmark.

Poverty Street   270 feet   Very Severe   (1970)
Start on the terrace at the foot of the first groove right of the gully.
1   40 feet. Follow the groove into a steep corner. Hand-traverse left on poor rock and climb the bulge above, then move rightwards into the grassy recess.
2   120 feet. Traverse left between the two sets of overhangs to reach a thin crack and follow this to a large terrace.
3   110 feet. Follow the crack to the top.

Medicare   270 feet   Severe   (1970)
A better way up this area of rock than the previous route. Start at another groove 15 feet right of the previous route.
1   40 feet. Climb the groove direct to the grassy recess.
2   130 feet. Move right for 10 feet, then go through the overhangs into a scoop. Follow this and easier rock to the grassy terrace.
3   100 feet. Move across to the rib and finish up this.

LOWER CENTRAL CLIFF

This is the largest area of the cliff, getting steadily higher as the Central Rake rises. It is marked by a number of ribs which mark the lines taken by the main routes. The routes on the right of the buttress rate with the best on the cliff.

Saxifrage Rib   260 feet   Very Difficult
A vague line which even fails to make the top of the cliff. It provides easy but not necessarily secure access to the Upper Central Cliff should it be required. Start at the foot of the ill-defined rib. Follow the rib direct in a few pitches on poor rock to the Central Rake.

Manchester Rib 270 feet Severe (1950)
A much better alternative to gain the Central Rake; this route
takes the more prominent rib just to the right. Start at a groove
on the right-hand side of the rib.
1 100 feet. Climb the groove and its right wall to a stance level
with the foot of a grass-filled cleft on the right, the Pis-Aller.
2 90 feet. Follow the rib on its right wall, until easier climbing
leads to a grassy ledge.
3 80 feet. Gain the detached block on the right then get
established on the main face. Continue up easier rock to the
pinnacle at the top of the rib.

★ **Pis-Aller Rib** 470 feet Severe (1912)
A good route with a nice finish up an interesting arête which is
typical of the cliff. It takes the prominent rib in the centre of the
cliff which starts some 100 feet up. Start below the rib.
1 100 feet. Climb easily on rock and vegetation to the terrace
at the mouth of the Pis-Aller cleft (which the route sensibly
avoids).
2 40 feet. Go rightwards across the steep wall to belay in a
groove on the far edge.
3 90 feet. Follow ledges up to a wide crack, go up this then
move right into a groove on the edge of the rib. Climb this to a
grassy ledge.
4 80 feet. Climb up left of the rib to ledges and follow these up
rightwards to belay on the edge.
5 80 feet. On poorer rock, climb over a pinnacle, then avoid the
slab above by climbing the loose groove on the right and follow
the ridge to a stance.
6 80 feet. The ridge now falls back to a serrated knife-edge.
Follow this and the rocks beyond, finishing in the top of Grass
Pitch Gully.

★ **Yellow Buttress** 510 feet Severe (1912)
One of the better routes on the cliff taking a direct line up the
buttress just left of Grass Pitch Gully. Start at the foot of the
buttress below yet another rib.
1 100 feet. Scramble up mixed ground, then climb the cracked
rib on the right to a ledge.
2 100 feet. Climb the obvious weakness in the slab above, with
a move left to a ledge at 50 feet and then go back right to follow
the continuing line with interest to a grassy ledge. Continue up
the rib to ledges overlooking the gully.
3 50 feet. Join the rib on the left and follow it to the top of the
main buttress.
4 110 feet. Regain the heathery ridge and follow it and the
grassy groove on the left at times, loose rock in places, to
another stance overlooking the gully.
5 110 feet. Continue up to the pinnacles at the top of the
buttress.

6 40 feet. Move left to join the previous route and follow it into the top of Grass Pitch Gully.

Grass Pitch Gully   500 feet   Very Difficult   (1911)
The obvious gully line to the right; a route which no longer lives up to its name. It gives two short pitches then a long scramble to the site of the old grass pitch. Above this easier climbing leads to a bay and an easy exit leftwards.

Lichen Ridge   450 feet   Very Difficult   (1911)
An interesting route with a fine gendarme, the usual amount of vegetation and a little loose rock. Start at the foot of the ridge to the right of the gully.
1   100 feet. Climb rock and heather to a steepening.
2   60 feet. Ascend the left-hand side of the vegetated wall.
3   100 feet. Climb the arête above then scramble up to the foot of the gendarme.
4   40 feet. Either climb the crack in the gendarme direct on interesting holds or circumvent it by moving down a little and traversing left until it is possible to climb back onto the ridge.
5   90 feet. Continue along the ridge to belay below the final wall.
6   60 feet. Climb the wall on the right, or with more difficulty on the left.

Avalanche Gully, the deep gully bounding the Central Cliff to the right, is dangerously loose.

THE WESTERN SLABS
In general this area is as equally unattractive as the Eastern Cliffs, being vegetated and lacking definite lines. However as it is more continuous the existing routes are described in outline.

Leo's Wall   400 feet   Very Difficult   (1950)
A loose and vegetated route up the slabs just right of Avalanche Gully. Start near the foot of Avalanche Gully. Climb up tending right to a heather terrace (150 feet). Continue up the vegetation until the route steepens again, then ascend to the left of a shallow depression in the centre of the face, to finish with another dose of heather and loose rock.

Several hundred feet right of Avalanche Gully is the obscure break of **Civil Servant's Gully** which runs diagonally leftwards up the cliff. The foot of this can be reached direct over broken rock but take your umbrella!

Fox Route   210 feet   Very Difficult   (1950)
Another little vegetated gem, taking the slabs right of Civil Servant's Gully; start at the foot of this. Climb first to the right, then to the left of the shallow groove in the slabs to a belay at

60 feet. Continue for another 60 feet until below a small tower. Traverse right across the overhung slab below this until it is possible to climb up to the top of the tower. Scrambling remains.

About 100 feet right of the start of Civil Servant's Gully is the more obvious **Raven Gully** running directly up the cliff; this provides a feasible descent.

Oppenauer Slab   180 feet   Very Difficult   (1950)
This is the large, but usually wet, slab forming the left side of Raven Gully, best avoided except in a drought. Start just left of the foot of Raven Gully and climb direct up the smooth slab to a belay about 15 feet below the steep edge of the red slab above. Traverse up and right to gain the red slab and follow its right edge to the top.

On the steep right edge of Raven Gully is **Raven Buttress** (200 feet, Very Severe), an unbalanced route with little difficulty except for a bulge at mid-height. The last attempt to beat the vegetation is the vague line of **Dobbin** (160 feet, Very Difficult).

NANTLLE VALLEY and CWM SILYN

Cwm Silyn lies on the northern side of the Nantlle Ridge separating the Pennant and Nantlle valleys, below the highest point on the ridge, Carnedd Silyn. The cwm is backed by an impressive arc of cliffs, nearly a mile in length, overlooking the moorland which slopes gradually down into the Nantlle valley. The west side of the moorland drops down slightly to form a hollow which contains two lakes and is dominated by the most impressive cliffs.

There are four main cliffs, each of which is described in more detail below. The leftmost is Trwyn y Graig which is rather inconspicuous above two tiny lakes on the moor. Both it and its higher companion on the right, Craig Fawr, are rather broken cliffs giving old-fashioned climbing on excellent rock. The best of the cliffs is Craig yr Ogof which towers above the twin lakes, Llynnau Cwm Silyn. This cliff offers a fine range of climbing from hard test-pieces to classic Diffs. On the right of the cwm the vegetated mass of Clogwyn y Cysgod lies in almost perpetual shadow on the western wing of the cwm.

The normal approach to the twin lakes is from Bryn Gwyn, at O.S. ref. SH 496 511. This is the farm on the moorland at the end of a very narrow road (signposted to Vronlog Quarry) which leaves the Llanllyfni-Nantlle road about ⅔ of a mile from Llanllyfni at O.S. ref. SH 481 521.

When travelling from Nantlle, turn left for Llanllyfni just before a small council estate and opposite the entrance to Dorothea quarries. Go through some narrow slate cuttings to reach a few houses, Tan yr Allt, after ½ a mile. The road to Bryn Gwyn is the first on the left after this. Bryn Gwyn is about a mile and a half up this road. Cars should be left in the field just through the gate. This is private land so please do not drive across the field to save a few hundred yards of walking. The road continues as a narrow grassy track which leads through three blocked gates to the Llynnau Cwm Silyn.

Another approach is possible from Drws y Coed with much more walking. This may be convenient for those intending to traverse the Nantlle Ridge after a route. Follow the second approach for Y Garn from the lay-by near Drws y Coed. After passing through the gate onto the open mountainside, above the upper farm buildings, turn right and follow an old track round below Cwm Ffynnon into the valley of the Afon Craig Las. Near the head of this, bear up the slopes to the right and over the shoulder by two small marshy lakes into Cwm Silyn. This approach to the cliffs takes about 1 ½ hours, roughly twice as long as the other approach.

Craig y Bera (Kite Crag) O.S. ref. SH 545 540

This ruinous cliff, rising from a wasteland of scree, dominates the northern side of the Nantlle valley between Rhyd Ddu and Nantlle. Despite the obvious poor quality of its rock, to which the screes bear silent witness, the cliff gives a few worthwhile routes, including the fine and exposed Angel Pavement. It offers good views and interesting rock features to the climber able to cope with the nature of the rock.

Great care is required in the handling of the very friable rock which is often loose on a small or large scale. Multiple belays are advisable as even apparently solid rock may disintegrate under load. The grades of routes should only be treated as rough guides, as apart from Angel Pavement which is relatively solid and well used, most of the routes see few ascents and much depends on the individual climber's capacity in handling poor material.

The wide central buttress of Pinnacle Ridge with a stone wall rising to it dominates the scene. On its right, across a scree-filled descent gully is Sentries' Ridge. On the left of Pinnacle Ridge and at a higher level is a smaller loose buttress.

It is possible to descend any of the main gullies; the one to the right of Pinnacle Ridge is the most usual but it is as loose as the rest.

Access to this cliff is contentious and direct approaches are more likely to be contested. The simplest approach, and not as circuitous as it first appears, follows the path up Mynydd Mawr which starts at Planwydd in the Cwellyn valley until it is possible to contour across beneath the cliff.

An alternative, which appears to be tolerated by the appropriate farmer at present, gains the cliff at its left-hand end from much farther down the valley near the lay-by at O.S. ref. SH 537 533. This uses a faint path running up rightwards towards the boundary wall, until a steep grind up the screes left of the wall gains the cliff.

The direct approach from Drws y Coed, although commencing on a right of way, is likely to be resisted by the farmer. Please do not do anything to prejudice the position as people are working hard to improve the situation.

To the left of the main mass of Pinnacle Ridge, at a higher level, is a smaller buttress with two routes.

Reason in Revolt 340 feet Hard Severe (1952)
Note the name and go elsewhere. If still keen, start at the foot
of a slabby area, below and to the left of the small buttress.
1 90 feet. Follow steep and loose rock, right of heather, to a
large belay.
2 40 feet. Continue on better rock.
3 50 feet. Go across a grassy rake, then climb more steeply to
a stance with two spike belays.
4 100 feet. Take a chimney-crack on the right to a heather field,
then follow the steep and loose rib on its left with difficulty to a
break and poor belays.
5 60 feet. Continue steeply to the top and safety.

No Highway 250 feet Hard Severe (1952)
A fair route on better rock than its neighbour (which isn't saying
much). Start at the foot of the right-hand edge of the buttress.
1 50 feet. Climb the left-hand side of the ridge to a ledge.
2 50 feet. Move left back onto the face, and climb to another
ledge beneath a line of overhangs.
3 70 feet. Go directly up to the overhang and go round it on
the left to gain a fine exposed leftwards traverse. Follow this to
reach a ledge which leads back to the right-hand edge.
4 80 feet. Go easily to the top.

To the right is the main buttress of Craig y Bera, Pinnacle Ridge,
giving the best climbing on the cliff. The buttress contains a
series of slabby rakes interspersed with steep walls building up
rightwards to the crest of the ridge. Its most obvious feature is
a huge triangular slab, which is taken by the start of Angel
Pavement.

★ **Angel Pavement** 600 feet Severe (1946)
An excellent route but only recommendable to confident parties
as protection is poor, the rock often questionable and the pitches
long. The route follows the narrow gangway slipping past the
steep walls in the centre of the buttress in positions of high
exposure. Start at the foot of the expanse of slab, some 30 yards
left of the wall.
1 150 feet. Climb the slab, easier towards the left, but
everywhere with a striking lack of protection, to a large grassy
terrace. Thread belay at its right-hand end.
2 150 feet. Climb diagonally left across the steep slab on good
holds, then continue directly up the undulating slab to a second
grassy ledge below an overhang. Thread belay in the crack on
the right.
3 100 feet. Follow the narrow slab to the left of the overhang
in a fine exposed position, then climb more broken rock to a
small ledge.
4 150 feet. Climb the rib on the left and go up to grass,
continue into a corner and trend left beneath steep walls to reach
ledges.

5   50 feet. Continue up more broken rock to the top.

A pointless variation at Very Severe, avoiding the best of the route, follows the steep slab leading rightwards from the top of pitch 2 to gain easy ledges and Pinnacle Ridge.

Guardian Angel   250 feet   E3   (1970/1984)
A serious loose route taking the more prominent right-hand of the two grooves in the steep wall overlooking Angel Pavement. An early precursor of the South Stack horrors. The rusting karabiners on the old aid pegs tell their own tale. 'The crux traverse is rather loose' – 1971 guide(!). Start on the grassy ledge above the first pitch of Angel Pavement and below small twin grooves leading to the right-hand and more obvious groove.
1   50 feet. 5a. Climb either groove to belay on a large (detached) block.
2   120 feet. 5c. Move directly into the main groove and climb it with difficulty past two pegs until a line of holds leads left to the arête. Follow this to a small ledge, move up left then make a rising traverse back right on disposable holds, loose blade runner, to the arête and the security of pitch 4 of Primrose Path. Follow this to a grassy ledge.
3   80 feet. Follow the ledge up left then climb directly to the top as for Pitch 5 of Primrose Path.

The groove left of Guardian Angel, which terminates in a cornice of loose blocks, has been left for the next generation (with full body armour).

Primrose Path   440 feet   Very Difficult   (1949)
This route takes the narrow slab above and parallel to Angel Pavement, giving a good open route after a poor start. Start right of Angel Pavement in the second bay to the left of the wall.
1   140 feet. Climb a heathery corner until it divides, then follow the vegetated right-hand branch to a large grassy ledge. This point can be reached more pleasantly but with less protection by climbing the first pitch of Angel Pavement and traversing right.
2   70 feet. Amble up the fields on the right to a cave below a groove.
3   65 feet. Start up the left wall of the groove, then follow a slab up leftwards until it is possible to move back to a grassy ledge at the top of the groove.
4   85 feet. Traverse out onto the left edge of the slab overlooking Angel Pavement, and follow this airily to a hidden grassy ledge above.
5   80 feet. Follow the ledge up left until a short corner and wall above lead to a sudden finish on scree.
150 feet of loose scrambling remains to the top of Pinnacle Ridge.

Pinnacle Ridge   400 feet   Difficult   (1905)
Pleasant and typical ridge climbing but rather loose in places.
Start just left of the foot of the pinnacle gives the route its name.
Climb the pinnacle either by its left edge or by the corner to the
right (200 feet). Continue up the ridge to the top, taking care with
a particularly loose section at 30 feet.

The obvious spiky ridge on the far side of the descent gully
gives:

Sentries Ridge 350 feet   Difficult   (1910)
The guidewriter can do no better than to maintain the tradition
and quote from Archer Thomson's classic original description:
'The ridge is notched and carved into 14 pinnacles or
gendarmes. All yield to direct assault. The second involves a
tricky horizontal traverse of 18 feet round an overhanging
protuberance, with a stiff vertical chimney to follow. The ridge
has a moderate average gradient, but some of the sites attained
are singular, and, as each gendarme completely screens the rest,
a certain unexpectedness is a feature of the climb. It promotes
hilarity.'
For those who find the unexpectedness overwhelming, an easier
way is usually possible to the right.

Y Garn (The Cairn)   O.S. ref. SH 551 526

This crag consists essentially of two ridges high on the slopes
of Y Garn and it is seen splendidly outlined against the sky from
the road between Beddgelert and Rhyd Ddu. Both of the ridges
give excellent climbing in fine situations and provide an
appropriate way of starting the traverse of the Nantlle ridge.

The left of the two ridges, which is longer and easy angled, is
taken by the minor classic Eastern Arête. The steeper right ridge
is followed by Mallory's Ridge. The short Western Arête offers
only scrambling.

The cliff is best approached from the public footpath to Cwm
Pennant which leaves the Rhyd Ddu to Nantlle road at a sharp
bend a little way out of Rhyd Ddu. As space here is limited, it
will often be necessary to park in the car park at Rhyd Ddu –
only 5 minutes walk away. Follow the path until well above the
enclosed fields before turning rightwards to ascend more
directly to the cliff.

The cliff can also be reached less directly from the Nantlle Valley
starting on the right of way past Tal y Mignedd as for the next
crag and then contouring across the slopes of Y Garn.

A direct approach to the cliff from Bwlch Gylfin is not permitted by the local farmer.

It is possible to descend the Central Gully between the Eastern Arête and Mallory's Ridge, although the summit of Y Garn is only a short distance away and marks the start of the classic Nantlle Ridge.

The first route starts about 200 feet left of Eastern Arête at a wall which runs up the hillside to meet the cliff.

Reunion Cracks   160 feet   Severe   (1948)
This takes the steep and slimy black crack immediately above the wall. Often not at all pleasant! Start from the wall and follow the crack steeply at first to a ledge at 50 feet. Climb the right-hand crack over the overhang to another possible stance. Steep but easy climbing leads to the finish.

★★ Eastern Arête   410 feet   Very Difficult   (1905)
A fine and popular route on good rock, giving a natural mountaineering start to the Nantlle Ridge. Start at the edge of the ridge, just before the entrance to Central Gully on the right.
1 100 feet. Gain the body of the ridge, then follow a chimney and grooves to a stance beneath a nose.
2 30 feet. Climb the short steep nose to finish awkwardly on a sloping ledge.
3 80 feet. Follow the corner above to a slabby wall, and then go rightwards to a large ledge.
4 100 feet. Climb the awkward crack on the right, then follow another steep wall above.
5 100 feet. Go easily up the edge for 80 feet then climb a difficult final V-groove. Scrambling remains to the top.

★ Mallory's Ridge   380 feet   Very Severe   (1911)
A good route giving excellent climbing at a reasonable standard for the grade, except for the thin fourth pitch which has seen off some notable climbers in less than perfect conditions. The route follows the backbone of the ridge which is to the right of the ridge as a whole. Start about 20 feet up to the right from the foot of the ridge.
1 50 feet. Climb a rib to the right-hand end of a wide heather bay.
2 80 feet. Follow ledges up right round the corner and into a groove on the edge of a steep slab via some obvious spikes and continue to a small overhang. Swing back left to a good ledge on the front face.
3 80 feet. Climb up for a few feet then move out right to the edge above the steep slab and follow this and the groove above to another good ledge below a steep nose.

4 80 feet. 4c. Move round the corner to the right and traverse up right with increasing difficulty until it is possible to climb up past a small ledge to a large terrace.
5 50 feet. Climb the crack in the wall above to a stance amongst the pinnacles that litter its top.
6 40 feet. Continue up the ridge to the summit cairn.

The crux (pitch 4) can be avoided by a number of alternatives; the steep nose above the stance can be climbed direct – slightly easier but looser than the usual route or a traverse left can be made to a large grassy ledge (possible belay), from which a short difficult corner is climbed to regain the original route at the terrace.

Western Gully to the right of Mallory's Ridge contains no rock, and the Western Arête beyond is short and offers only broken scrambling.

Craig Trum y Ddysgl (Crag of the Ridge of the Bowl)

O.S. ref. SH 543 520

Craig Trum y Ddysgl is the large broken cliff tucked away in the secluded upper reaches of Cwm Tal y Mignedd below the summit of Trum y Ddysgl on the Nantlle Ridge. It is not really worth the walk unless one is in an exploratory frame of mind.

The cliff is generally vegetated, but less so on the right where two bands of lighter-coloured quartzite, separated by a shallow gully, are followed by the only routes.

The cliff can be approached from the Nantlle valley by taking the right of way through the lower pastures, passing Tal y Mignedd Uchaf, and after gaining the open hillside, trending up left into the upper part of Cwm Tal y Mignedd.

South Buttress   450 feet   Very Difficult   (1920)
The left rib is wider and more quartz marked than the other. It is broken by several grassy ledges and contains a prominent large slab high up. Start at the foot of the rib at the right-hand end of a ledge directly above a small cave.
Climb a dirty groove on the right of the slabs to a cave at 60 feet and continue up the rib to a grassy ledge. A crack on the left leads to the foot of the large slab. Go left and climb a crack to gain the col behind a prominent tower on the left of the slab. Continue up the broken arête above the tower to the top.

North Buttress   400 feet   Difficult   (1920)
A fair climb which avoids the main difficulties, some of which may have been climbed by the real explorer. Start at the foot of

the right-hand rib, between two patches of red rock.
1 40 feet. Climb straight up, then go leftwards to a grassy patch. The quartzy bulge above leads to belay on the right.
2 70 feet. From the left-hand end of the ledge follow a cracked nose to a platform overlooking the gully.
3 60 feet. Follow ledges into and up a large corner on the left of a thin rib. Gain the rib from a high ledge and follow it to a stance and belay below a steep wall.
4 80 feet. Climb the wall to a ledge at 20 feet and scramble up to a belay at the foot of a steep slab level with the large slab on South Buttress.
5 40 feet. Move across to belay below the cleft on the left of the slab.
6 60 feet. Climb the cleft to the top of the slab.
7 50 feet. Easy climbing leads to the top of the buttress.
Scrambling leads to the top of the crag.

Trwyn y Graig (Nose of the Crag)   O.S. ref. SH 520 505

This small rather broken crag rises out of the heather above two small marshy lakes on the shoulder to the east of the Llynnau Cwm Silyn. It forms the leftmost area of rock visible from the main lakes, and is some 300 yards east of Craig Fawr.

The main part of the crag is composed of a tall slabby buttress on the right, liberally sprinkled with heather ledges and terminating in a fine nose after which the crag is named. This buttress gives Overhanging Chimneys, the only worthwhile route on the crag. To the left is a shallow gully, The Recess. Left of this the crag diminishes in height to give a smaller buttress before fading into the hillside. A broad heathery ledge, the Heather Belt, crosses the cliff at about 50 feet; the better climbing is above this.

An easy descent is possible on either side of the cliff; but please respect the fences.

At the left-hand end of the Heather Belt is a small buttress split by a deep-cut chimney.

Deep Chimney   135 feet   Difficult   (1925)
A good diversion on the way to the top of the mountain.
Start in an alcove guarded by a detached column below the Heather Belt and directly underneath the chimney.
Climb a 30-foot crack and an easy rib to the Heather Belt. Scramble up to the foot of the chimney 50 feet above. Struggle over the flat-topped chockstone at the bottom then continue steeply for 30 feet on good holds to the broad ridge at the top of the crag. About 150 feet of pleasant scrambling remains.

Beyond this buttress is a slightly higher buttress with overhangs at the bottom and a fine white arête on the left above. This is bounded on the right by a shallow vegetated hollow, **The Recess**. This can be climbed direct (160 feet, Very Difficult) but it is usually wet and hardly recommended. The next route lies up its right-hand wall.

The Recess Route 210 feet Severe (1925)
After gaining the Heather Belt below The Recess, this route goes out right to finish up the slanting groove on the left of the final nose of the buttress. The lower part of the route is poor, but the upper section is pleasant, though not nearly as good as Overhanging Chimneys. Start below the Heather Belt and immediately below The Recess.
1 50 feet. Go up a little rib to the Heather Belt.
2 70 feet. Climb easily up The Recess for 20 feet and then follow the right wall to a ledge. The short chimney on the right leads to another ledge.
3 30 feet. Climb a difficult crack on the wall above to a small ledge and then squeeze right into The Closet ('a damp enclosure with four walls but no roof').
4 60 feet. Escape up a short crack on the right, then trend rightwards up the slanting break to the ledge at the top.

The next climb is the best on the cliff and maintains a high level of interest to the top of the cliff.

★ **Overhanging Chimneys** 330 feet Severe (1925)
An old-fashioned and somewhat artificial route but well worthwhile and on excellent rock. Start at the lowest point of the cliff to the right of the final nose.
1 70 feet. Climb up leftwards to a huge leaning flake, then go diagonally right up the wall above to the Heather Belt.
2 80 feet. Climb up leftwards to reach the foot of the right-hand crack in the wall above and follow this with interest until a traverse leads left to a stance below the first overhanging chimney.
3 40 feet. Struggle awkwardly up the chimney to a ledge.
4 65 feet. Climb the steep crack just right of the corner and then the rib above to a ledge. Ascend the second overhanging chimney above to a ledge below the nose.
5 75 feet. Step round to the right into a groove and go up this until it steepens. Move right into the third overhanging chimney and climb this until a steep crack on the left leads to the top of the nose.
Scrambling remains to the top of the crag.

Many variations exist to the original route which indeed goes out of its way to find difficulties, but none is worthy of description except for:

Direct Finish – **Terror Infirmer**   70 feet   Severe   (1952)
A good exposed pitch up the front of the nose from the stance
at the top of pitch 4.
Climb the flake in the chimney above the belay and move up left
to the foot of a groove. Follow this to easy ground and the top.

At the right-hand end of the Heather Belt is a 30-foot high pillar.
Tower Chimney, 300 feet, Difficult, a very broken route, reaches
and follows the cleft behind this.

A poor girdle traverse has also been recorded, **The Scarf**, Very
Difficult, 1928. This begins up Tower Chimney, traverses across
the top of pitch 2 of Overhanging Chimneys into the first
overhanging chimney, follows this then goes left to finish up the
left wall of the Recess.

Craig Fawr (Big Crag)   O.S. ref. SH 518 502

Although the largest of the Cwm Silyn cliffs, Craig Fawr is rather
broken and easy-angled. It offers long easy mountaineering-
style routes with many grassy and heathery ledges but good
rock (which is more than can be said for some cliffs in the
Cwellyn area).

The cliff is separated from Craig yr Ogof to the right by a wide
couloir. The main part of the cliff consists of a long narrow
buttress which slants up from right to left and is bounded on
both sides by grassy gullies. The deeper right-hand gully is
separated from the wide couloir by a subsidiary buttress.

The cliff is reached from the twin lakes up the scree slope which
descends from its left-hand bounding gully. A faint path
contours across the heather ledges at the base of the cliff, linking
it to Trwyn y Graig to the left and Craig yr Ogof to the right.

Descent is possible down either of the grassy gullies or down
the main couloir, although most parties attempting these routes
will be intending to visit the top of Carnedd Silyn.

Engineers' Climb   600 feet   Very Difficult   (1925)
A good long route following the obvious line up the crest of the
main buttress. The easiest line can be hard to follow but all the
major difficulties can be turned if necessary. Start about 150 feet
above the scree where the left-hand gully becomes more defined
and begins to slant to the left.
1   70 feet. Climb a short groove and the crack above, then follow
the rib on the right to a large ledge.

Cwm Silyn

1	Trwyn y Graig	S	Great Stone Shoot
2	Craig Fawr	F	Four Pitch Gully
3	Craig yr Ogof	R	Kitchen Rake
4	Clogwyn y Cysgod	K	Little Kitchen
A	Amphitheatre Gully	B	Bedrock Gully

2 80 feet. From 20 feet right of the gully, move up left and onto a small ledge. Step left into a wide crack and go up this then traverse right and climb a short groove lead to easier ground. Follow this to a ledge.

3 40 feet. Traverse up left until overlooking the gully, then climb direct to a pinnacle.

4 90 feet. From the grassy ledge above follow more ledges up left until it is possible to regain the crest of the buttress to the right. Go round the corner and up sloping ledges to belay below a short wall and two obvious towers.

5 60 feet. Climb the crack in the corner of the left tower to easy ground and go up left to belay below a short step.

6 100 feet. Ascend the step and the one above, then easy scrambling leads to a large terrace below the final tier.

7 110 feet. Climb to the foot of the square-cut tower above. Traverse a short distance right to a cleft and follow this and slanting cracks in the wall above to the top of the tower.

8 50 feet. Easy climbing leads to a cairn.

150 feet of scrambling lead to the top of the crag.

The next climb is short and begins high on the right wall of the final tier and is best approached from the top of the cliff down the gully between the main buttress and the subsidiary buttress on its right.

Bankers' Buttress   150 feet   Severe   (1939)
Pleasant if rather obscure. Start about 150 feet down the gully and a few yards right of an obvious grassy terrace.

1 110 feet. Move out left then climb straight up to a small ledge. Follow a fault sloping up right to a narrow grassy ledge. Move right and climb up to a narrow slab leading up to a corner.

2 40 feet. Climb up the slab, difficult at first, to the top.

The subsidiary buttress on the right of the main cliff is taken the pleasant but indefinite **LMH**, 400 feet Moderate (pre-1926).

Craig Yr Ogof   O.S. ref. SH 517 501

This is by far the best crag in the area, offering a wide variety of climbing in fine mountain situations. The crag is described in a number of sections which differ in their climbing characteristics for reasons of geology, direction of outlook and the amount of drainage they take.

From the lakes the most prominent feature of the crag is the great Nose of rock above the obvious central cave which gives the crag its name. The rush-covered Ogof Terrace runs left from the cave, dividing the face on the north side of the Nose into two tiers. Two dark gullies slant up the lower tier on the left-hand side of the main face to meet the Ogof Terrace where it finishes near the top of the right-hand gully.

The Nose, which narrows as it rises above the cave into the summit ridge of the cliff, has two facets; the North Face, the essence of which lies above and to the left of the Ogof and the West Wall, an area of steep grooves and overhangs, between the Ogof and the slab to the right. Prominent on the Nose is a grassy ledge, Sunset Ledge, some 200 feet above the screes which is visited by many routes in this section.

The slab to the right of the Nose is the sunny Great Slab which rises direct to the summit ridge some 400 feet above. Beyond the Great Slab is the rather broken South-West Buttress and right again the squat Amphitheatre Buttress. To the right again, between Craig yr Ogof and Clogwyn y Cysgod, is the Great Stone Shoot, the normal descent route.

The cliff is reached from the twin lakes by an unremitting grind up the obvious worn paths in the scree.

The Great Stone Shoot provides a simple, if long, descent route for climbs which reach the top of the cliff. Please respect the fence at the top. Alternatively, for mountaineers climbing with sacks, a more pleasant descent can be made down the ridge above Clogwyn y Cysgod directly to the parking place.

EASTERN SECTION
This consists of two appropriately-named gullies, Black on the left and Green on the right, together with their enclosing buttresses. All of the routes in this section finish near the top of Green Gully and from there it is only an easy scramble to the foot of Artist's Climb which offers a pleasant continuation to the top of the crag. Alternatively, descent can be made via a path which leads diagonally down into the large easy couloir to the left.

The wide, broken and vegetated **Heather Rib** marks the beginning of the climbing on the face although this was relegated by the previous guidewriters only to 'be useful to a large party of inexperienced climbers on a cold day'. Pleasant sections of moderate climbing are punctuated by periods of laborious rambling in heather. To the right again and taking the sharp rib bounding the left edge of Black Gully is a much better route.

Craig yr Ogof

1	Sunset Rib	D	10	Crucible	HVS
2	Black Gully	VD	11	Outside Edge Route	
3	Nirvana Wall	S			VD
4	Green Gully	HVS	O	Ogof Terrace	
5	Artist's Climb	D	S	Sunset Ledge	
6	Brutus	E2	G	The Great Slab	
7	Ogof Direct	E1	12	Aquarius	VS
8	Oblique Route	S	13	Upper Slab Climb	S
9	Desifinado	HVS	14	West Arête	VS

★ **Sunset Rib**   330 feet   Difficult   (1913)
A good natural line which, if combined with Artist's Climb, provides a pleasant way to the summit without the risk of encountering crowds. The route is rather well-worn and care should be taken in places, particularly at the short wall above the notch on pitch 2. Start at the foot of the rib.
1   90 feet. Climb the rib to a large heather ledge which runs left into the depression between the rib and Heather Rib. The final section is harder than the grade but can be avoided easily.
2   80 feet. Traverse right along a narrow ledge until good holds can be followed up and slightly left to a notch on the crest of the rib. Move up left to a ledge then go back up right with care and some difficulty to some spikes. Continue just left of the crest to a larger notch and good spike belays.
3   60 feet. Climb easily up heather ledges to reach a point overlooking Black Gully just above its dividing rib.
4   60 feet. Continue pleasantly up just right of the knife-edge to a huge belay on the crest again.
5   40 feet. Go easily on to the top of Black Gully.

Black Gully   230 feet   Very Difficult   (1933)
The left-hand of the two gullies, with a cave near the bottom, which is full of the usual gully contents. Start about 100 feet up the gully where it narrows.
1   50 feet. Climb the first step on the right, then continue up the groove to belay in the cave.
2   40 feet. Follow the narrow chimney then move up to a rib that divides the gully.
3   110 feet. Climb the right-hand branch to a terrace and follow this to a groove. Ascend this and then easier gully climbing leads to a belay.
4   30 feet. Scramble to the top.
It is possible to escape from the gully at the top of the dividing rib on pitch 3 by traversing left to join Sunset Rib in the middle of its pitch 3 and follow this to the top.

Nirvana Wall   310 feet   Severe   (1925)
A good route with an awkward crux which takes a line up the left wall of the buttress between Black and Green Gullies. Start about 30 feet below the first step of Black Gully.
1   50 feet. Gain the heather ledges on the wall of the gully and follow these up to belay beside a large flake level with the cave in the gully.
2   40 feet. Climb to a ledge on the right, then follow the slanting groove back leftwards to a large pinnacle.
3   60 feet. Follow ledges up left to below the obvious nose in the centre of the buttress. Gain the grassy ledge above and climb left into a groove which leads up right to a stance beneath a bulge.

4 40 feet. Gain the recess splitting the bulge with difficulty on elusive holds and continue to ledges and a terrace.
5 120 feet. Climb the right-hand wall of the next section until scrambling leads into the top of Green Gully.

Green Gully   240 feet   Hard Very Severe   (1970)
An unusually hard route of its type, which is well protected but is normally very wet and slimy. A route which is unlikely to achieve popularity. Start by scrambling up to the chimney at the start of the gully proper.
1 100 feet. Climb the chimney or the groove to the left, then continue more easily up the gully bed to belay where the gully narrows.
2 100 feet. Climb to a bulge at 20 feet, where the gully closes to a crack. Negotiate this and follow the crack above with difficulty to a resting place at 45 feet. Move up a little and then climb the slabby left wall to grass. Ascend this to a large flake belay at the end of the Ogof Terrace.
3 40 feet. Move up into a niche, step onto the right wall, then climb up and left on good holds to a grassy finish.

The next route goes up to the final ridge of Craig yr Ogof and starts some distance above the finishes of the previous routes.

Artist's Climb   145 feet   Difficult   (1925)
Not a route that is worth seeking out for itself but it is a good continuation to the previous routes in order to reach the summit ridge. The final section is shared with Ordinary Route and Outside Edge Route which arrive from the other side of the Nose. The start of the route is reached by a scramble up from the top of Green Gully. Gain and climb a 20-foot crack behind a pinnacle some 40 feet up from the top of the gully, then continue across a terrace and go up onto another terrace close under the ridge. Start at a V-chimney near the right-hand end of this terrace.
1 45 feet. Climb the chimney to the ridge.
2 100 feet. Move right onto the crest of the ridge and climb easily to the step in the ridge above. Go over this to large spikes and scrambling on the summit ridge.

OGOF NOSE – NORTH FACE
The main substance of this face is the upper wall above the Ogof Terrace which harbours a number of shallow grooves which slant slightly to the left. The grooves are rather blank and incut holds are uncommon, but the rock itself is firm and rough. Unfortunately the area takes a lot of drainage and as it faces north it takes a long time to dry out, so that it is less frequently in condition than the rest of the cliff. The routes will be found harder than the grade would suggest in wet conditions.

232

Craig yr Ogof

1	Oblique Route	S	5	Codswallop		E2
2	Eureka	E1	6	Jabberwocky		E2
3	Bandersnatch	E3	7	Bourdillon's Climb		E4
4	Crucible	HVS	8	Penates		HVS

The lower tier of the face, below the Ogof Terrace, is mostly vegetated to the left and easy-angled on the right. The climbing here contributes little to the routes up the face.

The first route, which traverses the upper part of the wall, starts above the lower tier.

Jones's Traverse   210 feet   Very Severe   (1958)
The easiest climb on the upper wall which takes the obvious rightwards-trending line of ledges from the top of green Gully to Sunset Ledge. Pleasant climbing and in a good position in the middle of the steep wall make it worth doing in good conditions. Start in the bay at the top of Green Gully.
1   50 feet. Go easily across heather ledges to a large block belay.
2   60 feet. 4b. Continue along the ledges to reach a corner. Move across onto a sloping ledge which is followed by more heather. Follow this into another corner and step down to a triangular ledge at the top of pitch 3 of Brutus.
3   50 feet. 4c. Move up round the corner and ascend a short wall to a good ledge. Follow a descending traverse to the grassy ledge at the top of pitch 4 of Ogof Direct.
4   50 feet. 4c. Climb up right and go across under the overhang. After a step right pleasant slabs lead diagonally up right to Sunset Ledge.

The next route begins up the impressive crack in the right wall of Green Gully, then trends rightwards up the steep walls of the upper tier.

★ **Brutus**   260 feet   E2   (1966)
A fine varied route. A strenuous crack leads to steep wall climbing. Start at the top of the first pitch of Green Gully.
1   70 feet. 5a. Gain the grassy ledge below the steep crack in the right wall of the gully. Climb the crack past two bulges to a small grassy bay.
2   50 feet. 4a. Follow the open chimney at the back of the bay to the Ogof Terrace. Move rightwards along this for 25 feet to belay at a flake at the foot of a shallow groove.
3   60 feet. 5c. Start up the groove then move right onto the arête. Climb this to a resting place at 40 feet, then continue slightly left to gain the ledges of Jones's Traverse. Move up left to a stance.
4   80 feet. 4c. Climb up for a few feet and step right onto a sloping ledge. Climb the leaning groove on the right to reach another ledge at 40 feet. Move right then go up to the right on good holds to belay on a large ledge.
The ledge below the final pitch of Outside Edge Route is easily reached around the corner to the right.

The area immediately to the right of Green Gully in the lower tier is particularly vegetated and wet. Farther right again directly below the cave is a fine grey rib.

★ **Ogof Direct** 370 feet E1 (1952)
A very good route which follows the relatively easy rib to the Ogof Terrace and then the awkward grooves left of the cave. Start about 20 feet up the field of rushes on the left of the rib. This can be reached directly or from the screes on the right via a heather ledge.
1 35 feet. Move along the ledge above on the right into a short corner. Climb the left wall of the corner and step right onto the ledge at the top.
2 120 feet. 4b. Step right onto the rib and follow it to a grassy ledge below two short corners. Climb either corner, the right is easier, to another ledge. Step back left onto the main rib and ascend this to the cave. Belay well back.
3 70 feet. Cross the terrace to a peg belay just to the left of the groove on the left-hand side of the cave.
4 75 feet. 5c. Move up rightwards into the groove and climb it to a small ledge at 40 feet. Move up right with difficulty to a sloping ledge and continue up right in a fine position to better holds which are followed up to a grassy ledge below another smaller overhang.
5 70 feet. 5a. Continue with difficulty up the slanting groove above to a ledge at 25 feet. Move right and climb another corner to easier rocks leading up to the ledge below the final pitch of Outside Edge Route.

★ **Desifinado** 330 feet Hard Very Severe (1964)
A steep, sustained and exposed route which starts on the North Face and moves through the overhangs on the right of the Ogof to reach Crucible on the West Wall then returns leftwards to finish up Ogof Direct. Start as for Oblique Route.
1 120 feet. As for pitch 1 of Oblique Route.
2 60 feet. 5a. Traverse right out of the cave in an exciting position between two sets of overhangs into a bottomless corner. Move up onto a ledge on the right and climb straight up into the bottom of the large overhang-capped corner of Crucible.
3 80 feet. 5a. Step left round the block and climb diagonally left to a niche below a large square-cut overhang. Move out left and climb a diagonal crack until a traverse left can be made to the grassy ledges at the top of pitch 4 of Ogof Direct.
4 70 feet. 5a. As for pitch 5 of Ogof Direct, continue with difficulty up the slanting groove above to a ledge at 25 feet. Move right and climb another corner to easier rocks leading up to the ledge below the final pitch of Outside Edge Route.

Variation
3a   90 feet. E1. Move left above the block, and follow the groove
above. Instead of going right as for Crucible, continue straight
up passing a square-cut overhang on the right then move left
round a second overhang to a ledge. Traverse left again to join
pitch 3 of the normal route.

Oblique Route   330 feet   Severe   (1946)
A poor and rambling route which takes an obvious line into the
right-hand side of the cave, then crosses the Ogof Terrace to
finish up Green Gully. The climbing up to the cave takes one of
the main drainage lines from the Ogof Terrace. Start at a rib
composed of huge blocks on the right-hand side of the steep
open gully which descends from the right-hand end of the cave.
1   120 feet. Climb the rib to where it peters out in loose rock
then traverse left across the gully to a quartz ledge. Climb the
slabby left wall of the gully into the cave.
2   90 feet. Cross the terrace to the left-hand side of the cave.
Move up onto the continuation of the ledge and follow this
leftwards for to a flake belay at the foot of a shallow groove at
the end of pitch 2 of Brutus.
3   80 feet. Continue along the ledge until it again disappears.
Step down and across the top of a chimney to gain the
continuation of the terrace. Follow this to a large flake belay in
Green Gully.
4   40 feet. Move up into a niche, step onto the right wall, and
then climb up and left on good holds to a grassy finish.

OGOF NOSE – WEST WALL
This is the complex area of grooves and overhangs between the
Nose and the Great Slab. Again it takes on something of a
two-tier structure: a diminishing line of overhangs runs
rightward from the Ogof, and below it the rock is relatively
easy-angled.
Above the right-hand side of the Ogof is a large corner which
leads up to a large overhang just below Sunset Ledge. This
corner is the main feature of the third pitch of Crucible which
turns the large overhang on the right. The corner is also visited
at its foot by Desifinado, described in the North Face section.
Crucible reaches the corner by a long leftward traverse which
crosses the lower line of overhangs where they peter out on the
right. The leftwards traverse of Crucible begins from a ledge in
the centre of the wall, below the steep impressive groove capped
by a small overhang which is taken by Codswallop. The ledge
also provides the stance of Bandersnatch which continues up
the wall to the left of the groove. Eureka goes directly through
the obvious large rock-scar between the corner of Crucible and
the groove of Codswallop, having gained the wall through a
weakness in the lower overhang. The grooves in the arête to the

right of Codswallop are followed by the exposed second pitch of Jabberwocky and the clean-cut corner which terminates the wall to the right is taken by Bourdillon's Climb.

Most of the routes on the wall are worth doing and some are of exceptional quality in fine position. The rock is basically very sound but there is a surprising number of insecure blocks and spikes about and the rock-scar indicates that some of these have departed in catastrophic fashion. The wall dries out much faster than the north side of the Nose although dampness can make a significant addition to the difficulties on some routes.

All of the routes finish on Sunset Ledge, from which descent is usually made by reversing the first pitch and a half of Ordinary Route. This is straightforward and obvious.

Eureka 240 feet E1   (1966)
A worthwhile eliminate route through Crucible with two short hard sections. Start as for Oblique Route at the rib to the right of the open gully.
1 60 feet. Climb the rib of pitch 1 of Oblique Route to belay where that route traverses left across the gully.
2 90 feet. 5b. Go over a bulge and climb up rightwards to the perched block below the corner on the second pitch of Crucible. Move left to a weakness in the overhangs and climb straight through this to the sloping ledge on Crucible. Continue up a groove until it is possible to step left to a small stance.
3 90 feet. 5b. Move down right into a groove and climb this to reach a short diagonal crack on the right. Follow this onto the right arête then continue more easily to the ledge below the final groove of Crucible. Climb the groove to Sunset Ledge.

Bandersnatch 210 feet E3   (1982)
A direct line between Codswallop and Eureka following the groove which is crossed by Eureka's 3rd pitch. Some hard climbing with poor rock and dubious protection. Start by scrambling up to overhangs at 40 feet above which a smooth rib leads up the perched block on pitch 2 of Crucible.
1 80 feet. 5a. Move up right to the overhangs and go through them to gain a slabby rib via a leftward-slanting groove. Follow the rib via shallow grooves to reach the perched block. Climb up and right to belay as for Crucible.
2 130 feet. 5c. Climb the blank groove above the left end of the ledge, via the left wall, to gain a deeper groove. Follow this to join Crucible under the overhang and finish as for this up the groove to the right.

To the right in the lower half of the wall is a depression containing a confusing area of ribs and grooves. The next two routes begin in this depression. Crucible starts up the twin grooves on the right side of the depression, then traverses left into the groove which bounds the depression on the left; Codswallop takes the right-hand grooves direct.

★★ **Crucible**   300 feet   Hard Very Severe   (1963)
A classic route which takes the easiest line on the wall. It trends diagonally left across the wall to reach the large overhang high on the wall then turns it on the right. Start on the right-hand side of the depression below the twin grooves.
1   100 feet. 4c. Climb the left-hand of the twin grooves to a small overhang and step right into other groove. Go up this then move back left to a large triangular overhang at 60 feet. Move left into another groove and go up this for a few feet. Step right above a roof and follow easier climbing up rightwards to a stance below the central groove of the wall.
2   80 feet. 5b. Move down leftwards onto a large perched block. Climb the corner above past an overhang (peg) and go up left to gain a sloping ledge. Step left round the corner into a groove then go down and left again to gain a sloping gangway. Follow this leftwards to reach the foot of an obvious corner. Go up this for a few feet to a small stance beside a large block.
3   120 feet. 5a. From the top of the block step left into another groove and follow this and its right-hand rib until it is possible to regain the main corner. Ascend this past a bulge to a small ledge. Traverse right across the slab and then go delicately up to the roof. Move right into a niche and go right again to gain a slabby groove. Follow this to Sunset Ledge. The slab at the top of this pitch is often wet which adds to the interest.

The original version of this route took the left-hand groove direct to the overhang at 60 feet, followed the second pitch as described to the sloping ledge, then took a higher line into the main corner which it then took direct to the normal finish. This is harder than the route as described.

★ **Codswallop**   230 feet   E2   (1968)
A good route taking the obvious main groove of the upper wall. Start as for Crucible at the right side of the depression.
1   100 feet. 5a. Climb either of the grooves until level with the triangular overhang at 60 feet, then continue direct to gain the stance below the main groove.
2   130 feet. 5b. Ascend the groove to a small overhang, then move up left to gain a crack. Climb this to a small ledge and follow the left wall of the groove past the left side of the main overhang. Traverse right into an easy groove which leads to Sunset Ledge.

★★ **Jabberwocky**   210 feet   E2   (1970)
A fine enjoyable route with an exposed second pitch up the grooved arête to the right of Codswallop. The difficulties have

increased due to the loss of a large wobbly hold (by devious means!). Start below the arête in a grassy groove about 20 feet left of the edge of the Great Slab.

1 100 feet. 5a. Climb the groove to a grassy ledge. Move up left onto the arête and follow its right edge by the easiest line to a sloping stance below the steep upper wall.

2 110 feet. 5c. Move out left from up the small overhang to gain a spike, then go back up right into the main groove. Climb this with difficulty past a peg then move out left to gain an exposed gangway. Follow this easily up left until it is possible to move right across a slab in a fine position to gain the arête on the right. Move right into a shallow groove which is followed to Sunset Ledge.

Bourdillon's Climb (Briggs' Climb) 210 feet E4 (1956/1978)
A taxing climb with poor protection and friable rock which takes the groove in the smooth wall to the right. Start as for Jabberwocky in a grassy groove about 20 feet left of the edge of the Great Slab.

1 120 feet. 5a. Follow the groove past ledges to a bulge at 50 feet. Traverse out left onto the slab and climb back rightwards up the slab into the corner. Climb the corner, moving right at the top onto a sloping ledge.

2 90 feet. 6a. Move into the subsidiary corner on the left and climb this and the flake above to a resting place. Follow the groove with continuing difficulty to a niche, then traverse left to join the easy finishing groove of Jabberwocky.

Penates 160 feet Hard Very Severe (1963)
A short but interesting climb taking the wall right of Bourdillon's Climb. Start at a short slab just left of the edge of the Great Slab.

1 100 feet. 5a. Climb the slab then the short wall above to gain the arête. Follow this to a ledge at 60 feet where the wall steepens. Step left on to the wall and climb it with difficulty to a ledge, then follow a groove to a perched block.

2 60 feet. 5a. Climb the corner above the block to the ledge at the top of pitch 1 of Bourdillon's Climb. Gain the steep crack on the right and follow it for 15 feet until it is possible to move out right to a ledge on Outside Edge Route. Follow this to the stance.

★ **The Ogof Traverse** 500 feet Hard Very Severe (1964)
A pleasant collection of pitches traversing both walls of the Nose. Start as for Penates at a short slab just left of the edge of the Great Slab.

1 100 feet. 5a. As for pitch 1 of Penates.

2 80 feet. 4c. Climb the corner above the block to the ledge at the top of pitch 1 of Bourdillon's Climb. From the left-hand end of the ledge move down until a line of holds leads left to reach the stance of Jabberwocky. Step down left again and go round the corner to the stance of Crucible.

Craig yr Ogof
The Great Slab

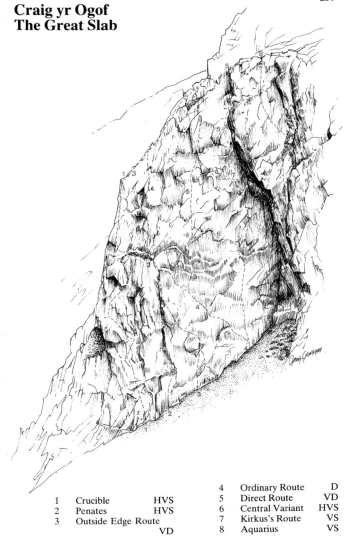

			4	Ordinary Route	D
1	Crucible	HVS	5	Direct Route	VD
2	Penates	HVS	6	Central Variant	HVS
3	Outside Edge Route		7	Kirkus's Route	VS
		VD	8	Aquarius	VS

3   80 feet. 5b. Pitch 2 of Crucible.
4   80 feet. 5a. Pitch 3 of Desifinado.
5   50 feet. 4c. Reverse pitch 3 of Jones's Traverse.
6   60 feet. 4b. Reverse pitch 2 of Jones's Traverse.
7   50 feet. Reverse pitch 1 of Jones's Traverse.

THE GREAT SLAB
This fine slab of rock reaches up the west side of Craig y Ogof for almost four hundred feet to the summit ridge. It is a popular resort for the lower-grade climber, having good rock and a sunny aspect. All the routes are worth doing and there are many other possibilities besides the routes described. The Slab is climbable virtually anywhere, however there are often few obvious landmarks once on a route and on some it is quite easy to lose the line.

About 50 feet up the centre of the main slab is a depression containing grassy ledges which reach out towards the left edge of the slab. These are visited by Ordinary Route which then takes a rising leftward line across Sunset Ledge to finish up the brow of the crag.

The main slab to the right of Ordinary Route is divided by three ledgy breaks trending diagonally up right. These are not very apparent in some lights and tend to disappear from view altogether when actually on the slab. The first of these consists of two grassy rakes about 10 feet apart which rise from the ledges on Ordinary Route. The lower of these ends at the top of the first pitch of Kirkus's Route and the upper steepens into the small corner taken by both of the Kirkus's Route variations. The middle break connects Sunset Ledge with the top. of pitch 2 of Kirkus's Route, and the upper break provides the unpleasant finish for Direct Route which gains it up the centre of the Slab.

High on the right of the main slab and separated from it by a corner which runs the full height of the cliff is the Upper Slab. Upper Slab Climb gains this slab from the South West Buttress farther right. The corner itself is the starting point for Aquarius which escapes rightwards from its damp confines. Kirkus's Route and its variants follow the main slab just left of this corner.

★★★ **Outside Edge Route**   420 feet   Very Difficult   (1931)
A classic route of its grade, taking a good line up the edge of the slab with an exposed finish above the nose of the crag. Start 20 feet right of the edge of the slab below a large semi-detached block.
1   70 feet. Climb a rightward-trending groove to gain the block by its right edge.

2 80 feet. Move up steeply to the next ledge and then make a fine ascending traverse across the wall to the left arête. Follow this to ledges where Ordinary Route arrives from the right.

3 40 feet. Continue up for 20 feet to Sunset Ledge and move left to belay at its left-hand end, beyond the open groove of Ordinary Route.

4 50 feet. Cross the grass to the left and move leftwards round ribs into a groove. Climb this to a large grassy ledge in a fine position on the brow of the buttress.

5 80 feet. Climb up then go left to a wide crack. Follow this as it steepens until it is possible to step left onto the rib. This leads more easily to a junction with Artist's Climb and Ordinary Route.

6 100 feet. Easy climbing in a good position leads up the ridge to the top.

Direct Start: 70 feet. Severe. This is only a little harder than the original line, starting at the extreme left-hand edge of the slab and climbing up slightly rightwards to the left side of the block at the top of the first pitch of the normal route.

★★ **Ordinary Route** 360 feet Difficult (1926)
The original route of the slab following a rising leftward line of ledges to Sunset Ledge and taking the open groove and slabs above. Start at a pedestal 20 feet above the scree and some 40 feet left of the right-hand corner of the slab.

1 90 feet. Climb the short polished wall on the right, then follow easy ledges up leftwards to belay below a broken groove.

2 70 feet. Continue diagonally left to the edge of the slab and continue up to Sunset Ledge. Go along the ledge for 15 feet to belay below an obvious open groove.

3 80 feet. Follow the groove to a short slab at 40 feet, climb this and the nose above to belay on a ledge where the angle eases.

4 120 feet. Go round to the left and climb easily to the step in the ridge above. Go over this to large spikes and scramble up the summit ridge.

Variations:
Inside Variation. 100 feet. Difficult. From the top of pitch 1, follow the broken groove above past a stance to eventually rejoin the original route at the short slab on pitch 3.

Inside Finish 100 feet. Very Difficult. From the foot of the short slab on pitch 3, traverse right to join Direct Route. Follow this for a few feet, then climb the steep exposed crack above to the top of the cliff, moving left when the angle eases.

Direct Route   360 feet   Very Difficult   (1927)
A good route which is marred by the finish which is often
covered with stones and earth. It takes a direct line up the
left-hand side of the main slab to reach the highest of the three
breaks. This is followed up rightwards to finish in the right-hand
corner of the slab. Start as for the Ordinary Route at a pedestal
20 feet above the scree and some 40 feet left of the right-hand
corner of the slab.
1   100 feet. Follow the first pitch of the Ordinary Route to its
belay, then continue 10 feet up the broken groove taken by
Inside Variation to a stance and belay.
2   80 feet. Ignoring the leftward-trending break of Inside
Variation, climb straight up for 25 feet to another ledge, move
awkwardly up right, then traverse up left for 15 feet to gain a
shallow groove at the left-hand end of a line of small overhangs.
Follow the groove for a few feet then traverse right to ledges on
the middle break of the Slab.
3   80 feet. Go up trending slightly left to a grassy ledge below
two short grooves. Start up the left-hand groove, then gain the
other groove and follow it to the left end of another line of small
overhangs. Move up left and then back right to a good ledge at
the start of the upper break.
4   100 feet. Carefully follow the break up right into the corner.
Climb this with disheartening protection past a large ledge, to
finish up the slab on the left of the corner. Great care should be
taken on this pitch not to knock stones down on to parties below.

Central Variant   320 feet   Hard Very Severe   (1952)
An artificial but worthwhile route which moves left from Kirkus's
Route to find a more difficult line up the middle of the slab. Start
as for Kirkus's Route.
1   90 feet. Pitch 1 of Kirkus's Route (or of Kirkus's Direct).
2   70 feet. 5a. Go easily up left to gain the small corner at the
end of the upper of the two rakes which run up from Ordinary
Route. Climb the corner for 10 feet to a small spike, then traverse
left above the small overhangs and continue up leftwards to
reach the middle break at the top of pitch 2 of Direct Route.
3   80 feet. Climb more or less straight up to the upper break as
for pitch 3 of Direct Route.
4   80 feet. 5a. Go up left to a small overhang and climb the thin
crack on its left. Continue up the groove and slab above to
another overhang which is taken by the crack on its right. Easy
climbing leads to the top.

★★ Kirkus's Route   310 feet   Very Severe   (1931)
A fine slab climb giving sustained climbing to the top of the cliff.
It takes a nearly direct line up the right side of the slab to finish
just above the step in the summit ridge. Start as for Ordinary
Route.

1 90 feet. 4b. Climb the short polished wall as for Ordinary Route to gain some ledges, then move up to the forked diagonal crack above. Climb the crack, following the right-hand branch round a corner into a niche. Continue up more steeply to a stance on blocks.
2 70 feet. 4b. Move delicately left across a groove to gain small holds leading to a line of holds running leftwards. Follow these to a large spike. Step left into a groove and follow this to belay on the middle break.
3 70 feet. 4c. Climb slightly rightwards up a smooth slab to a small overhang. Surmount this direct to reach a stance on Direct Route.
4 80 feet. 4c. Climb up to large holds below an overhang directly above. Pass the overhang on its right. Easier climbing now leads up leftwards to the summit ridge.

Kirkus's Direct   300 feet   Hard Very Severe   (1951)
A good climb with some exciting delicate sections. Start 15 from from the right-hand corner of the slab.
1 80 feet. 5a. Climb the wet slab to an overhang and pull round this to the foot of a shallow groove which leans to the right. Follow this awkwardly until it eases at the top of the groove. Traverse left past flakes and step down to the stance at the top of the first pitch of Kirkus's Route.
2 80 feet. 4c. Go easily up left to gain the small corner at the end of the upper of the two rakes which run up from Ordinary Route, as for Central Variant. Climb the corner for 10 feet to a small spike, then step right onto the rib. Continue up the thin crack above until it is possible to move left to an easy groove. Follow this rightwards to join Kirkus's Route near the top of its second pitch. Belay as for that route.
3 140 feet. 5a. Move right into the corner on the right of the slab and follow it to a small overhang. Climb the crack on the left to a mossy area then step left and continue directly up the slab about 10 feet from the corner to reach the upper break in the slab and a junction with Direct Route. Follow Direct Route carefully to the top.

UPPER SLAB AND SOUTH-WEST BUTTRESS

Above and to the right of the Great Slab is a smaller facet of slab, the Upper Slab, which is separated from the main slab by a corner. To the right of the Upper Slab is a broken and complex area of ribs and grooves which is delineated on the right by Amphitheatre Gully. This is the South-West Buttress which contains rather a lot of vegetation and is often wet. The Upper Slab is separated from the South-West Buttress by a shallow gully. This is followed by the lower section of Aquarius which then takes a direct line up the Upper Slab. The Upper Slab Climb starts well to the right and gains the heathery terraces at mid-height from which it traverses left to climb the left edge of the Upper Slab. West Arête takes a vaguer line up the right edge of the Buttress.

Aquarius   330 feet   Very Severe   (1966)
A reasonable climb, but the first pitches are always wet even in a good summer. If very wet they may well be found to be considerably harder than the grade might suggest. Start below the corner at the right-hand side of the Great Slab.
1 60 feet. 5a. Go up to the base of the corner and climb its left wall for about 15 feet until it is possible move right to join the corner itself. Follow the corner past a niche to gain a short slab on the right. Climb the shallow groove on the left of the slab and then step left to belay on a small ledge.
2 80 feet. 4c. Move right into the bed of the gully and follow it to where it narrows and steepens. Step left and climb the groove to a grassy ledge and continue up the slab on the left to a ledge.
3 60 feet. Continue up the slab to a grassy area on the right below the main part of the Upper Slab.
4 130 feet. 4c. Go up and left across the slab. Continue straight up past a line of small overhangs near the top to finish easily.

★ **Upper Slab Climb**   380 feet   Severe   (1931)
A wandering route which finds a fine exposed finish. Start about 40 feet right of the corner at the right-hand side of the Great Slab, at a grassy groove just right of an obvious double overhang.
1 70 feet. Ascend the groove to a niche then climb its left wall until the groove can be regained and followed to a large grassy ledge.
2 120 feet. Climb the corner on the left for 20 feet, move left and go up the slab to a small ledge in a corner below an overhang. Traverse left and follow the narrowing slab to heather ledges and a belay over on the left.
3 50 feet. Follow the grassy rake down to the left to join Aquarius. Climb the corner and steep grass to a small grassy ledge.
4 140 feet. Go down to a narrow ledge above the overhang on the slab and follow this out left until near the edge. Climb up and slightly right to gain a shallow groove which leads up left to a heather ledge overlooking Great Slab (and a junction with Direct Route). Traverse back right onto the Upper Slab and go diagonally right to the top.

Another route covering similar ground has been claimed – **Kangie's Crawl** (200 feet, Very Severe) but this is not sufficiently independent to warrant description.

West Arête 210 feet Very Severe (1970)
A clean and attractive route up the right-hand arête of the
South-West Buttress. Start below the arête, in the left-hand of
three grassy grooves.
1 70 feet. 4c. Climb the groove for 30 feet until level with the
base of a crack in the left wall. Gain the crack and follow it to
the large ledge at the top of pitch 1 of Upper Slab Climb.
2 50 feet. 4c. Continue up the smooth groove just left of the
arête to gain a sloping ledge.
3 90 feet. 4c. Climb the steep groove above the stance for 10
feet, then step left into a crack on the arête. Climb up and left to
a shallow depression which leads in fine position to the top.

Rib and Tower 450 feet Difficult (1936)
A poor, rambling and vegetated route taking a line up the left
wall of Amphitheatre Gully. Start about 50 feet below and to the
right of West Arête, at the foot of a rib just left of Amphitheatre
Gully. Climb the rib to a grassy ledge at 90 feet, then take the
next section slightly on the left for 60 feet. Follow the rib again
for 50 feet to a large terrace. Stroll up this for 100 feet to the foot
of some grassy ribs converging on a grassy tower about 100 feet
above. Climb the rightmost rib to the tower and pass this easily
on the right.

Amphitheatre Gully is wet and not recommended as a descent
route.

AMPHITHEATRE BUTTRESS
This is the huge sprawling mass right of Amphitheatre Gully.
Despite its size it is not as good as its namesake, offering only
isolated pitches and much grass.

Original Route 500 feet Difficult (1925)
Best avoided, although some more interesting rock does appear
at the finish. Start on the left of the buttress, near the gully. Climb
short slabby buttresses and much heather for 200 feet to an
extensive field. At the far end of the field the buttress narrows
and an narrow arête leads to the top.

Gotogo 130 feet Very Severe (1970)
A vegetated route up the slabby lower section of the buttress
right of Original Route. Start at the lowest point of the slabs at
a slabby groove.
1 130 feet. Climb the groove to a small overhang, then go
diagonally left up a crack to a stance below another overhang.
Move back right and climb the obvious groove until it is possible
to step left onto the rib. Follow this to a large terrace.

High up in the Great Stone Shoot and well seen during descent is a short steep tower in the right wall of Amphitheatre Buttress; this gives two routes.

Tower of Strength   110 feet   Severe   (1955)
A good steep route up the obvious crack and chimney in the centre of the tower. The original route avoids the main difficulties of the crack but the variation makes up for this deficiency. Start on the ledges above the gully and below the chimney, just left of a yellow rock-scar.
1   110 feet. Climb the cracked wall to the foot of the steep crack. Go up the wall on the right of the crack for 5 feet, then move right round the corner and follow a more broken crack until holds lead back left to the foot of the chimney. Climb the chimney to a ledge and then the top.
The direct variation is Very Severe 4c and takes the crack direct to the base of the chimney.

Afterthought   120 feet   Severe   (1967)
Takes a line up the right side of the tower. Start at the foot of the curving groove just right of the yellow rock-scar.
1   120 feet. Gain the groove from the right and follow it to a ledge at 60 feet. Move up left to go through the overlap, then traverse 10 feet right to an easy groove which is climbed to the top.

Clogwyn y Cysgod (Cliff of the Shade)

O.S. ref. SH 512 501

This is the brooding vegetated cliff on the western arm of Cwm Silyn. It is separated from the Great Stone Shoot by a wide expanse of easy ground. This cliff no doubt has its devotees (somewhere) but to most the copious vegetation and drainage are a good reason for avoiding it until the temperature is below freezing.

The cliff is frequently greasy even during a drought (remember them?). Some dedication – or indeed masochism – is required to unearth or even repeat the routes.

It flaunts the only aid point left on a non-artificial route in the area. Is no free-spirited botanist able to remove this?

The cliff is bounded on the left by Four-Pitch Gully, which faces Craig yr Ogof and is very conspicuous from the Great Slab although almost invisible from the floor of the cwm. Immediately right of the gully is the first significant buttress of the cliff which is conspicuous because of the huge overhangs at

Clogwyn y Cysgod

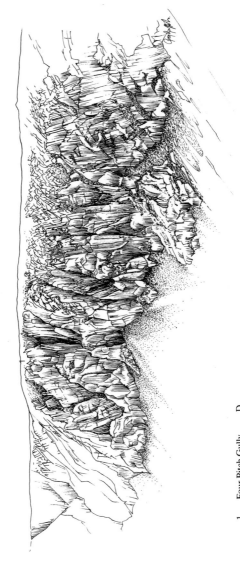

1	Four Pitch Gully	D
2	Little Kitchen	
3	Bedrock Gully	VD

247

mid-height. Below the overhangs it is broken by large grassy terraces, but on the right continuous rock, taken by Atropos, reaches up to the indefinite groove on the right of the overhangs. To the right of the buttress is a wide vegetated weakness and farther right another broken buttress.

In the centre of the cliff is an amphitheatre out of which rises a dark ravine, the Little Kitchen. The grassy Kitchen Rake leads up left from the Amphitheatre and is separated from the Little Kitchen by the steep rib taken by Sideline. To the right of the Little Kitchen and beyond another very vegetated buttress is an impressive deep and dripping cleft, Bedrock Gully. The right wall of this is the steep and narrow Flintstone Rib. Beyond this feature the cliff falls back into a large vegetated depression. The last climbing on the cliff lies on the rather indistinct buttress to the right of this depression.

The approach from the lakes up the screes on the right-hand side of the cwm is obvious if tiring. Descent is best made (carefully) down Kitchen Rake which finishes near the top of Four-Pitch Gully.

Four-Pitch Gully   310 feet   Difficult   (1912)
This gully slants from left to right at the left edge of the cliff, finishing near the top of The Kitchen Rake and Little Kitchen. There is much loose scree in the bed of the gully. Start below the gully, slightly right of its main line.
1   50 feet. Climb a little chimney and go past a block until a steep grassy ledge leads to a belay.
2   90 feet. Scramble up scree to an impressive cave.
3   90 feet. Exit through a high tight hole and go up the left wall above. Scramble up again to a belay below a loose wall.
4   80 feet. Climb the wall, then broken ground, to a final steep and vegetated wall which is followed to the top.

Eyrie   320 feet   Hard Very Severe   (1965)
This route rambles up the vegetated terraces to the indefinite groove on the right of the conspicuous overhangs on the left side of the cliff. It turns the overhangs by the crack on their left, taking in some impressive scenery. Start directly below the overhangs.
1   160 feet. Difficult and exciting climbing on vegetation leads up to the groove on the right of the overhangs.
2   100 feet. Climb the groove to the first roof, then traverse diagonally left to the crack on its left side. Follow this to a belay.
3   60 feet. Continue straight up for 20 feet then trend left to the top.

Atropos   420 feet   Hard Very Severe (1 pt. aid)   (1966)
This takes the steep wall which rises leftwards to the right of Eyrie, then makes an exposed finish above the overhangs.
Start in an indefinite gully about 40 feet right of Eyrie.
1   160 feet. Climb the dirty gully for 50 feet until an obvious gangway with a crack at the back leads up to the left. Follow this to a small pinnacle.
2   100 feet. Ascend the steep wall above the pinnacle and gain a shallow groove (one sling for aid on a blunt spike). Climb the groove and traverse left at the top to an obvious spike belay.
3   100 feet. From the top of the spike, step awkwardly onto the arête on the left. Climb the arête to the roof, then move left into a bottomless groove. Climb this, then trend left along an obvious traverse to join Eyrie at its third stance.
4   60 feet. As for Eyrie, continue straight up for 20 feet then trend left to the top.

Beyond the vague gully which is taken by the start of Atropos is a broken buttress with no routes. This is bounded on the right by the easy watercourse which leads up into the amphitheatre below the Little Kitchen. Running up left from the amphitheatre is the **Kitchen Rake** which is only a walk apart from an easy 15 foot wall a short way up. The **Little Kitchen** itself contains a pitch of piled boulders, some of which are loose, and is scarcely to be recommended. Between the two is a rib giving the following route:

Sideline   150 feet   Very Severe   (1962)
Start below the centre of the rib, high up in the amphitheatre. Climb vegetated rocks on the left then go rightwards up a small slab to gain a grassy chimney-crack. Climb this for a few feet, then step right into a slabby groove round the corner. Follow the groove and the shallow chimney above to a stance on the left at 80 feet in the wider grassy chimney. Continue easily straight up to the summit ridge.

About 200 feet down to the right from the entrance to the Little Kitchen is another conspicuous gully, Bedrock Gully. A route, **Sweep Wall** has been done up its left arête.

Bedrock Gully   300 feet   Very Difficult   (1933)
This dark narrow gully is usually very wet indeed and cannot in the slightest respect be advised as a summer climb. In the winter it can offer a good ice climb. The left-hand branch has now had a winter ascent, but despite advertisement in the last guide still lacks a summer ascent: it has some fine examples of hanging slime.

Flintstone Rib   300 feet   Very Severe   (1962)
A loose route taking the prominent rib which bounds Bedrock Gully to the right. Start at the foot of the rib, just inside the gully.

1   80 feet. Climb up steep loose rock and grass until it is possible to step right onto the front of the rib below a steep slab. Climb this diagonally rightwards over a bulge on the arête, then traverse left to a small stance overlooking the gully.

2   120 feet. Climb straight up behind the stance into a groove, then step left onto a slab. Go up this for a few feet and then step back right into the groove which is followed to a large grassy ledge. Move right and go up a chimney to another grassy ledge.

3   100 feet. Grassy scrambling up the ridge leads to the top.

On the right of Flintstone Rib is a shallow indefinite gully, then a wide vegetated depression. At the right end of this is a steep buttress with a smooth front. The next route follows a groove on the left side of this buttress.

Cysgodian Creep   300 feet   Very Severe   (1970)
Start below the buttress. Gain a grassy rake and follow it to a short wall just below the steep part of the buttress. Surmount the wall, then move left into a slabby groove which slants up left. Climb the groove past a bulge to easier climbing and a large grassy ledge at 100 feet. Continue up the break for 40 feet, then follow vegetation to the top.

To the right again the cliff falls back into a confused area of heather terraces and short buttress; the indefinite **Colin's Gully** takes in a line up here.

Craig Cwm Dulyn (Crag of the hollow of the black lake)

O.S. ref. SH 497 492

This small steep crag which rises above the inner end of Cwm Dulyn offers the only continuous climbing on the northern slopes of Mynydd Craig Cwm Silyn. Even this crag is very vegetated and the existing routes have required extensive gardening to become possible. Further attention may again be needed before subsequent ascents.

The cliff lies in a pleasant secluded position above the llyn. The crag is easily accessible and is situated low enough to sometimes be in condition when higher crags are shrouded in mist. However because of the vegetation, it remains greasy for long periods.

The crag juts out from the surrounding hillside and is topped by a hidden meadow. Near its right-hand end is a short gully divided into two branches by a narrow heather rib. Immediately left of the gully is a long easy-angled buttress with a conspicuous rock-scar at about mid-height.

The main wall of the crag rises above the vast steep heather-covered slope left of this buttress. Towards the left-hand side of the wall is an impressively smooth leftward-facing groove which steepens towards the top: this is Dulyn Groove, the only good route on the cliff. Farther left, beyond the heather slope, various isolated ribs of good grey rock appear from the heather before an easy rake marks the end of the crag.

Cwm Dulyn is easily reached in 20 minutes over the moor from Bryn Gwyn on the usual approach to Cwm Silyn. However, it is possible to drive to within 10 minutes easy walk of the cliff by following the service track for the reservoir to its end at SH 488 498. This track is approached via Nebo and the Caernarfon – Porthmadog road (A 487) and is perfectly adequate for motor vehicles. From the parking place go through the gate and follow either side of the lake until below the cliff.

The quickest descent route from the cliff is the easy rake on the left. The best route for returning to the parking-place, if no gear has been left at the foot of the crag, lies down the easy grass slopes on the right (west) of the crag. The short steep gully at the right-hand end of the crag is not recommended as a means of descent.

The east end of the crag left of the main wall but right of the easy rake contains some pleasant scrambling. The first outcrop right of the easy rake consists of a slab with an overhang at the bottom. The crack which splits this is about 60 feet long and Severe. Farther right a rib of clean rock, **Ebon Ridge** 160 feet, Very Severe, rises from the heather and provides some pleasant climbing if rock is rigidly adhered to. The route finishes up an obvious overhanging corner above a terrace.

The main wall of the crag is reached by scrambling for 30 feet up the rather slimy and unpleasant gully on the left of the heather slope, until an exit left can be made into the bracken. Bracken and heather then lead up right to the foot of the obvious leftward-facing corner taken by Dulyn Groove. Non-orienteers may prefer to abseil into the corner.

Just left of Dulyn Groove is another groove with a small retaining wall. Left again is a shorter groove slanting up left; this is taken by the next route.

Zip Groove   120 feet   Very Severe   (1970)
An interesting pitch if clean, now very overgrown, but still hardly worth the visit. Start in the heather-bracken field, immediately below Dulyn Groove.

1   120 feet. Climb shattered blocks about 10 feet left of Dulyn Groove, then traverse left to a large spike. From the top of this, follow the shallow groove up left for about 40 feet until easier ground is reached. This leads to a belay at the top of the crag.

★ **The Bodysnatchers**   130 feet   E3   (1988)
The groove left of Dulyn Groove. Start from blocks.
1   130 feet. 6a. Climb the groove past a trickly overlap. Finish up an awkward off-width crack; large runners.

★ **Dulyn Groove**   140 feet   E3   (1970)
A fine sustained pitch, both delicate and strenuous, with a difficult and impressive finish. The grade assumes that the route is clean. Start directly below the groove as for Zip Groove.
1   140 feet. 5c. Follow the groove, awkward at first, to a resting place at 30 feet. Bridge up to the bulge above and pass this to another resting place. Move out onto the slabby left wall and go up it for 10 feet before making a rising traverse to good footholds on the left arête. Step up then traverse back right into the groove. Ascend this with difficulty to a grassy finish.

The right facet wall of Dulyn Groove is impressively smooth and steep. The arête of this is:-

★★ **Red Shift**   120 feet   E4   (1989)
An exhilarating route taking the right-hand arête of Dulyn Groove. Start as for Dulyn Groove by abseiling down from a large spike some 40 feet down from the crag top. Large thread belay.
1   120 feet. 5c. Climb the first few feet of Dulyn Groove until a horizontal ledge can be hand-traversed into the middle of the wall. Move up to gain a good side hold, then go up and rightwards to the arête. Climb the arête for a few feet on its right then swing round left and climb a short crack. Pull back right and gain a small groove in the arête itself. At the top, step slightly right and pull over the bulge to the wall above. Climb the wall for a few feet then move back left to gain a good spike and belays just above.

Right of the arête the wall is very vegetated and forms a short overhanging corner on the right, where it meets the longer lower-placed buttress on its right. The last route of any consequence ascends the front of this buttress.

Quest for Corbeau   240 feet   Very Severe   (1953)
The first section of the buttress to the rock-scar is quite pleasant and interesting, but after that the route gradually degenerates into tedious heather scrambling. Start in the gully near the right-hand end of the crag, where the buttress steepens and a vegetated ledge runs left round to its front.

1   80 feet. Traverse left along the ledge and round a rib formed by a huge perched block. Go up the crack on the left side of the block for 10 feet then climb up left into a steep little groove with a tiny overhang formed by a suspect block. Move up to the overhang, swing left onto the rib and step up to a small ledge just below the rock-scar. Climb a loose but easy shallow groove on the left to the scar, then traverse the scar up right to ledges.

2   70 feet. Climb the broken groove above tending right until it is possible to scramble up left to the top of the buttress, where it abuts onto the main crag.

3   90 feet. Scramble up the jungle ahead, eventually fighting out onto the rib and fresh air on the left.

The left-hand and subsidiary branch of the gully have given a grassy route (**Irish Mail** 220 feet, Difficult) which eventually traverses left to finish up the last pitch of Quest for Corbeau. The rib between the two branches of the gully has also been climbed (**Loosenard** 200 feet, Severe), but neither route is worth describing in detail. The buttress to the right of the gully is vegetated.

MOEL HEBOG

The fine peak and viewpoint of Moel Hebog offers little to attract the discerning rock-climber. There is much rock here, but an equal or greater amount of vegetation which dominates most of the routes. The climbing that exists is on two cliffs which both face east. The more southerly Summit Cliff overlooks Upper Cwm Cloch and the main cliff, Y Diffwys, encircles the head of Cwm Bleiddiaid. Both cliffs are slow to dry because of the quantity of vegetation. When the cliffs are dry enough to be pleasant, most climbers will have their sights set on more interesting places.

The easiest approach to the cliffs is via the normal walker's path from Beddgelert. This leaves the Beddgelert – Rhyd Ddu road about ½ mile north of the village and follows a private road to Cwm Cloch Farm. The well-marked path runs right from here onto the hillside then follows the grassy spur running down from the summit between Cwm Cloch and Cwm Bleiddiaid. The cliffs of Y Diffwys are obvious in the back of the cwm on the right as one approaches the upper section of the path. The Summit Cliffs lie much farther up on the left of the path.

Y Diffwys (The Precipice)   O.S. ref. SH 567 476

This, the main cliff of Moel Hebog, is some 400 feet high, although much is vegetated and easy-angled. It is split into two sections by a steep rake, the Companionway, which runs from left to right up the centre of the cliff. The South Cliff lies to the left and above the rake and the North Cliff below it on the right. The Companionway offers the quickest descent for climbs on the left-hand side of the North Cliff.

SOUTH CLIFF
This is the large broken and vegetated cliff above the rake. The cliff is concave with a complex rib and groove structure. The routes are long and indefinite and defy detailed description (even by the first ascensionists).

Omega (350 feet, Difficult) takes a vague line up the slabby left-hand side of the buttress halfway between the walker's path and the central depression taken by **Bending Groove** (440 feet, Very Difficult, 1938). A very heathery route, **Anaconda** (380 feet, Very Difficult, 1953) takes a line diagonally right from the foot of Bending Groove; two other routes **Caterpillar** (380 feet, Very Difficult, 1950) and **Lodestone** (300 feet, Difficult, 1950) take even fainter lines farther to the right. This is an area for a true explorer.

The **Companionway** is the obvious easy rake which begins at an easy chimney facing south and runs diagonally up right between the two cliffs. In descent, keep well to the right to avoid the upper reaches of Tension Crack on the North Cliff.

NORTH CLIFF
The North Cliff, below and to the right of the companionway, is about 400 feet high. To the right of the Companionway the first obvious feature is a steep narrow gully which is taken by Tension Crack. To the right again, before a less obvious break, is a compact area of rock with two pleasant routes. The cliff to the right is dominated in its lower half by large overhangs above wet slabs and grooves. These overhangs fade out to the right, leaving a more heathery area before a huge patch of heather at about 50 feet, the Maidan, from which rises Maidan Gully. On the right of Maidan Gully is an easier-angled buttress.

Tension Crack   265 feet   Severe   (1950)
A good wet struggle. Start at a depression below an over-hanging crack, with a cave above, some 60 feet right of the initial chimney of the Companionway.
1 45 feet. Climb a short wall to reach the overhanging crack. Follow this leftwards to a grassy recess then continue more easily for 25 feet into the cave.
2 90 feet. Chimney up out of the cave on the left, then climb a strenuous wall beside the crack and step left to a narrow ledge. Continue straight up the grassy bed of the main groove to a stance where it narrows and steepens again.
3 70 feet. Continue up the crack for 10 feet to a small chockstone, then traverse upwards across the left wall and go delicately back into the crack above the impasse. Belay on the right.
4 60 feet. Scramble up to reach the Companionway.

Compression   430 feet   Very Severe   (1956)
An interesting climb when in good condition. Start a few yards right of Tension Crack at an inconspicuous rib.
1 60 feet. Follow the rib on small holds to a small stance.
2 120 feet. Traverse slightly right to a crack beneath the overhang. Follow slabs up for 20 feet to a thin crack, and go up to a second overhang. Climb over this at its right-hand end, and belay in a sort of gully to the right.
3 250 feet. Continue easily in several pitches up dirty slabs to the ridge.

Ignition   340 feet   Very Severe   (1970)
A pleasant route making the most of the buttress right of Tension Crack. Start on a rush-covered ledge beneath the obvious break to the right of Tension Crack.

1   60 feet. Climb the rib on the left then a groove to gain a leftward-sloping gangway. Follow this to a wet crack which is taken to an large grassy ledge. Large belay on the left.

2   80 feet. Move onto the slab above the belay and cross it to another grassy ledge on the left. Continue up the grass to a groove between two ribs. Follow the steep crack in the left wall until the rib can be gained and followed to the overhang at the top. Step left across a groove and go up the obvious corner crack to a grassy ledge on the skyline.

3   100 feet. Climb straight up for 20 feet, then traverse the pleasant slab on the right until the left edge of the overhang can be gained. Go back across the top and continue up on easy ledges to a large block belay.

4   100 feet. Easy climbing up heathery ledges gains the Companionway.

Redog   490 feet   Hard Very Severe   (1971)
A good climb on excellent rock towards the right of the central section, taking the left edge of the reddish slab capped by a huge overhang about 100 feet left of the Maidan. The foot of the slab is gained from the right. Start at a bulge, about 30 feet left of Chinaman and 20 feet right of two steep shallow grooves which run straight up to the bottom right-hand corner of the slab.

1   80 feet. Surmount the bulge, climb straight up for 15 feet then make a rising traverse left into the upper part of the right-hand groove. Climb this or the left rib to grassy ledges. Move left and go up to the highest ledge in the left-hand groove. Peg belay.

2   110 feet. Traverse out to a grassy ledge on the left edge of the slab. Go up near the edge, move right over a bulge, then step back left to continue near the arête to a ledge at 60 feet. Enter the groove above and climb it to a small triangular overhang. Step right to a crack and climb this and the wall above to grassy ledges. Peg belay.

300 feet of the usual mixed grass and rock leads to the top.

Chinaman   420 feet   Very Difficult   (1950)
A poor, vegetated climb which is based around the rightward-slanting chimney-groove line to the left of the Maidan.
Start at the foot of the chimney, about 30 feet left of the depression below the left-hand side of the Maidan.

1   120 feet. Climb the chimney for 20 feet, then traverse left to heather ledges which are followed up leftwards to the foot of a wide groove. Move right out of this immediately and follow more heather rightwards to regain the original groove. Small spike belay on the right rib.

2   80 feet. Go up the bed of the groove into a dark little hole (the Opium Den). Climb out of this on the right and continue up to the foot of a terrace. Move up left for 10 feet on a break which leads onto the front of the buttress and belay.

3   220 feet. Continue leftwards along the break then follow easy rocks in a direct line to the top.

David Bailey on Penamnen Groove, Carreg Alltrem.
Photo: Paul Williams

Terry Gifford on Angel Pavement, Craig y Bera.
Photo: Ian Smith

Maidan Gully   430 feet   Severe   (1951)
The obvious big gully above the Maidan gives one good steep
pitch before it deteriorates. The route then follows Maidan
Buttress to the top. Start on a grassy ledge above some easy
rocks 30 feet right of Chinaman and at a scoop running up to
the left corner of the Maidan.
1 60 feet. Climb the thin crack in the bed of the scoop for 30
feet until a move right can be made to the Maidan. Scramble up
to a small cave (the Shrine) with a thread belay on the right.
2 70 feet. Walk up the Maidan to the gully.
3 80 feet. Climb awkwardly into the crack above and follow it
into the bed of the gully. Scramble up to belay below a short
step in the gully.
4 50 feet. Go up for 10 feet then follow a ledge to the right and
climb up rightwards to a stance on Maidan Buttress.
5 170 feet. Follow the crest of the buttress, on perfect rock, to
the top.

Maidan Buttress   445 feet   Difficult   (1951)
A good route which follows the buttress to the right of Maidan
Gully. Start at a chimney at the foot of the buttress, 30 feet to
the left of the narrow pink slab on the right of the buttress.
1 50 feet. Climb the chimney or the rib on its right to a stance.
2 50 feet. Walk left to the foot of the pink slab.
3 60 feet. Follow an exposed ledge round the corner to the left
to a ledge on the edge of the main buttress. Climb straight up
the wall above to a small terrace below a dyke.
4 75 feet. From the right-hand end of the terrace, climb up to
a niche. Step left and gain a second niche a few feet higher. Go
up the wall to the left, overlooking the Maidan, until the angle
eases and a stance is reached.
5 40 feet. Go up the edge to another stance.
6 170 feet. Follow the crest of the buttress, on perfect rock, to
the top.

Pink Slab   400 feet   Severe   (1950)
This agreeable route follows the obvious reddish wet slab
towards the right-hand side of the North Cliff. Start as for Maidan
Buttress.
Follow the first two pitches of Maidan Buttress to the foot of the
slab. Climb the slab direct on small holds and go up to a stance
and thread belay on top of a hanging pulpit. Step left and
continue up the slab until two grooves lead into a scoop. Climb
up left and follow a short steep wall on good holds to gain the
trough above. Continue up for 70 feet to a clean rib which leads
to the top.

Two Chimney Route   300 feet   Very Difficult   (1950)
An old-fashioned climb. Start as for Maidan Buttress.
Ascend the first chimney of Maidan Buttress, then continue up
the more strenuous 80-foot chimney above. Scramble up to a
terrace and follow it leftwards to finish up the pleasant rib at the
top of Pink Slab.

To the right of the start of Maidan Buttress is a small buttress
of good rock split by three steep fissures. **Toy Crack Climb**,
Difficult, (1953) takes the right-hand of these and gives pleasant
chimneying.

Finally, for true heather specialists, a high-level traverse of the
North Cliff has been climbed. This starts up Maidan Buttress and
finishes on the Companionway.

Explorer's Traverse   580 feet   Difficult   (1950)
A horticultural ramble in a good position.
1, 2, 3   160 feet. As for Maidan Buttress.
4   100 feet. Continue leftwards then go up a slab to a small
grassy patch. Climb the second slab on the left to gain the
Maidan, and move across to a stance near the gully.
5   45 feet. Walk across for 15 feet then climb up a slabby scoop
trending leftwards to reach the rib above the Opium Den of
Chinaman. Follow this to a grassy stance.
6   30 feet. Wend up left to a stance on the edge.
7   50 feet. Continue traversing, ascending slightly, to gain a
prominent spike. Climb over this, and move across the top of a
steep chimney to reach a fine block belay 10 feet beyond.
8   60 feet. Ramble on easily on the same course to arrive at the
right-bounding rib of the upper gully of Compression. Follow
this up to a ledge leading into the gully, and go along to a stance
below a short groove.
9   35 feet. Climb the groove to a stance.
10   100 feet. Continue up easily to emerge a few yards from the
top of the Companionway.
It is possible to escape upwards at many points when one has
had a surfeit of vegetation.

THE ROCK OF AGES

At a slightly lower level than Y Diffwys on the northern slope of
Cwm Bleiddiaid is an attractive little outcrop of excellent rock. It
has many short pitches of about 40 feet.

THE SUMMIT CLIFFS O.S. ref. SH 567 467

These rather broken crags, overlooking upper Cwm Cloch, bound the eastern side of the summit plateau for about three-quarters of a mile. The cliffs are split in the centre by a large gully, Glyndwr's Ladder (otherwise known as Simnai Foel Hebog). Only two routes exist and these offer much scope for variation. The buttress on the left of the gully, South Buttress, contributes the following route:

Pursuer's Folly 240 feet Very Difficult (1952)
Start at the lowest point of the buttress, immediately to the left of the bottom of the gully.
1 70 feet. Climb directly up the front of the buttress to the base of a double groove. Step round the sharp dividing nose to the right, and continue up the trough above for 20 feet. Move back left, then go right again at the top to the grassy terrace. Good block belay.
2 30 feet. Walk to the foot of the main wall and climb a depression on the right for 15 feet to reach a ledge 20 feet out from the gully.
3 60 feet. Climb the slab from the left-hand end of the ledge for a few feet, then traverse to the left edge. Continue up this, over a block, to belay above.
4 80 feet. Scramble diagonally leftwards across the best of the available material, and gain the left edge above a vertical arête. Go along the narrow ridge to the summit plateau.

Glyndwr's Ladder 250 feet Easy (c.1400)
A solo test-piece of its time: the gully offers a few short pitches interspersed with noisy scree and good rock scenery.

On the right of the gully is Ladder Buttress. The lower tiers of the buttress alongside the gully have been climbed at Very Difficult standard, but the only continuous route here is:

May Rib 150 feet Difficult (1954)
To the right of Ladder Buttress is an isolated rib, formed by a series of short walls and topped by a longer one. Start at the bottom of the rib.
Climb up three short walls to a stance at 40 feet. Ascend the obvious crack in the centre of the wall above, move round left into a corner then go back to the rib (60 feet). Follow a narrow quartz-streaked ridge to the final wall which is taken on the left to easy rocks and the top.

Graded list of climbs in order of difficulty

Back again, to entertain and infuriate, is a list of the main routes in descending order of difficulty. The majority of the newer routes have not been included as they have had very few, if any(!), repeats and cannot accurately be compared with existing routes.

E7
Dream Topping (6c)
Llanberries (6c)
Strawberries (6b)

E6
Light Years (6c)
Psyche 'n Burn (6b)
Potency (6b,6b)

E5
Honorary Grit (6c)
Unreal Finish (6c)
Surreal Mcoy (6c)
Raving Lunatic (6b)
Surreal (6b)
Dwmsday (6a,6b)
Fingerlicker Direct (6b)
Raging Bull (6b)
Heading for Heights (6b,5c)
The Cry (6b)
Weirpig (6b)
Hitler's Buttock (6b)
Balance of Power (6a,5c)
Glasnost (6a,5c)
Death Can Be Fatal (6a)
Hang 'em High (6a)
Groove of Horror (6a)
Marathon Man (6a)
Mongoose (6a)

E4
Bananas (6b)
Poacher (6b)
Sexual Salami (6b)
Compromising Positions (6b)
Cardiac Arête (6b)
Penicillin (6b)
Tramgo (6a)
Zukator (6a)
Wailing Wall (6a)
Crimson Cruiser (6a)

Equinox (6a)
The Toit (6a)
Sonic Sinbin (6a)
Spare Rib (6a)
Dune Child (6a)
Sultans of Swing (6a)
Bigger Bug (6a)
Psycho (6a)
The Moon (6a)
The Widowmaker (6a)
Bing The Budgie (6a)
Vulture (6a)
Fingerlicker (6a)
Bourdillon's Crack (5a,6a)
Sleeping Beauty (5c)
Non-dairy Creamer (5c)
Danger Days (5c)
Sybilla The Pun (5c)
Leg Break (5c)
Curved Air (5c)
Starship Trooper (5c)
Marshall Hearts (5c)

E3
The Fugitive (6b)
The Atomic Finger Flake (6a)
Vulcan (6a)
Void (6a)
Cidwm Girdle
Hogmanay Girdle (6a)
Cream (6a)
Neb Direct (6a)
Croaker (6a)
Mangoletsi (6a)
Tall Dwarfs (6a)
Pellagra (6a)
Hot Rats (6a)
Ringwraith (6a)
Blade Runner (6a)
Darkside (6a)
Technical Master (6a)
Venom (6a)

E3 contd.
Pengo's Eliminate (6a)
Fear (6a)
Terraqua (6a)
Dwm (free) (6a)
Central Wall (5c,5c)
Samurai Groove (5c)
Perdido Street (5c)
Nosferatu (5c)
Erebus (5c)
Green Wall (5c)
Dulyn Groove (5c)
Titanium Man (5c)
Silly Arête (5c)
Integral Direct (5c)
King Kong/Troubador Connection (5c)
Poker (5c)
Heartline (5c)
Plastic Nerve (5c)
Scarecrow (5c)
Slopey (5c)
Bandersnatch (5a,5c)
Geireagle (5c)
Freudian Slip (5c)
Chance Encounter (5b)

E2
Clean Edge (6a)
Dragon (6a)
Itch (6a)
Johnson's Wall (6a)
Orodruin (6a)
Burlesque (6a)
Return of the Horsemen (5c)
Jabberwocky (5a,5c)
Riparian (5c)
Civetta (5c)
Endgame (5c)
Erection (5c)
Tensor (5c)
Vector (5c)
The Grasper (5c)
Castell Girdle (5c)
Straw Dogs (5c)
Extraction (5c)
Daddy Cool (5c)
Steel Fingers (5c)
The Deceiver (5c)
The Wasp (5c)

Primus (5c)
Lonely Edge (5c)
The Weaver (5c)
The Sting (5c)
Nimbus (5c)
Pincushion (5c)
The Olympiad (5c)
Overhanging Cracks (5c)
Hardd (5c)
The Struggler (5c)
The Snake (5c)
Brutus (5a,4a,5c)
Falcon (5c)
The Oxbow Incident (5c)
Raven's Nest Wall (5c)
Sisyphus (5c)
Blinkers (5b)
Integral (5c)
Cheap Trick (5b)
The Muleman (5b)
Groan (5b)
Glwm (5b,5a,5b,5a)
The Burner (5b)
Death Wisher (5b)
Codswallop (5a,5b)
Gormenghast (5b)
Titus (5b)
Ferdinand (5b)
Penamnen Groove (4c,5c)

E1
Toreador (5c)
Cursor (5c)
Valour (5c)
First Slip (5c)
The Spook (5c)
Wall of Ghouls (5c)
Anagram (5c)
Ogof Direct (4b,5c,5a)
Eureka (5b,5b)
Crocadillo (5b)
Diadic (5b)
Pretzel Logic (5b)
The Jackal (5b)
Zwm (5b)
Final Exam (5b)
Peuterey Girdle (5b)
One Step in the Crowds (5b)
Ivy Crack (5b)

E1 contd.
The Ent (5b)
Muscles (5b)
Torero (5b)
Ace High (5b)
Acoustic Flake (5b)
Condor (5b)
Skerryvore (5b)
Laser Crack (5b)
The Plum (5b)
Valerian (5b)
Barbarian (5b)
Tarantula (5b)
Dislocation (5b)
Grim Wall Direct (5b)
Thirty-nine Steps (5a)
Femaelstrom (5a)

HVS
Crucible (4c,5b,5a)
Vindaloo (5b)
Great Feet (5b)
Eifionydd Wall (5b)
Silver Crow (5b)
Gwaed (5b)
Chwys (5b)
Picador (5b)
Fiddler on the Dole (5b)
The Straighter (5b,4c)
Ectoplasm (5b)
Bovine (5b)
Niobe (5b)
Aquila (5a)
Fratricide Wall (5a)
The Fang (5a)
Leg Slip (5a)
Space Below My Feet (5a)
Gethsemane (5a)
Belshazzar (5a)
Biggles (5a)
Monkey Puzzle (5a)
Slipway (5a)
Soft Touch (5a)
Agoraphobia (5a)
Maybelline Finish (5a)
Javelin (5a)
Helsinki Wall (5a)
Sunset Traverse (5a)
Salamanda (5a)

Vestix (5a)
The Matador (5a)
Gothic Grooves (5a)
Bucket Rider (5a)
G-string (5a)
Earthsea (5a)
Flake Wall (5a)
Holloway (5a)
Plasma (5a)
Meshach (5a)
Vertigo (5a,4c)
Stromboli (5a)
Mean Feat (5a)
Tantalus (5a)
Kestrel Cracks (5a)
Y Broga (5a)
Scratch Arête (5a)
Bovril (5a)
Maelstrom (4c)
The Curver (4c,4c)
Kellogg Crack (4c)
Gallop Step (4c)
Hyll-Drem Girdle (4c)

VS
Mallory's Ridge (4c)
Striptease (5a)
Double Criss (5a)
Grotto Direct (5a)
Nifl-Heim (4c)
Alcatraz (4c)
Titan (4c)
Kirkus's Route (4b,4b,4c,4c)
Touch and Go (4c)
Oakover (4c)
Congl (4c)
Grim Wall (4c)
Forte Strapiombo (4c)
Peachpla (4c)
The Liquidator (4c)
Sphincter (4c)
Pear Tree Variation (4c)
Grotto (4c)
Right Touch (4c)
Overcome (4c)
Gwastadnas (4c)
The Chateau (4c)
Great Western (4c)
Plumbline (4c)

VS contd.
Strangeways (4c)
Oxine (4c)
The Castle (4c)
In Memoriam (4c)
Sheerline (4c)
Pinky (4c)
Nazgul (4c)
Astonall (4c)
Carol Crack (4c)
The Brothers (4c)
Avalon (4c)
Olympic Slab (4c)
Hedera (4c)
Thin Wall Special (4c)
Merlin (4c)

Clapton's Crack (4c)
One Step in the Clouds (4c)
Mensor (4c)
Shadrach (4c)
Oxo (4c)
Inverted Staircase (4c)
Shake (4b)
Leviathan Direct (4b)
Via Gellia (4b)
Lavaredo (4b)
Lightning Visit (4b)
Clonus (4b)
Split Finger (4b)
Scratch (4b)
Yogi (4b)

First ascents

AL and VL in brackets indicate alternate and varied leads respectively. The number of any points of aid known to have been used during a first ascent is given in brackets after the name of the route. Where a route was originally given an artificial grade this is indicated by an A grade in the brackets.

c. 1400   **Glyndwr's Ladder** (Moel Hebog)   O Glyndwr (on-sight solo)
A strong English party failed to follow!

1900's   **The Gwynant Crack**   The Pioneers
'The wall is split by a crack which invites the super-gymnast. The last eight feet are devoid of holds and overhangs. The only ascent on record was made by an expert with the aid of five other experts stationed on the top of the rock.'

1905   **Castell Cidwm Gully**   W P Haskett Smith
'Here there are two capital bits which make one wish to have either four hands or four feet, as most of the excellent handholds are towards the same side of the gully, and most of the equally fine footholds are just out of reach on the opposite side.'
W P H S, 1905 C.C.Journal
'It has three pitches. The first is a dark wet cave at 40 feet high, which is climbed to the right of the capstone, where one bush assists and another impedes the progress of the climber.'
1926 guide
'This route can hardly by regarded as much of an achievement, for there is only 15 feet of climbing.'
New Climbs 1966

1905   **Wolf's Buttress** (Castell Cidwm)   W P Haskett Smith and party

1905   **Pinnacle Ridge** (Craig y Bera)   W P Haskett Smith, G Hastings and party

1905   **Eastern Arête** (Y Garn)   W P Haskett Smith and party
'Passing through some fallen blocks at the very foot you are forced to the left, and find a square angle, and mounting on a sort of wardrobe on the right you work up in the angle. Personally I found it a place where, when the second man joined me on the top of the wardrobe, my peace of mind was substantially increased.'
1905 C.C.Journal

1909   **Lockwood's Chimney** (Bustach)   A Lockwood
' . . . provides amusement for all who wish to salve an idle conscience by a brief spell of energy.'

1910   **Sentries' Ridge** (Craig y Bera)   J M A Thomson, H O Jones, K J P Orton

1911 Easter   **North Gully, Central Ridge** (Llechog)   H M F Dodd, J M A Thomson

*'On the stiff upper passage the leader could certainly be
aided, but on the lower this would hardly be possible.'*

H R C Carr on North Gully

1911 Easter	**The Grey Gully and Wall** (Llechog) H O Jones, Miss B Jones, K J P Orton, Mrs Orton

*Not by the line described which was climbed by B K
Barber and A S Pigott on 12 June 1938.*

*'An easy scramble is succeeeded by 70 feet of climbing
similar to that in the Bracket Gully of Lliwedd.'*

1911 Easter	**Five Cave Gully** (Llechog) H O Jones, R Todhunter (AL), L Noon

*'Todhunter and Noon boldly bid for a Gargantuan mouth
away on the left.'*

1912 C.C.Journal

*'A second but steeper groove is then tackled, and a
mantelshelf five feet higher attained. Both these grooves
entail a strenuous struggle, whose severity the second
man can only slightly mitigate with a push. The third man,
meanwhile, is wedged in the cave, but his opportunities
for anchoring are hardly adequate.'*

J M A Thomson

1911 Easter	**Adam Rib** (Craig Cwm Du) J M A Thomson and party

*A fine start to exploration on a new crag. They avoided the
final pitch by traversing into Eden Gully. The final pitch
and the more direct line described were climbed by G H L
Mallory and R Todhunter in September 1912.*

1911 Easter	**Knight's Move Climb** (Craig Cwm Du) J M A Thomson and party

*The present start was first climbed by M W Guinness, G L
Reid and Miss Hughes on 30 May 1925.*

1911 Easter	**Grass Pitch Gully** (Craig Cwm Du) J M A Thomson and party

*'Leader needs 30 feet of rope and anything likely to assist
him in clinging to precipitous vegetation.'*

*The grass pitch disappeared in 1945 (but it is not known
who disappeared with it!).*

1911 Easter	**Lichen Ridge** (Craig Cwm Du) J M A Thomson and party

*'Conscientious adherence to rock ensures an agreeable
climb.'*

Little is known about the initial exploration of Craig Cwm Du but Thomson
initially pioneered 12 routes which varied from Moderate to exceedingly
difficult. One of them: 'A certain gully pitch has characteristics that are
unique within the combined knowledge of our party.' Thomson's party
did however return at Whitsuntide, staying at the Snowdon Ranger Hotel.
It consisted of: W A Brigg, W P Haskett Smith, Dr L Noon, Mrs Orton, Prof.
K J P Orton and of course Thomson. On the Friday evening they ascended
a new route of some interest at Castell Cidwm. On the Saturday they did a
new gully on Mynydd Mawr which yielded a 'pretty climb with an airy face
finish. The East Ridge of Y Garn, destined some day to become a favourite
expedition occupied Sunday. The last day was devoted to Llechog.'

1911 Whit	**The Mermaid Climb** (Llechog) J M A Thomson, W P Haskett Smith, W A Brigg

'It will be gathered at once from the name that this climb presents to the eye an attractive front, but tails off not far from the middle.'

H R C Carr

1911 Whit   **The Central Rib** (Llechog)   J M A Thomson, W P Haskett Smith, W A Brigg

'It will be gathered that steadiness and precision of movement are necessary throughout the climb. The leader cannot be aided. The rock is of splendid quality, and, to the best of my recollection, not a single fragment was removed. To strong parties, and to them only, the Central Rib can be recommended without reserve.'

1911 Jun. 18   **Black Rib** (Llechog)   J M A Thomson, H O Jones, Mrs Orton

'A leaf on the right has to be seized at a given moment with a stretching reach, otherwise the problem is apt to prove puzzling and to cause ingeniously intricate poses of the body.'

1912 C.C.Journal

1911 Jun. 18   **Torpedo Route, Cloister Climb** (Llechog)   J M A Thomson, H O Jones, Mrs Orton

'As Cloister Climb was our third ascent of the day, our party may possibly have slightly overrated its difficulty, but we were certainly impressed with the severity of some of the passages encountered.'

1911 Sep.   **Eastern Gutter, Trinity Buttress** (Llechog) G H L Mallory, H E L Porter

Both of these routes were 'lost' for many years due to poor descriptions (there must be a moral here for all first ascensionists!).
Trinity Buttress was rediscovered in June 1938 by B K Barber, A S Pigott and F Solari.
Eastern Gutter had to wait until 4 May 1980 for its reidentification and the second ascent by H I Banner and M Yates.

1911 Sep.   **Mallory's Ridge** (Y Garn)   H E L Porter, G H L Mallory

A fine climb which was unjustifiably neglected: it had acquired a notorious reputation for difficulty and looseness and so was omitted from Carr's guide.'
The line described was taken on the second ascent on 18 September 1949 by E W Dance, W Gordon, G Eglinton.
The two variations to the crux pitch were climbed by : D Clutterbuck, P L B Pilling on 10 August 1951; and H Storey, F Gandy on 15 July 1956.
'In Cumberland the first question one is always asked about Wales is, "But isn't the rock very loose?" There is much more rock in Wales.'

John Laycock, 1912 F.R.C.C. Journal

1911 Sep.	**Four Pitch Gully** (Clogwyn y Cysgod) G H L Mallory, R Todhunter *The start of climbing in Cwm Silyn and it is rather surprising that they did not go for the Great Slab.*
1912 Sep.	**Pis-Aller Rib** (Craig Cwm Du) R Todhunter, G H L Mallory *Repeated by R B Clayton, G W Wood on 15 May 1950 and thinking it to be new they called it Beer-Cellar Rib.*
1912 Sep.	**Yellow Buttress** (Craig Cwm Du) G H L Mallory, R Todhunter
1913	**Sunset Rib** (Craig yr Ogof) R Todhunter, G L Keynes, R Muhlberg
1913	**Trinity Buttress** (Llechog) R Todhunter, G L Keynes, H A H Percy, G H L Mallory *Another lost route which was finally located and reascended by B K Barber, A S Pigott and J R Jenkins on 15 May 1938.*
1920 Whit	**The South Buttress, The North Buttress** (Craig Trum y Ddysgl) E W Steeple, G Barlow, A H Doughty
1925 Apr. 10	**The Overhanging Chimneys** (Trwyn y Graig) E Downes, H R C Carr, W McNaught *'Calling loudly upon the patron saint of the locality, the leader explores the smooth vertical face with eager fingers. The saint, responsive to so urgent a request, opens a cunning little cavity in the rock precisely where it is least expected and most desired. The thankful climber is now able to swing out boldly across the wall and quickly gains the security of the chimney.'* *Maurice's Crack at the start of pitch 2 was climbed by M W Guinness, M S Gotch, H R C Carr and W McMillan on 25 August 1925.* *The Direct Finish was climbed by A J J Moulam, J H Longland, F Mayo, J L Longland on 13 April 1952.* *'. . . and then enter the crack. The manoeuvre is strongly reminiscent of the start of the Kern Knotts Crack. The crack itself is just as steep as the Cumbrian rival, but demands delicate balance rather than strenuous exertion.'*
1925 Apr. 10	**Engineers' Climb** (Craig Fawr) E Downes, G A Lister
1925 Apr. 12	**Deep Chimney** (Trwyn y Graig) H R C Carr, W K McMillan, W McNaught
1925 Apr.	**The Recess Route** (Trwyn y Graig) E Downes, H R C Carr, E Hewitt, W McNaught, W K McMillan
1925 Apr.	**Artist's Climb** (Craig yr Ogof) H R C Carr, D Hewitt
1925 Apr.	**Amphitheatre Buttress**: Original Route (Craig yr Ogof) M G Bradley, B F K O'Malley
1925 Aug 22	**Nirvana Wall** (Craig yr Ogof) H R C Carr, W K McMillan *'Hardly the height of attainment.'*

1971 guide

1925   **L.M.H.** (Craig Fawr)   Oxford University Women's Mountaineering Club party
The party was from Lady Margaret Hall.

1926 Apr. 4   **Ordinary Route** (Craig yr Ogof)   D R Pye, W R Reade, C A Elliot, N E Odell
The Inside Variation was climbed the same day.
The Inside Finish was climbed by J B Joyce on 8 September 1935.

1926   'The Climbers Guide to Snowdon and the Beddgelert District' by H R C Carr
'We are bold enough to hope that this book may weaken the monopoly of Lliwedd in the Snowdonia area, for it is time that the claims of other cliffs received a more general recognition.'

1927   **Direct Route** (Craig yr Ogof)
The origin of this route is in doubt but C F Kirkus probably added the lower section a few years later.

1928   **The Scarf** (Trwyn y Graig)   E Downes, H R C Carr, Evelyn Ritchie, B H Bathurst
A girdle of the crag above the heather belt†.
'Two long strides are taken to the left, where the climber is embarrassed by impending eaves!
                                                          1926 C.C. Bulletin

1928   **Kirkus's Climb** (Clogwyn yr Oen)   C F Kirkus, C G Kirkus

1931 May 31   **Kirkus's Route** (Craig yr Ogof)   C F Kirkus, G G Mcphee
Also known as Right-Hand Route.
They climbed separate finishes. Mcphee's finish was closer to the modern finish which was recorded by G C Band and E A Wrangham on Central Variant on 13 April 1952.
Variation start by Ordinary Route by J M Edwards, G H D Edwards on 2 August 1931.

1931 Whit   **Non-Engineer's Climb** (Craig Fawr)   R D Graham, G W Anson
100 feet above and left of Engineers' Climb.

1931 Jly 14   **Outside Edge Route** (Craig yr Ogof)   J M Edwards, C H S R Palmer
The Direct Start was climbed by D Clutterbuck, H L Kool, on 2 July 1951.

1931 Jly 14   **Upper Slab Climb** (Craig yr Ogof)   C F Kirkus, A B Hargreaves, A W Bridge

1932 Sep.   **Septentrionale** (Clogwyn Holland)   R Elfyn Hughes
1932 Sep.   **Milky Way** (Craig Fach)   R Elfyn Hughes
1933   **Pi** (Quartz Slab)   R Elfyn Hughes
An easy-angled slab at 67284492.

1933 Mar. 26   **Bedrock Gully** (Clogwyn y Cysgod)   J M Edwards
1933 Mar. 26   **Sweep Wall** (Clogwyn y Cysgod)   J M Edwards
The arête left of Bedrock Gully.

1933 Sep. 6   **Black Gully** (Craig yr Ogof)   G G Cruikshank
It is amazing that there were still gullies left to explore as late as 1933.

1934 Sep.	**Betimes** (Craig y Clipiau) R Elfyn Hughes	
1934 Sep.	**Whiles** (Craig y Clipiau) R Elfyn Huges	
	The chimney to the right of Thin Wall Special buttress.	
1934	**Forest Wall** (Bustach) T C G Tilby, W R Reade	
1935 Apr. 19	**Little Kitchen** (Clogwyn y Cysgod) J M Edwards	
	The right-hand branch of the gully right of Four Pitch Gully.	
1936 Jly 22	**Rib and Tower** (Craig yr Ogof) J E Q Barford, R B Kemball-Cook	
	The route differs slightly from the original which follows Fay Cee Rib more closely.	
1938 Jly 9	**Bending Groove** (Moel Hebog) H T Jackson, P Wareing, S Styles	
	A scrappy route up the depression in the centre of the upper mass.	
1938 Aug. 12	**Jezebel** (Craig Cwm Du) B K Barber, A S Pigott, J E Byrom	
	A large loose gully on the left-hand side of the crag.	
1939 May	**Banker's Buttress** (Craig Fawr) J E Byrom, J Lomas	
1939	**Lone Buttress** (Moel Siabod) C W F Noyce	
1945 Jly 8	**Fay Cee Rib** (Craig yr Ogof) B Wright	
	The sharp rib on the left of Amphitheatre Gully.	
1946 Jly 5	**Angel Pavement** (Craig y Bera) C P Brown, A J J Moulam	
	The Direct Finish was added by A J J Moulam, Miss V A Jones on 17 March 1952.	
1946 Aug. 4	**Oblique Route** (Craig yr Ogof) C P Brown, J P Cooper	
	The main part to the cave had been descended earlier by J P Cooper and party after reaching the Ogof in 1935.	
1947 Dec. 25	**Christmas Climb** (Craig y Dyniewyd) P O Work, E S Trickett	
1948 Jun. 16	**Reunion Cracks** (Y Garn) P R Hodgkinson, J Gianelli	
1949 Feb. 24	**Residents' Wall** (Llechog Facet) P O Work, G W Staunton	
1949 Jun. 4	**Jericho** (Craig yr Ogof) R G Folkard, P Wilkinson	
	A route leading out of the subsidiary gully 250 feet below the top of the Great Stone Shoot.	
1949 Jun. 5	**Gardener's Gully** (Trwyn y Graig) R G Folkard, A J Hyde	
	The damp line which The Recess avoids.	
1949 Sep. 17	**Slab and Groove** (Llechog) E W Dance, W Gordon	
1949 Sep. 18	**Nadroedd** (Llechog Facet) E W Dance, W Gordon	
	The leaning heathery buttress on the right-hand side of the North Bluff.	
1949 Oct. 16	**Primrose Path** (Craig y Bera) P R Hodgkinson, J Gianelli	
1949 Dec. 29	**Eve's Folly** (Craig Cwm Du) J T Hughes, K E Oldham	
1950 Jan. 6	**Two Chimney Route** (Moel Hebog) P O Work, D E Pullin	
	'A good bad weather route starting 10 yards to the right of a point directly below Pink Slab.'	
1950 Apr. 9	**Lamb's Leap** (Castell Cidwm) D Sutton, W Gordon	
1950 Apr. 9	**Manchester Rib** (Craig Cwm Du) R B Clayton, M Fenton	
	Climbed in error for Pis-Aller Rib.	

1950 May 12	**Leo's Wall, Fox Route, Oppenauer Slab** (Craig Cwm Du) R B Clayton, G W Wood *The 1971 guidebook describes these routes as being recommended when the cliff is intolerably crowded.*
1950 May 26	**Gash Wall** (Craig y Dyniewyd) A J J Moulam, P R J Harding, G Dyke
1950 Jun. 9	**Caterpillar** (Moel Hebog) P O Work, B E Nicholson *A line up to and passing a triangular alcove which can even be seen from outside Beddgelert Post Office – if one looks in the right direction.* *The start of a perverse enthusiasm for this rather unfashionable cliff.*
1950 Jun. 9	**Chinaman** (Moel Hebog) P O Work, B E Nicholson
1950 Jun. 15	**Maidan Variant** (Moel Hebog) P O Work, T Jepson *'An intriguing route including introductions to the Shrine and the Maidan without sacrificing direct upward progression.'.*
1950 Jun. 22	**Omega** (Moel Hebog) P O Work, G W Staunton
1950 Jun. 25	**Finale Wall** (Castell Cidwm) N A Thomson, G Eglinton *Also recorded as Finals Wall.*
1950 Jly 1	**Two Pitch Buttress** (Moel Hebog) T W Hughes *Right of Pink Slab and Toy Crack Climb.*
1950 Jly 3	**Explorers' Traverse** (Moel Hebog) P O Work, T W Hughes
1950 Jly 13	**Pink Slab** (Moel Hebog) P O Work, M Rowland, G W Staunton
1950 Jly 15	**Lodestone** (Moel Hebog) B E Nicholson, G W Staunton *A line to the left of the Companion Way rake.*
1950 Jly 25	**The Bar Steward** (Llechog Facet) F G Dennis, R C Davies *A shallow ridge on the right-hand side of the Lower Cliff.*
1950 Aug. 3	**Tension Crack** (Moel Hebog) F Ashton, F Gough, G W Staunton, P O Work
1951 Mar. 28	**Hound's Head Buttress** (Pant Ifan) A J J Moulam, G J Sutton *The first route at Tremadog. The route was blasted in 1963.*
1951	**North Chimney** (Bustach/Moelwyns) S Styles
1951 Easter	**Easter Parade** (Craig Stwlan) S Styles, R W Willmer
1951 Apr. 17	**Great Chimney Wall** (Bustach) C R Upton
1951 May 13	**Shadrach** (Bwlch y Moch) A J J Moulam, G W S Pigott, D Thomas
1951 May 18	**Maidan Buttress** (Moel Hebog) J Derry, D Meigh
1951 Jun. 7	**Colin's Gully** (Clogwyn y Cysgod) C B Wilson, E A Wrangham, J F Adams, A Wailes-Fairbairn *A vague gully near the right-hand end of the cliff.*
1951, Jun. 9	**Maidan Gully** (Moel Hebog) E W Dance, G Eglinton, A E Davies *Even in 1951 new gullies still appear!*
1951 Jun. 9	**The Greenhouse Roof** (Llechog Facet) K B Oldham, P Wadsworth, G Eglinton *Above and to the right of the Bar Steward.*

1951	**Kirkus's Direct** (Craig yr Ogof) V Ridgeway and party	

Pitch 3 was added by B Ingle, R G Wilson on 20 May 1963.

1951 Jly 12   **Creagh Dhu Wall** (Castell)   J Cunningham, W Smith, P Vaughan
The first of the raiders – and not the last!
Variation Finish: D T Roscoe, A J J Moulam.
Variation pitch one: A Beanland, C T Jones in November 1957.
'The description given in the interim guide was insufficient to identify the climb. Here is a better one . . . '

1956 C.C.Journal

1951 Jly 12   **Valerie's Rib** (Bwlch y Moch)   P Vaughan, W Smith, J Cunningham

1951 Jly 23   **Belshazzar** (Bwlch y Moch)   P Vaughan, K V Ingold
Quite a hard lead; by 1956 the route had been graded Extremely Severe.

1951 Sep. 3   **Canyon Rib** (Aberglaslyn)   P O Work, T Blackburn

1951 Oct. 7   **South Chimneys** (Bustach/Moelwyns)   S Styles, H Morris

1951 Dec. 25   **Christmas Route** (Moel Hebog)   C R Upton, T Weir
A line to the right of Chinaman.

1952 Mar. 8   **Rienetta** (1 pt. aid) (Bwlch y Moch)   A J J Moulam, D Thomas
'Crux (hard in nails). Make a difficult mantelshelf up left onto a grassy ledge, with aid from a sling round the (re-inserted) chockstone.' This climb has suffered from two large rockfalls. On both occasions it was cleaned and reclimbed by C J Phillips.

1952 Mar. 17   **No Highway** (Craig y Bera)   A J J Moulam, Miss V A Jones

1952 Mar. 22   **Quest for Corbeau** (Craig Cwm Dulyn)   A J J Moulam, J M Barr

1952 Apr. 13   **Terror Infirmer** (Trwyn y Graig)   A J J Moulam, J H Longland, F Mayo, J L Longland
Between Overhanging Chimneys and The Recess Route.

1951 Apr. 13   **Central Variant** (Craig yr Ogof)   G C Band, E A Wrangham
Finishing up what is now the finish to Kirkus's Route. The present finish was climbed by B Ingle, G Rogan on 12 May 1966.

1952 May 8   **North Route** (Moel Hebog)   P O Work, Miss R J Ruck
The right-hand edge of Maidan Buttress.

1952 May 20   **Pineways** (Aberglaslyn Pass)   P O Work, B E Nicholson
Start at a giant boulder by the Fisherman's Path 200 yards up stream from the bridge.

1952 Jun. 15   **Evasion** (Wrysgan)   M J O'Hara, S Styles, D Esmond

1952 Jun. 15   **Floating Rib** (Bustach/Moelwyns)   M J O'Hara, H Morris, D Esmond

A line to the right of Y Drafel evading the challenge of the big quartzy slab by an obvious left to right fault, left of the nose.

1952 Jun. 22   **Reason in Revolt** (Craig y Bera)   A J J Moulam, W R Craster
He had climbed here before and should have known what to expect.

1952 Jly 3   **Pursuer's Folly** (Moel Hebog)   P O Work, Miss R J Ruck

1952 Jly 5   **Ogof Direct** (8 pts. aid) (Craig yr Ogof)   A J J Moulam, G W S Pigott, W Bowman
'The challenge of this awe-inspiring face was taken up by many before the successful ascent. Most of those who failed finished up the upper part of Green Gully. Eight pitons were used on the first ascent and several are essential. At least one etrier has been found useful.'

1955 Supplement

The day started with 17 people most of whom were left at the Ogof when the ascent was completed late in the day. The Direct finish, now incorporated into the description was climbed with 1 point of aid by H Smith, R Handley and C T Jones on 11 August 1956. The aid had been reduced to 2 points by 1966. First free ascent unknown..

1952 Aug. 28   **Corner of Roots** (Bustach)   J M Edwards, H C Bryson
The corner left of Lockwood's Chimney.
'Brush past a fallen tree to a grassy ledge with a small forest.'

1952 Aug. 28   **The Tenth Rib** (Bustach)   J M Edwards, H C Bryson

1952 Aug. 31   **Side Entry** (Bustach)   J M Edwards, H C Bryson, A Shutt

1952 Dec. 13   **Chic** (Clogwyn yr Oen)   A J J Moulam, W R Craster, C W Brasher
Variations have been done by many people. In particular, R Elfyn Hughes wandered all over this face.
The theme song for this ascent was California Here I Come.

1953   **Grey Slab** (Wrysgan)   D H Jones, G Williams

1953 Apr. 5   **Creeper** (Bustach/Moelwyns)   M J Harris, J Neill

1953 Apr. 5   **Slick** (Clogwyn yr Oen)   A J J Moulam, J A F Watson, R G Hargreaves
Some of this had been climbed by R Elfyn Hughes in 1932.

1953 Apr. 11   **One For The Road** (Clogwyn yr Oen)   A J J Moulam, J M Barr
Pitches 5 and 6 were added by J Neill, A T Griffith in 1955.

1953 Apr. 12   **Bent** (Clogwyn yr Oen)   A J J Moulam, J M Barr
A similar line had been climbed earlier by R Elfyn Hughes in 1932.

1953 Apr. 12   **Orange Outang** (Clogwyn yr Oen)   A J J Moulam, J M Barr

1953 Apr. 12   **Pied Piper** (Clogwyn yr Oen)   A J J Moulam, J M Barr

1953 Apr. 12	**Oxo** (Wenallt) J R Lees, G D Roberts, W A Trench
	'. . . *those spurning the use of various not very*
	substantial bushes will use a piton for a belay.'
1953 Apr. 15	**Pinky** (Clogwyn yr Oen) I G McNaught-Davies, C W
	Brasher
	The upper pitches were done on the same day by T F
	Mawe, D Thomas, E M Herbert.
1953 Apr. 15	**Toy Crack Climb** (Moel Hebog) P O Work, Miss R Busby
	The right-hand of three fissures to the right of Two
	Chimney Route..
1953 Apr. 15	**Anaconda** (Moel Hebog) P O Work, Miss R Busby
	Midway between Bending Groove and Caterpillar.
1953 May 16	**Betimes** (Craig y Clipiau) G C Curtis, J Neill, M J Harris
	The original route up the central depression, later taken
	by Depression Direct.
1953 May	**Waney Edge** (Wenallt) G D Roberts, W A Trench
	At the right-hand side of the cliff.
1953 Jun. 2	**Y Drafel** (Wrysgan) D H Jones, G Williams
1953 Jun. 2	**Taith y Pererin** (Wrysgan) G Williams, D H Jones
1953 Jun. 12	**Honeysuckle Wall** (Craig y Llyn) D H Haworth, Miss J M
	Tester
1953 Jly 19	**Block** (Clogwyn yr Oen) A J J Moulam, J H Longland, J V
	Rusher
	Pitches 4 to 6 C Bramfitt in June 1953.
1953 Jly 27	**Y Gelynen** (Wrysgan) R Davies, G Williams
1953 Aug. 16	**Africa Rib** (Craig y Clipiau) R Buckland, J Neill
1953 Aug. 16	**Depression Direct** (Craig y Clipiau) M J Harris
	The first pitch only: pitch 2 added by E Beard in 1965.
1953 Aug. 16	**Usher's Dilemma** (Craig y Clipiau) R Buckland, J Neill
	The Eagle Finish: J R Lees, K C Gordon in April 1961.
1953 Sep. 5	**Yggdrasil** (Bwlch y Moch) D R Fisher, E A Wrangham, A
	Tissieres, R R E Chorley
	'*A feeble climb, except for the crack at the top of the rake*
	on Shadrach Buttress.'
1953 Sep. 6	**Double-Criss** (Craig y Clipiau) C J S Bonington, C W
	Brasher
1953 Sep. 6	**Thin Wall Special** (Craig y Clipiau) C J S Bonington, C W
	Brasher
1953 Nov.	**Carol Crack** (Wenallt) G D Roberts, J Lines
1953 Dec. 12	**Pocked Wall** (Craig Stwlan) M J Harris, J Neill
1953 Dec. 12	**Original Route** (Alltrem) A J J Moulam, G J Sutton
1953 Dec. 12	**Bay Groove** (Alltrem) A J J Moulam, J M Barr
1953 Dec. 12	**Route II** (Alltrem) G W S Pigott, J M Barr
1953 Dec. 12	**Green Gully** (Carreg Flaen-Llym) M J Harris, J Neill
	'*Very vegetated and slimy with dirty scrambles between.*'
1953 Dec. 13	**Backstairs** (Gesail) M J Harris, J Neill
	Halfway up Backstairs Gully to finish on Sheerline
	Buttress.
1953 Dec. 13	**Bramble Buttress** (Gesail) M J Harris, J Neill

| 1953 Dec 16 | **Bandolier Traverse** (Clogwyn yr Oen)   G J Sutton, M J Bailey |

A varied girdle traverse of the crag.

1953 Dec. 19   **Princess** (Gesail)   M J Harris, J Neill

1953 Dec. 19   **Scratch** (Pant Ifan)   A J J Moulam, W R Craster

'Only the crux is hard, but it is inescapable.' 'Crux. Climb the crack in the corner, by a dirty layback (the aid of pitons may be needed if the rocks are greasy).'

1953 Dec. 20   **Poor Man's Peuterey** (Pant Ifan)   G J Sutton, J Gaukroger

Originally this started up what is now the lower part of Borchgrevinck.

1953 Dec. 20   **Clutch** (4 pts. aid) (Gesail)   A J J Moulam, W R Craster, J F Mawe

'Four pitons required as climbing aids.'

1953 Dec. 20   **Sheerline** (Gesail)   D R Bell, D Thomas

1953 Dec. 25   **Christmas Curry** (Bwlch y Moch)   A J J Moulam, J M Barr

The upper part of the Micah Eliminate was climbed in 1954 by M J Harris and the lower part was added later by A Strapcans, R Brown.
The Treemudrock Finish: C T Jones in 1968.
The Finish of Moments: G Gibson in 1978.

1954 Jan. 2   **Hogmanay Hangover** (Pant Ifan)   M J Harris, J Neill

Pitch 1 and 2: S G Moore, C T Jones, G A P Knapp, K J Clark on 9 June 1954.

1954 Jan. 3   **Badger's Buttress** (Pant Ifan)   G J Sutton, G C Band

200-300 ft left of Olympic Slab.

1954 Jan. 4   **Olympic Slab** (Pant Ifan)   J K Disley, Miss S Cheeseman

Pitch 1 was added by B D Hogan, C T Jones in 1958.

1954 Mar. 28   **Hail Bebe** (Bwlch y Moch)   A J J Moulam, J M Barr

1954 Mar. 12   **Shake** (Bwlch y Moch)   G D Roberts, W A Trench

1954 early   **Vaughan's Crack** (Wenallt)   P Vaughan

A hard variation start to Carol Crack.

1954 Apr. 4   **Ave Atque Vale** (Pant Ifan)   M J Harris, J Neill

A route up the left-hand side of Peuterey Buttress.

1954 May 2   **May Rib** (Moel Hebog)   T W Hughes, W Wynn

An isolated rib on the right-hand edge of Ladder Buttress.

1954 May 9   **Tu Tin Tut** (Craig Cwm Trwsgl)   M J Harris, J Neill, D Thomas

1954 May 23   **Treasurer's Wall** (Wenallt)   P Hampson, W V Lamb, E Siddall

Another variation start to Carol Crack.

1954 Jun. 11   **Gam Bay** (Aberglaslyn)   A J J Moulam, Mrs E Upton

A route on the mass of rock north of the buttress with Tunnel Rib.

1954 Jun. 26   **Pastures New** (Craig Cwm Trwsgl)   G W S Pigott, W R Craster

*'Halfway along this cliff between the north-west corner
and the gully is a vague rib line. Take this line, most of the
rock being avoided on vegetation, then break through the
overhangs above by quite arbitrarily an interesting slab.
Quite artificial and unworthy.'*

1954 Jun. 26   **Fresh Woods** (Craig Cwm Trwsgl)   M J Harris, J Neill
*The steep broken buttress beyond the gully. A very poor
climb.*

1954 Jun. 26   **Owl** (Craig Isallt)   M J Harris, J Neill
*Reaches and breaks out right from the overhangs in the
centre of the face. Called 'Muddle' by Oread parties.
' . . . hard, vegetated and messy.'*

1954 Jun. 26   **Sloe Passage** (Craig Isallt)   G W S Pigott, W R Craster
The second buttress right of Owl.

1954 Jun. 26   **Ivy Buttress** (Craig Isallt)   G W S Pigott, W R Craster
1954 Aug. 1   **Bovril** (Wenallt)   D McKelvey, L Rogerson, Miss M Dutton
1954 Sep. 4   **The Castle** (Gesail)   M J Harris, J Neill
1955 Jan. 30   **Mimsy** (Castell)   G D Roberts, J Neill
Left of the jungle on the left-hand part of the crag.

1955 Feb. 6   **Lucretia** (4 pts. aid – A2) (Pant Ifan)   R R E Chorley, M J
Harris, D C Bull
*An early aid route on Avalanche Buttress. 'Three pitons
and one etrier used on the traverse.*

1955 Apr. 16   **Weep** (Pinacl)   A J J Moulam, Miss P D Chapman
*A line on the three-tiered Craig Dau between the quarry
incline left of Wrysgan and the waterfalls stream.*

1955 Apr. 17   **Much Ado About Nothing** (Pant Ifan)
*A variation finish to Hound's Head Buttress. Ascended on
a top-rope by some of C T Jones, B Hogan, R Morgan, R
Yates.*

1955 Apr. 24   **Jane** (Craig y Llyn)   D E Fielding, S Wiseman
In the neighbourhood of Honeysuckle Wall.

1955 May 7   **Worker's Playtime** (Pant Ifan)   W H Little, S Bodsworth,
Miss B Boughton
Twenty feet right of Hound's Head Pinnacle.

1955 May 14   **Tumbleweed** (Craig y Gelli)   D H Briggs, E W Dance
*A vegetated route starting at the foot of the woody
groove-chimney.*

1955 May 14   **Pothook** (Craig y Gelli)   G W S Pigott, R R E Chorley
1955 May 21   **Strapiombo** (Pant Ifan)   D D Whillans, G J Sutton
*'One of the most exhausting climbs in the district.'
After the first ascent it was acknowledged to be both
impressive and strenuous.*

1955 May 30   **Primrose Path – Perdition** (Craig y Bera)   A J J Moulam,
Miss P D Chapman
*'Above everything is horrid. Up and left a bit to the edge:
Climb over rattling rocks here and finish up the vertical
scree.'*

1955 Jun. 1   **Verti-Veg** (Craig y Llyn) D McKelvey, S Wiseman, B Wright, Miss B Warbrick
A death route right of the gully.

1955 Jun. 4   **Fork** (Bustach/Moelwyns) A J J Moulam, J Neill, Miss P D Chapman

1955 Jun. 5   **Oakover** (Bwlch y Moch) A J J Moulam, G W S Pigott

1955 Jun. 5   **Knell for a Jackdaw** (Bwlch y Moch) G R Robson, J Neill, G W S Pigott

1955 Jun. 5   **Glade Way** (Bwlch y Moch) G W S Pigott, A J J Moulam, G R Robson, J Neill
On Ivy Buttress, Craig Bwlch y Moch, which fell down in the 1970s.

1955 Jun. 11   **Whittington** (Castell) J I Disley, J Neill
'From below the big corner a traverse right not far above the ground (from which it could be reached at many points – but only by painful penetration of thorny jungle) looking for and finding the easy way up the face but only at the right-hand end.'
1956 C.C.Journal

1955 Jun. 26   **Niobe** (2 pts. aid – A1) (Castell) G R Robson, D H Briggs, J Neill
'The lower overhang is made easier by use of an etrier (and one piton for protection), and the upper one by a piton for direct aid (and another for protection).'

1955 Jly 3   **Tantalus** (Castell) H I Banner, J Neill (or was it A T Griffith?)
The route originally finished up Niobe. The new finish was added in 1964 (1 pt. aid) by D Yates, G Simpkin.

1955 Jly   **Asahel** (Craig y Clipiau) R James, R L Roberts

1955 Jly   **Reptile Route** (Craig y Clipiau) Miss P Langley, R James
Via the nose to the left of Africa Rib.

1955   **Misty Wall** (Craig y Llan) B Cooke, E C Webb
Above the village of Dolbenmaen. The left-hand buttress. Direct variations by J N Millward, P Janes, J Welbourne, R Handley on 30 March 1956.

1955 Jly 6   **Arrow Slab** (Llechog) J O'Sullivan, T Williams

1955 Jly 6   **Cross Slab and Arête** (Llechog) J O'Sullivan, T Williams
Situated on the left of the buttress, left of the Central Gully.

1955 Aug. 27   **Aquila** (aid) (Craig y Llyn) H I Banner, J Neill
'This climb only escapes an A grading by virtue of the use of inserted pebbles and slings where pitons and etriers would be more comfortable.'
The variation start was climbed by C T Jones at Easter 1969.

1955 Sep. 3   **Breakfast in Bed** (Craig yr Ogof) M F W Holland, I C Bennett
A line up an obvious weakness in the steep left-hand wall of the gully starting 150 feet below the top of the Great Stone Shoot.

1955 Sep. 3	**Tower of Strength** (Craig yr Ogof) M F Holland, I C Bennett *The direct version was climbed by H I Banner, R G Wilson on 22 April 1962.* *The original route done in 1955 was called* **Breakfast in Bed** *and the direct version in 1962 was claimed as Tower of Strength.*
1955 Sep. 21	**Flake Wall** (Bustach/Moelwyns) D D Stewart, T Kellett
1955 Sep. 25	**Callunacy** (Craig y Llyn) D thomas, J Neill, M J Harris *Ribs right of an open gully, 80 yards left of Honeysuckle Wall.*
1955 Sep. 27	**Helsinki Wall** (1 pt. aid) (Pant Ifan) J H Longland, B E H Maden *'Climb the slab behind the stance for 15 feet with aid from a piton on the way to a large clump of heather, then traverse left to small footholds and a small ledge (hand-inserted piton). Then climb a series of cracks to 6 feet from the top, step right and mantelshelf into or round a thorn bush.'*
1955 Sep. 27	**Nifl-Heim** (Bwlch y Moch) H I Banner, Miss E M Baldwin *The final crack was added in 1963 by D R Fisher and party.*
1955 Nov. 20	**Oberon** (Bwlch y Moch) A J J Moulam, J Neill, J B Gass, Miss P D Chapman
1955 Dec. 24	**Slab Route** (Craig Isallt) F J Fisher, Miss B N Bird, D Penlington, Miss B Goodwin *Slabs at the left-hand end of the cliffs.*
1955 Dec. 25	**Pear Tree Variation** (Pant Ifan) H Smith, H Drasdo, F Davies *So called because of the difficulty in the pronunciation of Peuterey.*
1955 Dec. 27	**Breeze Buttress** (Bwlch y Moch) J H Longland, A J J J Moulam *Up the right-hand face of the buttress.* *'Much vegetation. Start; penetrate the vegetation to where this steepens.'*
1955 Dec. 28	**Strangeways** (Pant Ifan) H Smith, H Drasdo *'Unfortunately the brambles are tenacious and painful and a prospective party must ponder whether the suffering is worthwhile. Once the rock is reached the climbing is delightful.'*
1955 Dec. 31	**Nos Calan Rib** (Pant Ifan) J H Longland, P Gordon *On the buttress to the right of Hound's Head Pinnacle and a little way left of Porker's Gully.* *'Moss, gorse, oaks etc.'*
1956 Jan. 4	**Limpopo** (Pant Ifan) J H Longland, H B Carslake, P Gordon, R E Kandall *100 feet right of Olympic Slab on the left-hand side of Verdant Buttress.* *'Very vegetated. Not advised . . . a variety of undergrowth rockeries, trees . . . '*

1956 Jan. 8	**Gallop Step** (Bustach) J I Disley, Denise Morin
1956 Apr. 2	**Left-Hand Route** (Craig Isallt) J N Millward, J Welbourne, P Janes
	A route up the left-hand side of Ivy Buttress.
1956 Apr. 2	**Easter Wall** (Craig Isallt) J N Millward, P Janes, F Allen
1956 Apr. 15	**Merlin** (Bwlch y Moch) A J J Moulam, B A Jillott
	Pitch 2 was climbed by C E Davies, A Cowburn in 1958.
	The Direct Finish: H Smith and party in 1959.
	Pitch one suffered a rock-fall in 1986; reclimbed to the left by P Williams, C Whitehead.
1956 May 26	**Bourdillon's Climb** (VS, A3) (Craig yr Ogof) T D Bourdillon, H G Nicol (AL)
	Originally named Briggs' Climb.
	"This climb had been attempted on numerous previous occasions. The name commemorates, in spite of the objections of the party concerned, an attempt on 18th March 1956 by D H Briggs and D P Davies, during which for the first time a considerable height was reached on the line which was eventually used by the successful party.'
	14 pitons were used on the first ascent and as they were so loose on the main pitch Nicol took the lead as he was the lighter of the pair.
	Probable second ascent with 6 pts. aid by R Evans, M Yates in May 1970.
	First free ascent by M Fowler, C Rowe in 1978.
	There is a slight confusion as in the 1964 C.C. Bulletin it states that B Ingle and R G Wilson made a free ascent of Briggs' Climb. Perhaps this happened during their ascent of Penates. It is however most unlikely that they freed the main pitch of what is now referred to as Bourdillon's Climb.
1956 May 28	**Anniversary Waltz** (Bustach) (A2) T D Bourdillon, M H Westmacott
	The second pitch was climbed using several pegs. The same team with M P Ward had first tried the route on 29 May 1954 – hence the name.
1956 Jun. 2	**Left-Hand Route Direct** (HVS, A2) (Craig Isallt) R Handley, J N Millward
	The thin crack requires 2 pitons.
1956 Jun. 3	**Ash Tree Wall** (Craig Isallt) J N Millward, R Handley
1956 Jly 8	**W.O.B.** (Pant Ifan) D H Briggs, A J J Moulam
	While others bathed. The route described is a more difficult version of the climb. The Pagoda Finish up the groove was so called because 'A Chinese film was being made in Nant Gwynant.'
1956 Aug. 7	**Stromboli** (Pant Ifan) H Smith, C T Jones
1956 Aug. 10	**Swept Wall** (Craig Isallt) J N Millward, Mrs M Millward
1956 Sep.	**Compression** (Moel Hebog) A Neale, J Knowles
1956 Sep.	**Sunset Slabs** (Llechog) A Neale, J Knowles

1956 Sep. 16	**Javelin** (Gesail) D P Davies, D Thomas, J Neill, M J Harris
	The final pitch was climbed by D Yates, G Simpkin in 1964.
1956 Sep. 18	**Penamnen Groove** (1 pt. aid) (Alltrem) R D Downes, Miss J E M Clark
1956 Oct. 6	**Raven's Nest Wall** (aid) (Pant Ifan) G W S Pigott, A Birtwistle
	'A number of pitons were used, mainly for protection.'
1956 Oct. 6	**Pincushion** (16 pts. aid – A2) (Pant Ifan) D P Davies, M J Harris, R R E Chorley
	First free ascent H Barber 1976.
	Numerous attempts had been made on this climb by different parties. By 1958 the aid had been reduced to 6 points and by 1966 to 3 points.
1956 Oct. 7	**Krakatoa** (Pant Ifan) C T Jones, G Eveson
1956 Oct. 13	**Two Face Girdle** (Pant Ifan) C T Jones, G Eveson
	'The abseil was caused by the leader slipping off whilst indulging in rope antics.'
1956 Oct. 21	**Fresher's Folly** (Castell Cidwm) R Wilson, C Buckley
	On the buttress across the stream left of the south wall of Afon Goch, starting left of a dark cave.
1956 Oct. 27	**Arctic Girdle** (Pant Ifan) C T Jones, A Pryke, M G Hanson
	A girdle traverse of Peuterey Buttress.
1956 Oct. 28	**Seven League Chimney** (Pant Ifan) C T Jones, M G Hanson
	On the right of Hound's Head Pinnacle.
1956 Nov. 10	**The Next of Kin** (1 pt. aid) (Pant Ifan) C T Jones, M G Hanson
	Up the gully from Helsinki Wall.
1956 Dec. 8	**Rock 'n Roll** (Pant Ifan) C Pryke, N Knight
	The second wedge-shaped buttress 200 feet right of Hound's Head Pinnacle.
1956 Dec. 24	**Eifionydd Wall** (Pant Ifan) C T Jones, G Eveson, M J Hanson, K J Clark
1956	**Via Gellia** (Craig y Gelli) M J Harris, J Neill, R F Jones
1956	**Orodruin** (3 pts. aid) (Pant Ifan) C T Jones
	Rediscovered, climbed with 1 point of aid and named by F E R Cannings, M A Toole in March 1966.
1957 Jan. 19	**Great Western** (Pant Ifan) C T Jones, M J Hanson
1957 Mar.	**Triangulum** (Bwlch y Moch) H Smith, H Fox, J R Sims, C T Jones
	A route which crossed Hail Bebe.
1957 Mar.	**Grim Wall** (Bwlch y Moch) H Smith, C T Jones, H Fox
1957 Apr. 22	**Borchgrevinck** (Pant Ifan) C T Jones, J R Sims
	Originally this started up what is now the lower part of Poor Man's Peuterey.
1957 May 19	**Bovine** (1 pt. aid) (Wenallt) C E Davies, B D Wright, D McKelvey
1957 Jun. 9	**Oakway** (Gesail) C E Davies, R D Wright, Miss E Millington

At the right-hand end of Princess Buttress.

1957 Jun. 9   **The Brothers** (1 pt. aid) (Bwlch y Moch)   C T Jones, B A F Jones
The Direct Finish: D Yates, T Parker in 1968.

1957 Jun. 23   **Andromeda** (Craig Fach)   S R G Bray, M Blamey
The ubiquitous Elfyn Hughes climbed a similar line in 1932.

1957 Jly   **Mean Feat** (Craig y Clipiau)   R James, P Vaughan

1957 Sep. 1   **Twr** (Carreg y Fran)   R Elfyn Hughes, C West, R West

1957 Oct.   **Oak Tree Wall** (Pant Ifan)   C Pryke, A Fisher
On the buttress right of Rock 'n Roll.

1957 Nov.   **Right Touch** (Gesail)   R James, Miss A Marshall
A V-chimney in the centre of the Midas Buttress.

1957 Nov.   **Touch and Go** (Gesail)   R James, P Benson
The crack above the V-groove was climbed by M Crook, H Walton in 1976.

1957 Nov.   **Foul Touch** (Gesail)   R James, P Benson, M Connelly

1957 Nov.   **Rombold** (1 shoulder aid) (Castell)   A Beanland, C T Jones
Variations around Creagh Dhu Wall.

1958 Jan. 2   **Pigtail Grooves** (Carreg y Fran)   T J Fraser, R Elfyn Hughes

1958 Mar. 20   **Cottage Buttress** (Pant Ifan) (A2)   C J Mortlock, J Cole
An assault on the jungle left of Hound's Head Gully.

1958 Apr. 6   **Girdle Traverse** (Craig y Clipiau)   R James, J M Benson, P H Benson
A 400-foot line which went at HVS.

1958 May 11   **One Step in the Clouds** (Bwlch y Moch)   C T Jones, Ray Moseley

1958 May 26   **Jones's Traverse** (Craig yr Ogof)   C T Jones, B D Wright, A Cowburn
The first two pitches had previously been climbed by C P Brown and J P Cooper on 4 August 1946.

1958 May   **The Maelstrom** (Bustach)   C T Jones, C E Davies, C Pryke
' . . . the most serious undertaking in the valley.'
' . . . climbed with some trepidation and a lack of ability to retreat.'

1958 Jun. 15   **Romulus** (Wrysgan)   G Rees, A F Mason
The central rib left of Babylon.

1958 Jun. 20   **Agog** (Wrysgan)   R L Roberts, E Thomas, G Dwyer, R Dwyer
The Tower Finish: J R Lees, R R Wilson in April 1961.

1958 Summer   **Daufaen** and **Honeysuckle Corner** (Wrysgan)   R L Roberts, G Dwyer, E Thomas
Pitches 1 and 2 only. Honeysuckle Corner: J R Lees, G Moffat in April 1961.

1958 Jly 5   **The White Streak** (Wrysgan)   G Dwyer, R L Roberts

1958 Jly 15   **Little Corner, Gangway** (Wrysgan)   R L Roberts, G Dwyer
The lines to the right of Y Gilfach.

1958 Jly 15	**Babylon** (Wrysgan) G Dwyer, R L Roberts
1958 Jly 22	**Y Gilfach** (Wrysgan) R L Roberts, G Dwyer, E Thomas
1958 Aug. 16	**The Barbarian** (10 pts. aid – A2) (Pant Ifan) C T Jones, C E Davies, Miss E Millington, M King

'The corner was very grassy and the party took 10 hours and ten pitons.' Climbed free by J Brown some time later. An enigmatic contemporary record stated that in 1956 H Smith made an artificial climb up the diedre directly above the lower parts of Scratch (16 pitons).

1958 Aug. 23	**Tiercel** (1 pt. aid) (Castell) C E Davies, W A Trench
1958 Sep. 7	**Inverted Staircase** (Craig y Clipiau) R James, A F Mason, G Rees
1959 Feb. 7	**Ferdinand** (Wenallt) J Brown, C T Jones

'At present this is the hardest free climb in the Nant Gwynant – 1960.'

1959 Feb. 21	**Jones's Crack** (Craig y Clipiau) C T Jones

*The original route up the buttress, **Tarry**, Was by M J Harris, J Neill, on 16 August 1953.*

1959 Apr. 4	**Agrippa** (Pant Ifan) H Smith, Shirley Thomas

Between W.O.B. and Raven's Nest Wall.

1959 May	**Torero** (1 pt. aid) (Wenallt) J Brown, D D Whillans

'Next to Ferdinand it is the most formiddable undertaking in the valley.'

1959 Jun.	**Lightning Visit** (Alltrem) R James, C T Jones
1959 Oct. 10	**Waspie** (Clogwyn yr Oen) J R Lees, R H Newby
1959	**The Bastion** (Bwlch y Moch) (A1) C E Davies, B D Wright

The main pitch, which needed several pitons, is now part of Venom.

1960 Feb. 26	**Primus** (2 pts. aid) (Hyll-Drem) J Brown, C E Davies

The first attack on a very fierce crag.

1960 Mar. 13	**Leg Slip** (Bwlch y Moch) J Brown, C E Davies

Direct Start (2 pts. aid) R Edwards, R Haycroft on 20 September 1964.

1960 Mar. 13	**First Slip** (1 pt. aid) (Bwlch y Moch) J Brown, C E Davies
1960 Mar. 27	**Dwm** (3 pts. aid) (Castell Cidwm) J Brown, H Smith

The start of modern climbing at Cidwm.

'Dwm was the hardest of the first routes, and it was hardly surprising that the great final roof yielded only with aid from pegs.'

New Climbs 1966

H Smith led the last pitch which was running with water and thus required aid. It is likely that less aid would have been needed if the rock had been dry.

1960 Easter	**Hardd** (1 pt. aid) (Hyll-Drem) J Brown, G D Roberts, N Drasdo

'We had been told that Hardd contained the hardest move on British rock and although the author of this statement was hardly in a position to speak with authority, we knew he was a good climber. Rumour had it that Whillans had

> *"jumped" on to a hold, somewhere on the cliff when normal tactics had proved inadequate. Others had raved over the "trundling" from the cliff's overhanging crest on to the road below. The commonest "legend" of all was of those who had gone to climb and stayed to watch.' Dave Cook, 1966.'*
>
> *Direct Finish: M Boysen and party (2 pegs and a sling) on 17 September 1961.*

1960 Mar. 26   **Vector** (2 pts. aid) (Bwlch y Moch)   J Brown, C E Davies
A tremendous route which is one of Brown's masterpieces.
One piton was used on the ochre slab and another was used to exit from the groove on the top pitch prior to the excavation of good holds. Vector has retained much of its early reputation although the excessive number of falling leaders is now past – unfortunately for the spectators below.

1960 Mar. 27   **Hyll-Drem Girdle** (Hyll-Drem)   J Brown, G D Verity
The Maybelline Finish: (2 pts. aid) C Boulton, D Cook (AL) on June 8 1965.

1960 Apr. 17   **Dorcon** (Wrysgan)   R H Newby, J R Lees

1960 Apr. 23   **Fratricide Wall** (1 pt. aid) (Alltrem)   C T Jones, A S Jones, A Daffern

1960 Apr.   **Avalon** (Gesail)   C T Jones, E Siddall

1960 Apr.   **Acropolis** (Gesail)   C T Jones, M J Hanson

1960 Jun. 26   **Vertigo** (1 pt. aid) (Castell Cidwm)   J Brown, B D Wright
The route started off as HVS, later got downgraded and is 'thankfully' for most climbers, back to its original grade.

1960 Sep.   **The Wasp** (5 pts. aid) (Castell)   J Brown, C E Davies
On pitch 1 two slings were used on chockstones. On pitch 2 a sling was used for the bulge, then two pegs.

1960 Sep. 26   **The Curver** (Castell Cidwm)   J Brown, C T Jones
Another route which was HVS, got downgraded, and then intimidated VS leaders for some years.

1960 Nov. 13   **Slack** (Clogwyn yr Oen)   I F Cartledge, J R Lees
Alternative Finish: N Gough in May 1966.

1960 Dec. 4   **Mars** (Craig Fach)   I F Cartledge, J R Lees, K C Gordon
1960 Dec. 4   **Orion** (Craig Fach)   K C Gordon, I F Cartledge, J R Lees
1960   *Snowdon South guidebook by J Neill and Trevor Jones published.*

> *'Tremadoc in particular is becoming very popular. However much mountaineers of the old school may regret cliffs which are divorced from mountains, the most doubtful must admit that rock climbing as a sport of its own, quite apart from mountaineering, has come to stay and flourish. Tremadoc and the other cliffs here described are no longer relegated to days when it is too wet for higher things, but are sought out because they provide routes as attractive for their own sakes as any in Snowdonia. It is hoped that Snowdon South will draw off*

*some of the crowds from Llanberis; but it should be
emphasised that nobody need forsake the tops who does
not want to.*

Wilfrid Noyce, June 1960

1961 Jan. 19	**Clapton's Crack** (Bwlch y Moch)	G Clapton, T Lloyd
1961 Mar. 20	**Lavaredo** (Alltrem)	R James, K Forder, I F Campbell
1961 Mar. 24	**Yogi** (Bwlch y Moch)	G Hodgkiss, M Shannon
1961 Mar. 24	**Boo-Boo** (Bwlch y Moch)	M Edwards, N Crofton
1961 Apr. 3	**Striptease** (Bwlch y Moch)	J Brown, C E Davies

1961 Jun. 2 **The Grasper** (5 pts. aid) (Bwlch y Moch) J Brown, D Thomas bach
A piton low down and four slings were used for aid on the first ascent.

1961 Jun. 4 **The Fang** (Bwlch y Moch) J Brown, C E Davies
The direct variation was added by M Boysen and party in 1962.

1961 Jun. 9 **Space Below My Feet** (aid slings) (Wrysgan) J R Lees, D W Walker

1961 Jun. **The Neb** (Bwlch y Moch) J Brown, D Thomas bach
Pitch 2: M H Lewis, M G Davies in 1968.
Neb Direct (2 aid wedges) (Bwlch y Moch)*was possibly first done by B Brewster.*
First free ascent H Barber.

1961 Jun. **Nimbus** (1 pt. aid) (Bwlch y Moch) J Brown, C Goodey

1961 Aug. **Kestrel Cracks** (Bwlch y Moch) C T Jones, C E Davies
Pitch 1 had been climbed by J Brown, D Thomas bach as the start of The Neb.

1961 Sep. 16 **The Toit** (2 pts. aid) (Pant Ifan) J Brown, J R Allen, C E Davies
First free ascent S Haston c. 1982.

1961 Sep. 16	**The Mole** (Craig y Clipiau)	K H Forder, E Forder
1961 Sep. 17	**Forte Strapiombo** (Bustach)	F Corner, B Thompson
1961 Oct. 15	**Kellogg Crack** (Bustach)	B Thompson, F Corner
1961 Oct.	**Sphincter** (Gesail)	C T Jones, J H Swallow
1961 Dec.	**Alcatraz** (Pant Ifan)	M Boysen and party
1961 Dec.	**Holloway** (Pant Ifan)	M Boysen and party
1961 Dec.	**The Plum** (2 pts. aid) (Bwlch y Moch)	R James, D Yates
1961	**Overhanging Crack** (2 pts. aid) (Craig y Clipiau)	J Brown, D Thomas bach
1961	**Leviathan** (Alltrem)	C T Jones, G Holmes

1962 Mar. 24 **Scratch Arête** (1 pt. aid) (Pant Ifan) B Ingle, R F Jones
Originally the overhang was avoided by climbing the thin crack on the right with an aid peg.

1962 Apr. 20 **Vulcan** (15 pts. aid) (Pant Ifan) B Wright, C Goodey
It is reported that B Brewster climbed this free but is very unlikely. Probable first free ascent by R Fawcett in Spring 1977.

1962 Apr. 22	**Cyclops** (Clogwyn y Gigfran)	B D Wright, C E Davies
1962 Apr. 22	**Titan** (Clogwyn y Gigfran)	C E Davies, B D Wright, D Alcock

1962 Apr. 28   **Tramgo** (several pts. aid) (Castell Cidwm)   J Brown, C J S
Bonington
The aid was two pegs and at least three slings.
'*In 1962 Brown was back once more, this time to assault
the overhangs on the right of Dwm. He climbed a fierce
crack which split several roofs, and called it Tramgo, after
the Tramgo Towers in the Andes. It was a fairly short but
vicious route, and tales of the leader hanging horizontally
by fist jams, and being unable to raise his hands above his
head at the top were alarming to say the least.*'

New Climbs 1966

*The route developed a tremendous reputation and if the
grapevine is correct has seen few ascents. Certainly the
vegetation that builds up in the crack seems to bear this
out.*
*First free ascent: J Moran (with G Milburn, S Horrox) on 1
June 1978.*

1962 Apr. 28   **Hors d'Oeuvre** (Castell Cidwm)   C T Jones, C E Davies
(AL)

1962 May   **Y Broga** (Bwlch y Moch)   D M Jones, H Morris, G
Williams

1962 Jun. 10   **The Last Post** (1 pt. aid) (Alltrem)   C T Jones, R F Jones
1962 Summer   **Sideline** (Clogwyn y Cysgod)   R G Wilson, D Sanders
1962 Jly 8   **Slate** (Clogwyn yr Oen)   J E Roberts
1962 Jly/Oct.   **Meshach** (1 pt. aid) (Bwlch y Moch)   R James, A
Earnshaw, M Petrovsky

1962 Oct.   **Falcon** (9 pts. aid – A2) (Pant Ifan)   R James, M Petrovsky
First free ascent by J Clements in 1964.

1962 Oct. 14   **Tornado** (Craig y Gelli)   N Gough, J G Thomas, R E J
Gough

1962 Oct. 20   **Flintstone Rib** (Clogwyn y Cysgod)   P Crew, B Ingle (AL)
1962   **Peachpla** (Craig y Llyn)   C A G Jones and party
1963 Mar. 19   **Cancer** (Pinacl)   J E Roberts, C Bloor
1963   **Soft Touch** (Craig y Gesail)   K Wilson, D Blackwell
P Trower and S Lowe added the startin 1976.

1963 May 18   **Penates** (Craig yr Ogof)   B Ingle, R G Wilson
*They started up Briggs' Climb and the final crack was
added later in the year.*

1963 May 25   **The Straighter** (Castell Cidwm)   J H Swallow, A Cowburn
'*He had some trouble with the ascent in the middle of a
rainstorm, and when at last he came down, the relief of
his second, who sprained his ankle getting away from the
crag, was short lived! Swallow was soon back with a
replacement and completed the route in more favourable
conditions.*

1966 New Climbs

'*Swallow had a fine year with his new route on Castell
Cidwm, and made a contribution to the anti-peg
movement by his second ascents of Agrippa (Craig yr
Ysfa) and The Groove on Llech Ddu, both with*

considerably less aid than on the first ascent.
Unfortunately some of the younger generation cannot be
said to be doing the same and keep setting precedents
which some of us may find difficult to understand.'

P Crew, 1966 New Climbs

1963 May 25   **Crucible** (1 pt. aid) (Craig yr Ogof)   B Ingle, R G Wilson
The high line was taken on the second pitch.
First free ascent pre-1976, unknown.
'Undoubtedly the most important event of 1963 was
Ingle's new route on Craig yr Ogof, Cwm Silyn. This route
takes a superb line up a very improbable-looking piece of
rock and is comparable to Vector for quality and difficulty.
It is to be hoped that this route will re-establish free
climbing on Craig yr Ogof, which has been used for a long
time as a peggers' playground. Most of the numerous
confusing pegs in various parts of the cliff have now been
removed.'

P Crew, 1964 New Climbs

1964 Jan.   **Mangoletsi** (1 pt. aid) (Pant Ifan)   H I Banner, B Ingle
The finish described was climbed by P Gomersall in
Spring 1977.

1964 Feb.   **Victimisation** (Pant Ifan) (Artificial)   R James, D A Jones
Considerable aid was employed. This route was later to
be replaced by Fingerlicker.

1964 Feb. 9   **The Fox** (Craig y Carlwm)   J Harwood, R A High (AL)
400 yards east of Craig y Gesail, the central of three
buttresses.

1964 Mar. 31   **Hedera** (Bwlch y Moch)   J Brown, J Cheesemond
1964 Mar.   **Tensor** (2 pts. aid) (Castell)   J Brown, C E Davies
"Again Brown appeared on the scene after an absence of
some years to add his Tensor, climbed with extra pegs on
subsequent ascents by later parties. The roof was climbed
free by H Barber.

1964 Apr. 1   **The Croaker** (4 pts. aid) (Bwlch y Moch)   J Brown, J
Cheesemond, B Sharp
First recorded as Cracker.
Climbed free by R Fawcett in 1976.

1964 Apr. 5   **The Struggler** (1 pt. aid) (Pant Ifan)   B Ingle, C T Jones
1964 Apr. 25   **Grotto** (Bwlch y Moch)   T Heatherley, A Davies
1964 Apr. 25   **Mensor** (Castell)   D Alcock, A Cowburn
1964 Apr. 29   **Cursor** (3 pts. aid) (Craig y Gelli)   D Alcock, S Williams
First free ascent A Sharp, D Lewis in May 1978.

1964 Apr.   **Toreador** (Wenallt)   R Edwards and party
1964 May 24   **Iolyn** (Castell)   D Thomas bach, G D Roberts
1964 May   **Salix** (Castell)   D Thomas bach, A Cowburn, T Heatherly
1964 May   **Pellagra** (2 pts. aid) (Castell)   J Brown, J Cheesemond, K I
Meldrum
First free ascent P Livesey in 1976.

1964 Jun. 3   **Diadic** (Bwlch y Moch)   E Penman, A Harris

| 1964 Jun. 28 | **Whale** (Alltrem)   H I Banner, A J J Moulam |
| 1964 Jly 18 | **The Fly** (Craig y Carlwm)   D E Burgess, J Harwood (AL) |

1964 Jly 18 **The Fly** (Craig y Carlwm)   D E Burgess, J Harwood (AL)
Towards the right-hand end of the cliff.

1964 Jly 19 **Mistral** (Wrysgan)   N Gough, W Johnson

1964 Sep. 10 **Biolet** (Craig y Carlwm)   J Harwood, S Janvrin (AL)
The arête on the right-hand buttress on the left-hand part of the cliff.

1964 Sep. 27 **Glwm** (Several pts. aid) (Castell Cidwm)   J Clements, A Bell (AL)
'It involved an alarming second pitch, traversing into the centre of the crag on loose pegs. That day it became clear that prussiks were an asset on Cidwm, for a peg came out on the second, and he found himself spinning in space 10 feet away from the nearest rock and unable to get back.'
1966 New Climbs
The above description was sufficiently off-putting to deter not a few parties from setting foot on Castell Cidwm over the next eight years.
The present variation to pitch 2 was worked out by the same team in June 1965.

1964 Oct. 3 **Central Wall** (2 pts. aid) (Castell Cidwm)   A Bell, J Clements (AL)
The line had been spotted as a possible weakness up the wall but it had defeated quite a few strong parties prior to the first ascent.
First free ascent: W Wayman, T Jepson in May 1977.

1964 Oct. 4 **Desifinado** (1 pt. aid) (Craig yr Ogof)   B Ingle, A 'Richard' McHardy (AL)
The variation was climbed by W S Lounds and D Mathews on 15 April 1969.

1964 Oct. **Zukator** (7 pts. aid) (Bwlch y Moch)   P Crew, A Harris
All in all a tour de force rather than an aid pitch. Of the seven pegs which were placed horizontally below the top bulge to rest and consolidate before the final push, it is likely that one peg was used to gain height rather than for resting. During the ascent a large part of the final overhang fell off necessitating panic measures.
Pitch 1 done in March 1963.
First free ascent P Livesey, J Sheard in 1976.

1964 Oct. **Ectoplasm** (Clogwyn yr Oen)   N Gough, A Hughes
1964 Nov. **Plasma**(Clogwyn yr Oen)   N Gough, A Hughes
1964 Autumn **Tiros** (4 pts. aid) (Bwlch y Moch)   R James, D H Jones
Later to be incorporated in Cream.

1964 **G-String** (1 pt. aid) (Bwlch y Moch)   R James, C Goodey
1964 **Molar** (1 pt. aid) (Bwlch y Moch)   D Yates, G Simpkin
1964 **Civetta** (aid sling) (Alltrem)   J V Anthoine, R James
First free ascent G Tinning in 1979.

1964 **Leviathan Direct** (Alltrem)   A J J Moulam
1964 **Valour** (3 pts. aid) (Bwlch y Moch)   D Yates, D H Jones

> *Pitches 2 and 3 only. Aid was used on pitch 3. The first part of pitch 2 was climbed later by N Gough and the complete route was first climbed in 1967 by F Cannings, D Peers.*

1964	**Cat Walk** (Upper Wrysgan)	N Gough, A Hughes
1964	**Ash Tree Slabs** (Upper Wrysgan)	N Gough, S Glass
1965 Apr. 7	**Plumbline** (Gesail)	C E Davies, G Holmes
1965 Apr. 10	**Integral** (1 pt. aid) (Pant Ifan)	J Brown, C E Davies
1965 Jun. 13	**The Erg** (some aid) (Castell Cidwm)	J Clements, R Beasley

> *The aid was a peg and sling on pitch 2 and slings and a peg on pitch 3.*
> *Pitch 2 was climbed free by L R Holliwell, L E Holliwell in 1966.*
> *First all free ascent: R Fawcett, C Shorter in April 1980.*

1965 Oct.	**Eyrie** (Clogwyn y Cysgod)	M Boysen, A Williams

> *A mysterious route so the grade needs a public health warning.*

1965 Oct.	**Cidwm Girdle** (6 pts. aid) (Castell Cidwm)	J Clements, D Potts

> *'Cidwm held one last problem – the Girdle. At first glance it appeared impossible, but an assault lasting several weekends showed the feasibility of the climb. The barrier proved to be the slab between The Straighter and The Erg. Clements fell of it once, but the complete route finally succumbed over two days in October, and was revealed as the most difficult undertaking on the cliff.'*
>
> 1966 New Climbs
>
> *It was described in 1966 as 'Probably one of the most arduous undertakings in Wales. It is a formidable route of unrelenting difficulty and steepness traversing the crag from right to left.'*
> *'It is a high-level girdle, following geological weaknesses, with all the climbing in exhilarating situations.'*
> *Yet another description which was to deter or unnerve subsequent parties.*
> *First free ascent: P O'Donovan, P Williams (AL) on 12 August 1983.*

1966 New Climbs commented that on Castell Cidwm 'Not much that is obvious remains for those with an eye for a new line: but this has so often been proved wrong in the past who knows what the future holds?'.

1965 Oct. 9	**Vestix** (Craig y Clipiau)	R Newcombe, G Ashton

> *Pitches 2 and 3 had been climbed respectively by R James and E Beard respectively.*

1965 Oct. 17	**Sisyphus** (1 pt. aid) (Castell)	R Edwards, C Boulton
1965 Dec. 27	**Valerian** (1 pt. aid) (Pant Ifan)	H Smith, I Sanderson
1965	**Congl** (Craig Rhiw Goch)	R James, B James, R Rowlands
1965	**Mur Dena** (Craig Rhiw Goch)	R James, P Fletcher, D Rowlands

1966 Feb. 9	**Castell Girdle** (1 pt. aid) (Castell) R Edwards, C Boulton
1966 Feb. 27	**Geireagle** (2 pts. aid) (Bwlch y Moch) R Edwards, J Edwards

A name which has the unusual distinction of having been spelt in five other ways in its previously printed forms.

1966 Mar. 19	**Little Rocker** (Llechog Facet) D E Alcock, K J Wilson

An obscure second on an obscure climb. The climb remained obscure.

1966 Mar. 19	**Nazgul** (Carreg y Fran) D T Roscoe, B D Wright
1966 Mar. 20	**Atropos** (1 pt. aid) (Clogwyn y Cysgod) M Boysen, A Williams, J Jordan

This route contains the last aid point in the Cwm Silyn area. Go for it!

1966 Mar. 20	**Aquarius** (Craig yr Ogof) B Ingle, G Barrow

They took a less direct line on the first pitch which was climbed as described by M P Hatton, J A Maguire in September 1966.

1966 Easter	**The Chateau** (Gesail) R James, J Wilkinson
1966 Apr. 9	**Erebus** (3 pts. aid) (Pant Ifan) R Edwards, D Blythe

First free ascent R Fawcett in 1976.

1966 Apr. 12	**Burlesque** (Bwlch y Moch) R Newcombe, A Campbell

Now harder since a jug came away in 1981.

1966 Apr. 14	**Terra Nova** (1 pt. aid) (Craig y Llyn) C T Jones, A J J Moulam
1966 Apr. 24	**Astonall** (Gesail) C T Jones, A J J Moulam, N A J Rogers, Mrs J Rogers
1966 May 13	**Scuffer** (1 pt. aid) (Craig y Llyn) G Rogan, B Ingle (AL)

The right-hand side of the square-cut gully to the right of Aquila.

1966 May 14	**Tarantula** (Castell) D Yates, I C Lowe, Miss F L Crawford
1966 May 15	**Femaelstrom** (Bustach) S Wroe, T Howard
1966 May 19	**Strider** (Carreg y Fran) D T Roscoe, B D Wright
1966 May 30	**Brutus** (3 pts. aid) (Craig yr Ogof) B Ingle, G Barrow

First free ascent: unknown.

1966 May	**Deceiver** (Carreg y Fran) D T Roscoe, B D Wright
1966 Jun. 11	**Carlwm Corner** (Craig y Carlwm) R F Burns, J Harwood

The left-hand ection of the face.

1966 Jun. 19	**Rib and Groove** (Alltrem) S C Tunney, C Osborne, R Poole
1966 Jun.	**The Spook** (1 pt. aid) (Hyll-Drem) S Tattersall, R Dixon (AL)
1966 Jly 7	**Dentist's Debut** (Upper Wrysgan) A J J Moulam, P F J H O'Donoghue
1966 Jly 7	**Central Gully** (Upper Wrysgan) A J J Moulam, P F J H O'Donoghue
1966 Jly 31	**Itch** (1 pt. aid) (Pant Ifan) L E Holliwell, L R Holliwell

Climbed free by A Sharp.

1966 Aug. 17	**Via Nimbus** (9 pts. aid – A2) (Bwlch y Moch) G Farnsworth, C McDonald. G Pemberton

Graham Parkes on Central Wall, Castell Cidwm.
Photo: Chris Craggs

Norma Elliott and Terry Gifford on Adam Rib, Craig Cwm Du.
Photo: Kevin Borman

'Climb the overhanging corner of the cave with the aid of nuts to a wooden wedge at the roof. Peg up the cracks above (9) until it is possible to traverse left to the top of the crag.' Later to be replaced by *Void.*

1966 Aug. 21   **The Burner** (Hyll-Drem)   R Evans, I R Esplin
'No pegs needed for aid or protection.'

1966 Aug. 22   **Helix** (2 pts. aid) (Craig Cwm Trwsgl)   R Edwards, E G Penman

1966 Aug. 27   **Eureka** (Craig yr Ogof)   L E Holliwell, L R Holliwell
The first of the Holliwells' impressive new routes in North Wales.

1966 Sep. 10   **Poker** (Hyll-Drem)   L E Holliwell, L R Holliwell

1967 Jan. 25   **Birthday Route** (Craig Stwlan)   D J Ashton, B J Blackhall

1967 Mar. 19   **Gothic Grooves** (1 pt. aid) (Pant Ifan)   C J Phillips, E Edkin
The Rookery Nook Variation: J Moran, G Milburn, S Horrox in October 1977.

1967 Mar. 24   **The Prow** (5 pts. aid) (Hyll-Drem)   R Evans, E Jones
'Climb the chimney using three pegs for aid.' Free climbed by M Griffiths, R Griffiths 25 May 1983 renamed: Raging Bull.

1967 Apr. 23   **Great Feet** (Craig y Clipiau)   R Newcombe, G Ashton
Pitch 2 R James, J M Benson, P H Benson in 1958.

1967 Apr. 29   **Chwys** (1 pt. aid) (Bwlch y Moch)   M Lewis, H G Davies

1967 May 7   **Psycho** (aid) (Carreg y Fran)   D T Roscoe, J M Brailsford
One piton was used at 20 feet and the crack was climbed mainly on inserted slings.

1967 May 13   **The Hump** (Clogwyn Holland)   A J J Moulam, H Drasdo

1967 May   **The Ent** (Clogwyn y Gigfran)   J Brown, C E Davies

1967 May   **Shelob** (Clogwyn y Gigfran)   J Brown, C E Davies

1967 May 29   **Agoraphobia** (Pant Ifan)   A Willmott, W Church

1967 May 29   **Thumbelina** (Clogwyn yr Oen)   B St J Phillips, C Phillips

1967 Jun. 27   **Fandango** (2 pts. aid) (Pant Ifan)   A Willmott, J Brown
On Avalanche Buttress, Craig Pant Ifan – it fell down in 1981.

1967 Jly 2   **Gay** (Carreg y Fran)   A J J Moulam, N Drasdo, H Drasdo

1967 Jly 8   **Green Wall** (Alltrem)   A J J Moulam H Drasdo

1967 Jly 23   **Afterthought** (Craig yr Ogof)   R Hughes, A J J Moulam (AL)

1967 Aug. 9   **Tyke's Wall** (Carreg y Fran)   J Barker
Second did not finish owing to heavy rain.

1967 Oct. 15   **Dislocation** (2 pts. aid) (Upper Wrysgan)   R J Eddington, J F Kerry
Climbed free in 1978 by M Griffiths and A Moller.

1968 Mar. 10   **Vindaloo** (Bwlch y Moch)   G Tabbner, R Smith

1968 Apr. 15   **Axeminster** (Bwlch y Moch)   M H Bayliss, P J Bayliss, V G Atkins
The variation: A Green, K Latham, C Fryer in 1973.

1968 Apr.   **Gwastadanas** (Nant Gwynant)   C E Davies, G Holmes

1968 May 26   **Crossover** (Clogwyn yr Oen)   B St J Phillips, M Phillips

1968 Jun. 9   **Codswallop** (1 pt. aid) (Craig yr Ogof)   R Evans
(Unseconded on the main pitch)
*First claimed free ascent: J Hart, S Isherwood on 18 July
1976.*

1968 Jly 7   **Yoghurt Miscellaneous** (Upper Wrysgan)   S F Gleeson,
Miss S Shallcross, D R Headley, Miss B Thomson

1968   **Tight** (Clogwyn yr Oen)   A J J Moulam, E Hammond

1969 May   **Split Finger** (Craig y Llyn)   C T Jones, R Conway

1969 May   **Clonus** (Craig y Llyn)   C T Jones, R F Jones, A J J
Moulam

1969 Jun. 12   **Little Plum** (Carreg y Fran)   L Noble, J M Brailsford, D T
Roscoe

1969 Jun. 12   **Red Wall Crack** (Carreg y Fran)   J M Brailsford, D T
Roscoe, L Noble

1969 Jun.   **Thirty-Nine Steps** (Craig y Llyn)   C T Jones, S Williams

1969 Nov. 23   **Last Slip** (1 pt. aid) (Bwlch y Moch)   D G Peers, K Martin
Right of Leg Slip.

1969   **Titus** (Bustach/Moelwyns)   R Newcombe, G Ashton

1970 Mar.   **Slipway** (Bwlch y Moch)   R Cane, A de Cousel

1970 May 8   **Ignition** (Moel Hebog)   M Yates, Judy Yates

1970 May 18   **Jabberwocky** (1 pt. aid) (Craig yr Ogof)   R Evans, Judy
Yates, M Yates
Climbed wearing old RAF boots.
*Earliest claimed free ascent: J Hart, S Isherwood on 29
June 1975.*

1970 May 22   **Zip Groove** (Craig Cwm Dulyn)   R Evans, M Yates

1970 May 23   **Gotogo** (Craig yr Ogof)   R D Kift, L W P Garland (AL)

1970 May 23   **West Arête** (Craig yr Ogof)   M Yates, R Evans (AL)

1970 May 30   **Medicare, Poverty Street** (Craig Cwm Du)   J Gosling, G
Mcnair

1970 Jun. 13   **Green Gully** (Craig yr Ogof)   M Yates, Judy Yates
*Previously top-roped by E A Dance and others around
1952.*

1970 Jun. 14   **Cysgodian Creep** (Clogwyn y Cysgod)   R Evans, M Yates

1970 Jly   **Touch Up** (Gesail)   K Toms, G Upton
Replaces **Ek Borge** *by C T Jones, E Siddall, R F Jones in
August 1961 and* **Touché** *by C E Davies, D W Walker.*

1970 Aug. 15   **Resurrection** (Llechog)   J Perrin, N J Estcourt, M Yates
*A fine discovery which solved a long-standing problem
which had been totally ignored by most climbers.*
*2 pegs were used for aid while gardening. The gaunt red
crack first atttempted in 1911 by Archer Thomson, who
had written:.*
*'A brief survey did not disclose to me any line of ascent up
the face. We climbed the secondary edge on the left for
some distance; then a very delicate traverse to the main
edge was made in vain for this was found to be quite
impossible.'*

1970 Sep. 19   **Guardian Angel** (2 pts aid) (Craig y Bera)   M Yates, C T
Jones, Judy Yates
First free ascent (?): M Crook, D Farrant on 30 June 1984.

1970 Sep. 27	**Paranoia** (Bustach) C Phillips, T Taylor (AL)
1970 Oct. 18	**Dulyn Grooves** (several pts. aid) (Craig Cwm Dulyn) R Evans, B Wyville
	The route had been attempted on several occasions by this team and others without aid.
	First free ascent: M Fowler, A Baker on 20 June 1982.
1970	**Groan** (Bustach/Moelwyns) R Newcombe, D Davies
1971	*'Cwm Silyn and Cwellyn' guidebook published.*
1971 Apr. 14	**Foxtrot** (2 pts. aid) (Bustach) Z Leppert, J Blears
	The slab and overhang above the second pitch of Gallop Step.
1971 Apr. 18	**Silly Arête** (Pant Ifan) J Pasquill, J Nuttall, R Evans
	One of the best routes in Wales.
1971 Apr. 18	**Hot Pants** (Wrysgan) J R Lambertson, R Carrick
1971 Apr. 25	**Samurai Groove** (2 pts. aid) (Hyll-Drem) B Wyvill, D Mossman
	A free version climbed by P Thomas in 1979 to give an outrageous route.
1971 May 21	**Redog** (Moel Hebog) M Yates, Judy Yates
	Even guidebook work hadn't put them off this cliff.
1971 Aug. 6	**The Deceiver** (2 pts. aid) (Craig y Llyn) G Rigby, K Bentham
	The route described incorporates a direct finish added by N Gough, M Creasey in May 1975.
1972 Apr. 23	**Acrophily** (Castell Cidwm) C H Taylor, M R Sinker (VL)
1972 Aug. 4	**The Riparian** (Craig Rhiw Goch) J Perrin, A Cornwall
1972 Aug 6	**Endgame** (Craig Rhiw Goch) J Perrin, T Clare
1972 Aug. 14	**The Green Wall** (1 pt. aid) (Wrysgan) J Perrin, A Cornwall
1972 Aug. 14	**Gethsemane** (Wrysgan) J Perrin, A Cornwall
1972 Aug. 15	**The Wanderer** (Wrysgan) J Perrin, J Balmer
	Alternative Start: M Griffiths, E Jones in August 1981.
1972	**Remembrance** (Clogwyn yr Oen) J Perrin, A Skuse
1972	**The Ox Bow Incident** (2 pts. aid) (Bustach) D Cook, A Evans (AL)
1972	**Dark Side** (aid) (Bwlch y Moch) G Upton, K Toms
	*Climbed free in 1978 by G Gibson and renamed **A Vengeance**.*
1973 Mar. 18	**Hindleburg** (1 pt. aid) (Craig y Gelli) J de Montjoye, E S Hindle
1973 Mar. 25	**Troubador** (Hyll-Drem) J Perrin, D Britt (AL)
1973 May 7	**Hogmanay Girdle** (2 pts. aid) (Pant Ifan) J Perrin, P Basterfield
	Little of this was new. Pitches 6, 7 and 8 had been climbed in the opposite direction by H Smith, I Sanderson in 1965 as part of Valerian. The final pitch had been climbed in 1967 by D Yates and party.
	Tension traverse on pitch 4 freed by R Fawcett by mistake whilst on Psyche 'n Burn.

First free ascent of all of pitch 4 by A Pollitt, S Andrews 1985.

1973 May 26 **Slabby Flues** (Pant Ifan)   C L Jones, M H L Hewer
1973 Jly 23 **Phidl** (Craig y Clipiau)   P Morris
Pitch 2 was climbed in 1958 by R James.

1973 Jly **Ivy Crack** (Pant Ifan)   P Rigg, M Ryan, P Sinclair
1973 **Raspberry** (Clogwyn Holland)   J C Bucke, J R Mason
1974 Feb. 26 **Crocadillo** (Pant Ifan)   A Sharp, S Humphries
Only the first pitch was new. The final crack had been climbed earlier by J Perrin. The groove was climbed in 1977 by J Moran, M Crook, D Bailey.

1974 Apr. 8 **Gremlin Groove** (Upper Wrysgan)   J F Kerry
1974 Apr. **Caravansoreye** (Gesail)   C Dawes, R Williams, I Pritchard, H Jones
1974 Jun. **King Kong** (Hyll-Drem)   R Evans, H Pasquill
1974 Jly **Pretzel Logic** (Bwlch y Moch)   A Rouse, B Hall
Most, if not all, of this had been climbed by I Edwards and others.

1974 Sep. **The Exterminating Angel** (Craig Cwm Trwsgl)   J Perrin, D C O'Brien
1974 Oct. 4 **Dragon** (aid) (Bwlch y Moch)   J Dunwell, J Parry
First free ascent July 1978 by M Griffiths.

1975 Apr. **The Second Coming** (Craig Cwm Trwsgl)   J Perrin, M Boysen
1975 Apr. **Peuterey Girdle** (Pant Ifan)   M Gough, M Creasey
1975 May 5 **Vulture** (Bwlch y Moch)   A Sharp, C Dale
The first of the hard Tremadog crack routes.
Vulture Direct: A Pollitt (unseconded) on 19 September 1982.

1975 May 11 **Fingerlicker** (Pant Ifan)   P Livesey, Jill Lawrence
Free climbs most of Victimisation. This ascent caused some controversy at the time due to the two yo-yos employed (!).
Direct Finish: J Redhead, A Pollitt on 29 May 1982.
On the first ascent of the Direct Finish, Redhead, climbing only in underpants (!) due to the heat, stopped for 10 minutes in one position. When asked why he pointed to the topless woman sunbathing in the meadow below!

1975 May **The Widening Gyre** (Craig Cwm Trwsgl)   J Perrin, P Doncaster
1975 Jun. 1 **The Snake** (Bwlch y Moch)   A Sharp, C Dale
The first free route to venture onto the Vector Headwall.
1975 Jun. 16 **Extraction** (Bwlch y Moch)   C J Phillips, M Crook
1975 **The Ceremony of Innocence** (Craig Cwm Trwsgl)   J Perrin, I Nightingale
1975 **Void** (1 pt. aid) (Bwlch y Moch)   R Edwards, I Ponfret
Superseded Via Nimbus.
First free ascent by R Fawcett in February 1976.
1976 Apr. 27 **Venom** (Bwlch y Moch)   I Edwards, W Turner, T Riley

The Girdle Traverse of Carreg Hyll-Drem.
Photo: John Cleare

Rusty Baillie on the final moves of Aquila, Craig y Llyn.
Photo: John Cleare

Bonington climbing to his Dwm, Castell Cidwm.
Photo: John Cleare

Richard McHardy on Craig yr Ogof (Either Desifinado 1st ascent or Ogof Traverse!). *Photo: Ingle/Crew?*

The first pitch was climbed as a direct start to Leg Slip (1 pt. aid): C J Mortlock. The main pitch was part of The Bastion (1959).

1976 May 1   **Cream** (Bwlch y Moch)   P Livesey, R Fawcett, E Clapton
Supersedes Tiros.

1976 May   **Mere Anarchy** (Craig Cwm Trwsgl)   M Boysen, J Perrin

1976 May   **Terraqua** (aid) (Pant Ifan)   S Cathcart
Climbed free in January 1980 by K 'Chipper' Jones.

1976 Aug. 8   **In Memoriam** (Clogwyn yr Oen)   D R M Bailey, R J Shimwell
Named in memory of Tony Booth.

1977 Jan. 2   **Wanda** (Pant Ifan)   J Moran, M Crook, P Deans
'The block of the final pitch appears to be held together by faith, hope and congealed mud. I'm not going near it again.'

1977 Feb. 26   **Scarecrow** (Pant Ifan)   J Moran, D Hollows

1977 Apr. 29   **Steelfingers** (Pant Ifan)   J Moran, P Williams

1977 Apr.   **Tachyphouse** (Gesail)   S Cathcart, P Waters

1977 Apr.   **Tall Dwarfs** (Pant Ifan)   J Moran, M Crook, P Williams

1977 Apr.   **The Moon** (Craig y Llyn)   S Cathcart, P Waters

1977 May   **The Mongoose** (Bwlch y Moch)   P L Gomersall, A Evans, J Moran
So called because it eliminated The Snake. A route with an interesting history. Originally climbed with side-runners in Void it was climbed without by P Gomersall in June 1980, then soloed 'the easy way' by P Burke and finally soloed DOWN by R Fawcett.

1977 Jun. 5   **Marathon Man** (Bwlch y Moch)   R Fawcett, C Gibb
One of the bolder routes at Tremadog.

1977 Jun. 5   **Pippikin** (Pant Ifan)   P Gomersall, E 'Bonny' Masson, J Moran

1977 Summer   **The Matador** (Wenallt)   M Crook, S McCartney

1977 Summer   **The Death Wisher** (Wenallt)   M Crook, S McCartney

1977 Oct. 2   **The Olympiad** (Pant Ifan)   J Moran, S Horrox, G Milburn

1977 Oct. 16   **Bing the Budgie** (Wrysgan)   D Bailey, M Griffiths
Variation by M Griffiths, E Jones in August 1981.

1977 Oct 24   **Touchstone** (Gesail)   J Moran, A Evans

1977 Oct.   **Lavrol** (Alltrem)   J Moran, S Horrox, D Banks

1977 Nov. 3   **Straw Dogs** (Craig y Clipiau)   M Crook, D R M Bailey
Probably climbed earlier by several other parties including M G Mortimer.

1977   **Spare Rib** (Pant Ifan)   P Gomersall, E 'Bonny' Masson
Pitch 2 only. Pitch 1 P Gomersall June 23, 1979.

1977   **Sunset Traverse** (Hyll-Drem)   B Wyvill, R Evans

1978 Jan 5.   **The Sting** (Bwlch y Moch)   R Edwards, P Williams

1978 Jan. 14   **Groove of Horror** (1 pt. aid) (Pant Ifan)   R Edwards, D Roberts (seiged) P Williams
First free ascent Summer 1978 by B Hannon.

1978 Jan. 15   **Daddy Cool** (Bwlch y Moch)   D Roberts, P Williams (AL) R Edwards

1978 Jan. 24	**Salamanda** (Bwlch y Moch) R Edwards, M R Edwards *Possibly Salamander or Salamandra!*	
1978 Jan. 24	**Heartbreak Hotel** (Bwlch y Moch) P Williams, D Cuthbertson	
1978 Jan. 25	**Fiddler on the Dole** (Bustach/Moelwyns) D R M Bailey, M Crook, M Griffiths	
1978 Feb. 7	**Earthsea** (Bwlch y Moch) R Edwards, M R Edwards	
1978 Feb. 12	**Curved Air** (Pant Ifan) L McGinley, R 'Strappo' Hughes *'Comparable to Archangel.'*	
1978 Feb. 12	**The Liquidator** (Craig y Clipiau) M Crook, M Griffiths	
1978 Mar.	**Anagram** (Bwlch y Moch) B Wintringham, M Wintringham	
1978 Mar.	**Electric Edge** (Pant Ifan) M Griffiths, G Griffiths	
1978 Easter	**Poacher** (1 pt. aid) (Wenallt) P Burke, G Kent *First free ascent R Fawcett in 1980.*	
1978 Apr. 29	**Starship Trooper** (Bwlch y Moch) P Thomas *'I lost my heart . . .'*	
1978 May 29	**Blood on the Tracks** (Llechog) C E M Yates, H I Banner	
1978 May	**Going Straight** (Bustach/Moelwyns) M Griffiths, P Denham	
1978 May	**Condor** (Wrysgan) M Griffiths, M Crook	
1978 Jun. 18	**Strawberry** (Clogwyn Holland) M Griffiths, M Griffiths, P Denham	
1978 Jun.	**Sybilla the Pun** (Craig y Llyn) P Gomersall, P Livesey	
1978 Jun.	**Chance Encounter** (Craig y Llyn) P Livesey, P Gomersall, E Masson	
1978 Jun.	**Sasquatch** (Upper Wrysgan) M Griffiths, P Denham	
1978 Jly 16	**Freudian Slip** (Bwlch y Moch) B Wintringham, A D Baker	
1978 Jly 24	**Hot Rats** (Bwlch y Moch) S Cathcart, G Griffiths *Food was scarce that Summer.*	
1978 Jly 25	**Y Taith** (Wrysgan) D Johnson, R Griffiths	
1978 Jly 30	**Oblatron** G Gibson, M Hewitt	
1978 Jly	**Chim-chu Roo** (Upper Wrysgan) M Crook, M Griffiths, P Denham	
1978 Jly	**Buzby** (Upper Wrysgan) M Griffiths, P Denham	
1978 Aug. 25	**Wailing Wall** (Craig y Llyn) P Livesey, C Crawshaw	
1978 Aug. 27	**Heartline** (Bwlch y Moch) S Cathcart, G Griffiths *Climbed earlier as **Bloodsucker** by G Gibson, J Perry.*	
1978 Aug. 28	**Timeslip** (Bwlch y Moch) S Cathcart, G Griffiths	
1978 Aug. 29	**Rattlesnake Finish** (Bwlch y Moch) G Gibson, J Perry	
1978 Aug.	**Erewhon** (Clogwyn yr Oen) M Griffiths, A Prellas (AL)	
1978 Sep. 1	**The Finish of Moments** G Gibson, J Perry	
1978 Sep. 27	**Final Exam** (Bwlch y Moch) M Griffiths, M Crook	
1978 Sep. 28	**Brys** (Craig y Clipiau) M Griffiths, A Moller	
1978 Sep.	**Leg Break** (Bwlch y Moch) P Livesey, P Cobley *A climb taking a similar line, The Last Gasp, was climbed by G Gibson, J Perry on 12 August 1978.*	
1978 Sep.	**Blinkers** (Bwlch y Moch) P Livesey, A Livesey, A Taylor	
1978	**High Kicks** (Bwlch y Moch) D Cuthbertson, M Duff *Climbed earlier by G Gibson, J Perry and called **The Singe**.*	

1978	**Titanium Man** (Castell) K Robertson, I Laughton
1978	**Greenpeace** (Alltrem) P Gomersall, E Masson
1979 Apr. 15	**Bombshell** (Bwlch y Moch) G Gibson, J Walker
1979 Apr. 16	**Integral Direct** (Pant Ifan) D Humphreys, B Sutton, P Williams
1979 May 29	**Sometimes** G Gibson, J Walker
1979 May 31	**Sorry Sally** (Castell) A Evans, S Tansey, S Beresford
1979 May	**Skerryvore** (Clogwyn yr Oen) M Griffiths, P Elliot, E Jones
1979 May	**Oblatron** (Bwlch y Moch) G Gibson, R Hewitt, D Beetlestone
1979 May	**Sometimes** (Bwlch y Moch) G Gibson, J Walker
1979 Jun. 1	**One Step in the Crowds** (Castell) A Evans, S Tansey, S Beresford
1979 Jun. 24	**Cruel Tone** (Castell) G Gibson, I Barker
1979 Jun. 24	**Walk On By** (Castell) G Gibson, I Barker
1979 Jun. 24	**Hey!** (Gesail) G Gibson, I Barker
1979 Jly 1	**Back to Nature** (Pant Ifan) G Gibson, J Walker
1979 Jly 3	**Magic Mushroom** (Bwlch y Moch) S Peake, P Walsh
1979 Jly 5	**Broken Edge** (Bwlch y Moch) S Peake
1979 Jly 21	**Hurricane** (Craig y Gelli) M Crook, D Farrant
1979 Jly 30	**New Management** (Bwlch y Moch) S Peake, G Griffiths
1979 Jly	**Laser Crack** (Pant Ifan) M Griffiths, K Robertson, S Peake
1979 Aug. 30	**Biggles** (Hyll-Drem) M Griffiths, R Chamberlain
1979 Aug. 31	**Caligula** (Wenallt) M Griffiths, R Chamberlain
1979 Aug. 31	**Picador** (Wenallt) M Griffiths, R Chamberlain
1979 Aug.	**Zwm** (Castell Cidwm) F Crook, K Crook
1979 Sep.	**Perdido Street** (Craig y Llyn) W Wayman, W Walsh
1979 Sep.	**The Gamekeeper** (Wenallt) B Chamberlain, M Griffiths
1979 Oct.	**Pulsar** (Castell) F Crook, K Crook
1979	**The Jackal** (Bwlch y Moch) M Crook, M Griffiths
1979	**Quakerman** (Pant Ifan) D Cuthbertson, M Griffiths, K Johnson
1979	**Fear** (Pant Ifan) S Cathcart, G Griffiths
1979	**Silly Billy** (Pant Ifan) P Williams, M Griffiths, D Pyecroft
1979	**Savage Man** (Bwlch y Moch) S Cathcart, G Griffiths
1979	**Solitaire** (Bwlch y Moch) M Duff, T Dailey
1979	**Footless Frenzy** (Bwlch y Moch) S Cathcart, G Griffiths
1979	**Technical Master** (Pant Ifan) M Griffiths
	Improved by the collapse of Fandango.
1980 Feb.	**The Weaver** (Bwlch y Moch) P Williams, C Shorter
	Some of this had been climbed earlier by J Brown.
1980 Mar. 2	**The Atomic Finger Flake** (Bwlch y Moch) J Redhead, P Williams (AL) C Shorter, K Robertson
	P Williams had done the route with some aid the day before.
	The first of a new wave of hard routes at Tremadog by this talented climber.
1980 Mar. 15	**Sexual Salami** (Pant Ifan) J Redhead, K Robertson, C Shorter
	'A brilliant finger-searing modern test-piece.'

1980 Mar. 30	**Bananas** (Bwlch y Moch) J Redhead, K Robertson *A sensational route with the sensational grade of 7a. Now considered to be 6b.*
1980 Mar.	**Strawberries** (Bwlch y Moch) R Fawcett (unseconded) *A route with an interesting ethical history. On his succesful ascent Fawcett pre-placed and clipped runners from his previous days high point. A subsequent ascent by J Moffatt was made in three pitches. The first true free ascent was made by J Woodward in 1982.* *First on-sight flash ascent S Glowacz August, 1987.*
1980 Mar.	**Penicillin** (Bwlch y Moch) J Redhead, R Fawcett *Claimed earlier the same month as* **Big Bug**. *'Gary's got a problem!'*
1980 Apr. 8	**Hang 'em High** (Castell Cidwm) J Moran, G Milburn *The first of the super-routes to go. So did the first ascent team as the wind was at gale force and neither person fancied hanging around for any of the other superb lines that were so obviously waiting to be done.*
1980 Jun.	**The Fugitive** (Wenallt) M Crook, M Griffiths
1980 Apr. 1	**Plastic Nerve** (Pant Ifan) G Gibson, S Keeling
1980 Apr. 12	**Ace High** (Gesail) G Reid, A Creaigh
1980 Apr.	**Sultans of Swing** (Bwlch y Moch) J Redhead, P Williams *P Williams, J de Montjoye had done pitch 1 two days earlier.*
1980 Jly 30	**Clean Edge** (Bwlch y Moch) P Elliott, J Cousins, G Dady
1980 Aug. 22	**Sonic Sinbin** (Pant Ifan) G Moffatt, S Law
1980 Sep. 5	**Emily Street** (Bwlch y Moch) Elizabeth Masson, P Gomersall, P Livesey
1980 Oct. 2	**Dune Child** (Pant Ifan) J Moffatt, M Griffiths
1980 Oct.	**The Emerald** (Craig y Clipiau) M Griffiths, C J Hicks
1980 Oct.	**Johnson's Wall** (Craig y Clipiau) M Griffiths, C J Hicks
1980 Oct.	**Wall of Ghouls** (Upper Wrysgan) M Griffiths, C J Hicks
1980 Nov. 18	**Cheap Trick** (Castell) K Telfer, P Dickens
1980 Nov.	**Nosferatu** (Wrysgan) M Griffiths (unseconded)
1980 Nov.	**Gormenghast** (Bustach/Moelwyns) M Griffiths, C J Hicks
1980 Dec. 7	**Cardiac Arête** (Pant Ifan) J de Montjoye, V Thomas
1980 Dec.	**Crimson Cruiser** (Craig y Clipiau) R Fawcett, P Williams
1980	**Non-Dairy Creamer** (Craig y Clipiau) R Fawcett, P Williams *The Non-creaming Dairy Start was added by M Griffiths, E Jones in June 1981.*
1981 Jan.	**The Wildebeest** (Hyll-Drem) S Haston, G Tinning
1981 Jan. 26	**Gwaed** (Bwlch y Moch) M Roberts, C Jones
1981 Mar. 15	**Lonely Edge** (Castell) G Gibson, D Beetlestone
1981 Mar. 29	**Hitler's Buttock** (Pant Ifan) J Redhead, J de Montjoye, J Perrin, P Williams
1981 Mar. 30	**Jackdaw on the Edge of Time** (Castell) M Crook, D Farrant

Y Gelynen, a superb VD on Craig yr Wrysgan.

Photo: George White

John Middleton on White Streak, Craig yr Wrysgan.
Photo: George White

1981 Mar.	**Pengo's Eliminate** (Pant Ifan) S Haston, M Griffiths, M Crook	
1981 Mar.	**The Weirpig** (Hyll-Drem) S Haston (solo)	
1981 Apr. 17	**Marshall Hearts** (Craig y Llyn) S Cathcart, M Cameron	
1981 Apr.	**Return of the Horsemen** (Craig y Clipiau) M Griffiths, M Crook	
	First pitch by M Griffiths, E Jones in July 1980.	
1981 Apr.	**The Widowmaker** (Clogwyn yr Oen) M Griffiths, M Crook	
1981 Apr. 18	**Life In A Day** (Pant Ifan) G Gibson, D Beetlestone	
1981 Apr. 19	**Silver Crow** (Pant Ifan) M Crook, M Mitchell	
1981 Apr. 19	**Bigger Bug** (Castell) G Gibson, D Beetlestone	
1981	**Ringwraith** (Pant Ifan) M Griffiths, M Crook	
1981 May	**Danger Days** (Craig y Llyn) S Cathcart, P Stott	
1981 Jun. 18	**Muscles** (Gesail) C Jones, S Smith	
1981 Jly 14	**The Ebb Tide** (Bustach/Moelwyns) M Griffiths, E Jones	
1981 Jly 15	**Acoustic Flake** (Bustach/Moelwyns) E Jones, M Griffiths	
1981 Jly 16	**Mr. Flibbertigibbet** (Bustach/Moelwyns) M Griffiths, E Jones	
1981 Jly	**Psyche 'n Burn** (Pant Ifan) J Moffatt	
	Along with Strawberries the most significant new route at Tremadog for years. 'No-one else but me can hang on those holds.'	
1981 Jly	**The Muleman** (Craig y Clipiau) M Griffiths, E Jones	
1981 Aug. 2	**Slopey** (Llechog) H I Banner, C E M Yates	
1981 Aug. 20	**Sleeping Beauty** (Bustach) C Shorter, M Creasey	
1981 Aug.	**Y Lloer** (Wrysgan) M Griffiths, E Jones	
1981 Sep. 2	**The Tumor** (Pinacl) E Jones, M Griffiths	
1981 Sep.	**Louis Wilder** (Upper Wrysgan) M Griffiths (solo)	
	In memory of Gordon Tinnings.	
1981	**Peth Bras** (Craig y Clipiau) E Jones (solo)	
1981	**Re Entry** (Bwlch y Moch) R Chamberlain, G Thomas	
1981	**Quimbo** (Bwlch y Moch) P Elliot, K Robertson, N Green	
1982 Mar. 13	**Jill the Thrill** (Castell) S Reid, S Wilkinson	
1982 Mar. 13	**Holly Tree Variation** (Castell) S Reid, S Wilkinson	
1982 Mar. 13	**Brass** (Castell) S Reid, S Wilkinson	
1982 Apr.	**Surreal** (Pant Ifan) Dominic Lee, Daniel Lee	
	Variation: The Unreal Finish 12 May 1982 by A Pollitt, M Wilson.	
1982 May 9	**The Anvil** (Craig Rhiw Goch) A Pollitt, J Perrin	
1982 May 29	**Sheer Resist** (Bwlch y Moch) A Pollitt, J Redhead	
1982 Jun. 15	**Bandersnatch** (Craig yr Ogof) M Fowler, A Baker	
1982 Jly 24	**Erection** (Llechog) H I Banner, Judy Yates, C E M Yates	
	A long-standing problem of Jim Perrin's.	
1982 Aug. 7	**Pin Up** (Alltrem) G Gibson, M Lynden	
1982 Aug. 14	**Zarquon** (Llechog) H I Banner, C E M Yates	
1982 Nov. 13	**Blade Runner** (Pant Ifan) A Pollitt, C Parker, H Ford	
1982 Nov. 20	**Death Can Be Fatal** (Craig y Llyn) A Pollitt, P Bailey	
	Climbed on-sight in mistake for The Moon.	

1982	**Badger by Owl-Light** (Clogwyn yr Oen) M Griffiths, E Jones
1982	**The Falconer** (Alltrem) M Crook, H Walton
1983 Apr. 24	**Non Stop** (Gesail) G Gibson, N Harvey
1983	*Tremadog guidebook published.*
1983 Apr.	**First Blood** (Hyll-Drem) M Crook, M Griffiths
1983 May 25	**Raging Bull** (Hyll-Drem) M Griffiiths, R Griffiths
	At last the Prow goes free to give a horrific pitch.
1983 Jun. 2	**Compromising Positions** (Hyll-Drem) C Gore, S Haston
1983 Jly	**Bychan** (Craig y Llyn) J Brown, D Jones
1983 Aug.	**Dal y Twrch** (Bustach/Moelwyns) M Griffiths, B Skadding
	'Means Catch-the-Mole.'
1983	**Emotional Crisis** (Bwlch y Moch) A Andrew, A Hardcastle
	An accurate portrayal of the leaders feelings!
1983	**Ryan's Son** M Griffiths, E Jones
1984 May	**Raving Lunatic** (Hyll-Drem) P Littlejohn, M Campbell
1984 Jly 1	**Special 'K'** (Craig y Clipiau) D Bailey, W Shackell
1984 Sep. 4	**Rhych Y Din** (Pant Ifan) M Roberts, S Barking, C Edwards
1984 Sep. 5	**Scallywag** (Wrysgan) D Bailey, F Filzek
1984 Sep. 6	**Limited Edition** (Pant Ifan) P Gomersall, E Masson
1984 Sep. 8	**The Sandbagger** (Pant Ifan) P Gomersall, E Masson
1984 Oct.	**Dream Topping** (Bwlch y Moch) M Atkinson
	Sieged over several days. 'I thought Dream Topping was
	instant, I didn't know it took eight days to prepare.'
1984	**The Steal** (Pant Ifan) A Bailey, R Haszko
1984	**Stormy Weather** (Pant Ifan) A Bailey, R Haszko
1984	**Beyond the Cosmos** (Craig y Llyn) M Crook, D Cuthbertson
1984	**Fishbox** (Wenallt) J Redhead, D Towse
	Direct Finish: Climbed with 2 points of aid by M Crook.
1984	**Psychedelic Cult** (Wenallt) M Crook, M Brothers
1984	**Surreal M'coy** (Pant Ifan) J Moran
1985 Jan. 11	**Tamlin** (Pant Ifan) M Lewis, E Davies
1985 Jan. 11	**Saffron Sunset** (Pant Ifan) B Drury, D Jones
1985 Apr. 24	**Bad Reputation** (Wrysgan) P Wright, R Barker
1985 Apr. 26	**Stained Class** (Wrysgan) P Wright, R Barker
1985 May 6	**Cnychwyr** (Bwlch y Moch) F Hall, J Pitts, I Jones
1985 Jun. 28	**Omerta Crack** M Lewis, E Davies
1985 Jly 24	**Conrod** (Wrysgan) E Jones (solo next to hanging rope)
1985 Nov. 15	**Bigger Bug Start** M Lewis, E Davies
1986 May 12	**Megalomania** (Rhiw Goch) P Wright, M Barker, M Walker
1986	**In Homage to a Hound** (Wenallt) J Silvester (solo)
1986 May	**Quite Easy for Bigheads** (Bwlch y Moch) C Smith, I Jones
	Crux climbed by R Fawcett in 1982. 'Dead Steady!'
1986 Jun.	**Honorary Grit** (Craig y Llyn) J Dawes
	'The best move in Wales.'

1987 Feb.	**Harvey Proctor's Spanking Groove** (Pant Ifan) D Lampard, N Bonnet, A Phizacklea
1987 May 4	**Llanberries** (Bwlch y Moch) J Dawes
	'Make a dynamic move for a thumb sprag, go up to a faint pod and then out to a sloper. Mantel this (crux) and continue . . . '
1987 Jly 31	**The Seraphic Sanction** (Craig Cwm Trwsgl) D Lampard, A Phizacklea (AL)
1987 Jly 31	**The Iconoclastic Exit** (Craig Cwm Trwsgl) A Phizacklea, D Lampard
1987 Jly 31	**The Killing Fields** (Craig Cwm Trwsgl) A Phizacklea, D Lampard (AL)
1987 Jly 31	**Day of Reckoning** (Craig Cwm Trwsgl) D Lampard, A Phizacklea (AL)
1987 Aug. 1	**Gwyddbwyll** (Hyll-Drem) R Griffiths, E Jones
1987	**Total Bull** (Hyll-Drem) G Smith, P Hawkins
1987	**Bleed for the Dancer** (Clogwyn Du) A Greenwood (solo)
1987	**The Witching Stick** J Silvester, S Howe
1987	**Cunnyson** J Silvester, C Dale
1987	**The Pain and the Ecstasy** (Pant Ifan) J Redhead, M Crook
1987 Oct. 2	**The Jewel in the Crown** (Gesail) C Greatwich, G Russell
1987 Nov. 11	**Poison Ivy** (Gesail) C Greatwich, C Lloyd, C Benette
1987 Dec. 25	**Jumble Tumble** (Gesail) C Greatwich, C Lloyd, C Benette
1988 Feb. 27	**Wild Horses** C Greatwich, G Russell
1988 Mar. 26	**Smarter than the Average Bear** (Bwlch y Moch) T D Hughes, D J Jacques
1988 Apr. 3	**Food for Thought** (Gesail) A Woodward, C Greatwich
1988 May 10	**Balance of Power** (Castell Cidwm) P Littlejohn, J de Montjoye
	A bold on-sight lead.
	'Thought I'd wear something bright for the photos.' - light grey trackies and a pale blue T-shirt – I ask you!
1988 May 10	**Potency** (Castell Cidwm) P Littlejohn, J de Montjoye
	'Pat had abbed the line and placed a peg the previous week. Worries of inadequate protection were starting to bother him even as we were driving over from the Gwynant. His reasoning was that, as the crux was going to be gaining the peg, he should place another, lower. It was: he didn't.'
	This was the second of two tremendous routes that were to inspire Littlejohn to drag Cidwm into the Eighties.
1988 May 11	**Bay of Pigs** (Hyll-Drem) P Littlejohn, J de Montjoye
1988 May 15	**Rowland Rat** (Gesail) C Greatwich, A Woodward, C Benette
1988 May 21	**Cuckoo Waltz** (Bustach/Moelwyns) J Beasanty, J McQueen. P Semmar, J Maskis
1988 May 26	**Rain Shadow** (Hyll-Drem) P Littlejohn, J de Montjoye
	Also known as Welsh Water Subversion.

| 1988 May 26 | **Going for Gold** (Hyll-Drem)   P Littlejohn, J de Montjoye |
| 1988 May 27 | **Heading for Heights** (Castell Cidwm)   P Littlejohn, J de Montjoye (AL) |

'We were still pumped from the previous day, having climbed two new routes at Carreg Hyll-Drem. Pat knew that there were good holds to go for, but thought his only hope of reaching them was to jump. He got them statically. The strong bastard'

1988 May 29	**Dion** (Hyll-Drem) D Griffith, G Jones
1988 Jun.	**Flare Up** (Hyll-Drem) J de Montjoye, P Littlejohn (AL)
1988 Jun. 4	**Dwmsday** (Castell Cidwm) S Monks, P Littlejohn (AL)
1988 Jun. 5	**Glasnost** (Castell Cidwm) P Littlejohn, S Monks (AL)
1988 Jun. 5	**Light Years** (Castell Cidwm) P Littlejohn (unseconded)

Steve, the second, couldn't follow.

1988 Jun. 5	**Tumbledown** (Gesail) C Greatwich, A Woodward
1988 Jun. 5	**Golfball** (Gesail) C Greatwich, C Lloyd, A Woodward
1988 Jly 1	**Peachstone** (Upper Wrysgan) S Howe, G Smith
1988 Jly 1	**Neusk Prospect** (Upper Wrysgan) G Smith, S Howe

Or is it Nevski Project?

| 1988 Aug. 6 | **The Bodysnatchers** (Craig Cwm Dulyn)   S Howe, I Jones |

A mega-route in all senses of the word; strenuous, technical and strictly space-walking.

| 1988 Oct. 1 | **Drug Test** (Pant Ifan)   C Greatwich, C Benette |

Part of the groove on pitch 2 was followed by an earlier route Next of Kin.

1988 Oct. 16	**The Shining** (Gesail) C Greatwich, A Woodward
1988 Oct. 22	**Equinox** (Castell Cidwm) P Littlejohn, T Jepson
1988	**Bombproof Runner** (Pennant) C Phillips, J Tombs

An E3 5c on the 3rd outcrop from the road.

| 1989 May 11 | **Red Shift** (Craig Cwm Dulyn)   D Lampard, I Jones, D Green |

Appendix of Recent Information

Just before the guidebook went to the printer David Bailey (after consultation with locals Elfyn Jones, Wayne Shakell and Pete Wright) provided some further information on the Moelwyns. The details either fill in gaps, amplify, or correct the existing script.

CLOGWYN Y BUSTACH

Southern Cross   200 feet   Very Severe
A very photogenic line crossing on to the steep wall at half-height. One hard move at the start of the second pitch leads to fine views of the harder wall climbs. Start as for South Chimneys.
1   70 feet. As for South Chimneys.
2   130 feet. 4c. From the grassy ledge take the obvious traverse line across the right wall to the main face (an unprotected long reach). Follow the groove to an arête, which is followed to the top.
First ascent: D Bailey, R J Shimwell in 1974.

CLOGWYN YR OEN

On the headwall between Pinky and Skerryvore is:

Saline Solution   115 feet   Hard Very Severe
A reachy route taking a line up the large flake just left of the tree-filled crack of Pinky.
1   115 feet. 5b. Climb the face of the flake going first left then right, with a crank or two thrown in for good measure to the final cracks of Pinky. Finish up the right-hand crack.
First ascent: D Bailey, E Jones on 7 August 1978.

Slant   240 feet   Very Severe
A good route which leads to an amazing finish above the final stance of Slick. Start on the mossy slab to the right of the rib of Slick.
1   70 feet. Climb dirty slabs to belay on the left of the detached flake.
2   90 feet. 4b. The steep groove on the left is taken to a ledge. Step left round the corner and go diagonally up the slab towards the cave on Bent.
3   50 feet. 4a. Continue more or less up the corner to a stance above the right edge of the slab.
4   30 feet. 4b. The steep left-hand crack in the wall on the right is awkward to start and gives surprisingly exposed climbing to easy ground.
First ascent: A J J Moulam, G D Roberts on 26 December 1971.

CRAIG YR WRYSGAN

Nosferatu has lost its peg runner and is now thought to be E4.

UPPER WRYSGAN

To descend from routes on the left-hand end of the crag follow the top farther to the left and descend a grassy shoot towards a small lake. From Auction Wall routes merely follow the grassy rock ramp down to the right-hand end of the wall.

D.Y.W.A.M   110 feet   Very Difficult
Start at the extreme left-hand end of the crag just above an old level leading into the cliffs. A good little route.
1   40 feet. Step on to the wall and climb the steep crack to a ledge below the obvious corner.
2   70 feet. Bridge up the corner until a hand-traverse leads out rightwards. Finish up Cave Arête. At this point 'Do you want a medal?'
First ascent: R J Shimwell and party.

Cave Arête   110 feet   Difficult
Start as for D.Y.W.A.M above the level.
1   35 feet. Climb the wall to a chimney which leads to a large stance.
2   75 feet. Go straight up the arête, trying to keep to the left edge.
First ascent: B St J Phillips, D Sneath, J W Morris on 4 October 1967.

Headcross   110 feet   Difficult
Start 30 feet right of Cave Arête.
1   60 feet. Climb the large groove and take the left-hand crack to a ledge. Hand-traverse into Cave Arête and go up to another large ledge.
2   50 feet. Step round the block on the ledge and go across the slab. Follow the wall above then ascend the arête to finish.
First ascent: D R Headley, Miss S Shallcross on 22 June 1968.

No Thanks   100 feet   Very Difficult
Start 10 feet left of Cat Walk.
1   60 feet. Climb the wall and crack above to a large ledge below some slabs.
2   40 feet. Continue up the slabs to the top.
First ascent: R J Shimwell, D Bailey (solo) on 8 April 1974.

To the right of Chim Chu Roo is an unbroken 80-foot wall – Auction Wall. The climbing is steep and there are some very painful finger pockets. In the main text the routes go from

Sasquatch to Gremlin Groove. Protection on most of the lines is minimal and the landings are festooned with ankle-snapping boulders.

Louis Wilder is thought to be E5 as it gives a very hard and serious pitch. There is no gear, no easy escape and no prospect of jumping off without serious injury. It is very seldom led, although it has been climbed on numerous occasions with the aid of a high runner (at the top!).

Wall of Ghouls   80 feet   E3   (1980/1986)
The wall just left of Gremlin Groove above the obvious rock scar – the scene of some uncalled for vandalism. The original start went up the flake now lying in pieces on the ground. The new start is much harder.
1   80 feet. 6a for the tall. Just to the right of the scar are several pockets. Using these, progress on the wall above is sometimes possible. Continue carefully past a loose flake to the steep crack which leads to the finish. A good pitch.
First free ascent: E Jones (solo)

★ **Elf Wall**   80 feet   E3
The wall right of Gremlin Groove gives interesting climbing on good rock.
1   80 feet. 5c. Climb the bulging wall on reasonable pockets to a small ledge. Trying moves then lead left to another ledge. Finish up the slab above.
First ascent: E Jones (solo) on 24 May 1987.

The Very Low-Level Girdle   50 feet   6a/b
Keeping as close to the ground as possible (without actually touching it!) traverse from left to right across the wall. The hardest section is from Louis Wilder into Gremlin Groove. If you can then reverse it all you must be either popping pills, a short arse with arms like Arnold Schwarzenegger, or a super cool rock-jock.

Peruvian Parrot   80 feet   Severe
A slight route. Start by scrambling up to the terrace under Johnson's Wall.
1   80 feet. Just left of the steep wall (with a peg in) is a large flake. Climb the right-hand side of the flake to a ledge. Step right and follow the blunt rib to the top.
First ascent: P Wright (solo) on 1 July 1986.

Johnson's Wall should be E3 6a
'Do NOT move right on to the hollow-sounding jug, as it came off when I did the route on 16 June 1984. Instead finish directly above the tiny niche to reach easier ground and the top.'

CRAIG DAN YR YSGOL (Cliff under the school)   O.S. Ref. 701 456

This steep cliff is underneath Ysgol y Moelwyn in the centre of
Blaenau Ffestiniog. It is best approached by driving past Kwik-Save
and turning right at the swimming pool, just before the school
playground. At the end of the road follow the path down through the
trees to the cliff. The approach lasts about one minute. There are
several short problems but the best two lines at present are:

Dunces' Corner   40 feet   Hard Very Severe
Above the graffiti-decorated wall is an obvious groove-cum-ramp.
Start below the small roof in a corner.
1   40 feet. 4c. Climb thinly up to the roof, traverse left, then go up
into the groove. This is followed boldly to the top. Belay on the school
railings (or not if it is likely to cause 'a fence').
First ascent: E Jones (solo) circa 1979.

Vertical Playground   40 feet   E2
The right-hand side of the steep wall capped by an overhanging
groove.
1   40 feet. 5b. Step steeply on to the wall and stretch up to an obvious
finger-hold. Climb into the niche (peg and wasp's nest) and swing
boldly up the overhanging groove (peg) to a tree belay at the top.
First ascent: W Shakell, D Bailey, R Barry on 20 April 1989

CARREG HYLL-DREM

Spooks   80 feet   E4
A minor route starting from the stance of Primus.
1   80 feet. 5c. Move up and left from the sharp rib to reach a short
crack. Continue straight up to a detached pinnacle and finish up the
obvious groove above.
First ascent: P Littlejohn, M Hardwick on 1 June 1988.

The Big Six Fun Box (E5 6b) is the 'fun to do' overhanging wall 20 feet
left of The Weirpig. It should be reserved for a torrential rainstorm
when it will be found to be totally dry.
First ascent: P Pritchard, T Hodgson on 13 March 1988.

One Fine Day   150 feet   E5
Start 6 feet left of the arête of Wildebeest, below a line of thin cracks
leading to a downward-pointing flake.
1   80 feet. 6a. Gain the thin cracks from the left and move up to the
flake. Pull up leftwards over the bulge to a small ledge just right of
Gwyddbwll. Step up and right, then climb up past an obvious
undercut to reach some sloping ledges. Continue up a steep groove
immediately left of Hardd to its slab, then go up the continuation right
of the overhang to the stance of the original route.

2   70 feet. 5c. A sensational pitch. Climb the short corner above the stance to the obvious rising traverse line. Follow this for 30 feet past a large spike, then, keeping low round a bulge to an obvious exit and easy ground.
First ascent: P Littlejohn, T Jepson on 20 April 1988.

CARREG ALLTREM

Alltrem Arête   130 feet   Very Severe
Start as for Lightning Visit.
1   55 feet. 4a. As for pitch 1 of Lightning Visit.
2   75 feet. 4c. Follow the obvious crack in the left wall of Lightning Visit to the hanging arête. Climb this via a dubious spike to the top.
First ascent: W Shakell, G Carter on 19 June 1989.

Leviathan Direct Variation Finish   100 feet   Very Severe
2a 100 feet. 4b. Climb the crack to the top, then go strenuously up the arête on good holds to the top.
First ascent: C Knowles, A Bateman on 31 July 1983.

★ **Rainbow Warrior**   220 feet   E3
A tremendous traverse line with a strenuous and sustained pitch in a stunning position. Start as for Fratricide Wall.
1   70 feet. 5a. As for pitch 1 of Fratricide Wall.
2   70 feet. 5c. Climb the steep and awkward stepped wall to the right of the stance to regain the traverse on Fratricide Wall. Follow this until below the final steep corner, runner. Step down and move round (loose spike) into Lightning Visit. Hanging belay on a small flake plus some large nuts.
3   80 feet. 5c. Step right on undercuts and make a totally committing bridge into Penamnen Groove. Climb to the roof and step right and layaway through the roof then continue rightwards past a steep crack. Step right again into an even steeper green and greasy crack which is followed to a notch. Swing blindly round towards the final 10 feet of Lavaredo Wall, which is followed to the top. A cracking pitch.
First ascent: D Bailey, W Shakell (AL) on 22 June 1989.

Ahab   50 feet   E1
Start at the left-hand end of the crag.
1   50 feet. 5c. Ascend the crack which has an overhanging start.
First ascent: J Tombs (solo) on 5 June 1988.

CRAIG RHIW GOCH

Big River   120 feet   Hard Very Severe
Right of Mur Dena's starting pinnacle is a steep rib with the crack of Smiler's Route on the right.

1   40 feet. 5a. Step right into a small niche in the rib and go over steep bulges above to a stance.
2   80 feet. 5a. Layback to the steep crack on the left, then go up and leftwards across ribs and grooves to the direct finish of Congl. Follow this to the top.
First Ascent: D Cook, C Hoyland (AL) on 19 April 1981.

Betws y Coed Area

A Crafnant area guidebook is currently in preparation and adjacent to this valley are several crags which have not appeared in a guidebook since 1970. As interest in this area is now increasing, the original information is given below as well as information about the latest development. Perhaps someone will be stimulated to write a definitive guidebook before long

CRAIG DINAS   O.S. ref. 808 538

The cliff is formed of twin buttresses close above the Silver Fountain Hotel on the A5 about 1½ miles out of Betws y Coed. The rock is compact, hard and generally sound, but becomes inordinately slippery in damp or rainy conditions. The main section is steep, with many overhangs, and it is characterized by a blunt pillar (The Boulder) leaning against it over on its right-hand side. The pillar is defined by a crack on the left (Gull's Nest Crack) and a cave/rift (The Cavern) on the right, and just to its right an incipient gully cuts a final rib (Moss Rib, Severe) off from the cliff.

The Nurgler   150 feet   Severe
The best route on the crag – varied and in a good position. Start at the foot of the obvious crack left of The Boulder.
1   45 feet. Climb the crack (Gull's Nest Crack) and belay on the wall behind the top of The Boulder.
2   50 feet. Step on to the belay and go up to a bulge. Traverse right to the rib, round it, and go up to another bulge. Go right again by an apparently loose block, and step back on to it. The steep wall above enables grass to be reached on the left, where there is a poor belay.
3   55 feet. Instead of the easier grassy groove, traverse left under the overhang, round the heathery corner, and go up the easy buttress.
First ascent: R James, C T Jones in 1953.

Gull's Nest Crack had been done in 1930.

The Bolder Way   135 feet   Very Severe
A good route, but the first pitch is rather artificial. Start at the
foot of Gull's Nest Crack.
1 45 feet. Take the indefinite crack slanting up the wall of The
Bolder, right of Gull's Nest crack.
One can also climb the overhang on the left corner of the
Boulder, to the crack, and escape leftwards.
2 90 feet. Climb straight up to the overhang above and traverse
with difficulty below it. At its left-hand end a short crack and a
groove lead to a bulge and easier ground.
First ascent: I Richardson, D Williams in July 1958. Pitch 1
variation by J F Kerry on 19 December 1967.

Main Wall Climb   150 feet   Hard Severe
A good and well-protected climb. Start about 10 feet left of Gull's
nest crack. Climb to a small gorse on small holds to a sloping
ledge. Traverse left and go up until good spikes lead right under
the overhang to a groove on its right. finish straight up.
First ascent: G Arnold, J F Kerry in October 1964.

Dinas Mawr Eliminate   150 feet   Hard Very Severe
A very good route for a small cliff. Start 25 feet left of the corner
formed by the blunt pillar (Gull's Nest Crack) which is the most
obvious feature of the upper crag.
1 80 feet. Climb the green, shattered scoop for 20 feet, then
traverse slightly left. A layback crack in the overhanging bulge
above, leads to a small ledge and flakes. Climb the crack to the
right to a sloping, grassy ledge.
2 70 feet. Enter the obvious V-groove and go up until it is
blocked by an overhanging bulge. Ascend the bulge direct and
scramble to the top.
First ascent: J F Kerry, J D Roberts on 10 September 1968.

Scrub Way   140 feet   Severe
Good, steep climbing which soon relents. Start at a flat-topped
stone below a steep groove on the corner of the buttress.
1 30 feet. Go up steeply to the small oak.
2 135 feet. Cross the groove delicately to the rib on the right,
which is climbed to grass above (possible belay above right of
two jammed blocks). As the groove overhangs, step past the
belay and go round to the slab. Ascend the slab and a crack to
join Bolder Way.
2a 135 feet. Ascend the groove (possible belay) then follow the
groove to the roof and exit right. Finish up slabs.
First ascent: J Richardson, D Williams in July 1958.

By-Ways 145 feet Severe
Interesting but vegetated. Start at short crack 20 feet left of Scrub
Way.
1 35 feet. Ascend the crack and continue up the slab to a grassy
ledge and small belay below the heathery groove.
2 110 feet. Get onto the slab left of the groove, then return to it.
This leads to easy ground. A short crack and a step right lead to a
good belay. Finish easily up the cracked wall and through gorse.
2a 110 feet. Go to the top left corner of the slab to below a steep
groove (possible belay). Finish up the awkward crack.
First ascent: J Richardson, D Williams in July 1958.

Crossways 275 feet Very Severe
A pleasant girdle of the crag. Start as for By-Ways.
1 35 feet. Ascend the crack and slab of By-Ways.
2 75 feet. Take the slab left of the groove, step back to it and
continue to the overhang. Cross the right wall and continue traversing
slightly downwards under the overhangs. Two spike belays.
3 15 feet. Step down and scramble into the next groove, on Scrub
Way.
4 35 feet. Go down a step and traverse the wall. Pull up under the
bulge and step round to the grey slab. Cross it to the top of The
Boulder.
5 50 feet. step onto the belay and go up to a bulge (as for Nurgler).
Traverse right to the rib and round it, then go up to another bulge. Go
right again by an apparently loose block, and step back onto it. The
steep wall above leads to grass and a poor belay on the left.
6 15 feet. Cross the grassy groove and go up to a belay on the right.
7 75 feet. Traverse right under the upper overhang to the top of
Moss Rib.
First ascent: J Richardson, D Williams in 1958.

CLOGWYN CYRAU (Cliff of Edges)   O.S. ref. 789 571

This is the rocky knoll north-east of Betws-y-Coed. It overlooks the
car-park by Pont y Pair, the bridge at the north-western end of the
village, and from this point six buttresses arranged in two tiers of
three may be seen.

The TOP TIER, from left to right consists of:
(a) The main buttress of Clogwyn Cyrau.
(b) Conway Buttress, with the top of a right-angled corner just visible
in the centre.
(c) Little Buttress, right of a definite depression.
These three crags form the skyline, the third of them having trees on
its summit.

The LOWER TIER is 300 feet below and is almost hidden in the trees. It extends further to the west. From left to right again, the buttresses are:
(d) Craig Cynhelier, a short steep wall, further west than the upper cliffs and close above the end of the forest track.
(e) The Central Slabs below and between the Main Buttress and Conway Buttress.
(f) Little Wall, directly below Little Buttress.
Cars must be left in the car-park at Pont y Pair, since the sign-posted road to the cliffs is restricted to Forestry Commission vehicles. About 100 yards past the foresters' houses a well-made walk, the Jubilee Path, zigzags through the trees to the summit, passing between Craig Cynhelier and the Main Buttress. Another path goes off to the right 50 yards up it and leads past Central Slabs and along the top of Little Wall. There are almost no climbs of more than 100 feet on Clogwyn Cyrau. However, the rock is usually excellent and the routes are very steep. The crags are often in sunshine when the highest mountains are in thick cloud, or rain.

MAIN CLIFF
This is the dominating section of the cliff as seen from Betws y Coed. It is reached most easily by following the Jubilee Path to a right elbow, then continuing rightwards on to the screes below the crag. the routes are described from left to right.

Holly Groove   80 feet   Moderate
The floral groove at the left-hand end of the cliff, immediately left and set slightly back from the wall, forming the first main feature of the cliff.

The Ramp   100 feet   Hard Very Severe (1 pt.)
Climb the groove of Jingling Wall for a few feet then step left onto the steep wall. Climb this and the overhung crack above. Climb diagonally right across the wall and take a short corner right of an overhang in the centre (aid peg).

★ **Jingling Wall**   100 feet   Severe
A good and varied route. Start below an obvious V-groove behind a holly at the left-hand end of the main face. Climb the groove to a large ledge on the right. Traverse back across the groove and go along a good ledge to a groove which provides the finish.

Bomber's Wall   100 feet   Hard Severe
Start 30 feet right of the previous routes below an obvious corner at the top of the cliff. Go straight up the wall via a large flake to the Jingling Wall stance. Finish up the corner.

Hangover   110 feet   Hard Very Severe
The main overhanging wall of the crag. Start 20 feet left of the recessed area at the right-hand end of the overhangs. Climb direct to a stance below the main overhangs. Go up 12 feet and climb the yellow wall diagonally rightwards, to cross the overhangs at the right-hand end.

Central Route   80 feet   Severe
Start at a short wall 20 feet right of the overhangs below a long grass ledge at 20 feet. Ascend the wall to the ledge. Climb diagonally rightwards to a short corner right of a nose then step left round the nose and go up to a ledge. The short corner right of the bulge and the groove above lead to the top.

Long Climb   150 feet   Very Difficult
Start as for Central Route, take the wall to the grass ledge. From the right-hand end of the ledge step right and go up to gain a good traverse line. This leads to a corner at 40 feet. Climb the corner and its continuation above to more broken ground. Finish diagonally rightwards.

Consolation   70 feet   Very Difficult
Immediately right of a large oak and 40 feet left of a group of firs.

Panorama   230 feet   Very Severe
A fine girdle in a good position, with excellent protection. Start at a stance on top of a perched pillar at the western end of the crag. First stance of The Ramp.
1   35 feet. Traverse down to the right to the top of the groove on Jingling Wall.
2   40 feet. Continue easily to a large flake then move awkwardly under the overhangs and descend a few feet to a stance.
3   60 feet. Cross a rib to gain a groove above the grass ledge on Central Route, then cross the wall on the right delicately to a small stance in the centre of the wall.
4   30 feet. Step up and go round the corner avoiding the large ledges by a traverse slightly downwards. Cross a vertical wall to gain a corner then go up a rib on the right to a small stance.
5   45 feet. The corner above leads to an obvious diagonal line leading to the top of the crag.

CONWAY BUTTRESS
Moving east over a bramble-engulfed boulder-field leads to a short crag. The ground slopes up under the left wall and behind a large tree is an indefinite groove. The routes are described from left to right.

Wall Climb   60 feet   Severe
The wall just right of the groove is followed by a move or two up the easing arête.

Waterloo 70 feet Very Severe
The arête direct gives an amusing climb, with 1 peg low on the arête.

Conway Corner 70 feet Severe
The prominent right-angled corner is excellent.

Diagonal Climb 100 feet Difficult
A steep and exposed climb starting as for Conway Corner. A few feet up the corner go out right, then traverse across the face on good holds crossing below a rib. Continue past two small trees then finish up a little corner.

Academy 70 feet Hard Severe
30 feet right of Conway Corner. Climb through the brambles for a few feet and move left to a short corner with a remarkable pocket. Move up and right to a shallow groove and climb this to a small overhang. Step left and finish up the wall.

Precedent 85 feet Very Difficult
Start 40 feet right again below an obvious corner at the top of the cliff. Climb a series of grooves and corners leftwards to gain the main corner at 60 feet. Climb this direct to the top.

Stripper 80 feet Severe
Start as for Precedent but move right and take the arête to the top.

50 feet right below a tree that grows up over a small overhang halfway up the cliff is:

Tree Climb 100 feet Very Difficult
Start about 15 feet right and below the tree. Go up and across to the tree on good holds. Climb the tree and the rock above.

The Bat 110 feet Very Severe
Reach the tree direct up a crack, and continue up to the left of the Direct Line.

LITTLE BUTTRESS has three 40-foot routes.

CRAIG CYNHELIER is under 60 feet in height.

CENTRAL SLABS
The buttress is reached by walking 50 yards up the Jubilee Path and taking the path off to the right. The routes are broken at first until the big cave to the right of the conifers.

Depression   110 feet   Very Severe
Climb the short wall to the first niche of the cave. Move into the upper niche then traverse left, peg, and round the corner. Step left and finish direct.

Earthworm Direct   100 feet   Very Severe
Follow Depression into the upper niche than surmount the big overhang by the obvious diagonal crack (big chocks or Friends).

Earthworm   100 feet   Very Severe
Follow Depression to the first niche then move right for 10 feet and ascend diagonally rightwards to finish.

The Fate of Icarus   100 feet   Very Severe (3 pts. aid)
Start 50 feet right of Earthworm. Climb the slab and wall to the cave. Go over the overhang at its right-hand end and traverse left on the obvious line to gain the arête. Finish up the arête.

The routes are now rather overgrown.

LITTLE WALL
There are about 6 routes up to 70 feet in length.

SWALLOW FALLS BUTTRESS   O.S. ref. 765 588

This steep little buttress overlooking Swallow Falls opposite the hotel. It is best reached by the footpath from the Ugly House Bridge.

★ **Traditional**   120 feet   Severe
A good climb taking the left-hand side of the crag starting only 30 feet above the riverside path. A 10-foot block stands in the base of an overhanging groove. Start on the left side of the block.
1   45 feet. Climb on to the top of the block, step out right into a groove and ascend this to a ledge below a right-angled corner.
2   25 feet. Climb the crack that splits the right wall. Tree belays on the long terrace.
3   25 feet. Climb the weakness near the left edge of the wall to reach a ledge and tree belay below the final wall.
4   15 feet. Climb the wall starting just right of the slight nose.
First ascent: H Drasdo, N Drasdo, G D Roberts, M Feeley on 25 December 1964.

CLOGWYN YR ADAR

An 80-foot crag in the Lledr Valley which deserves to be kept free from the hordes. From Blaenau Dolwyddelan following a lane south-westwards for one-and-a-third miles until the crag can be seen behind Coed Mawr farm. The farmer is at present prepared to allow up to four climbers at a time on the crag, providing that respect is shown to the property. The crag has been visited since the 1960s but details were withheld until the blitz of 1988 when locals 'discovered' the crag.

Mabel's Route   70 feet   Very Difficult
Start just to the left of central vegetation by a boulder field.
1   30 feet. Follow a low shelf sloping up to the right and climb the corner moving right at its top to a large ledge and trees.
2   40 feet. On the left is an overhanging wall. Climb to the right of this up a wall, then an arête, to the top.
First ascent: A Green, K Latham, D Hughes on 19 August 1972.

Gringo   80 feet   Hard Very Severe
Start to the right of the central vegetation.
1   50 feet. Climb the left edge of a green slab then a curving crack. Hand-traverse left and gain a niche. Go left round the rib to a stance.
2   30 feet. Take the bulging wall above via a crack.
First ascent: A Green, K Latham on 19 August 1972.

Tarantula   120 feet   Severe
Start on the left-hand buttress below an S-shaped crack.
1   30 feet. Traverse leftwards up a gangway to its end, avoiding the huge in situ spiders.
2   50 feet. Make a bold move over the bulge on the right then traverse right past the crack up a short wall to some loose blocks.
3   40 feet. The obvious sloping gangway on the left is followed on small holds to the top.
First Ascent: A Green, K Latham, D Hughes on 19 August 1972.

The rhyolite main crag, first girdled by Mel Griffiths has a bulge which guards entry onto the face at 15 feet. From left to right the 1988 routes are:

Genericon Limits   100 feet   E5
1   100 feet. 6b. From a good peg on the lip of the bulge, move right, then go straight up to good holds. Head straight for a porthole and finish directly over the bulge.
First ascent: G Smith, S Howe, P Williams, M Crook in April 1988.

*** Bloodbank   100 feet   E5
A superb left-trending line. Start just right of a rust streak.
1   100 feet. 6b. Move up, 2 pegs, to a block on the left. Gain the left-trending crack, then climb through the centre of the overlap. Go up the wall to a break, then move left and go up a flake to a break, thread runner on the right. Continue up past an undercut to a jug, peg, and finish leftwards to a ledge, thread, and the top.
First Ascent: S Howe, G Smith on 7 April 1988.

Boss Talkers   100 feet   E5
1   100 feet. 6b. From the block on Bloodbank, swing right to jugs, peg, and climb the fine wall to a break, old peg and thread. Continue through a niche and go up a wall to a final crack.
First ascent: S Howe, G Smith, M Crook on 6 April 1988.

Noble Horse   100 feet   E2
1   100 feet. 5b. Climb the wall to a pink thread, then step left and go up to a peg. Climb the groove/crack above to the break. Ascend the flake above to finish up the crack of Boss Talkers.
First ascent: S Howe, P Kirton on 22 May 1988.

** Hustlers, Beats and Others   100 feet   E2
1   100 feet. 5b. Climb straight up to a pink thread, then trend right up the wall on good holds.
First ascent: M Crook, G Hughes, S Howe, E Felson on 7 April 1988.

John Damocleese   100 feet   E4
1   100 feet. 6b. Ascend the wall below the holly moving left to a thread. Hard moves lead to a peg then a slab is followed to a break. Continue up the slab finishing leftwards.
First ascent: G Smith, S Howe in April 1988.

** Enterprise Allowance   100 feet   E2
1   100 feet. 5b. Start up the obvious crack in the right-hand side of the crag and follow it to where it fades. Finish up John Damocleese past a peg.
First ascent: S Howe, Sue Harland on 6 April 1988.

Whisper of the Axe   100 feet   E4
1   100 feet. 5c. To the right of Enterprise Allowance gain an earthy hollow from the right and go up to the base of a slab, Friend 2. Move right and climb the slab, then take the wall above, thread, to the top.
First ascent: S Howe, G Smith on 5 April 1988.

On the left-hand buttress is a superb route which gives the best climbing on the crag.

★★ **The Cheshire Cat**   100 feet   E5
1   70 feet. 6a. Climb past a block on good holds to 'the grin.' Enter this and pull over the roof to a thread. Go straight up, then walk right, 2 pegs, to belay at a small thread.
2   30 feet. 5c. Climb the groove, peg on the right, and continue direct using holds on the left.
First ascent:G Smith (unseconded) on 7 April 1988.

PONT-Y-PANT CRAG   O.S. ref. 759 540

Situated in the Lledr Valley above the A470 Betws y Coed to Dolwyddelan road is this fine little outcrop. So far the following bare details have been received. The lines go from left to right, starting just right of a big boulder, and they can easily be located by the in situ pegs.

No Coaches   (E2/3 6a) by G Smith, N Dixon, E Stone.
The crack to the right of the big boulder.

Unnamed   (E3 6b), peg, By E Stone, G Smith.
The crack in the centre of the wall.

Unnamed   (E3 6a), 2 pegs, by S Howe.
The left-hand edge of the wall near the arête gives an intimidating line.

A Gathering of Old Men   (E4 6c), 3 pegs, by N Dixon.
An utterly desperate route. Most climbers don't get off the ground.

The Good Booklet   (E5 6b) by G Smith, E Stone.

Unnamed   (E2 5c) by E Stone.

316

Index

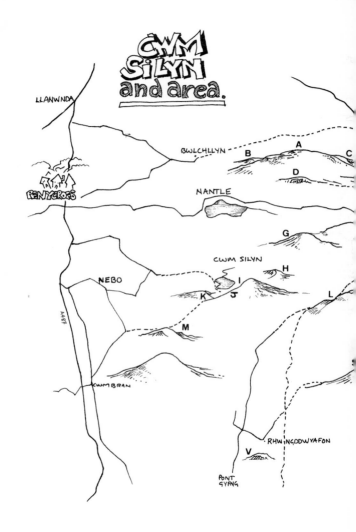

CWM SILYN and area.

LLANWNDA

BWLCHLLYN

PENYGROES

NANTLE

CWM SILYN

NEBO

A487

KWMBRAN

RHWINGDDWYAFON

PONT GYFNG

A B C D G H I J K L M V

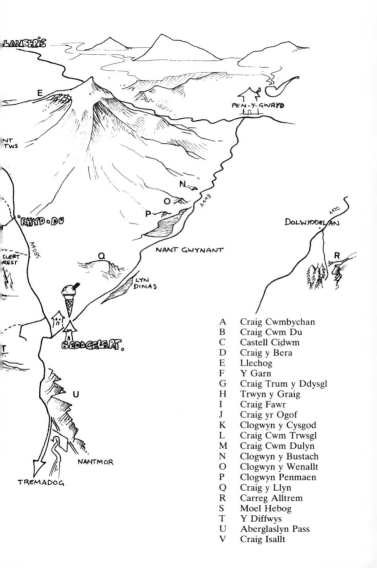

A   Craig Cwmbychan
B   Craig Cwm Du
C   Castell Cidwm
D   Craig y Bera
E   Llechog
F   Y Garn
G   Craig Trum y Ddysgl
H   Trwyn y Graig
I   Craig Fawr
J   Craig yr Ogof
K   Clogwyn y Cysgod
L   Craig Cwm Trwsgl
M   Craig Cwm Dulyn
N   Clogwyn y Bustach
O   Clogwyn y Wenallt
P   Clogwyn Penmaen
Q   Craig y Llyn
R   Carreg Alltrem
S   Moel Hebog
T   Y Diffwys
U   Aberglaslyn Pass
V   Craig Isallt

RESCUE

In the event of a serious accident where assistance is required, a message giving all the factual information about the person(s), location (crag, climb, pitch etc.) should be passed on to the North Wales Police by dialling 999.

The Police will contact the respective Rescue Team and as co-ordinators will obtain further assistance (e.g. helicopter) as directed by those effecting the rescue.

After an accident, please report in writing directly to the Hon. Secretary, Mountain Rescue Committee, 18 Tarnside Fold, Simmondley, Glossop, Derbyshire, giving particulars of: date of accident, extent of injuries, name, age and address of the casualty, details of the M.R.C. Equipment used and the amount of morphine used (so that it can be replaced). Normally this will be done by the local Police and/or the Rescue Team involved, who will also require the names and addresses of the persons climbing with the injured party.

Avoid making rash or unconsidered statements to the press; refer any jounalist to the mountaineer who has overall charge of the rescue.

HELICOPTER NOTES
In the event of a helicopter evacuation ALL climbers ON and OFF the cliff should take heed. A helicopter flying close to the cliff will make verbal communication between climbers difficult, and small stones will be dislodged by the rotor downdraught. All loose equipment must be secured and climbers in precarious positions should try to make themselves safe. A smoke grenade may be dropped from the helicopter to give wind direction.

The persons with the injured party should try to identify their location. No attempt should be made to throw a rope to the helicopter, but assistance should be given to the helicopter crew if requested.

A helicopter will always be flown into the wind to effect a rescue and on landing there are three danger points; the main rotor, the tail rotor and the engine exhaust. The helicopter should not be approached until directions to do so are given by the air crew.

RESCUE

In the event of a serious accident where assistance is required, a message giving all the factual information about the person(s), location (crag, climb, pitch etc.) should be passed on to the North Wales Police by dialling 999.

The Police will contact the respective Rescue Team and as co-ordinators will obtain further assistance (e.g. helicopter) as directed by those effecting the rescue.

After an accident, please report in writing directly to the Hon. Secretary, Mountain Rescue Committee, 18 Tarnside Fold, Simmondley, Glossop, Derbyshire, giving particulars of: date of accident, extent of injuries, name, age and address of the casualty, details of the M.R.C. Equipment used and the amount of morphine used (so that it can be replaced). Normally this will be done by the local Police and/or the Rescue Team involved, who will also require the names and addresses of the persons climbing with the injured party.

Avoid making rash or unconsidered statements to the press; refer any jounalist to the mountaineer who has overall charge of the rescue.

HELICOPTER NOTES

In the event of a helicopter evacuation ALL climbers ON and OFF the cliff should take heed. A helicopter flying close to the cliff will make verbal communication between climbers difficult, and small stones will be dislodged by the rotor downdraught. All loose equipment must be secured and climbers in precarious positions should try to make themselves safe. A smoke grenade may be dropped from the helicopter to give wind direction.

The persons with the injured party should try to identify their location. No attempt should be made to throw a rope to the helicopter, but assistance should be given to the helicopter crew if requested.

A helicopter will always be flown into the wind to effect a rescue and on landing there are three danger points; the main rotor, the tail rotor and the engine exhaust. The helicopter should not be approached until directions to do so are given by the air crew.

John Middleton on Slack, Clogwyn yr Oen.
Photo: George White

Africa Rib, Craig y Clipiau, a Moelwynion classic.
Photo: Paul Williams

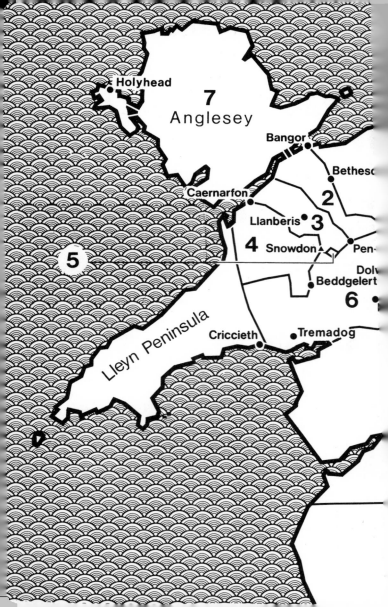